understanding
MONEY

EDWARD SHAPIRO

The University of Toledo

Harcourt Brace Jovanovich, Inc.

New York   Chicago   San Francisco   Atlanta

TO MY MOTHER

ISBN: 0-15-592876-7

Library of Congress Catalog Card Number: 75-382

Printed in the United States of America

PREFACE

The standard textbook in money and banking treats the institutional, structural, historical, empirical, and analytical or theoretical aspects of the subject. It is primarily in this regard that the present volume differs from other books: this book focuses almost exclusively on the analytical or theoretical aspects—on what might be called the "economics" of money and banking. The book is concerned with the meaning of money, the way in which the banking system creates money, how the total money stock is controlled, and—most important—how changes in the money stock affect income, output, and prices, according to both the Keynesian and the monetarist views of the process. The book is not concerned with the advantages and disadvantages of branch banking or those of membership or nonmembership in the Federal Reserve System, nor the provisions of various banking acts, the evolution of banking from colonial times to the present, the composition of the Board of Directors of Federal Reserve Banks, and the like. This approach is taken in the belief that too many students fail to obtain a clear understanding of the more basic aspects of money and banking when they are confronted with an overabundance of all kinds of material.

Exactly where these analytical or theoretical aspects begin and where the other aspects of money and banking end is not something on which all will agree, but few will deny that the major theoretical question is how money influences the economy's total spending and—through spending—the level of prices, output, and employment. To answer this question, one obviously must begin with some understanding of what money is and what determines how much money there is. Parts I and II are concerned with these two questions. Part I begins with an examination of the meaning of money in Chapter 1, introduces the T-account in Chapter 2 and employs this device to trace the movement of money from one holder to another, and shows in Chapter 3 how the commercial banking system may increase and decrease the money stock through its lending and investing activities. Part II introduces the Federal Reserve, covering the mechanics of money stock control in Chapters 4 and 5 and the choices among the tools of control in Chapter 6. Chapters 7 and 8 examine the way Treasury operations affect the money supply, and Chapter 9 provides an overview of Part II.

Part III turns to the major question of the influence of money on aggregate economic activity. The questions of the way in which and the extent to which changes in the money stock influence the level of economic activity are answered differently by Keynesians and monetarists. Part III begins with a preview of the difference and then pursues it in some detail. The focus is analytical, but empirical and historical material is also introduced. Chapter 14 looks specifically at some of the empirical evidence submitted by both the Keynesians and the monetarists, and Chapter 16 traces the history of monetary policy since World War II from the perspective of the Keynesian–monetarist debate.

Part IV, "Money in the International Economy," begins with a chapter on the nature of the balance of payments. A chapter dealing with the primary question of the balance of payments adjustment mechanism follows: adjustment under the gold standard, adjustable pegs, and flexible exchange rates are analyzed in that order. The final chapter in Part IV surveys the dramatic developments in the international monetary system from 1970 through the fall of 1974.

The objective has been to develop the analytical aspects of money and banking in a way that is understandable to all readers, including those who have difficulty with algebra or graphics. An ability to manipulate equations and Marshallian and Keynesian crosses is not required. The one exception occurs in Chapter 5, where—try as one will—algebra cannot be avoided. Apart from this, reliance is entirely on plain, carefully written English.

The book is intended to serve as the basic text in the kind of short first course in money and banking that takes a nontechnical approach to the subject and that emphasizes its theoretical aspects—especially how the stock of money affects the income level. The book does not assume the student already has a solid grasp of the material presented in the introductory economics course. Because it does not have the usual prerequisite of that introductory course, the book also may be used as a supplement to the introductory economics course by those who want to pursue the study of money in greater depth.

If the book helps in any way to make elementary monetary economics more understandable, it will have served its purpose—whoever its readers may be.

Edward Shapiro

CONTENTS

part four: MONEY IN THE INTERNATIONAL ECONOMY

part one
MONEY

one

THE MEANING OF MONEY

The receipt of a paycheck and the expenditure of its sum on goods and services or the setting aside of part of it as saving has come to be so much a part of the average person's day-by-day living that we give no more thought to it than to any other routine activity. However, when we look below the surface, the fact that it is money which we receive in payment for our labor services or whatever else we may have to sell and the fact that it is money which we use to make payment for whatever we want to buy turn out to be among the most important facts of economic life.

Such routine transactions as paying the month's rent, buying the day's groceries, or meeting the next installment on the car all depend, of course, on a person's having available the money he needs for these purposes. But much more basically, the ability of millions of people to carry out such transactions every day depends on the very fact that there does exist in the economy this thing we call money. There is no better way to gain a real appreciation of the importance of this thing's existence than to visualize what would happen in our contemporary economy if money should suddenly cease to exist. There would just as suddenly be no means by which most of the millions of exchange transactions that now occur every day could be carried out. If there were no money in the system, there would be no way consumers could secure the goods they regularly purchase, or alternatively there would be no way merchants could sell the goods they are in business to sell. Goods would remain unsold on store shelves. Merchants who are unable to dispose of what they have on hand would have neither any reason to order more goods nor the means to pay their suppliers for more goods. This cessation of orders would, of course, quickly work back through distributors and wholesalers to manufacturers. Production would virtually come to a halt, workers would be laid off, and factories would close down. Even if some firms along the line wanted to try to keep things going with hopes that the problem would be solved before long, they would be powerless to do anything about it. For example, a manufacturer who might have preferred to maintain production with the unmarketable output temporarily going into his inventories would find his hands tied. Without money he could not pay his workers, purchase raw materials, or make the payments for all the other supplies he needs in order to keep on turning out whatever commodities he produces.

The economy would find itself in a peculiar type of bind: practically everybody would like to see a restoration of normal economic activity, but nobody would be able to do anything to bring this about, try as he might, if money has somehow disappeared from the economy. And as long as the economy is without money, production would be way down and unemployment would be up as much as production was down. It is a situation like this that brings out most dramatically the unparalleled importance of money in a modern economy: money, which is powerless in itself to produce anything, is yet so powerful that its absence means that virtually nothing will be produced.

One can say that, in its potential impact on production, the existence of money is far more important than an uninterrupted flow of such basic products as steel or automobiles. Almost like clockwork, a strike occurs every few years against a basic industry like automobiles or steel. As soon as such a strike begins, business analysts proceed to make their estimates of what the strike will cost in terms of lost production, lost sales, and lost payrolls for various possible durations. The costs tend to rise more than proportionately with the length of the strike—an eight-week strike will "cost" more than twice what a four-week strike will cost—because each passing day spreads the impact out to more and more firms. The impact falls first on those firms whose production depends, in part or in whole, directly on orders from the firms in the struck industry and then radiates out to the firms whose production depends, in part or in whole, on orders from the firms whose production depends directly on orders from the firms in the struck industry, and so forth in ever widening circles. Yet even the record-breaking 116-day strike against the steel industry in 1959 did not paralyze the economy. By the fourth month of that strike, the remotest corners of the economy had probably begun to feel its impact, but the economy as a whole suffered no collapse of overall production or massive unemployment.

In contrast, an economy that suddenly found itself without money would suffer a complete breakdown long before four months had elapsed. It is ironic that money, whose creation in today's economy involves no more productive activity than the running of a few printing presses and the writing of some figures in the books of banks, can, potentially at least, have a much greater impact on the overall level of an economy's productive activity than even an industry like steel, which plays so vital and direct a role in that activity.

It is in order to see how crucially important the existence of money is to the working of the economy that we have looked here at the extreme situation of a complete disappearance of money. However, it must immediately be recognized that a complete disappearance of money is not something that could occur in practice. The existence of money is so very essential to the existence of the modern economy that the case of such an economy's being without money is a purely hypothetical one. Various economies have at times experienced circumstances under which those things that had long been used as money ceased to be so used, but we find that instead of the economy then being completely without money, some other thing or things begin to be used in place of the things no longer used. These new things, like cigarettes and cognac in Germany after World War II, may not be available in the quantities needed and may not be as convenient or efficient as was the "regular" money in mediating exchanges. But through an unsupervised process of mutual agreement people will begin to use such things as these as money simply because they must. The problems of exchange will be extremely difficult even with these things, but the alternative would be the total collapse of the economy and, one may add, the collapse of the inhabitants of that economy.

It is important to see that once these things come to be used as money, difficulties notwithstanding, it is appropriate to describe them as money itself and not in the substitute sense of something being *used* as money. These things, whatsoever they may be, *are* money by the fact that they display a property which, in the view of most economists, is the most important property a good must have if that good is to be money. This is that the good be generally acceptable by persons and firms in exchange for whatever goods and services they have to sell. As we will see below, in today's economy this means that currency and coin and demand deposits or checking balances in banks are money because these are the things through which exchanges are actually conducted—or, in a word, these are generally acceptable media of exchange.

BARTER

Although a modern economy could not function without money, this is not the same as saying that no exchange at all would be possible in such an economy without money. Some exchange, albeit a relatively limited amount, could occur through the barter of goods and services for goods and services. To be designated as barter exchange, the exchange would have to be mediated without the use of whatever at the time is money. If the things customarily used as money cease to be used and the people of necessity switch to things like cigarettes and cognac, the latter become money, and we cannot call the act in which the farmer exchanges his potatoes for cigarettes a barter exchange. However, if the farmer were to work out with a shoe dealer an exchange of so many pounds of potatoes for a pair of shoes, that would be barter exchange as long as neither potatoes nor shoes had come to be a commodity that the members of society find to be generally acceptable in exchange for goods and services.

The exchange by the farmer of his potatoes for cigarettes or cognac is, of course, just as much an exchange of one good for another as would be his exchange of potatoes for shoes. However, in the former case we may say that he is "selling" his potatoes, or that somebody else is "buying" his potatoes, because the exchange is one between potatoes and a good that is money. One "buys" goods with money and "sells" goods for money. In the latter case, we have an exchange in which neither good is money itself and which is therefore properly described as a barter exchange.

The reasons why a society will adopt some particular good as money—for example, cigarettes—in the event that the things ordinarily used as money cease to be so used, are apparent as soon as one sees the limitations of carrying out barter exchange. For example, barter exchange can occur only if there is what is called a "double coincidence of wants." In order that there be an exchange of potatoes for shoes between two parties, the party with shoes to trade must be willing to exchange shoes for potatoes, and the party with potatoes must be willing to exchange potatoes for shoes. If only one of these conditions is satisfied, obviously no direct exchange of potatoes for shoes is possible. However, if the farmer wants shoes and the shoe dealer doesn't want potatoes, the farmer may still be able to get the shoes he wants from the dealer. What is required is to extend the number of goods to three, four, or even more. If the shoe dealer states what good or goods he is willing to accept in exchange for shoes, an indirect exchange may be worked out. If his list includes motor oil and if either he or the farmer can find someone willing to exchange motor oil for potatoes, it is then possible for the farmer to obtain the shoes he wants by first exchanging his potatoes for motor oil and then exchanging motor oil for shoes. This same principle may be extended to a case in which the different goods held by four or more parties may be required to effect an exchange of two goods held by two parties. It is easy to see, however, that arranging such exchanges will become first difficult and soon impossible as the number of intermediate steps increases in this way.

A difficulty of another kind in any barter exchange is that of settling on the terms of exchange. The farmer wants shoes for potatoes, but there is a limit to how many pounds of potatoes he will give up for the pair of shoes he has in mind. Even after finding the party willing to exchange motor oil for potatoes, the farmer will not be able to get the shoes he wants at the maximum "price" he is willing to pay in terms of potatoes unless the terms on which he can exchange potatoes for motor oil and then motor oil for shoes are consistent with this maximum price.

In any economy in which there is money, the terms on which exchanges can be made do not have to be worked out but are known almost immediately. The thing that is money becomes what is variously described as the standard of value, the unit of account, or the common denominator of values. It becomes the thing in terms of which the values of all goods and services are expressed. If cigarettes came to be money, a pound of potatoes of given quality might at some time have a price in the market of, say, 2 cigarettes; similarly, a pair of shoes of the kind in question might have a price of, say, 24 cigarettes, and a quart of a particular grade of motor oil might have a price of, say, 4 cigarettes. By measuring the value of all goods and services in terms of the monetary unit or the unit of account, here 1 cigarette, the problem of measuring the exchange values of all goods and services is no more complicated than comparing their relative prices in terms of this particular monetary unit. In our illustration, the farmer would know immediately from the existing set of prices that the pair of shoes he wants will cost him 12 pounds of potatoes in the market. If he is willing to trade at these terms, he knows right off that he can obtain the pair of shoes at a price that does not exceed the maximum price he is willing to pay. He can simply sell 12 pounds of potatoes for money, here cigarettes, at the market price of 2 monetary units per pound and go to the shoe dealer and buy the pair of shoes he wants at the posted price of 24 monetary units.

In the case in which there is no good being used as money, the case we are assuming in order to see the problems of barter exchange, there would be no single price for each good like a pound of potatoes equals 2 cigarettes, a pair of shoes equals 24 cigarettes, etc. Each good would have as many values as there are other goods in the market. If potatoes were one of 100,000 different goods, there would be 99,999 different values for potatoes, one for each of the other 99,999 other goods for which potatoes could be exchanged in the market. The same would be true for every other of these 100,000 different goods. Altogether there would be just under five *billion* different exchange values for the total of 100,000 different goods.* Many of these billions of exchange values would be between pairs of goods that are rarely exchanged, so parties who sought to exchange such goods could not look to the market to find the appropriate exchange rate. Negotiations would be required to reach agreement on the terms of exchange. Such negotiations could be difficult enough in a barter exchange involving only two goods; imagine the difficulty in the case where the exchange between two such goods can only be accomplished indirectly by working through one or more other goods. Like other problems of exchange, this problem is practically removed if one of the goods is used as money. In an economy with 100,000 different goods, the number of exchange values or prices then drops from almost 5 billion to a mere 99,999. Each of the 99,999 goods will have a more or less well-established price in terms of that one good which is money, and so each of these 99,999 goods will have a more or less well-established exchange rate in terms of every other.

If the preceding difficulties encountered in barter exchange are not enough to convince one of how limited the possibilities of barter

---

*The overall number of exchange values is given by the following equation:

$$N = \frac{n(n-1)}{2} \text{ or } 4,999,950,000 = \frac{100,000(99,999)}{2}$$

in which N is the number of exchange values and n is the number of goods.

exchange are in anything but the most primitive economy, others can be noted. One of these arises from the fact of indivisibilities. If the farmer had a tractor that he wanted to trade for other goods, he could not use it to obtain shoes alone unless he was willing to acquire a life-time supply of shoes. If he wants an assortment of small quantities of shoes and various other goods whose values per unit are minor in comparison to the value of the tractor, it will be apparent that putting together the coordinated series of trades among what may be a half-dozen different parties at terms agreeable to all parties would be almost impossible. Of course, with money this problem disappears. The most valuable good can be sold for money, and units of money can be used to buy any desired quantities of the least valuable goods.

Another difficulty arises in exchanges in which both parts of the transaction do not occur at the same time. Suppose that the shoe dealer above had been willing to exchange a pair of shoes today for an agreed number of pounds of potatoes at a future date (when he expects to be off his diet). If both parts of the exchange occur at the same time, the farmer sees the shoes he is getting, and the shoe dealer sees the potatoes he is getting; the terms of the exchange can then be mutually agreed upon by the two parties for the particular units of the goods in question. But in the case of future payment, there is the likelihood that disagreement will arise; the shoe dealer may object to the quality, size, freshness, and other characteristics of the potatoes the farmer brings him in payment at that future date. Such differences between debtors and creditors are inevitable if the thing in terms of which the debt is expressed is anything but a product that is perfectly uniform, every unit being identical with every other unit. No two potatoes are identical, nor are any two units of many other goods. Yet barter exchange involves exchange of such goods for other goods.

A modern economy cannot operate without credit (future payment plus interest in exchange for present goods and services), but under barter conditions parties to exchange will be fearful of giving up goods today in exchange for goods in the future unless the good to be supplied in the future is precisely defined. In the modern economy money is just such a good, so, like other problems of barter, this one is effectively met in an economy that makes use of money. The thing that is money will be a thing that is uniform—every unit will be identical with every other unit. Other problems may arise between creditor and debtor, but with the amount owed by the debtor expressed in terms of the monetary unit, there can be no problem as to whether or not the debtor is repaying according to the terms of the agreement. One 4-ounce potatoe is not identical with another 4-ounce potatoe, but any one monetary unit within a nation is identical to every other monetary unit within that nation.

It is because of the difficulties of conducting exchange by barter in even a simple society that money came into being thousands of years ago. It is because of the sheer impossibility of conducting by barter the kinds of exchange that occur in a modern society that money is an indispensable part of that society. Over the years since money first appeared various things have served in that role in different societies. Early societies used such things as corn, cattle (which in Latin is *pecunia* and the source of the word "pecuniary"), wool, salt, sheep, and the like. The shortcomings of some of these things in terms of their lack of uniformity, durability, and divisibility made them less than ideal money, but it was items like these that were generally acceptable in early societies, so these items, came to be money. Later various metals like iron, copper, brass, and then silver and gold came into general use. Once the silver, gold, and other metals were issued by governments in coin form, there was uniformity as well as durability and divisibility in money. Today, of course, metals continue to be used in coinage, but the great bulk of the money supply in every economy is made up of paper currency and demand deposits of the banks.

THE CONCEPT OF GENERAL ACCEPTABILITY

Barter exchange plays a minor role in the economy today. Anyone who would like to dispose of some goods he owns and acquire other goods in their place does not ordinarily even think of resorting to barter. He simply sells his goods for money at the highest price he can get, and he uses the money to buy the other goods he wants at the lowest price he can find. He will today unhesitatingly accept coin, currency, or demand deposits for his goods, because he knows that the sellers of the goods he wants to acquire will also unhesitatingly accept these same things. They are, in a word, generally acceptable in exchange for all kinds of goods and services offered by all sellers in the market.

It is those things that have this particular property that most people think of as money. From this viewpoint, a workable definition of money is that money is anything generally acceptable in payment for goods and services and in settlement of debt. If we accept this definition, what things then actually qualify as money in the U.S. economy of today? We have a very brief list of items noted earlier: one is *currency*, which we will here understand to include coin as well as paper, and the other is *demand deposits*, or checking accounts. The latter are dollar amounts recorded in the books of the banks that the banks are committed to convert into currency on demand (immediately) by their owners, thus the name demand deposits. They also are viewed as dollar amounts that their owners can transfer to others by writing checks, thus the name checking accounts. Nothing but these two things is generally acceptable to those who offer goods and services for sale in the marketplace, and so nothing other than these two things falls within the limits of this particular definition of money.

The inclusion of currency among the things that qualify fully as money should raise no question, for none of us in this country has experienced a situation in which currency ceased to be generally acceptable in payment for goods and services. The inclusion of demand deposits, however, may raise a question in some minds. This in large part is the result of a confusion between demand deposits, or the actual amounts that are recorded to our credit in checking accounts at the banks, and the personal checks we draw against these accounts as a means of transferring dollars from our accounts to those persons and firms to whom we are making payments. These checks are never money but only the instrument by which the checking account balances that are money may be transferred in effecting payment.

After all, it is easy enough for anyone to write personal checks in any amount against any bank at any time (they may be written on scrap paper, as long as the legally necessary information is set forth), but these checks like any personal check will not be "generally acceptable" in payment unless the payees know that the check writer has a demand account in the bank shown on the check and, furthermore, believe that there is in that account an amount sufficient to enable them to "cash" the checks—i.e., convert them into currency—if they so desire, immediately on presentation at the bank. This is why a so-called certified check is generally acceptable; in this case, at the request of the writer of the check, the bank indicates on the face of that party's personal check that the stated number of dollars has been set aside from the person's account with which to make payment or to "cash" this check whenever it may be presented at the bank. The bank itself is said to "certify" that the amount indicated on the check will be paid on presentation of the check. Once one knows that a deposit of equal amount is there, so to speak, "behind" a check, as is always true in the case of a certified check, the check becomes generally acceptable, but it is still the *deposit* that is money and not the *check*, which is merely an order directing the bank to pay out the specified number of dollars from the deposit balance.

We earlier noted the possibility that the things which had long been money might under extraordinary circumstances cease to be money. For that to happen, these things, which we have now identified as currency and demand deposits, must have lost their general acceptability, and the question one immediately raises is: Under what conditions could this happen? The answer is: under conditions of hyper-inflation, of a truly runaway rise in prices. A price, after all, is nothing more than the number of currency units a seller asks in exchange for a unit of a particular good; hyperinflation is the situation in which the number of currency units asked per unit of goods rises at an extremely rapid rate. In the case of hyperinflation, the price level, say, more than doubling every day (and this has happened in some countries in the not too distant past—in Hungary in July 1946 prices rose 200 percent *per day*), the point is soon reached at which people flatly refuse to accept currency on any terms in exchange for goods they want to sell. Goods are then provided only in direct exchange for other goods, like ciga-rettes, coffee, and staple products. The farmer, for example, is unwill-ing to give up his potatoes for pieces of paper whose value is depreciat-ing so rapidly that he has no good idea of what it may be the very next day, let alone the next month or the next year. He reaches the point at which he will trade his goods only for other goods that he can use personally or that he knows will be acceptable to others and thus will have value in carrying out later trades for still other goods.

In the absence of such extremely rapid rises in prices, currency will maintain its general acceptability, but consistent with this are still cases in which demand deposits may not. For example, if banks have been forced to shut their doors as a result of a "run," which is an attempt by masses of depositors to convert all of their deposits into currency at the same time (and this country had a number of such experiences during the 1930s and earlier), people will refuse to accept checks in payment for goods and services, since checks transfer to them "demand" deposits that can no longer be converted into currency on demand. Here the unacceptability of checks need not be due to any doubt as to whether the writers of the checks have balances in the banks sufficient to cover the checks; it is simply because the banks themselves are unable to meet their obligation to provide currency in exchange for existing demand deposits. In these circumstances, only currency itself remains money, while inconvertible demand deposits lose this status. Again, it is to be emphasized that cases like those noted here are quite extraordinary, at least in the recent experience of the U.S. economy, so it is fair to say that both currency and demand deposits are ordinarily the things that qualify fully as money under the definition given.

Looking at these extraordinary cases is useful, however, because it helps to set straight one of the popular misconceptions about money. We may say that demand deposits are generally acceptable and there-fore are money, by the definition adopted above, because demand deposits are instantly convertible into currency. But we have still to explain why paper currency itself is generally acceptable. Contrary to the misconception so prevalent among laymen, these otherwise worthless pieces of green paper do not have this acceptability because the government has stored away behind every dollar's worth of this paper it issues a dollar's worth of gold or silver or even some fraction of a dollar's worth of these metals or any other commodity. The link between the currency you hold and a metallic reserve behind it has eroded over the past forty years to the point at which virtually none exists today in the United States. Still, paper currency has remained as generally acceptable as it ever was, despite this development. People who are aware of this development realize that they can no longer say with any accuracy at all that these pieces of paper have general acceptability because the government "backs" them with gold or silver. Many of these people fall back to the position that these pieces of paper have this property because people have "faith" in the government, without, however, specifying at all clearly what "faith" may mean in this context. If it means faith that the government will somehow see to it that the purchasing power or value of a unit of the currency will be prevented from depreciating rapidly or, what is the same thing, that the government will see to it that prices will be prevented from rising rapidly, the word does not seem altogether inappropriate. But faith in this sense, unlike the religious sense, is a very fragile thing and is a term better avoided. Furthermore, the essence of the question after all is strictly one of economics; and faith, at least in its ordinary meaning, is outside of economics.

It thus seems best to say that the general acceptability of currency is basically explained not in terms of any vague concept of faith but by the concrete economic fact that its purchasing power is kept reasonably stable. As noted earlier, a truly runaway rise in prices (hyperinflation) will make currency generally unacceptable—it will cease to be money as will anything else, like a demand deposit, that is convertible dollar for dollar into currency. Such extreme price movements occur only if government resorts to or permits a correspondingly extreme overexpansion of the money supply. One can thus also say that currency and demand deposits are generally acceptable because government restrains the growth in the amount of these things to the degree necessary to prevent rapid depreciation in the purchasing power of a unit of these things or, in other words, to prevent rapid rises in goods prices or in the number of units of these things required to purchase any particular good.

MONEY AND NEAR-MONEY

A great advantage in defining money as anything generally acceptable is that it provides a precise criterion for drawing the line between those things that are money and those that are not. As we have seen, the only things that qualify by this definition are currency and demand deposits. But with this great advantage comes an equally great disadvantage: the line drawn on this criterion denies the title of money to a number of things that are only one small step removed from those things given the title of money. The public at any time holds billions of dollars in the forms of currency and demand deposits, but it also holds many more billions of dollars in time deposits (i.e., savings deposits and other kinds of deposits not legally payable on demand) in commercial banks and in mutual savings banks, share accounts in savings and loan associations, savings accounts with credit unions, U.S. Savings Bonds, and other similar forms. Apart from currency and demand deposits, the other things in this list cannot be used in making payment for goods and services; they lack the property of general acceptability, which means they are not money by the definition earlier noted. But all these things have in common some other very important properties—they can in practice quickly, easily, and without appreciable loss be converted into currency or demand deposits, which means, of course, that they then have the property of general acceptability or they then have become money.

It is the fact that the public can so readily transform its holdings of these other things into the things which are money that is the source of the great disadvantage in defining money in terms of general acceptability. One of the most important magnitudes in economic analysis is the economy's stock of money, and what this magnitude is at any time obviously depends on what the adopted definition includes as money. If the public can with ease move billions of dollars back and forth across the line between currency and demand deposits, on the one side, and things like bank savings deposits and savings and loan share accounts, on the other side, it seems from an economic point of view that the things on the two sides of this line are not very different from each other, that they are close substitutes. This suggests that the use of a line so drawn to distinguish what is money from what is not money is somewhat artificial and as such might better not be drawn at all. Not to draw this line would mean that we would include as money not only currency and demand deposits, the things generally acceptable in payment, but also savings deposits in banks, share accounts in savings and loan associations, and other such things that can quickly, easily, and without appreciable loss be converted into currency and demand deposits. However, in trying to take this step we are driven back to a full appreciation of the great advantage of using the criterion of general acceptability as the basis for our definition of money: it is a precise criterion for drawing the line between what is and what is not money. Once we abandon this line and proceed to include other things like those mentioned, we do not escape the need to draw a line, but we do lose the only precise criterion we have for so doing.

It may be apparent that a new line will have to be drawn—not to do so is to turn the word "money" into something meaningless by allowing it to include anything and everything of value that the public holds. And while we cannot escape the problem, we also cannot solve it satisfactorily. For wherever one may choose to draw the new line, there are some economists who will say one has gone too far and others who will say one has not gone far enough. Most will agree in principle that the new line should be drawn to include all of those things held by the public that may be "quickly," "easily," and "without appreciable loss" converted into demand deposits or currency, but these words do not mean exactly the same thing to all persons—they are actually subject to fairly wide differences in interpretation. The more broadly interpreted, the more things will be included in the definition of money, and the larger will be the magnitude of the figure of the economy's stock of money at any date. The more narrowly interpreted, the smaller the figure will be at that date. Thus, the economy's money stock will be one figure according to one group and a quite different figure according to another group.

Instead of engaging in what could be an endless debate as to what should and what should not be included in a single definition of money, economists have sidestepped the problem in a familiar manner: by employing a number of definitions of money with appropriate adjectives to distinguish each from the others. As might be guessed, there is one definition that limits money to those things generally acceptable in payment for goods and services. This is the narrowest but still the most basic and most commonly used definition of all and, of course, limits money to the public's holdings of demand deposits and currency. It is this that we will mean by the word "money" in this book wherever it appears without any qualifying adjectives or phrases. Another definition, popularized by Milton Friedman of the University of Chicago, includes the public's holdings of time deposits in commercial banks as well as its holdings of currency and demand deposits. These two definitions are the ones most widely used, the former sometimes referred to as "money narrowly defined" and the latter as "money broadly defined." For short, the former is also described as M_1 and the latter as M_2.

Beyond these two definitions are the still broader definitions, which include other holdings of the public such as savings deposits in mutual savings banks, share accounts in savings and loan associations, U.S. Savings Bonds, credit union shares, and the like. Although we have seen that, like time deposits in commercial banks, these are only one step removed from the things counted as money by the narrow definition, the general practice among economists has not been to build up a series of broader and broader definitions of money—e.g., M_3, M_4, M_5—by adding each of these one by one to the definition just preceding. This is not to say that this is not done for particular purposes; —e.g., the *Federal Reserve Bulletin* regularly publishes figures for three measures of the money stock, and there are studies that make use of M_4 and beyond. However, for most purposes the usual practice is to include all of these things under the heading of *near-moneys*, conveying the idea that these things have a high degree of *moneyness* but are still not money in the fullest degree. Time deposits at commercial banks are, in this formulation, included under the heading of near moneys; but under the M_2 formulation noted above, they are added to currency and demand deposits to produce "money broadly defined."

Once we have these distinctions before us, there remains the specific task of drawing the line between things that are near-moneys and things that are not. As noted above, not all economists will draw the line in the same place, but practically all will agree that a list should properly include at least the following: time deposits in commercial banks, deposits in mutual savings banks, share accounts in savings and loan associations, U.S. Savings bonds, and U.S. Treasury bills. As of June 1974, the stock of money (currency and demand deposits) in the hands of the public was $280.9 billion (average of daily figures); the amount of the indicated kinds of near-moneys held by the public as of this date was estimated as $860.0 billion. If one believes that other assets—e.g., the cash surrender value of life insurance policies—properly belong in the list, the total dollar amount for near-moneys becomes substantially larger.

No question is likely to arise regarding the inclusion of the listed items, with the possible exception of Treasury bills. Unlike the more familiar U.S. Savings Bond, which the Treasury agrees to exchange for money without notice (any time after 60 days from issue date) at fixed redemption values, Treasury bills are a portion of the national debt that are exchangeable at the Treasury for money only at their maturity dates. However, the bulk of these bills are issued with a 13-week (91-day) maturity, which means that the holder of such bills is never more than 13 weeks from the date at which the amount involved will be paid in full by the Treasury. Actually, holders of these bills can at virtually a moment's notice turn almost any amount of them into money by selling them to other investors through the very efficient market that exists for such securities. They qualify fully under the requirements of being convertible into money "quickly," "easily," and "without appreciable loss." The same is equally true for other U.S. government securities like notes and bonds that happen to be within three months of their maturity dates.

One can perhaps better understand the nature of near-moneys by crossing over the line drawn here to look at several things that are almost near-moneys and might be called near-near-moneys. Here, for example, would be found the major portion of the national debt, which is made up of marketable Treasury obligations with a maturity greater than the 13 weeks of Treasury bills. Unlike U.S. Savings Bonds, these securities cannot be turned in to the Treasury for payment except at maturity (and maturity of some is 20 years or more away), but also unlike Savings Bonds holders of these securities can sell them freely in an open market that exists for this purpose. However, unlike Treasury bills, which may also be sold in this market, the longer maturities of these other Treasury obligations means that the prices at which they can be sold are potentially subject to considerable variation as interest rates in the market vary. Although the holder can sell quickly and easily at any time, he may find that at some times he can sell only at an appreciable loss. These U.S. government obligations thus fail to meet the third requirement set forth for near-moneys and so are left off the list of near-moneys that most economists would prepare.

It is in large part for this same reason that the public's holdings of bonds issued by private corporations are not counted as near-money. One can quickly and easily sell any bonds he holds of such corporations as General Motors or American Telephone and Telegraph, but again he cannot always sell such bonds at the price he paid for them. He cannot always sell such bonds without appreciable loss. The public's holdings of the common and preferred shares issued by corporations would have an even weaker case for inclusion as near-money than the bonds issued by these companies. The price volatility of the stock of even blue chip corporations like General Motors and American Telephone is familiar to anyone with the slightest acquaintance with the stock market. This volatility of stock prices, of course, works two ways—it means that a stockholder may at times convert his shares into money at appreciable gain. The same is also true at times for a holder of corporate bonds and U. S. government long-term securities. Although these things might therefore seem to more than meet the requirement for near-money, the requirement is more stringent. It is not enough that they may *at some times* meet or more than meet the requirement; to qualify as near-money, things must *at all times* be convertible into money without appreciable loss and, of course, quickly and easily. It appears from this that the line of demarcation between near-moneys and the things that are near to near-moneys is drawn essentially in terms of the requirement of convertibility into money without appreciable loss. For there are many things that can meet the requirements of quick and easy convertibility but not too many that can meet the other requirement as well.

Most of the things that come close to meeting the requirement, it should also be noted, are financial instruments of one type or another. There are no physical things, specific types of goods, that appear on anybody's list of near-moneys. There are, of course, all kinds of physical things that can be quickly and easily converted into money, if the owner is willing to accept whatever he can get and thus possibly suffer appreciable losses in the process. A person with a warehouse full of new steel plates, cigarettes, ballpoint pens, bowling balls, radios, scotch whiskey, coffee, or any other commodity can hardly look at his holdings of any of these goods as near-money. Unlike financial instruments, such as a U.S. Savings Bond or a savings account passbook whose very essence is the specific number of dollars printed on the bond or entered in the passbook, physical things have no specific number of dollars attached to them. Holders of such goods clearly have no assurance that they can at any time turn these goods into money quickly and easily, much less without appreciable loss.

Still, we should note that there are conditions under which some of these physical things, like cigarettes, which don't even qualify as near-money under present conditions may move all the way up to become money proper under other conditions. These are the conditions earlier summed up by the word "hyperinflation." Since hyperinflation means that the purchasing power of currency and demand deposits shrinks rapidly, it is another way of saying that the amount of physical things like cigarettes and cognac that a dollar's worth of currency or demand deposits can command in exchange shrinks rapidly. The same thing happens to the purchasing power of near-moneys, for $1 in near-money is by its very nature convertible into $1 of money, no more and no less. Accordingly, the amount of physical goods it will exchange for will decrease as rapidly as does the amount that money itself will exchange for. As was noted earlier, if the value of money (and of near-moneys) depreciates at an extremely rapid rate—i.e., if there is hyperinflation—then those things that were money will cease to be money, and certain physical things like cigarettes will come to be generally acceptable and thus come to be money. Also those things, like savings deposits, that were near-moneys will cease to be near-moneys. For if cigarettes became money, near-moneys would by definition be those things convertible into cigarettes quickly, easily, and without appreciable loss. None of the old near-moneys could begin to qualify, for they are convertible at fixed rates into currency or demand deposits and not into cigarettes.

Still, there would be a tendency for new near-moneys to appear. One can visualize savings accounts, shares in credit unions, and the like in which the saver's passbook showed so many *cigarettes* instead of so many *dollars*. These things would clearly be kinds of new near-money, for they would be things convertible quickly, easily, and without appreciable loss into what had come to be money. Actually, the customary forms of money would come back into use long before the situation had reached this state. Hyperinflations are eventually ended as the government "stabilizes the currency" by exchanging units of the almost worthless old currency for units of new currency (e.g., the German government in 1923 exchanged *one* new mark for 1 trillion of the old) and by terminating its policy of trying to finance itself by resort to the "printing press." Once this is done, commodities like cigarettes that may temporarily have achieved the status of money will be supplanted by the new "stable" currency.

Although a modern economy could hardly function effectively, even temporarily, with cigarettes or some similar commodity as its money, such an economy would offer us one small advantage: the explanation of what determines the money supply could be more direct and less involved than in the case where money is currency and demand deposits. If cigarettes are money, the rate at which the money stock grows would depend in part on the economy's capacity to produce cigarettes. The laws of production relevant to the output of any manufactured commodity would apply within limits here. But when the money supply is made up of currency and demand deposits, the economy's capacity to "produce" money is virtually unlimited. A pound of tobacco can make only a limited number of cigarettes, but a given quantity of paper and ink can make almost any dollar amount of money. To increase the amount, merely raise the denomination per unit of currency by any desired multiple. It is even easier in the case of demand deposits, for it is no more problem to record an entry of $10,000 in the books of a bank than it is to record an entry of $1.

It is, of course, the very fact that the mere act of production is nowadays no barrier to the infinite expansion of the money stock which makes it vital that the government guard against its own tendency at times to take actions that result in an excessive expansion of the money stock. A major reason for establishing monetary authorities with a certain degree of autonomy, like the Federal Reserve authorities in the United States, is to have some group specifically responsible for seeing to it that the money supply does not expand too rapidly—or too slowly. The basis on which the monetary authorities determine what are regarded as appropriate changes in the money supply and the particular actions by which they bring about these desired changes are obviously matters of great importance and matters to which considerable attention will be paid in later chapters. However, an obvious prerequisite to consideration of these and other equally important questions regarding money is to make as clear as possible what money is, and to do this has been the objective of this first chapter.

A CONCLUDING NOTE

There is more than a grain of truth in the cynic's remark that "Nobody knows what money is!" This is not to say that money has not been defined; definitions abound, but none satisfactorily answers the cynic's assertion. The most popular and least involved definition is that money is anything generally acceptable in payment for goods and services. We approached the concept of money in this chapter by first looking at this definition. We first approved it for its ability to pin down in tight fashion what things qualify as money, but we criticized it in the next breath for excluding absolutely things that differ only ever so slightly from the things that qualify as money. If they are so very close, might they not just as well be included as money?

There is no easy answer to this question, and it is not vital here that we somehow come up with one. Our purpose in this chapter has been merely to raise this and a few other basic questions pertaining to the meaning of money. In the first place, what makes anything money? When does that which is usually money cease to be money? Why are demand deposits money while checks are not? Where do we draw the line between money and near-money? Between near-money and almost near-money? To these questions we have provided what are at best only preliminary and partial answers. In so doing, however, we have at least developed some feeling for what we mean by this thing called money and also for what we don't mean—this is a foundation on which we will be building later.

two

MONEY IN MOTION: THE T-ACCOUNT

To provide a systematic treatment of many of the questions that arise in the area of money, we have a simple tool that enables us to follow step by step the effects of various actions taken by the monetary authorities, the commercial banks, the public, and other groups. This simple but indispensable tool is the T-account. Through it we can trace the effects of the actions of various groups on the balance sheet of each of these groups. This chapter introduces this tool and offers some illustrations of its use.

First of all, a balance sheet for an individual, a firm, a governmental unit, or any other entity that *owns* things and also *owes* things is a specially organized summary statement of the dollar values of these things at any particular date in time. Thus, an individual may prepare a list of the things he owns, or a list of his *assets*, with a dollar value attached to each. The dollar value of some of these assets can only be estimated, although professional appraisers can give him a fairly reliable figure for his house, furnishings, art objects, and the like. The value of any shares of stock of major corporations he may hold can be checked readily in the daily newspaper. The value of what he holds in near-money form like savings accounts at banks is whatever amount appears in his passbook. No estimating at all is ordinarily required in determining the dollar amounts for each item in the list of what he owes, the list of his *liabilities;* apart from the complication of accrued interest in some cases, these will be fixed dollar amounts as of any date. For example, the dollar amount owed on his house, his car, his charge account at the department store, and so forth. If we now subtract the total dollar amount of his liabilities from the total dollar amount of his assets, the remainder (which can be negative) is his *net worth.* With some qualifications, this may be viewed as the dollar amount he would have left for himself after using up whatever assets are required to pay off all his liabilities or debts.

What has been here described for an ordinary individual is true in principle but in much more complex form for the largest corporation in the land. For a corporation, the term *capital accounts* is ordinarily used instead of net worth, but it also is basically nothing more than the difference between the corporation's assets and its liabilities. However, in the case of the corporation, it is a measure of the stockholders' or owners' share in the assets of the company. Subject to considerable qualification, it may be viewed as the dollar amount that would be left for stockholders after using up whatever assets are required to pay off all the corporation's liabilities.

These three concepts provide the basis for what may be called the fundamental balance sheet identity, an identity being nothing more than a relationship that follows from a set of definitions and is in turn true by definition. This particular identity may be expressed as *assets − liabilities = net worth* or, alternatively, as *assets = liabilities + net worth.* Any transaction, such as the purchase of raw materials by a firm or the payment of a doctor bill by an individual, produces changes in the dollar amounts of particular assets, liabilities, and, in some cases, of net worth. The purpose of the T-account is to pinpoint the specific changes that occur as a result of any given transaction. It does not show the total amount of each asset and liability or the total amount for net worth on a particular date; it shows only the changes in these amounts produced by a given transaction, with a plus sign for an increase and a minus sign for a decrease. As may be apparent from the fundamental balance-sheet identity, for any one transaction there cannot be a change in only one item in the balance sheet; for any one transaction there must be at least two changes to maintain the balance between assets, on the one side, and liabilities plus net worth, on the other side.

Among the various possibilities are the following: an increase (decrease) in one asset may be offset by a decrease (increase) in another asset, and similarly an increase (decrease) in one liability may be offset by a decrease (increase) in another liability. An increase (decrease) in one asset not matched by a decrease (increase) in another asset is accompanied by an increase (decrease) in liabilities or in net worth. Similarly, an increase (decrease) in one liability not matched by a decrease (increase) in another liability is accompanied by an increase (decrease) in an asset or a decrease (increase) in net worth. Almost all of the transactions we will be dealing with involve only changes in assets and liabilities. Thus, we will find that a change in one liability not offset by a change in another liability will be matched by a change in an asset, and a change in one asset not offset by a change in another asset will be matched by a change in a liability.

Let us now turn to some particular transactions. We began the preceding chapter with a reference to several of a commonplace nature: the receipt by a worker of a weekly pay check and the expenditure of that full amount or the setting aside of part of it as saving. If the worker spends all that he receives, he may write checks for this amount in payment for what he buys. This is the first transaction we will examine. A second possibility and the second transaction that we will examine is that he spends this same total in part by writing checks and in part by paying out currency. The third and last transaction we will look into here is of a different nature, when the worker spends only part of the total received and puts the remainder into a savings account.

DEMAND DEPOSITS ARE TRANSFERRED

Suppose that John Jones, an auto worker in Detroit, receives for a particular week a pay check in the amount of $200 drawn by General Motors Corporation (GMC) against its checking account at the National Bank of Detroit (NBD), and suppose further that this worker also has a checking account at one of the offices of this same bank. If he has the bank credit the amount of the check to his account, the only effect of the transaction is that the

bank shows a decrease of $200 in one liability, the amount it owes to
GMC, and an increase in another liability, the amount it owes to Jones.
The T-account for the bank will show the entries labeled (a):

NATIONAL BANK OF DETROIT

Assets	Liabilities		
	Demand deposits:		
	GMC	−$200	(a)
	John Jones	+$200	(a)
	Demand deposits:		
	John Jones	−$200	(b)
	Others	+$200	(b)

Our interest here is primarily in the effect of the transaction on
the bank's T-account, but for completeness we may also set up T-
accounts for GMC and Jones. One possible set of entries that shows the
effects of this particular transaction follows:

JOHN JONES

Assets		Liabilities
Wages due	−$200	
Demand deposit	+$200	

GMC

Assets		Liabilities	
Demand deposits	−$200	Wages owed	−$200

If Jones now draws checks totaling $200 against his demand
deposit to pay some of his outstanding bills and to buy some goods for
"cash," the recipients of these checks are in the same position relative
to Jones that Jones was earlier relative to GMC. Although there is a
complication here in the fact that the recipients of these checks deal
with many other banks as well as the National Bank of Detroit, it does
no violation to the principle here being examined if we assume that all
of these recipients also deal with this same bank. Finally, if all the
recipients of Jones's checks simply deposit the checks to the credit of
their checking accounts, the result will be the entries labeled (b) in the

T-account given above for the bank. All of the recipients of Jones's checks are for convenience here lumped together as "Others." Clearly, there is again no change in the bank's T-account other than in the composition of its liabilities: a decrease of $200 in the amount owed to Jones and an increase of $200 in the amount owed to "Others." Whatever the total of the bank's demand deposit liabilities was before GMC drew the check for $200 in favor of Jones, that total is still the same at the present point, insofar as these transactions affect it.

Again for completeness, one may add here a T-account for "Others." Suppose that Jones disbursed the $200 by writing checks totaling $110 in payment of outstanding bills and totaling $90 in payment of goods purchased for "cash." The T-account for "Others" might then show the following:

OTHERS

Assets		Liabilities
Demand deposits	+$200	
Accounts receivable	−$110	
Goods on hand	−$ 90	

It would be possible to follow the $200 initially transferred by check from GMC to Jones and then from Jones to others through subsequent transfers as these others wrote checks and transferred the $200 to still others. However, the principle this simple transaction brings out is probably already clear: over a period of time, the same dollar of demand deposits may be used repeatedly in making payments. Of course, whoever owns any given dollar of demand deposits can use it only once, for the act of using it to make payment is the act of giving it up or transferring it to somebody else. Statistics show that the average dollar of demand deposits in the United States is now used about 70 times per year, or more than once per week on the average. It may be better to say this is the number of times per year that the average dollar of demand deposits "turns over" instead of saying that it is the number of times it is "used," because, unlike the many things that are *used up* as they are used, a dollar of demand deposits is a thing that may turn over an unlimited number of times without being used up in the slightest degree. It is, in a sense, an infinitely durable object. Our illustration above showed only two of these turnovers: from GMC to Jones and from Jones to others. Our illustration did not indicate the elapse of any particular interval of clock time, but tracing through what is involved in the actual process suggests that these two specific turnovers could quite plausibly occur within a period of a week or two.

CASH IS WITHDRAWN FROM THE BANKS

One may well object at this point that the preceding illustration is formally correct but somewhat unrealistic in that Jones would be more likely to "cash" his check and spend cash than to write checks. But payment by check is increasingly common, so the most realistic case today may be a combination of both. Suppose then that on pay day Jones wants $50 of cash or "pocket money." Among the things it owns or counts among its assets, every bank includes an amount of currency that it believes is sufficient to meet the ordinary demands its depositors may make upon it. If Jones presents the $200 check and takes $50 in currency and $150 in credit to his demand deposit, the bank's T-account will show three entries as follows:

NATIONAL BANK OF DETROIT

Assets	Liabilities
Currency −$50	Demand deposits:
	GMC −$200
	John Jones +$150

Note that there is in this case more than a shuffling of the bank's deposit liabilities. There has been a decrease in its assets of $50 and a decrease in its liabilities of $50, or −$200 + $150 = −$50. From the viewpoint of the public (here made up of only GMC and Jones), there has been an increase of $50 in one of its assets, currency or cash, and a decrease of $50 in another of its assets, demand deposits. Demand deposits, which are a liability to the banks that owe them, are, of course, an asset to the public who owns them or to whom they are owed. In terms of a T-account for the public, we then have the following two entries:

PUBLIC

Assets	Liabilities
Currency +$50	
Demand deposits −$50	

Recall that according to the basic definition of money given to us by the criterion of general acceptability, the only things that qualify as money are demand deposits and currency in the hands of the public. The definition of "public" excludes all firms that have demand deposits among their liabilities, which means that it excludes all commercial banks, but it includes all other business firms from GMC to the corner drugstore, all persons from the president of GMC to John Jones, all state and local governmental units, nonprofit organizations, and the like. By this definition of money and this definition of public, the public's holdings of money are unchanged by the transactions that produce the entries shown in the public's T-account above. The public now has $50 more in currency but $50 less in demand deposits.

It is apparent that the switch from demand deposits to currency does not change the *total* of money held by the public but changes only the *form* in which an unchanged total is held. What is not so apparent is that this switch in itself brings this $50 of currency from a location in which it was not a part of the total money stock to a location in which it is a part of that stock. Currency located in a bank teller's cash drawer or in the vault of a bank is not counted as part of the nation's stock of money; that same currency, however, is counted as part of the stock of money when it is in the hands of the public. It is obviously the same physical substance, no matter who holds it, but whether or not it is part of the stock of money does depend on who holds it.

Offhand this may seem to make no sense, for once we agree that currency is money, we should be able to say flatly that every dollar of currency represents a dollar in the total stock of money. But if we were to take this approach, it would mean that every time the public converted some of its demand deposits into currency, the total stock of money in the system would by this very act fall by that amount, since the public still has the same total for currency and demand deposits combined that it had before the switch but the banks now have that much less in currency than they had before. By the same argument, the public's action in switching any given amount of its currency holdings into additional demand deposits would be counted as an equal increase in the stock of money.

Instead of concluding that it makes no sense to exclude currency held in commercial banks and include only currency held outside these banks (i.e., by the public), it is more correct to conclude the opposite. By the basic definition, we view the stock of money as the number of dollars held in those forms that can be used directly to make payment—namely, currency and demand deposits. However much this total number of dollars may vary over time for other reasons, it should not vary merely because the public chooses to hold more of it in currency and less in demand deposits or vice versa. Of course, this same total will vary as the public at times converts *savings* deposits into money or vice versa; but there is no reason to compound the problem by defining money itself in a way that makes its amount change because the public shifts from the currency form of money to the demand deposit form of money.

The fact that the definition of money rules out bank-held currency as money must not be interpreted to mean that a dollar of currency held by the banks is a weak brother to a dollar of currency held by you or me. On the contrary, each dollar of currency held by the banks is quite commonly and appropriately described as a dollar of "high-powered money," as each of these dollars provides the basis on which the banks can create four or five dollars of new demand deposits, which means the addition of that number of dollars to the money stock. We must defer a fuller explanation of this phenomenon until we get to the subject of bank reserves and deposit creation in the next chapter. Here we only need recognize that to deny bank-held currency the status of inclusion in the money supply is not to deny it another and even more important status in the monetary system.

SAVINGS ACCOUNTS ARE CREATED

Implicit in the transactions underlying the entries in the T-accounts above was the assumption that Jones intended to spend the full $200 of his wage income for that week, the only question being whether he would carry out the spending by handing over currency or by transferring demand deposits. Alternatively, he may, of course, have decided to set aside part of the $200 of income as saving. If his decision was to save $20 and spend $180, he might still do as he did in the first T-account above, deposit the full $200 to the credit of his checking account. Then after disbursing the $180, his balance in the checking account would be $20 higher than before with this $20 viewed by Jones as saving. What is, of course, more likely, especially if he saves on a fairly regular basis, is for him to put the $20 into a near-money form. Unlike currency and demand deposits on which the holder gets no interest return, all forms of near-money have the advantage of providing the holder with some rate of return. Jones is faced with a sizable list of near-money alternatives, one of which is a savings account at the same bank at which he carries his checking account. Suppose he turns in the $200 check from GMC at his bank in exchange for a $180 credit to his checking account and a $20 credit to his savings account. The entries in the bank's T-account are those labeled (a).

NATIONAL BANK OF DETROIT

Assets	Liabilities		
	Demand deposits:		
	GMC	−$200	(a)
	John Jones	+$180	(a)
	Savings deposits:		
	John Jones	+$ 20	(a)

	Demand deposits:		
	John Jones	−$180	(b)
	Others	+$180	(b)

The immediate effect of this is a decrease in the stock of money; as a result of this transaction, the public's holdings of demand deposits are $20 less than they were. At the same time, the public's holdings of near-moneys are $20 greater than they were. After Jones disburses the $180 as planned for currently purchased goods and services and in payment of outstanding bills, the entries in the bank's T-account are those labeled (b), assuming as earlier that the recipients of Jones's checks all deposit those checks to the credit of their respective checking accounts at this same bank. Thus, starting with the check drawn by GMC against its account and ending at the present point, the net changes are $200 less in the GMC checking account, $180 more in the checking accounts of "Others," and $20 more in Jones's savings account. Arithmetically, this is the result we get by merely combining all the changes shown in the bank's T-account above. The two entries for Jones under demand deposits cancel out, and the entries that remain are the three entries described in the second preceding sentence.

A savings account at the bank where he has his checking account is only one of the many possible near-money forms into which Jones can put his saving. Which he chooses may make little difference to him. However, our definition of money is such that whether he puts these funds into a savings account at a commercial bank, on the one hand, or into any of the other possible near-money forms, on the other hand, does make a difference so far as its direct effect on the stock of money is concerned. Suppose that Jones already has or opens an account with the First Federal Savings and Loan Association of Detroit and puts the $20 of saving into that account. Starting again with the check for $200 drawn by GMC against its account, we will have the following entries in the T-accounts for the bank and the association.

NATIONAL BANK OF DETROIT

Assets	Liabilities	
	Demand deposits:	
	GMC	−$200
	John Jones	+$180
	First Federal	
	Savings and Loan	
	Association	+$ 20

FIRST FEDERAL SAVINGS AND LOAN ASSOCIATION

Assets		Liabilities	
Demand deposits	+$20	Share account of John Jones	+$20

We have assumed that Jones first deposited the full amount of his $200 check to his checking account and then wrote a check for $20 payable to the association in the same way that we earlier saw him writing checks payable to others. The association adds $20 to Jones's passbook balance with it and sends Jones's check to the bank, where the $20 is, of course, charged against Jones's checking account and credited to the checking account of the association. The T-account for the association shows a rise of $20 in the liability "Share accounts" and a rise of $20 in the asset "Demand deposits." As before, for convenience we are assuming that this savings and loan association happens to carry its checking account with the same bank at which Jones carries his checking account.

It comes as a surprise to many people that savings and loan associations, which to them seem to be banks much like other banks, have no choice but to carry demand deposits at commercial banks in order to be able to make payments by check. But a check, which is an order directing the payment of the indicated amount on demand, can be written only against deposits payable on demand, and it is only commercial banks that are legally permitted to maintain what are strictly demand deposit liabilities. Or, more correctly, only those banks that are legally permitted to maintain demand deposit liabilities are called commercial banks—this, it turns out, is the distinguishing feature of commercial banks. This distinction is not as sharp today as it was for the preceding half-century. A small number of mutual savings banks over the last few years have issued a new kind of deposit known as a "negotiable order of withdrawal," which is quite close to the conventional demand deposit. Nevertheless, so far at least the distinction remains a workable one. Only banks with conventional demand deposits are commercial banks. Among financial institutions with "bank" in their names, we find mutual savings banks, investment banks, mortgage banks, and still others, but none of these has demand deposits among its liabilities, so none of these is also a commercial bank.

What is the relevance of all this in the present context? Simply this. If Jones shifts $20 from his demand deposit to a savings deposit at the same bank (which must be a commercial bank because it has demand deposit liabilities), the total amount of money in the economy decreases by $20 and the amount of near-money increases by $20. But if, as in the last transaction above, Jones shifts $20 from his demand deposit to a savings and loan association (or to a mutual savings bank or to a credit union), the result is different: there is no decrease at all in the amount of demand deposits held by the public and, given an unchanged amount of currency held by the public, there is no decrease at all in the money supply, but there is an increase of $20 in the amount of near-money held by the public. In this case, new near-money comes into being, not at the expense of a decrease in the amount of money in the economy, but in addition to an unchanged amount of money.

It may appear that this difference is nothing more than a peculiarity that follows from the way the concept of the stock of money held by the public has been defined. One might argue in these terms: because you don't count commercial banks as part of the public, you should not count other financial institutions like savings and loan associations as part of the public either. Then the demand deposits held by the savings and loan associations will not be counted as demand deposits held by the public and, so far as the stock of money held by the public is concerned, the result above is the same whether Jones puts his $20 of saving in the bank or in the savings and loan association. This seems to be a convincing argument. However, the result noted is actually more than a matter of definition. If Jones shifts $20 from his demand deposit to a savings deposit at the National Bank of Detroit, for the bank it is in dollar terms merely an offsetting shift from one bank liability to another and thus a change that leaves the bank's assets unchanged. But if Jones shifts the $20 from his demand deposit to a share account at the First Federal (or to a mutual savings bank or to a credit union), the association shows an increase in liabilities *and* an equal increase in assets. The difference that follows from this may now be apparent. Commercial banks, savings and loan associations, mutual savings banks, credit unions, and other financial institutions all make loans. Specifically as a result of Jones's action, the First Federal now has available $20 in money that it did not have before. If a satisfactory borrower is available, the First Federal can make a loan of almost $20, something it could not have done if Jones had merely switched the $20 from his demand deposit to a savings deposit at the National Bank of Detroit. On the other hand, if Jones *had* merely switched the $20 at the bank, the bank would not by this action suddenly find itself with an almost equal amount of new funds that it could loan out.

The difference between these two cases would be very difficult to discern without the assistance of the T-accounts on pages 29 and 30. Our immediate purpose in these and preceding pages has been to show how one can employ the T-account to trace the effects of various transactions. In doing this, however, one gets into more than the mechanical manipulation of entries under assets and liabilities. Thus, it happens that the two transactions compared just above, the movement of funds from demand deposits to a savings deposit in the same bank versus the movement of funds from a demand deposit to a share account in a savings and loan association or to another thrift institution, lead us into one aspect of a major controversy in monetary economics. It seems from what we just saw that the public can add to the amount of funds available to borrowers by shifting deposits from one location to another. If millions of John Jones's were to shift funds to savings and loan associations in the way described in the illustration, it would appear that the associations could then provide an addition to the amount of funds being made available to borrowers that would not have been available if these funds had been left on deposit in the commercial banks. Suppose now that because of inflationary pressures or other reasons the monetary authorities are attempting to restrict the amount of funds being made available to borrowers to spend. Does an action such as that described then tend to thwart the policy the monetary authorities are trying to carry out? Some economists say yes and some say no. We will not pursue this difficult question, whose answer involves much more than an ability to trace transactions through T-accounts. However, such an ability is an indispensable prerequisite to making any progress toward answering this and many other questions confronted in this area.

A CONCLUDING NOTE

An almost endless number of other transactions, including some that bring in the Federal Reserve Banks and the U.S. Treasury, could be traced out in the same way as those we followed. The few to which we have limited ourselves were selected not only to show the way the T-account can be used as a tool—tracing any transactions will do this—but to shed light on the concepts of money and near-money to which the preceding chapter was devoted. In the following chapters we will be employing the T-account to illuminate many other concepts.

Over the years money has acquired a largely unwarranted reputation as something mysterious, whose innermost secrets have been revealed to or unraveled by only a select few. It is true that one does find in most areas of study only a handful of gifted scholars who operate at the outer fringes where the problems encountered seem so intractable as to be almost mysteries. But there are problems of money encountered closer to the other extreme that the average person has been conditioned to view as if they too were mysteries, even though they really are not. In some cases a good part of the mystery that surrounds these less difficult problems can be dispelled by almost anyone through resort to the simple, systematic device of dissecting transactions and tracing their elements through a series of T-accounts. We have provided a sample of this technique in this chapter.

three

BANK RESERVES
AND MONEY

In any pay period, General Motors Corporation and all other employers pay wages to John Jones and all other employees. Jones and the others in turn pay out these receipts to still others. We started out in Chapter 2 indicating that GMC already "had the money in the bank" to pay Jones and, by implication, the hundreds of thousands of its other employees, but we did not explain how the money got there. Presumably this occurred as dealers paid GMC for cars and trucks supplied, and the dealers in turn got the money as they received payment for the cars and trucks sold to the rest of us. This process indicates something about where each individual or firm gets the money it holds at any time and so also indicates something about the total amount of money everyone together, or the public as a whole, holds at any time. It also, therefore, would seem to say something about what determines the amount of money the public holds at any time. It is specifically this question to which we next turn, and the first step taken toward an answer is the negative one of pointing out that we cannot get an acceptable answer by any such approach as that noted above. When pursued to its extreme, that approach leads one to say that the amount of money that everybody holds at any time depends on the amount that everybody got from everybody else. This, we can all agree, is not much of an answer.

Still many people do try to explain the total amount of money in the system along these lines. As they see it, because each individual essentially determines how much money he personally will hold, therefore individuals as a group determine how much money they will hold as a group. Their collective decision accordingly determines the amount of money in the economy. The fallacy here is known as the fallacy of composition: what is true for each individual separately is not necessarily true for all individuals taken together. Each individual can and does, within certain limits, determine the amount of money he will hold, but all individuals combined cannot and therefore do not determine the amount of money they will hold as a group. Let us see why we get these opposite conclusions in the two cases.

An individual can increase the amount of money he holds by spending less money than the amount he receives as income, or by selling assets, or by borrowing. He can decrease the amount of money he holds simply by using the excess to support a higher level of consumption expenditures or to purchase assets or to pay off previous borrowings, if he has any. However, the appearance that all individuals can, through the same actions, control the amount of money they hold as a group is an optical illusion. What is overlooked is the fact that any one individual can increase (decrease) his holdings of money in the ways noted only because one or more other individuals have chosen to decrease (increase) their holdings. Each is getting money from or releasing money to others. But at any point in time there is a given total of money in the hands of the public, and it necessarily follows from this that everybody cannot simultaneously either get more money from everybody else or release more money to everybody else. The amount of money that happens to exist at a point in time is the amount of money that the public must necessarily hold at that point in time, but the amount of money that exists at a point in time is not an amount determined by the public. Broadly speaking, the public itself cannot change the amount of money available to be held, although the firms and individuals that make up the public may by their actions cause the existing amount of money to move from one pocket to another or from one checking account to another.

This assertion that the public itself cannot change the amount of money it holds would seem to be the grossest contradiction of what was said in the first chapter. For if it is true that the public can at will convert into money the hundreds of billions of dollars it holds in near-moneys (or vice versa), it most assuredly can in this way vastly change the amount of money it holds. Here, however, we must take note of a characteristic of near-moneys that we had no reason to concern ourselves with in the earlier chapter. Near-moneys are convertible into money quickly, easily, and without appreciable loss only if not too many holders of near-moneys try to convert at the same time. In principle, this is the same as the fact that demand deposits maintain their status as money only if not too many holders of demand deposits try to convert from this form of money into the currency form at the same time. Such attempts in years now far behind us spelled bank closings. Actually, if the holders of demand deposits and of near-moneys all tried to convert into currency at the same time today, emergency actions would be authorized by government to provide this astounding quantity of currency. But in actuality a massive conversion like this would occur only under the most extreme conditions, specifically, the conditions of hyperinflation, which in turn are conditions in which the amount of money itself is already growing by leaps and bounds. The public's conversion of its near-moneys into money is then not undertaken because it wants to increase its holdings of something so rapidly declining in value but merely as an unavoidable intermediate step in the process of getting out of near-moneys and into goods.

If we set aside these obviously extreme conditions, which the U.S. economy has not even approached since colonial times, may one not still argue that the public under quite ordinary conditions has the power to increase its holdings of money. For an uncomplicated example, suppose that Jones and a million others like him each decides to switch $1,000 from his savings account to his checking account at his bank; the result would be, as we saw in Chapter 2, an increase of $1 billion in the public's holdings of money. Cannot the public, then, at least to this extent, determine the amount of money that it holds?

That it can follows incontrovertibly as a matter of simple definition. An action like the one noted does in itself increase the stock of money in the hands of the public by $1 billion. However, this says only that the public can increase the money supply if the monetary authorities do not oppose such an increase. If, on the contrary, the monetary authorities have decided—say, because of developing inflationary pressures—that a decrease in the amount of money held by the public is in the best interest of the economy, they will take the actions needed to produce the desired decrease and in so doing will offset the increase that otherwise would have occurred.

The public is not the only group other than the monetary authorities which can take certain actions that tend to change the money supply. There are also actions taken by the U.S. Treasury and, most important of all by far, actions taken by the commercial banks. We will look at these actions of the commercial banks in some detail later in this chapter, but their importance in this regard may be immediately apparent from the fact that the money supply itself is composed primarily of the liabilities of the commercial banks. Demand deposits, which are nothing more than such liabilities, constitute over three-fourths of the money stock. It would then seem that if the commercial banks take actions which increase both their earning assets and demand deposit liabilities, they thereby bring into being demand deposits that did not previously exist, or they thereby increase the economy's money stock. In the same way, they take demand deposits out of existence and thereby decrease the money stock by taking the opposite actions.

The actual changes that occur in the public's money holdings over time in fact correspond closely with precisely such actions by the commercial banks. It is the public's willingness to take payment for what it sells in the form of demand deposits that makes this possible. Loans, which are one of the two major earning assets in the commercial banks' balance sheets, come into being through the purchase by the banks of borrowers' promises to pay, for which the banks make payment with newly created demand deposit liabilities. For example, the granting by all banks combined of, say, $100 million of additional loans to businesses and consumers will result in the entries labeled (a) in the following T-account. The borrowers exchange their promises to pay $100 million (plus interest) for $100 million added to their demand deposit balances. Investments or securities, which are the other major earning asset in the commercial banks' balance sheets, are purchased from their previous holders with payment again made with newly created demand deposit liabilities. This is illustrated in the T-account by the (b) entries. The sellers of the $100 million of securities take payment from the banks with that amount of newly created demand deposits, and the banks add that amount of securities to their earning

ALL COMMERCIAL BANKS

Assets			Liabilities		
Loans	+$100 million	(a)	Demand deposits	+$100 million	(a)
Securities	+$100 million	(b)	Demand deposits	+$100 million	(b)

assets. For the two transactions combined, there is an expansion in the banks' earning assets of $200 million and in the banks' deposit liabilities of an equal amount. With no change in the public's currency holdings, the $200 million increase in the public's demand deposit balances is that much of an increase in the money supply.

There is no question but that the commercial banks can increase or decrease the money supply through these actions of lending and investing. This is as incontrovertible as the conclusion that the public can increase or decrease the money supply through its actions of shifting balances from time to demand deposits or from demand to time deposits within the commercial banks. However, just as we noted above that the monetary authorities can offset such actions taken by the public, we note here that the monetary authorities can control the amount by which the commercial banks may expand their earning assets and thus create new demand deposits and thus enlarge the money supply. Recognition of the fact that the commercial banks can create money through their actions of lending and investing does not alter the fact that the monetary authorities in the final analysis can still determine the money supply by controlling this money-creating power of the commercial banks in a way to make the total money supply what the authorities want it to be.

A word of qualification: to say that the amount of money in the hands of the public is the amount it is because the Federal Reserve authorities want it to be that amount is not to say that the money supply for May 22, 1974, was $280.6 billion because the authorities wanted it to be precisely that amount on that date. The authorities cannot determine the size of the public's money holdings down to the last million as of a particular date. The fact that the money stock is affected by actions other than those taken by the monetary authorities means that those authorities can "have their way" only over a period of time. Thus, the stock of money may change over a period of a few months in a way that is contrary to the authorities' intentions, but over a longer period they can assert themselves and make the figure come close to the one they want.

Specifically, how do the monetary authorities control the amount of money in the hands of the public? We cannot answer this question in detail until Part II, but, to get off the ground, let us start out here with a short—and necessarily imprecise—answer and build from that. The Federal Reserve authorities control the amount of money held by the public by controlling the *sum* of the Federal Reserve Banks' currency and deposit liabilities and by dictating the minimum amount, in the form of currency or deposits at the Federal Reserve Banks, that the commercial banks must hold against each dollar of their deposit liabilities.

BALANCE SHEETS: FEDERAL RESERVE BANKS
AND COMMERCIAL BANKS

To get any meaning at all out of this answer requires as a first step the introduction of the Federal Reserve Banks into the picture, for it is primarily through control over the assets and liabilities of their Federal Reserve Banks that the monetary authorities exercise control over the money supply. Table 3–1 presents a simplified balance sheet or statement of condition, the name usually given to a bank's balance sheet, for the 12 Federal Reserve

TABLE 3–1

STATEMENT OF CONDITION
OF ALL FEDERAL RESERVE BANKS (in billions)
June 30, 1974

Assets		Liabilities	
Cash	$ 0.2	Deposits	$ 34.2
Gold certificates	11.5	Federal Reserve Notes	65.3
Loans	3.2	Other liabilities	6.5
U.S. Government securities	80.5	Capital accounts	2.2
Other assets	12.8		
	———	Liabilities plus	———
Total assets	$108.2	capital accounts	$108.2

STATEMENT OF CONDITION
OF ALL COMMERCIAL BANKS (in billions)
June 30, 1974

Assets		Liabilities	
Cash	$ 8.4	Deposits	$623.8
Deposits at Federal		Other liabilities	112.8
Reserve Banks	30.1	Capital accounts	61.6
Loans	529.0		
Investments	189.8		
Other assets	40.9		
	———	Liabilities plus	———
Total assets	$798.2	capital accounts	$798.2

Banks that make up the system of these banks. The table is highly condensed to show specifically only the particular asset and liability items we have need to look at here. Because the actual changes in the money supply are primarily in the form of changes in the demand deposit liabilities of the commercial banks, one can say little about the question of control of the money supply without looking into the balance sheet of the commercial banks. The second part of Table 3–1 offers an abbreviated balance sheet for the over 14,000 commercial banks in the United States as of the date given.

There is much that could be said in advance about the Federal Reserve Banks. They constitute what is called a central bank and are comparable to the Bank of England, the Bank of France, or the Deutsche Bundesbank. Like other central banks, the Federal Reserve Banks act as fiscal agents for the central government, assist the commercial banks in the collection of checks, handle the distribution of paper currency and coin, and perform other routine services. But some of the most important things that need to be said at the outset about the Federal Reserve Banks may be said by noting the major similarities and differences in the items found in the balance sheets for these banks and the commercial banks.

After adjusting for the fact that similar things sometimes carry different names, we find that several of the major assets and liabilities found in the balance sheet of the commercial banks have a counterpart in the balance sheet of the Federal Reserve Banks. On the asset side, commercial banks show "Loans," the total amount owed to the banks by the millions of individuals and firms who have borrowed for hundreds of purposes—to finance the purchase of a car, a house, a computer, a machine tool; to pay for doctors' services, vacations trips, raw materials, and machine repairs. On the asset side, the Federal Reserve Banks also show "Loans," a relatively small item. This amount at any date is the amount owed to the Federal Reserve Banks by the one and only group of borrowers they regularly deal with, the nation's commercial banks. The commercial banks lend to any person or firm deemed creditworthy and for almost any purpose and almost any time period; the Federal Reserve Banks lend only to the commercial banks, usually for short time periods (about 15 days), and typically only to enable the commercial banks to meet a temporary problem. The Federal Reserve Banks never seek to increase the amount of their loans as a means of increasing their income; most of the excess of income over costs of these banks is given to the U.S. Treasury. In contrast, the prospect of greater income and greater profits is what underlies an increase in the volume of loans made by the commercial banks.

Again on the asset side, commercial banks show "Investments," which is the term used to cover their total holdings of U.S. Government securities, state and local government obligations, and corporation bonds and stock (of negligible amount). The Federal Reserve Banks show a similar asset reported specifically as "U.S. Government securities" instead of the broader term "Investments" because the only kind of securities they purchase are U.S. Government obligations. Just as in making loans, commercial banks buy securities for the purpose of securing the interest income and earning a profit. In contrast, the Federal Reserve Banks' holdings of U.S. Government securities are never increased to increase interest income. Increases and also decreases in this asset item are effected solely to increase or decrease the *sum* of the amount of currency they issue and the amount of their other liabilities that are convertible into currency. We will turn in Part II to an explanation of how this most important control operation is carried out.

Once again, on the asset side, we find that both groups of banks show "Cash," a word here understood to mean currency (which in turn we are using to include coin as well as paper money). Apart from coin, which is issued exclusively by the Treasury, almost all cash in the monetary system is now in the form of Federal Reserve Notes, which, as we will see just below, are liabilities of the Federal Reserve Banks. This means that the small amount of cash shown among the assets of the Federal Reserve Banks is almost entirely coin. The amount of cash shown among the assets of the commercial banks, however, is made up almost completely of Federal Reserve Notes issued by the Federal Reserve Banks and coin issued by the U.S. Treasury.

Finally, on the asset side of the Federal Reserve Banks' balance sheet is the item "Gold certificates," the only place in the banking structure that this item is found. These amount to "warehouse receipts" for an equal amount of gold bullion held by the U.S. Treasury at Fort Knox and other locations, and the dollar amount of this item shown in the assets of the Federal Reserve Banks is only slightly less than the total physical gold stock (valued at $42.22 per ounce) held by the Treasury. Thus, one may say, in a sense, that the Federal Reserve Banks "own" this amount of gold and that they accordingly hold among their assets some fraction of a dollar's worth of gold for every dollar's worth of liabilities. The implications of this are of interest from an international viewpoint, and we will come to this in Part IV. Here we need only note that gold certificates are a major asset of the Federal Reserve Banks and appear among the assets of only the Federal Reserve Banks.

Shifting now to the liability side of our two balance sheets, we find another similarity: deposits appear as a major liability of both groups of banks. We already know what the deposit liabilities of the commercial banks are—the checking deposits and time deposits of

GMC, John Jones, and all the rest of us. What are the deposit liabilities of the Federal Reserve Banks? One thing they are *not* is deposits of GMC, Jones, or any other such firm or individual. No private firms, with the exception of commercial banks, and no individuals at all carry deposit accounts at any of the Federal Reserve Banks. Actually, about 90 percent of the deposits at these banks are held by the nation's commercial banks. Most of the remaining 10 percent of the deposit liabilities of the Federal Reserve Banks are assets of the U.S. Treasury. The Treasury has the legal authority to carry deposit accounts at the Federal Reserve Banks, and it chooses to make all its payments by drawing checks against these accounts instead of against demand accounts maintained at the commercial banks. The Treasury's deposits at the Federal Reserve Banks thus serve the same purpose as any firm's or individual's demand deposit at a commercial bank.

The commercial banks' huge deposit balances at the Federal Reserve Banks are there for a reason altogether different from the reason for the Treasury's deposit balance. The deposits of the commercial banks constitute one of the two assets that qualify as *legal reserves* for those commercial banks that are "member banks" of the Federal Reserve System (and for simplicity here we will assume that all commercial banks are member banks). The only other asset that qualifies as legal reserves is the currency held in the vaults of the commercial banks. As mentioned above, the bulk of the currency outstanding is in the form of Federal Reserve Notes. This is the largest single liability of the Federal Reserve Banks and one of the two major liabilities listed in the balance sheet in Table 3–1. What we now see is the fact that *the two commercial bank assets which qualify as legal reserves are the very same two items which appear as the two major liabilities of the Federal Reserve Banks.* To the commercial banks, a dollar's worth in one form is no different from a dollar's worth in the other form—each is a dollar's worth of legal reserves. To the Federal Reserve Banks, a dollar's worth of one liability is no different from a dollar's worth of the other. The commercial banks can move freely from one of these two assets to the other with no direct effect other than a change in the composition of their total assets, and the Federal Reserve Banks can similarly move freely from one of these two liabilities to the other with no direct effect other than a change in the composition of their total liabilities.

Although there is this parallel between these two assets of the commercial banks and these two liabilities of the Federal Reserve Banks, note that the convertibility between these two liabilities of the Federal Reserve Banks is exclusive to these banks. *No other bank of any kind anywhere in the financial structure has the power to print paper money or in effect to substitute a currency liability as a means of meeting a deposit liability.* For this reason, the Federal Reserve Banks can meet any requests by their commercial bank customers to exchange deposits for currency without the slightest difficulty or inconvenience. The commercial banks as a group, on the other hand, can encounter a problem in meeting their customers' demands for currency. They obtain additional currency not by printing it—there is no liability item for paper money outstanding in the balance sheet of the commercial banks—but by exchanging deposits at the Federal Reserve Banks for it. Because the amount of these deposits they have at the Federal Reserve Banks is not something they control, they have no way of securing more of these deposits if the monetary authorities don't want them to have more. If the commercial banks actually had unlimited access to deposits at the Federal Reserve Banks, they would not only have unlimited access to currency but complete control over the sum of these two asset items. As above noted, it is the sum of their deposits at the Federal Reserve Banks plus currency in their vaults that makes up their legal reserves, and it is the amount of these reserves that plays a key role in determining the amount of loans and investments the banks may own at any time. We turn now to look more closely at this role of legal reserves.

THE ROLE OF LEGAL RESERVES

In the field of banking, there is probably not a harder working word than the word "reserves"; it is commonly used in a dozen different ways by attaching a dozen different adjectives, of which "legal" is one. We will find it necessary to introduce several of these other adjectives a few pages hence. However, whether reference is to legal reserves or any other form, it is important to see that the word itself always refers to a *dollar amount*, measured usually as the sum of two or more particular assets or sometimes as the difference between two such sums. The most important of these dollar sums is the one measured as the sum of those two assets that count as legal reserves.

The adjective "legal" is appropriate as an identification of this particular dollar amount because it refers to the dollar amount that the commercial banks have on hand to meet requirements imposed on them by law. Banks are, of course, subject to hundreds of legal requirements, but that of first importance to us is the following: each bank must maintain among its assets a dollar amount in the form of cash in vault and deposits at the Federal Reserve Bank equal to a specified *percentage* of the dollar amount of deposits found among its liabilities. These percentage requirements are different at any time for demand deposits and time deposits and for different banks depending on the total amount of demand deposits and time deposits held by a bank. Furthermore, these percentage requirements vary over time as the Federal Reserve authorities raise or lower the percentages applicable to the demand and/or time deposits at the banks in all or in selected bank size classes.

Despite the complications produced by these variations, there is a crucially important underlying proposition that stands out unmistakably: *given any existing set of percentage reserve requirements, the upper limit to the amount of deposits which may be found among the liabilities of the commercial banks as a group is determined by the amount of legal reserves they hold as a group.* To express the same thing in slightly different form: if the commercial banks as a group have a dollar amount of legal reserves just equal to the amount required to satisfy the percentage reserve requirements on the dollar amount of their existing deposits, the amount of those deposits is at its upper limit. In this event, a prerequisite to an increase in the dollar amount of these deposits is either an increase in the dollar amount of legal reserves held by the commercial banks or a decrease in the specific percentage reserve requirement imposed on these deposits.

Since the Federal Reserve authorities decide what the percentage reserve requirement shall be and since they also control the dollar amount of those assets which qualify as legal reserves, it follows that the authorities can control the maximum amount of deposits the commercial banks may have on their books at any time. Beyond this, they can with these same powers also control the total amount of money in the hands of the public. In order to provide a simple numerical illustration of this conclusion, let us sidestep a series of complications by assuming that the commercial banks have deposit liabilities of the demand type only and that all commercial banks are subject to the same percentage reserve requirement, say 20 percent. We will also assume that all currency (which again includes coin) is issued by or is a liability of the Federal Reserve Banks (in other words, we assume that there is no currency issued by the Treasury). Adopting what may appear to be several rather drastic assumptions actually does not affect the conclusions to be reached here in any essential way; it merely enables us to reach the appropriate conclusions without needless complications.

Now suppose that on a particular date the liabilities of the 12 Federal Reserve Banks show $55 billion outstanding in Federal Reserve Notes (in denominations from 1 cent upward) and $30 billion in deposits owned by the commercial banks. These figures appear in the hypothetical balance sheet for the Federal Reserve Banks given as the first balance sheet in Table 3–2. As soon as we ascertain what part of

TABLE 3–2

FEDERAL RESERVE BANKS

Assets		Liabilities and Capital Accounts	
Gold certificates	$10	Federal Reserve Notes	$55
U.S. Government securities	65	Deposits of commercial banks	30
Loans	1	Other liabilities	4
Other assets	14	Capital accounts	1
		Total liabilities and	
Total assets	$90	capital accounts	$90

COMMERCIAL BANKS—BALANCE SHEET (a)

Assets		Liabilities and Capital Accounts	
Deposits at Federal		Demand deposits	$175
Reserve Banks	$30	Nondeposit liabilities	5
Cash in vault	5		
Legal reserves	35		
Loans	100		
Investments	50	Capital accounts	20
Other assets	15		
		Total liabilities and	
Total assets	$200	capital accounts	$200

COMMERCIAL BANKS—BALANCE SHEET (n)

Assets		Liabilities and Capital Accounts	
Deposits at Federal		Demand deposits	$200
Reserve Banks	$30	Nondeposit liabilities	5
Cash in vault	10		
Legal reserves	40		
Loans	115		
Investments	55	Capital accounts	20
Other assets	15		
		Total liabilities and	
Total assets	$225	capital accounts	$225

the $55 billion of Federal Reserve Notes is in the vaults of the commercial banks and what part is outside the commercial banks—i.e., in the hands of the public—we will be able to show the maximum possible amount of deposits the commercial banks may have outstanding and the maximum possible amount of money in the hands of the public. Suppose that the commercial banks hold $5 billion and the public holds the other $50 billion. This tells us that the commercial banks have a total of $35 billion in legal reserves, $30 billion on deposit at the Federal Reserve Banks and $5 billion cash in vault. Given the 20 percent reserve requirement, this amount of legal reserves is able to support a maximum of $175 billion of demand deposits at the commercial banks ($35 billion being 20 percent of $175 billion). This is the amount of deposits shown in the hypothetical balance sheet for all commercial banks labeled "Balance Sheet (a)" in Table 3–2. To get the figure for the money stock requires nothing more than the summing of the $50 billion of currency held by the public and the $175 billion of demand deposits held by the public. The money stock is, therefore, $225 billion.

With the same initial figures for the two Federal Reserve Bank liabilities, $30 billion in deposits held by the commercial banks and $55 billion in Federal Reserve Notes outstanding, a split of currency into $10 billion held by the banks and $45 billion held by the public would mean a maximum of $200 billion of demand deposits at the commercial banks and a maximum money stock of $245 billion. In Table 3–2, the hypothetical balance sheet for the commercial banks labeled "Balance Sheet (n)" fits this case.

It is worth noting that this illustration covers something that was simply asserted in Chapter 2. If the public exchanges some of its holdings of currency for demand deposits, that currency, once in the hands of the commercial banks, is no longer counted as part of the money stock. However, each dollar of that currency becomes a dollar of legal reserves (or what is sometimes called "high-powered money") and, in the present illustration, will form the support for $5 of the other form of money, demand deposits. The curious conclusion is that a dollar of currency ceases to be counted as a dollar in the stock of money when it passes from the public into the commercial banks but in the process becomes the basis for the creation of more than a dollar of the other kind of money, demand deposits.

EXCESS RESERVES
AND THE MULTIPLE EXPANSION OF DEPOSITS

In passing from Table 3–2's Balance Sheet (a) to its Balance Sheet (n), we simply asserted that the result of the movement of $5 billion of Federal Reserve Notes from the hands of the public into the vaults of the commercial banks would be, at a maximum, an increase in the public's holdings of demand deposits in the amount not merely of the $5 billion secured by the deposit of currency but of five times this amount, or $25 billion. This says that the public could end up holding $25 billion more in demand deposits, $5 billion less in currency, and thus on balance $20 billion more in money.

In turning to an explanation of this extraordinary result, we must recognize two fundamental facts at the outset: first, the already noted fact that the commercial banks are required to keep in legal reserves an amount equal to only a fraction of their demand deposit liabilities and, second, the fact that the commercial banks are essentially no different from other businesses in their pursuit of profits. In this pursuit, a banker typically looks far more contentedly at an extra $1 million of assets in the form of loans or investments than at an extra $1 million in the form of deposits at his Federal Reserve Bank or in the form of cash in the bank's vault. As nature abhors a vacuum, a banker abhors nonearning assets. Loans and investments are earning or interest-bearing assets, and legal reserves are not. An extra $1 million in the previous form may add from $50,000 to $150,000 per year to the bank's gross revenue; the same in the other form will not add a penny. The implications of this for the bank's profitability are obvious.

The relevance of both these facts will become apparent in the series of T-accounts and balance sheets we will now construct to show the process by which we get from Table 3–2's Balance Sheet (a) to its Balance Sheet (n). Note that in that table the second of the two balance sheets for the commercial banks is labeled not "(b)" but "(n)." A virtually endless time-consuming series of changes occurs in the process by which the banks get from (a) to (n), and we will show some of the steps in this endless series in terms of balance sheets (b), (c), and (d) that now follow.

Deposit Expansion Through Lending

Starting off with the public's deposit of $5 billion of its $55 billion of currency holdings with the commercial banks, the changes in the combined balance sheet for the banks are as follows:

COMMERCIAL BANKS

Assets	Liabilities
Cash in vault +$5	Demand deposits +$5

Or Table 3-2's Balance Sheet (a) with these changes inserted becomes Balance Sheet (b) below.

COMMERCIAL BANKS—BALANCE SHEET (b)

Assets		Liabilities and Capital Accounts	
Deposits at Federal		Demand deposits	$180
Reserve Banks	$30	Nondeposit liabilities	5
Cash in vault	10	Capital accounts	20
Legal reserves	40		
Loans	100		
Investments	50		
Other assets	15		
		Total liabilities and	
Total assets	$205	capital accounts	$205

Before the banks received this $5 billion in Federal Reserve Notes from the public, their legal reserves of $35 billion were just equal to 20 percent of their demand deposit liabilities of $175 billion, as indicated by the figures in Balance Sheet (a). Given the assumed reserve requirement of 20 percent, required reserves were $35 billion; the banks had legal reserves exactly equal to required reserves. The receipt of the $5 billion of currency from the public, however, adds $5 billion to legal reserves, while it raises required reserves by only $1 billion—that is, 20 percent of the $5 billion of new deposits that the banks provided in exchange for the public's $5 billion of currency. Or, in terms of the balance sheets, legal reserves rise from $35 billion to $40 billion, while required reserves rise from $35 billion (or 20 percent of $175 billion) to $36 billion (or 20 percent of $180 billion). In whichever way it is viewed, the result is that the banks now have $4 billion of what are known as *excess reserves*, which are simply the difference between legal reserves and required reserves.

Although bankers prefer interest-bearing loans and investments to noninterest-bearing legal reserves, they accept the inescapable fact that they must hold legal reserves of an amount sufficient to meet their percentage reserve requirements. But they need not hold legal reserves of an amount greater than this, and they find themselves doing just that now with legal reserves of $40 billion and required reserves of $36 billion. Of the $40 billion of legal reserves, $36 billion is immobilized by the reserve requirement, but the remaining $4 billion, or the amount by which legal reserves exceed required reserves, is available for use.

Suppose that the various banks around the country that just

acquired the $4 billion of excess reserves had been turning down the loan applications of creditworthy firms and individuals due to a lack of funds to lend. These banks apparently can now meet $4 billion of this demand for loans and will proceed to do so. The bank asset "Loans" accordingly increases by $4 billion as the banks acquire this amount of interest-bearing promises-to-pay from the borrowers. The offsetting balance sheet change depends on the form in which the borrowers take the $4 billion of funds. There are three possibilities: currency, credit to their demand deposits, or a combination of both. The first is entirely unrealistic. Although the third possibility is not entirely unrealistic—a few borrowers for special reasons may take currency—we will not be vary far off if we assume for simplicity that all of the borrowers take their loan proceeds in the form of credit to their checking accounts. Something close to this is in fact to be expected, since firms and individuals almost invariably borrow from the banks at which they are known, and these are the banks at which they carry their checking accounts. On this assumption, the T-account entries covering the combined loan transactions for all the banks involved are as follows:

COMMERCIAL BANKS

Assets	Liabilities
Loans +$4	Demand deposits +$4

And the balance sheet is now that indicated as Balance Sheet (c).

COMMERCIAL BANKS—BALANCE SHEET (C)

Assets		Liabilities and Capital Accounts	
Deposits at Federal		Demand deposits	$184
Reserve Banks	$30	Nondeposit liabilities	5
Cash in vault	10	Capital accounts	20
Legal reserves	40		
Loans	104		
Investments	50		
Other assets	15		
		Total liabilities and	
Total assets	$209	capital accounts	$209

Although the borrowers may all take the loan proceeds as credits to their checking accounts, they will, of course, in short order write checks in the amount of $4 billion to pay for current purchases or to pay outstanding bills. The borrowers, in acquiring additional assets in the form of a $4 billion increase in their checking account balances, have also acquired additional liabilities in the form of a $4 billion increase in their loans payable (or additional liabilities of something more than $4 billion if we were to be more exact and recognize accrued interest). Since they earn no interest whatsoever on the asset but do pay interest on the liability, borrowers are not likely to leave the loan proceeds sitting idly in their checking accounts. They will draw checks, and the persons and firms to whom they make payment will deposit these checks in their banks. As above, it would be completely unrealistic to assume that all of the recipients of these checks would exchange the checks at their banks for currency. Again, some part might be taken in currency, but for simplicity we will assume now as before that the recipients of all these checks deposit them to the credit of their demand deposits.

In our system, with over 14,000 commercial banks, we must now recognize the likelihood that there will be considerable redistribution of this $4 billion of new deposits among the banks. All of the recipients of the checks drawn by the borrowers against any one of the many banks that provided some part of the $4 billion in loans are not likely to have their accounts in that very same bank. They, of course, deposit the checks in the banks where they do have their accounts. What is involved then is the need for some banks to make payment to other banks as checks drawn by our borrowers against some banks are deposited by their recipients in other banks. This presents each of our lending banks, which must make payment, with no special problem, for each has in excess reserves an amount equal to the amount by which it increased its loans. Recall that collectively they had excess reserves of $4 billion and collectively they made additional loans of $4 billion. The actual transfer of the amounts to be paid by some banks and received by other banks could most readily be effected through the books of the Federal Reserve Banks, since each of our commercial banks has a deposit balance there. Thus, whatever the redistribution among the commercial banks of the additional $4 billion of demand deposits created by the banks which initially held that amount of excess reserves, there will be a corresponding redistribution of what is an unchanged amount of deposits that the commercial banks as a group have at the Federal Reserve Banks. On our assumption that none of the $4 billion was withdrawn from the banks in currency by either the original borrowers or by those to whom they made payments of $4 billion, there is also an unchanged amount of cash in the vaults of the commercial banks as a group. It then follows from these two observations that the total legal reserves of the commercial banks as a group are unchanged from the figures given in Balance Sheet (c).

This brings us to a major conclusion. *The banks as a group still find themselves with excess reserves after making additional loans and creating additional deposits of an amount equal to the amount of their excess reserves.* As noted above, the $4 billion of additional deposits in our illustration gets redistributed through the banking system as the borrowers of the $4 billion make payments to others, but these deposits remain on the books of the banks, which as a group show a deposit total of $184 billion in Balance Sheet (c). With the 20 percent reserve requirement, required reserves are now $36.8 billion instead of the $36 billion in Balance Sheet (b) with its deposit total of $180 billion. Legal reserves actually held, however, are still $40 billion, so the banks in the position described by Balance Sheet (c) show excess reserves of $3.2 billion (or $40 billion in legal reserves minus $36.8 billion in required reserves) in contrast to the $4 billion of excess reserves they had before they increased their loans by $4 billion. Increasing loans by $4 billion increased deposits by $4 billion, and this increased required reserves by $0.8 billion, which absorbed that amount of the original $4 billion of excess reserves and left the $3.2 billion we now find.

Deposit Expansion Through Investing

This $3.2 billion of excess reserves will be spread around among banks throughout the country, not necessarily excluding those that earlier held the original $4 billion of excess reserves. Like the original set of banks, these banks may be expected to acquire additional earning assets equal to the amount of their excess reserves. The next step may now be apparent: these banks make $3.2 billion of additional loans, and the borrowers take the proceeds in the form of $3.2 billion of additional demand deposits. Although this is very likely, let us take this opportunity to introduce an alternative that is also very likely: the banks with excess reserves purchase securities.

To pursue this alternative, let us suppose that the banks purchase $3.2 billion of U.S. Government and state and local securities from various dealers in such obligations. We immediately note this difference. When banks make loans, it is ordinarily to be expected that the borrowers will have the proceeds credited to their checking accounts at the banks from which they borrow. However, when banks buy securities, the sellers will not likely have demand deposit balances with each bank to whom they have sold. Most purchases and sales of securities by banks go through securities dealers, and, while each of these dealers by the nature of the business may sell to and buy from hundreds of banks, each one does not maintain hundreds of checking accounts. Accordingly, when our banks purchase the $3.2 billion of securities, they will pay the dealers with checks drawn against themselves, so-called cashier's checks, and not with newly created demand deposits. The dealers will promptly deposit these checks in the banks with which they do carry their deposit accounts. These banks in turn will secure payment from the bond-buying, check-issuing banks through a transfer of $3.2 billion in the deposit accounts carried by the various banks at the Federal Reserve Banks. The banks that purchased the $3.2 billion in securities will thus show an increase of this amount in one asset, investments, and a decrease of this amount in another asset, deposits at the Federal Reserve Banks.

Despite this initial difference between bank lending and bank investing, the important thing is that the two have the same final result on the dollar amount of the total assets and demand deposit liabilities of the banks as a group. Here the commercial banks *as a group* show a $3.2 billion increase in investments and a $3.2 billion increase in demand deposits, no different in magnitude from what we would have found if the banks had made $3.2 billion of additional loans instead of purchasing $3.2 billion of additional securities. Instead of the newly created demand deposits appearing originally among the deposits of the banks that make the loans, these deposits appear initially among the deposits of the banks that carry the accounts of the securities dealers. However, in both cases, the newly created deposits tend to get redistributed among the many banks in the system. For, just as the checks written by borrowers against their new deposits are deposited by their recipients in other banks, checks written by the securities dealers to pay for securities purchased to replenish their inventories are likely to be deposited by their recipients in other banks.

The purchase by the banks of the $3.2 billion of securities gives us the following entries in the T-account for the banks.

COMMERCIAL BANKS

Assets	Liabilities
Investments +$3.2	Demand deposits +$3.2

And the balance sheet is now that labeled (d) on page 53.

To go on now to Balance Sheet (e) and beyond would repeat what has been done in Balance Sheets (c) and (d) without adding anything to the principle already illustrated. As suggested by Balance Sheets (c) and (d), the banks within the system that find themselves with excess reserves as the process continues will make additional loans or investments equal to their excess reserves. Any one bank at any one time, in

COMMERCIAL BANKS—BALANCE SHEET (d)

Assets			Liabilities and Capital Accounts	
Legal reserves		$40.0	Demand deposits	$187.2
Deposits at Federal				
Reserve Banks	$30.0		Nondeposit liabilities	5.0
Cash in vault	10.0			
Loans		104.0	Capital accounts	20.0
Investments		53.2		
Other assets		15.0		
		———	Total liabilities and	———
Total assets		$212.2	capital accounts	$212.2

order to achieve what it regards as an appropriate balance between loans and investments in its portfolio, may devote its excess reserves entirely to one or the other or to some combination of both. This, as we have seen, does not affect the final outcome we are trying to explain. For the system as a whole, that final outcome is that the $4 billion of excess reserves acquired by the banks as a result of the public's deposit of $5 billion of currency provides the basis on which the banks expand their loans and investments by $20 billion. As the banks make additional loans and purchase additional securities totaling $20 billion, the banks create $20 billion of additional deposit liabilities. At this point the process comes to an end because the banks simply have no more excess reserves. Every dollar of the $4 billion of excess reserves that existed at the beginning has now ceased to be a dollar of excess reserves; these dollars have been reclassified one by one into required reserves. This was dictated by the banks' need to meet the 20 percent legal reserve requirement against the $20 billion increase in demand deposits that came into being dollar by dollar as the banks expanded their loans and investments by this amount.

With the process at an end, we find that the public holds $5 billion less in currency and $25 billion more in demand deposits; the banks hold $5 billion more in vault cash (currency) and $20 billion more in loans and investments. These are the results shown for the banks in Balance Sheet (n) back on page 45, where the "before" and "after" were presented side by side in the form of Balance Sheets (a) and (n). The preceding few pages have tried to bring out the essential mechanism by which the commercial banking system, once set into motion by an acquisition of excess reserves, moved from the position shown in Balance Sheet (a) to the quite different position shown in Balance Sheet (n).

THE PUBLIC'S DISTRIBUTION OF ITS MONEY STOCK
BETWEEN CURRENCY AND DEMAND DEPOSITS

We began this chapter by asserting that it is not the public who controls the amount of money it holds but the Federal Reserve authorities. However, having made this assertion, we seem to have proceeded thereafter in a way to disprove it. Consider the illustration in the preceding pages, which traced the effects of a decision on the part of the public to reduce its currency holdings by $5 billion and increase its demand deposits by $5 billion. Although the *immediate* effect of this decision is merely a change in the composition of an unchanged total of money held by the public, on our assumptions it sets into motion an expansion of bank lending and investing totaling $20 billion whose ultimate effect is an increase in the public's total money holdings by the same amount. The public's deposit of $5 billion of currency has been multiplied fivefold into a total increase in demand deposits of $25 billion, $5 billion originating through the currency deposit itself and $20 billion through the expansion of bank loans and investments.

If we had also examined the effects of the very opposite decision by the public—i.e., a *withdrawal* of $5 billion of currency from its demand deposit balances—we would have seen that this could set into motion a *contraction* of bank lending and investing totaling $20 billion whose ultimate effect would have been a *decrease* in the public's total money holdings by the same amount. The public's withdrawal of $5 billion of currency would have been multiplied fivefold into a total decrease in demand deposits of $25 billion, $5 billion originating through the currency withdrawal itself and $20 billion through a contraction of bank loans and investments. The two cases are exactly symmetrical, plus signs in the T-accounts for the one case would become minus signs in the T-accounts for the other.

We may now ask how anyone can deny that the public exercises considerable control over the amount of money it holds if the public can bring about changes of such magnitude by its decision to hold more or less of its money in currency form. Must we not agree that the public, if it so chooses, can run up the *total* of its currency plus demand deposits significantly if it is willing to increase the part of the total it holds in demand deposit form? Must we not also agree that it can run down the *total* of the two significantly if it decides to increase the part of the total it holds in currency form? From our own analysis above, the answer to these questions appears to be clearly affirmative. Appearances notwithstanding, the correct answer here is the same negative answer given earlier in this chapter to a related kind of question. On page 36 we noted that a million John Jones's could increase the public's money holdings by $1 billion if they each decided to switch $1,000 from their savings accounts at the commercial banks to their demand accounts. Although this much is in itself incontrovertible, the amount is not enough to permit the conclusion that these people thereby have the power to increase the money supply. If the Federal Reserve authorities don't want to see an increase in the money supply, they can in short order take the actions needed to offset this $1 billion increase. The final decision as to what the money supply shall be is theirs. We may now say the same thing in the case where the public exchanges some of its currency holdings for demand deposits. Although this transaction does not in itself change the money supply, it does enlarge the banks' legal reserves, creating excess reserves and thereby leading to additional bank lending and investing that does increase the money supply. But, again, if the Federal Reserve authorities don't want to see such an increase in the money supply, they can take the actions needed to offset it. The final decision is theirs. Specifically what these actions are and how they are carried out will be covered in Part II.

However, before we leave the present question, it should be seen that there is another and more basic reason why net deposits of currency by the public do not provide the banks with a basis for anything like a sustainable expansion in the money supply. The reason in short is that *net* deposits of currency by the public in the commercial banks as a group simply do not occur except on a temporary or seasonal basis. The banks as a group do enjoy a regular inflow of currency, for example, in January of each year, but this is nothing more than a post-holiday phenomenon that offsets in part the outflow that regularly occurs during the Christmas shopping season. It is also possible for individual banks to show an inflow of currency over a time period that is longer than a year and thus not seasonal, but other banks will then be showing an above average outflow of currency over a time period also longer than a year.

For the commercial banks as a group, the fact is that over the course of almost every year the public regularly withdraws currency on balance. We know that such withdrawals occur because the public's currency holdings do increase, as shown for recent years by the data in Table 3–3 below, and there is no place for the public to get this currency except from the commercial banks. If individuals convert some of their balances at savings and loan associations, mutual savings banks, credit unions or the like into currency, this does not change the amount of currency in the hands of the public by one dollar, for the currency held by all these financial institutions is already counted as

TABLE 3-3

U.S. MONEY STOCK
1956-1974 (in billions)

December	Currency	Demand Deposits	Total
1956	$28.2	$108.7	$136.9
1957	28.3	107.6	135.9
1958	28.6	112.6	141.1
1959	28.9	114.5	143.4
1960	29.0	115.2	144.2
1961	29.6	119.1	148.7
1962	30.6	120.3	150.9
1963	32.5	124.1	156.5
1964	34.3	129.5	163.7
1965	36.3	134.9	171.3
1966	38.3	137.0	175.4
1967	40.4	146.5	186.9
1968	43.4	158.1	201.5
1969	46.1	162.5	208.6
1970	49.1	172.2	221.2
1971	52.6	182.6	235.2
1972	56.9	198.7	255.7
1973	61.6	208.8	270.4
1974	64.2	213.0	277.2

Note: Averages of daily figures. Figures for 1974 are based on nine months.
Source: *Federal Reserve Bulletin.*

currency in the hands of the public. Those institutions will show an equal decrease in their deposit liabilities and in their cash in vault, but the public's currency holdings are unchanged by this. The fact that the public can get more currency only from the commercial banks follows, of course, from the fact that "the public" is defined as being everybody other than the commercial banks, the Federal Reserve Banks, and the U.S. Treasury. Since the public can get more currency only by drawing it out of the commercial banks, it follows that such withdrawals *tend* to reduce the amount of demand deposits held by the public. However, an examination of the record given by Table 3-3 shows that as the public increases its currency holdings each year, it enlarges the amount of its demand deposits as well. The only exception to this since 1956 is 1957, which was a year of recession. This simple statistical fact in itself should be enough to put to rest the wild idea still held by some people that the commercial banks as a group somehow build up their holdings of deposits over time through the deposits of currency by the public. The fact that these deposits are being expanded at the same time that the public is taking currency out of the banks conclusively rules this out as an explanation. For an explanation we are again forced back to the fact that the Federal Reserve authorities must have provided an amount of legal reserves sufficient to permit both an increase of currency in the hands of the public *and* an increase in the public's demand deposits. If over a period of time there is an increase in both, we may say that it occurred because that particular increase in the sum of the two was consistent with the increase in the stock of money that the Federal Reserve authorities wanted to see take place.

The monetary authorities' interest is in the money supply as a total and not in how that total is divided by the public between currency and demand deposits. In terms of its ability to command goods in the market, a dollar of one is no different from a dollar of the other. A growing economy requires a growing stock of money to handle the ever greater volume of transactions that accompany growth. The monetary authorities decide what an appropriate growth in the money stock is for any time period, but the public is left to decide how it will divide its total holdings of money between currency and demand deposits. If, then, the public chooses over time to keep an increasing fraction of the total in currency form, this tends to produce a drain on the reserves of the commercial banks. As we saw earlier, a given amount of currency in the vaults of the commercial banks will support a multiple of that amount in demand deposits (a multiple of five in our illustration with a 20 percent reserve requirement), but that same amount of currency in the hands of the public involves no multiple but enters the money supply on a dollar for dollar basis. Therefore, to the extent that the public is shifting toward holding a larger portion of its money in the currency form, the monetary authorities must see to it that the banks secure the larger amount of additional legal reserves required under these conditions to bring about any particular increase in the money supply that the authorities want to see take place.

The ratio in which the public chooses to hold currency and demand deposits is subject to some variation from year to year as may be seen by examining the data in Table 3—3. However, what is relevant to us here is that changes in this ratio in one direction or the other from one time period to another do not interfere with the ability of the Federal Reserve authorities to control the money holdings of the public over time. With the commercial banks subject to a given percentage reserve requirement, the authorities still control the money supply by controlling the *sum* of the currency the Federal Reserve Banks issue and the amount of the Federal Reserve Banks' other liabilities that are convertible into currency. To achieve any given growth in the money supply for any time period, this sum may be adjusted in fairly short order to cover any change in the public's currency/demand-deposit ratio. We will be returning to this question in more detail in Part II.

A CONCLUDING NOTE

There are many people who have always believed that only currency is money. To learn at some point that money, even in its narrowest definition, includes demand deposits comes as quite a surprise. As they learn a few other things that follow from this fact, their reaction is sometimes more than mere surprise. Some people are actually dismayed to learn that the bulk of the money supply is composed of what amounts to the liabilities of privately owned, profit-seeking business units known as commercial banks. Beyond this, some are perplexed to learn that the total amount of these liabilities which are money tend to increase and decrease as a result of the profit-oriented decisions of bankers to expand or contract the amount of loans they have outstanding or the amount of securities they hold. As a final step, some are stunned when they put the preceding together and recognize that so important a matter as the creation and destruction of money is closely related to the day-by-day actions taken by the commercial banks in their pursuit of profits.

An arrangement like this understandably appears to many to be one well designed to produce a disaster, and well it might in the absence of controls placed over it, primarily by the Federal Reserve authorities. How many billions of dollars the commercial banks may hold in total assets at any time, which in turn essentially determines the amount of deposits they will have outstanding at any time, depends primarily on the amount they hold of those special assets that qualify as legal reserves and on the amount of such assets they are required to hold for each dollar of their deposits—i.e., on the percentage reserve requirement. Both this dollar amount and this percentage are controlled by the Federal Reserve authorities.

However, given a situation in which the existing dollar amount of these legal reserves is more than that needed to meet the percentage requirement on the existing volume of deposits, what is the process by which the commercial banks as a group are able to acquire additional loans and investments and thereby create additional deposits equal to some multiple of this excess of legal reserves over required reserves? Our major purpose in this chapter has been to sketch the essentials of this multiple expansion process. Contrary to what is frequently believed by the average citizen, this process by which the commercial banks as a group increase their holdings of loans and investments is not one that depends on the prior deposit of currency or anything else in the banks by him or by the millions of other citizens. The public actually gets its holdings of money, the sum of its holdings of demand deposits and currency, as a result of the lending and investing activities of the commercial banks as a group. The reverse is incorrect: the lending and investing activities of these banks as a group do not occur as a result of the public's depositing money with these banks. In brief, the banks' lending and investing beget money; money does not beget the banks' lending and investing.

The amount by which the commercial banks are able to expand their holdings of loans and investments and thereby expand the money supply in any period of time is controlled by the Federal Reserve authorities. It is the purpose of the first chapter of Part II to look into the way these authorities exercise this control through their ability to vary bank reserves. The remaining chapters of Part II then go on to an examination of other aspects of this important question of controlling the money supply.

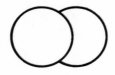

part two
CONTROLLING MONEY

four

THE FEDERAL RESERVE, BANK RESERVES, AND MONEY

How do the Federal Reserve authorities control the money supply? Although an adequate answer to so large a question is not without its intricacies, the basic element in any answer is as follows: *the Federal Reserve authorities control the money supply by controlling the amount of those assets held by the commercial banks which qualify as legal reserve assets and by dictating to the commercial banks the minimum amount of these specific assets that they must hold against each dollar of their deposit liabilities.* The two assets—and the only two assets—of the commercial banks that qualify as legal reserves are the deposits those banks carry at the Federal Reserve Banks and the currency in their vaults. Although the amount of currency they hold can be affected by the amount the Treasury has outstanding and, over short time intervals, by variations in the amount the public holds, nevertheless the Federal Reserve authorities can over time effectively control the total amount of these legal reserves by varying the amount of the Federal Reserve Banks' currency and deposit liabilities, which make up almost all of the commercial banks' reserves.

The critical role played by the amount of these reserves in influencing the amount of money that may exist in the economy at any time was examined in the preceding chapter. Our first task in this chapter is to examine the process by which the Federal Reserve Banks may bring about changes in the sum of their currency and deposit liabilities and to see in turn how these changes affect the legal reserves held by the commercial banks. The essentials of this process require little more for their explanation than the information that lies behind the balance sheets of the Federal Reserve Banks and the commercial banks. Condensed balance sheets for each set of banks were presented in the preceding chapter on page 39.

There, with the assistance of balance sheets and T-accounts, we traced through the essentials of the process by which the commercial banks' acquisition of additional earning assets in the form of loans and investments give rise to additional liabilities in the form of deposits. In very much the same way, but for altogether different reasons, the Federal Reserve Banks also acquire similar assets by making loans and purchasing securities and also typically pay for them initially by creating deposit liabilities. Growth in the deposit liabilities of the Federal Reserve Banks over time tends to be accompanied by growth in the Federal Reserve Note liabilities of these banks as some of these deposits are converted by the commercial banks into Federal Reserve Notes to meet demands by the public for currency. What we have then is a tendency toward parallel movements in the *sum* of the loans outstanding and securities held by the Federal Reserve Banks, on the asset side, and the *sum* of Federal Reserve Notes outstanding and deposits, on the liabilities side. This is only a tendency, since any specific rise in the sum of these two particular assets may be matched, for example, by a decline in the gold certificate asset with no change in any liability item. However, it is nonetheless true that the Federal Reserve authorities over time can deliberately vary the sum of the loans and security holdings of the Federal Reserve Banks in whatever way and to whatever degree is needed to effect any desired change in the sum of the Federal Reserve Note liabilities and deposit liabilities of those banks. For convenience in the following, we will look at a change in the amount of the loans or security holdings of the Federal Reserve Banks as if each were in every case initially matched by an equal change in the specific liability "Deposits of commercial banks."

THE FEDERAL RESERVE BANKS MAKE LOANS

For all practical purposes, lending by the Federal Reserve Banks is restricted to the commercial banks, so only the T-accounts of the two groups of banks are involved. A $100 million increase in Federal Reserve Bank loans outstanding will appear in the T-accounts as follows:

FEDERAL RESERVE BANKS

Assets		Liabilities	
Loans	+$100	Deposits of commercial banks	+$100

COMMERCIAL BANKS

Assets		Liabilities	
Deposits with Federal Reserve Banks	+$100	Borrowings from Federal Reserve Banks	+$100

The rate of interest, or the so-called discount rate, at which the commercial banks can borrow from the Federal Reserve Banks, the period for which they may borrow, the conditions under which they are permitted to borrow, and numerous other aspects are all important in this process, but the aspect of the process that is our immediate concern is the mechanical one: $100 million of additional borrowing by the commercial banks provides the banks with $100 million of additional *legal reserves*, other things being equal (and neglecting the complications of adjusting for interest paid on the borrowings). The banks have clearly added $100 million to their deposits at the Federal Reserve Banks, and, other things being equal, have therefore added $100 million to the total of their legal reserves. Instead of taking the proceeds of the loans as credits to their deposits at the Federal Reserve Banks, it would be possible for the commercial banks to take the $100 million in newly issued Federal Reserve Notes. The same increase in their legal reserve assets would then have been in the form of cash in vault instead of deposits at the Federal Reserve Banks, and the increase in the Federal Reserve Banks' liabilities would then have been in Federal Reserve

Notes outstanding instead of in deposits of the commercial banks. In either event, however, the commercial banks increase the amount of their legal reserves dollar for dollar with the increase in their indebtedness to the Federal Reserve Banks, other things being equal.

The reverse of this process in which the commercial banks pay off $100 million of their indebtedness to the Federal Reserve Banks would be shown by the same entries now given in the T-accounts with a minus sign in place of each plus sign. If the commercial banks repaid this amount by sending Federal Reserve Notes back to the Federal Reserve Banks, the commercial banks would show a −$100 million entry for cash in vault and the Federal Reserve Banks would show a −$100 million entry for Federal Reserve Notes outstanding. The other two entries would be as given in the T-accounts above with the plus signs again changed to minus signs.

The basic mechanics of Federal Reserve Bank lending to commercial banks involves nothing more than what is shown by these two T-accounts. Beyond the simple mechanics, however, lies the broad question of what is called Federal Reserve "discount policy," which includes such things as the rationale for and the actual actions taken by the Federal Reserve authorities from one time period to the next to encourage or discourage commercial bank borrowing from the Federal Reserve Banks. We will not get involved with these questions here. At the moment our concern is solely to see the fact that increases and decreases in the loans of the Federal Reserve Banks produce equal increases or decreases in the legal reserves of the commercial banks as a group, other things being equal.

To appreciate fully the importance of this fact, however, one also must see that it is the Federal Reserve Banks and only the Federal Reserve Banks that have the power to influence the amount of the commercial banks' legal reserves by varying the amount of their loans outstanding. One commercial bank with an excess of legal reserves can, if it so chooses, lend legal reserves to another bank, and the commercial banks as a group do this regularly on a large scale through what is called the "federal funds" market. However, no amount of such lending changes by $1 the amount of legal reserves the commercial banks as a group hold—it merely moves the existing amount around among the banks. For example, suppose that Bank B lends Bank A $1 million of legal reserves by having the Federal Reserve Bank transfer that amount from its deposit balance to the deposit balance of Bank A. This clearly involves no increase in the total of legal reserves, as is evident from the T-account entries for this transaction shown below. Later Bank A will repay Bank B by reversing this transaction. This, by the same argument, involves no decrease in the total of legal reserves.

COMMERCIAL BANK A

Assets	Liabilities
Deposits with Federal Reserve Bank +$1	Borrowing from Bank B +$1

COMMERCIAL BANK B

Assets	Liabilities
Deposits with Federal Reserve Bank −$1 Loan to Bank A +$1	

FEDERAL RESERVE BANKS

Assets	Liabilities
	Deposit of Bank A +$1 Deposit of Bank B −$1

A few banks at times borrow from the public by selling capital notes or bonds much in the manner that nonfinancial corporations regularly do. Again, borrowing of this kind leaves the total reserves of the banks unaffected, as is shown by the entries in the T-accounts below for such a transaction. By assumption the purchasers of the notes sold by Bank A (who become creditors of Bank A by said purchase but not depositor-type creditors) have their checking accounts at banks other than Bank A, so that Bank A takes away legal reserves from the other banks as it presents for payment the checks drawn by the note buyers against these other banks. The public itself, which includes these note buyers, shows only a switch from one asset, demand deposits, to another asset, notes.

By showing as we have here that commercial bank borrowing from other commercial banks or from the public is not a means by which the commercial banks as a group can secure additional legal reserves, we indirectly bring out the uniqueness of commercial bank borrowing from the Federal Reserve Banks. To the extent that we are concerned with the factors affecting the total amount of legal reserves held by the commercial banks as a group, the only kind of borrowing by the commercial banks with which we need to be concerned is their borrowing from the Federal Reserve Banks.

COMMERCIAL BANK A

Assets		Liabilities	
Deposits with Federal Reserve Bank	+$1	Capital notes outstanding	+$1

OTHER COMMERCIAL BANKS

Assets		Liabilities	
Deposits with Federal Reserve Bank	−$1	Demand deposits	−$1

FEDERAL RESERVE BANKS

Assets	Liabilities	
	Deposit of Bank A	+$1
	Deposits of other banks	−$1

PUBLIC

Assets		Liabilities
Capital notes	+$1	
Demand deposits	−$1	

THE FEDERAL RESERVE BANKS
BUY AND SELL SECURITIES

In its lending, each Federal Reserve Bank acts on loan applications from the commercial banks in its district, and each loan to each bank involves, so to speak, a visit by that bank to the Federal Reserve Bank's "discount window." In purchasing and selling U.S. Government securities, what is commonly referred to as *open market operations*, the Federal Reserve Bank of New York handles all such transactions for the whole system and in the process has direct contact with only some two dozen dealers in U.S. Government securities. When the Federal Reserve Bank of New York seeks to purchase some given amount of these securities, contact is made by phone with each of these dealers, and the planned purchase is made from those dealers who offer the lowest price at the time. The procedure is similar in the case of sales.

Although these transactions in the so-called open market are in this way effected through this relatively small number of dealers, in many cases the Federal Reserve Bank's purchases from dealers are matched by commercial banks' sales to dealers, so it is possible to look at these as if they were in fact purchases by the Federal Reserve Bank directly from the commercial banks, by-passing what in this event is the purely middleman role of the dealers. In the case of a $100 million purchase transaction of this kind, the entries in the T-accounts are as follows:

FEDERAL RESERVE BANKS

Assets		Liabilities	
U.S. Government securities	+$100	Deposits of commercial banks	+$100

COMMERCIAL BANKS

Assets		Liabilities	
Deposits with Federal Reserve Banks	+$100		
U.S. Government securities	–$100		

As in the case of a $100 million increase in loans outstanding, this increase of $100 million in U.S. Government securities held by the Federal Reserve Banks means an equal increase in the legal reserves of the commercial banks. In borrowing, the commercial banks secure an increase in their legal reserve assets by incurring an increase in their indebtedness to the Federal Reserve Banks; in selling securities to the Federal Reserve Banks, the commercial banks secure an increase in legal reserves by giving up an equal amount of another asset.

When the Federal Reserve Bank purchases U.S. Government securities from the public instead of the commercial banks, the results are somewhat different. To start off, let us suppose as before that the Federal Reserve Bank purchases $100 million of securities; this time, however, the ultimate sellers are individuals, life insurance companies, savings and loan associations, pension funds, or anybody else included as part of the public. No matter who the seller may be, as long as the seller is part of the public, the result here will be the same. As noted earlier, the Federal Reserve Bank will actually conduct its transactions through U.S. Government security dealers, but as before it is convenient here to view the transactions as if they were carried out directly with the public.

The Federal Reserve Bank will pay the sellers with checks drawn against itself, and the sellers of the securities will quite promptly deposit these checks to the credit of their demand deposits in the commercial banks with which they deal. These banks in turn will forward the checks into the Federal Reserve Banks and have the amount credited to their deposit balances. The entries in the T-accounts are then as follows:

FEDERAL RESERVE BANKS

Assets		Liabilities	
U.S. Government securities	+$100	Deposits of commercial banks	+$100

COMMERCIAL BANKS

Assets		Liabilities	
Deposits with Federal Reserve Banks	+$100	Demand deposits	+$100

PUBLIC

Assets		Liabilities	
U.S. Government securities	−$100		
Demand deposits	+$100		

The T-account for the Federal Reserve Banks turns out to be the same as before. No matter whether the commercial banks or the public sell the securities purchased by the Federal Reserve Banks, the result is an equal increase in the deposit liabilities of the Federal Reserve Banks and in the legal reserve assets of the commercial banks. Regardless of from whom they buy—and, indeed, regardless of what they buy—the Federal Reserve Banks essentially pay for whatever they purchase by issuing either deposit liabilities or Federal Reserve Notes. In the first instance, payment is almost invariably in the form of an increase in deposit liabilities, this being subsequently converted into Federal Reserve Notes only to the extent that the commercial banks and the public seek to hold a larger amount of paper money. Hence, the conclusion noted above: we derive the very same entries in the T-account for the Federal Reserve Banks whether they purchase from the commercial banks or from the public.

Unlike the T-account of the Federal Reserve Banks, that for the commercial banks is not the same in both cases. If the commercial banks are the sellers of the securities purchased by the Federal Reserve Banks, they show only an offsetting switch from one asset to another, from U.S. Government securities to deposits at the Federal Reserve Banks, with no entry at all on the liabilities side. But in the case in which the public happens to be the sellers, the commercial banks as a group show an increase in their demand deposit liabilities to the public as the public deposits the checks received in payment from the Federal Reserve Banks. This increase is then matched by an equal increase in the deposit balances of the commercial banks at the Federal Reserve Banks as the commercial banks send these checks up to the Federal Reserve Banks for credit to their deposit accounts.

Although the commercial banks in both cases gain the same $100 million in additional legal reserves, note that the increase in legal reserves is matched by an *equal* increase in their excess reserves only when the commercial banks are the sellers of the securities. In this case, their deposit liabilities are unchanged, which means that their required reserves are unchanged, which in turn means that their excess reserves are changed upward by the full $100 million addition to their legal reserves. In the other case, however, the means by which the commercial banks acquire the additional $100 million of legal reserves is through the $100 million of deposits that come into being as they credit the sellers of securities for the checks turned in to them. Assuming a percentage reserve requirement of 20 against these demand deposits, $20 million of the additional $100 million in legal reserves is absorbed in meeting the reserve requirement for the additional $100 million of deposits. Only the $80 million remaining is added to whatever amount of excess reserves the commercial banks may have already had. This difference has implications we will look into at a later point.

The next step in the present set of mechanics is to reverse the preceding process and trace the effects of the sale of U.S. Government securities by the Federal Reserve Bank for the same two cases: first, that in which the securities are purchased by the commercial banks and, second, that in which they are purchased by the public. Just as we saw that the commercial banks' *repayment* of loans to the Federal Reserve

Banks involved the very same entries in the T-accounts as the commercial banks' *borrowing* from the Federal Reserve Banks, except that each entry then carried the opposite sign, we see the very same thing here. If instead of buying the Federal Reserve Bank of New York sells $100 million of securities and the commercial banks buy this amount, the four entries in the T-accounts on page 69 remain as given, but the three plus signs become minus signs and the one minus sign becomes a plus sign. The commercial banks simply pay for the securities purchased by drawing down their deposit balances at the Federal Reserve Banks. This asset goes down $100 million, and another asset, holdings of U.S. Government securities, goes up by $100 million. The Federal Reserve Bank shows a $100 million decrease in both the asset and liability items entered in its T-account.

If the Federal Reserve Bank sells $100 million of securities to the public rather than to the commercial banks, we have the very same six entries as when the Federal Reserve Bank bought from the public, but again with the difference that each plus sign now becomes a minus sign and vice versa. If one starts off in this case with the fact that the Federal Reserve Bank receives payment for the securities sold with checks drawn by the purchasers against their commercial banks and traces the changes that occur in each of the three T-accounts on page 70 as these checks are collected, he will see how each of the signs is reversed from those given there to cover the situation in which the Federal Reserve Bank purchased securities.

What these basic mechanics bring out in unmistakable fashion is the fact that, other things being equal, Federal Reserve Bank purchases and sales of securities add to or subtract from the legal reserves of the commercial banks on a dollar for dollar basis. This parallels the fact developed above that increases or decreases in the amount of Federal Reserve Bank loans outstanding, other things being equal, add to or subtract from the legal reserves of the commercial banks on a dollar for dollar basis. As we saw there, commercial bank borrowing from the Federal Reserve Banks is unique in that it is only by borrowing from the Federal Reserve Banks that the commercial banks *as a group* can secure additional legal reserves through the act of borrowing. Again we have a parallel because, of all possible purchases of securities, it is only those by the Federal Reserve Banks that supply the commercial banks *as a group* with additional legal reserves.

Any one commercial bank, say Bank A, may be able to obtain additional legal reserves by selling securities even if the Federal Reserve Banks are not the purchasers. If another commercial bank, say Bank B, is the purchaser, the following T-accounts show that what Bank A gains in reserves Bank B loses, and this leaves unchanged the total legal reserves held by the commercial banks as a group.

BANK A

Assets		Liabilities
Securities	−$1	
Deposits with Federal Reserve Bank	+$1	

BANK B

Assets		Liabilities
Securities	+$1	
Deposits with Federal Reserve Bank	−$1	

Bank A may also succeed in getting additional legal reserves by selling securities even if neither the Federal Reserve Banks nor other commercial banks are buying. To do this Bank A sells securities to the public. The following T-accounts assume that Bank A sells $1 million in securities to nonbank purchasers who have their checking accounts at banks other than Bank A. In collecting the checks for $1 million, Bank A gains $1 million in its deposit balance at the Federal Reserve Bank, but it takes this amount away from the deposit balances of the other commercial banks at the Federal Reserve Banks.

BANK A

Assets		Liabilities
Securities	−$1	
Deposits with Federal Reserve Banks	+$1	

OTHER COMMERCIAL BANKS

Assets		Liabilities	
Deposits with Federal Reserve Banks	−$1	Demand deposits	−$1

PUBLIC

Assets		Liabilities
Securities	+$1	
Demand deposits	−$1	

A crucial question is whether all banks can do at the same time what Bank A has done here. All may possibly be able to sell securities at some price even if the Federal Reserve Banks are not buying, but *they cannot as a group expect to obtain any additional legal reserves in this way.* If the Federal Reserve Banks are not buying and all commercial banks are trying to sell (or some commercial banks are trying to sell but no commercial banks are buying), the only possible buyers left are the public, and they make payment by drawing down their demand deposit balances, a means of payment that does not provide the commercial banks with additional legal reserves. Assuming that all commercial banks together sell $100 million in securities to the public, the T-accounts are as follows:

ALL COMMERCIAL BANKS

Assets		Liabilities	
Securities	−$100	Demand deposits	−$100

PUBLIC

Assets		Liabilities
Demand deposits	−$100	
Securities	+$100	

For the commercial banks there is a matching decrease in their holdings of securities and in their demand deposit liabilities but no change in the amount of legal reserves held. On the assumption of a 20 percent legal reserve requirement, the decrease of $100 million in demand deposits does mean that $20 million of legal reserves previously classified as required are released to become $20 million of excess reserves, but again there is no change in whatever the pre-existing total of legal reserves may have been.

We see then that the buying and selling of securities by the Federal Reserve Banks, like lending by the Federal Reserve Banks, is unique in causing changes in the legal reserves of the commercial banks as a group. On any day thousands of loans are made by a long list of different types of lenders, varying from those by the Federal Reserve Banks at one end of the spectrum to the $100 loans by small loan companies to high-risk individual borrowers at the other end. But among these many types of lenders, only the Federal Reserve Banks create additional legal reserves in the course of expanding the amount of their outstanding loans or destroy existing legal reserves in the course of contracting the amount of their outstanding loans.

In a similar way, on any day there is a long list of different types—Federal Reserve Banks, life insurance companies, commercial banks, mutual funds, individuals, pension funds—who may be buying and selling U.S. Government, state and local, and corporate securities in the nation's bond markets, but in this list it is only the purchases and sales by the Federal Reserve Banks that tend to add to or subtract from the existing amount of legal reserves of the commercial banks.

The key to this repeatedly emphasized conclusion is the fact emphasized earlier that, apart from the qualifications needed to recognize the existence of currency issued by the Treasury, the only things that qualify as legal reserves are the two things that are the two major liabilities of the Federal Reserve Banks. The Federal Reserve authorities are able to control the sum of these two liabilities, and thereby in effect control the total of commercial bank legal reserves, merely by controlling the sum of the amount of loans and the amount of U.S. Government securities they hold in their portfolios. The amount of these loans outstanding is, to a degree, decided by the commercial banks, but the amount of securities held is completely a decision of the Federal Reserve authorities, and the latter can be adjusted to make the sum of the two whatever they want it to be and thereby make the sum of the Federal Reserve Note and deposit liabilities of the Federal Reserve Banks whatever they want it to be.

THE FEDERAL RESERVE AUTHORITIES CHANGE
THE PERCENTAGE RESERVE REQUIREMENTS

The foundation of the Federal Reserve authorities' control over the money supply is their ability to regulate the amount of legal reserves held by the commercial banks and their power to set the percentage reserve requirement that these banks must maintain against their deposits. Both are essential. The authorities would have little control over the money supply if they were to regulate the amount of reserves without also being able to set the percentage reserve requirements and no control at all if they were to set the percentage reserve requirements without also being able to regulate the amount of reserves. This does not mean that they must continuously raise or lower the percentage reserve requirement to be able to decrease or increase the money supply. They could set the percentage requirements at some level and, barring the most unusual circumstances, simply leave them at that level permanently. However, they must at the very least set them at some specific level (and a level appreciably above zero), or each commercial bank would be completely free to decide from day to day what total amount of cash reserves it felt was appropriate to hold against its deposit liabilities. Even in the absence of any legally imposed percentage reserve requirement, every bank would find it necessary to hold some cash reserves because it must always be ready to meet its depositors' ordinary demands for currency. But the Federal Reserve authorities could not exercise any close control over the total deposits in a system of thousands of commercial banks with each one making its own decision on this matter from day to day.

The actual system in this country is one in which a minimum legal reserve requirement is set by the monetary authorities. Depending on the level of this percentage, a given dollar amount of legal reserves can support a larger or smaller amount of money in the form of demand deposits. In Chapter 3 we assumed a 20 percent requirement, which gave us a 5 to 1 ratio, or $5 in demand deposits for every $1 in legal reserves. On the basis of this and other assumptions, if the commercial banks found themselves with $1 billion of excess reserves they could expand their loans and investments by a maximum of $5 billion, which would expand their demand deposit liabilities by $5 billion. That $1 billion of legal reserves, which previously had been excess reserves, would then have become required reserves, and the banks' existing legal reserves would all be needed to meet the legal reserve requirement against their now enlarged volume of deposits. The first balance sheet in Table 4-1 shows the banks in such a "loaned up" situation. It is assumed here for simplicity that the banks have only demand deposits and that all banks are subject to the same legal reserve requirement of 20 percent against these deposits.

Although the monetary authorities have made sparing use of it in recent years, they do have the power to vary this percentage requirement within certain limits set by Congress. The question we now turn to is the effect of any such variation on the amount of legal reserves of the commercial banks as a group, on the amount of earning assets they may be able to hold, and on the amount of demand deposits they may be able to support. The answer to the first part of this question is the easiest: changes in the percentage reserve requirements do not in themselves involve any change at all in the amount of the legal reserves of the banks. If the Board of Governors of the Federal Reserve System decides on such a change, they modify the appropriate regulations (known as Regulations D and M) and advise the commercial banks of what the new percentage requirements are, the date they become effective, and other matters of detail. This action, however, does not in

TABLE 4–1

COMMERCIAL BANKS—20 PERCENT RESERVE REQUIREMENT

Assets		Liabilities and Capital Accounts	
Legal reserves	$ 40.00	Demand deposits	$200.00
Loans and investments	170.00	Other liabilities	5.00
Other assets	15.00	Capital accounts	20.00
		Total liabilities and	
Total assets	$225.00	capital accounts	$225.00

COMMERCIAL BANKS—18 PERCENT RESERVE REQUIREMENT

Assets		Liabilities and Capital Accounts	
Legal reserves	$ 40.00	Demand deposits	$222.22
Loans and investments	192.22	Other liabilities	5.00
Other assets	15.00	Capital accounts	20.00
		Total liabilities and	
Total assets	$247.22	capital accounts	$247.22

COMMERCIAL BANKS—22 PERCENT RESERVE REQUIREMENT

Assets		Liabilities and Capital Accounts	
Legal reserves	$ 40.00	Demand deposits	$181.82
Loans and investments	151.82	Other liabilities	5.00
Other assets	15.00	Capital accounts	20.00
		Total liabilities and	
Total assets	$206.82	capital accounts	$206.82

itself change the amount of legal reserves the banks hold by as much as $1.

This conclusion suggests that changes in percentage reserve requirements as a tool of control differ from changes in the amount of Federal Reserve Bank loans to the commercial banks or in the amount of Federal Reserve Bank security holdings, since both of the latter tools operate directly on the amount of the legal reserves held by the commercial banks. Furthermore, unlike the mere change in Federal Reserve regulations required to effect a change in the percentage reserve requirement, a change in Federal Reserve Bank loans or security holdings involves actual operations in the market by the Federal Reserve Banks that are reflected directly in the assets and liabilities of those banks. The action of changing the percentage reserve requirement in contrast does not in itself affect the assets or liabilities of the Federal Reserve Banks in the slightest. This means that we need only the accounts of the commercial banks and the public to trace the direct effects of a change in the percentage reserve requirement.

Let us suppose then that the reserve requirement is reduced from the previously assumed 20 percent to 18 percent. In terms of the first balance sheet in Table 4–1, this action in itself does not change the dollar amount of legal reserves held by the banks. These were $40 (all figures here are in billions) before the percentage reduction and remain $40 after that reduction. What this action does—and all that it does directly—is to change the composition of the $40 of legal reserves from *$40 required* and *zero excess* to *$36 required* and *$4 excess*. Or it reduces required reserves by $4 and increases excess reserves by $4 (from an original zero level).

With the reserve requirement of 18 percent, each dollar of reserves is now able to support $5.55 of demand deposits. This 5.55 multiple may be derived by finding *DD*, or demand deposits, in the equation, $1 = 0.18($DD$), which simply amounts to finding that number that $1 is 18 percent of. More directly, this figure, which is called the *demand deposit multiplier*, is simply the reciprocal of the percentage reserve requirement; the multiplier equals 1/0.18, or 5.55, in the present case. A 25 percent reserve requirement would mean a demand deposit multiplier of 4—i.e., a dollar of legal reserves could support a maximum of $4 in demand deposits; a 10 percent requirement would mean a demand deposit multiplier of 10—i.e., a dollar of legal reserves could support $10 in demand deposits; and so forth.

With a reduction in the legal reserve requirement from 20 to 18 percent, the existing (and unchanged) $40 of legal reserves is able to support 5.55 × $40, or $222.2, of demand deposits, which is $22.2 more than the existing amount of deposits. Otherwise expressed, the $4 out of the $40 of reserves which became excess with the decline in the percentage requirement will provide support for 5.55 × $4, or $22.2, of additional deposits.

The banks are accordingly in a position to make loans to and purchase securities from the public in the amount of $22.2 billion. The entries in the T-account for the commercial banks would be as follows:

COMMERCIAL BANKS

Assets	Liabilities
Loans and investments +$22.2	Demand deposits +$22.2

The balance sheets for the commercial banks "before" the reduction in the percentage reserve requirement and "after" adjustment to that reduction are the first two given in Table 4–1. If we assume arbitrarily that the $22.2 figure for the banks is composed of $15 of additional loans and $7.2 of additional securities held, and that all of the additional $7.2 of securities were purchased from the public (as we must assume to prevent a change in the $40 billion figure for the total of legal reserves), the entries in the public's T-account would be as follows:

PUBLIC

Assets		Liabilities	
Demand deposits	+$22.2	Loans payable to	
Securities	−$7.2	commercial banks +$15	

In the reverse case, that of a rise in the reserve requirement from the initial 20 percent level to, say, a 22 percent level, required reserves against the initial $200 of deposits rise from $40 to $44 billion. Legal reserves, which as before remain unchanged in total at $40, do change in composition from *$40 required* and *zero excess* to *$44 required* and *minus $4 excess*, or a *deficiency of $4*. Or required reserves rise by $4 and excess reserves decline by $4 (from an original zero level).

The commercial banks could conceivably meet this deficiency by obtaining $4 of additional legal reserves, but as a group their only means of doing this is by borrowing from the Federal Reserve Banks or by selling securities to the Federal Reserve Banks. The monetary authorities presumably raised the percentage reserve requirement in order to force a contraction in commercial bank deposits and in the money supply, so they are not likely to permit the banks to avoid this outcome by supplying those banks with $4 of additional legal reserves through making loans and purchasing securities. If we take the extreme case in which the commercial banks are unable to get any additional reserves from the Federal Reserve Banks, what is the process by which they adjust to the deficiency? The process then reverses exactly that by which they adjust to an excess of reserves. In the illustration above of an excess of reserves, they expanded their loans and investments until the resultant rise in deposits called for $4 more in required reserves and thereby absorbed the $4 of what was previously excess reserves. In the present instance of a deficiency of reserves, they contract their loans and investments until the resultant decrease in deposits calls for $4 less in required reserves and thereby eliminates what had been a $4 deficiency of reserves.

A percentage reserve requirement of 22 means that each dollar of reserves is able to meet the requirement against $4.54 of deposits. The multiplier in this case is $1/0.22 = 4.5454$. Given this multiplier, the banks must reduce deposits by $18.18 to reduce required reserves by $4. The entries in the T-account are accordingly:

COMMERCIAL BANKS

Assets	Liabilities
Loans and investments −$18.18	Demand deposits −$18.18

The balance sheets for the commercial banks "before" the rise in the percentage reserve requirement and "after" adjustment to that rise are the first and third given in Table 4–1. If we assume arbitrarily that the total reduction of $18.18 in bank loans and investments happened to be composed of $5.18 billion in loans and $13 billion in securities, the entries in the public's T-account would be as follows:

PUBLIC

Assets		Liabilities
Demand deposits −$18.18		Loans payable to
Securities +$13.00		commercial banks −$5.18

Although the contraction process is the exact reverse of the expansion process, it may have been noted in our illustration that the results of the two are not symmetrical in all regards. The 2 percentage point decrease in the reserve requirement from 20 to 18 gave rise to an increase in excess reserves from zero to $4, and the 2 percentage point increase in the reserve requirement from 20 to 22 gave rise to a decrease in excess reserves from zero to −$4. At this step a symmetrical result. However, at the next step we found that the amount by which the banks were able to expand earning assets and deposits as a result of the $4 increase in excess reserves was $22.2, and the amount by which they were forced to contract earning assets and deposits as a result of the $4 decrease in excess reserves was the smaller amount of $18.18—a nonsymmetrical result. This difference is, of course, due to the fact that a change in the percentage reserve requirement changes the multiplier applicable to each dollar of legal reserves at the same time that it changes the way any existing amount of legal reserves is distributed between required reserves and excess reserves. Thus, the decrease from 20 to 18 percent raised the multiplier from 5 to 5.55, which raised the amount of deposits the $40 of legal reserves could support from $200 to $222.22 billion. Looked at in terms of excess and required reserves, the decrease from 20 to 18 percent reclassified $4 of reserves that had been required into excess, each dollar of which is available to support $5.55 of *additional* deposits. This gives us 5.55 × $4, or the $22.22 of additional deposits found as the total rises from $200 to $222.22 billion. In the opposite case of the rise in the percentage from 20 to 22, the multiplier declines from 5 to 4.5454, total deposits fall from $200 to $181.82, a decrease of $18.18 in contrast to the increase of $22.22 that followed from a decline in the percentage from 20 to 18.

From what we know about the operations of the commercial banks, it may be apparent that these equal decreases and increases in percentage reserve requirements are not symmetrical in a second but altogether different way: the response each will bring forth from the commercial banks. Decreases are enthusiastically welcomed and increases are even more enthusiastically opposed. Decreases permit a larger portion of any existing amount of assets to be held in earning form; increases force a larger portion to be held in nonearning form. One may also argue that a similar asymmetry will be found in the response of banks to lower and higher discount rates, but there is the significant difference that changes in discount rates affect directly only commercial banks that borrow from the Federal Reserve Banks, while changes in percentage reserve requirements affect directly all banks subject to those reserve requirements. These are important matters, and we will return to them after we have completed the construction of the necessary foundation. In this chapter we have put in a part of the foundation—we have traced through the basic mechanics of the process by which changes in Federal Reserve Banks' loans and holdings of securities and changes in commercial bank percentage reserve requirements affect the lending capacity of the commercial banking system.

A CONCLUDING NOTE

By merely varying the sum of the Federal Reserve Banks' loans and holdings of U.S. Government securities by whatever amount may be required, the monetary authorities are able to control the amount of legal reserves held by the commercial banks; by setting the minimum percentage reserve requirement the commercial banks must maintain against demand deposits, the monetary authorities are able to control the amount of demand deposits any given amount of legal reserves is able to support; and by controlling the amount of demand deposits, the monetary authorities are able to control the amount of money in the hands of the public, offsetting the effects of any shift by the public from demand deposits into currency or vice versa with appropriate changes in the amount of legal reserves held by the commercial banks.

Of these three statements, the first is true with virtually no qualification, the second is subject to some qualification, and the last requires greater qualification. The Federal Reserve authorities' close control over the amount of legal reserves would amount to an equally close control over the amount of money only if there were a rigid link between the amount of legal reserves and the amount of money. In order to introduce complications one at a time, we have proceeded in this chapter as if there were such a rigid link.

To recognize that the link is less than completely rigid is to recognize that there is some slippage between changes in legal reserves and changes in the money supply. At the same time, to recognize this slippage is in no sense to abandon the general conclusion that the Federal Reserve authorities control the money supply. The difference is a matter, not of control or no control, but of the degree of control. There is some controversy over how close a degree of control the Federal Reserve authorities are able to exercise, but it still seems to some specialists in this field that the authorities are able to keep the actual money supply, on the average, within a fraction of 1 percent of whatever level they want it to be over a period of around a quarter of a year.

Even if the Federal Reserve authorities can do this well, they still have less than complete control. In the next chapter we examine the major conditions that account for this slippage between changes in legal reserves and changes in the money supply.

five

THE SLIPPAGE
BETWEEN BANK RESERVES
AND THE MONEY SUPPLY

Only in a world quite different from that we know would the link between the amount of legal reserves held by the commercial banks and the money supply be perfectly rigid in the sense that any given change in the former would produce a fixed, predetermined change in the latter. Specifically, to get a link of this kind would require, among other things, that the following three conditions be satisfied:

1. The commercial banks have only demand deposit liabilities, no time deposit liabilities.

2. The commercial banks do not suffer a drain of currency as they expand their demand deposit liabilities, nor do they enjoy an inflow of currency as they contract their demand deposit liabilities.
3. The commercial banks are always "loaned up" to the limit set by the existing percentage reserve requirements and the amount of legal reserves held.

None of these conditions is fully or continuously satisfied in practice, which in each case introduces a degree of slippage between changes in the dollar amount of legal reserves and changes in the money supply. In the first part of this chapter we will examine these conditions one by one to see how the fact that each is not satisfied affects the change in the amount of money that any given change in the amount of legal reserves may produce. This essentially involves working through some additional mechanics of reserves, deposits, and currency, which will be done, as in preceding chapters, with T-accounts as far as possible. However, the nature of the questions faced here is such that some very basic algebraic expressions are unavoidable, and these are introduced as needed to back up the T-account presentations.

After working through these mechanics in three steps, we will turn in the second part of the chapter very briefly to the question of the implications of these conditions for Federal Reserve control of the money supply. Even if the Federal Reserve control over the amount of legal reserves were absolutely complete, this would not give the Federal Reserve authorities anything near complete control over the money supply unless the authorities could also somehow precisely offset or compensate for the slippages just mentioned. Complete precision in this sense is unattainable, but it would appear that the authorities can offset the slippages with sufficient precision to bring the money supply figure within a fraction of 1 percent of the figure aimed at over a period of approximately a quarter or so.

There is also an additional slippage problem—a fourth condition of a quite different nature from the other three—with which the authorities must cope. About 25 percent of the nation's demand deposits are held by banks that are not member banks of the Federal Reserve System and therefore are not subject to the reserve requirements set by the Federal Reserve authorities. Each of these banks is subject to reserve requirements set by the legislature of the state within which each is chartered, and these requirements may typically be met, at least in part, by assets other than cash in vault. In many states deposit balances carried with other commercial banks and holdings of U.S. government securities or of state securities may be used to meet at least part of the legal reserve requirement. This means that, even if the

Federal Reserve authorities were able to control precisely the sum of member bank deposits at the Federal Reserve Banks and member bank currency holdings, the amount of demand deposits held by all banks combined could vary as deposits move from member to nonmember or from nonmember to member banks. Thus, a shift in deposits to nonmember banks will mean that an unchanged total of member bank legal reserves will be consistent with an expansion of the deposit total for all banks combined, and the opposite in the case of a reverse movement.

' This source of slippage in the Federal Reserve's control over the money supply has become more serious in recent years as the proportion of total demand deposits held by the nonmember banks rose from 17 percent in 1960 to about 25 percent in 1974. To offset this slippage and thereby enable it to maintain closer control over the money supply, the Federal Reserve in January 1974 submitted to Congress a proposal to make nonmember banks subject to the same reserve requirements on demand deposits (and other deposits that perform a checking account function) that the member banks must meet on such deposits. If the Congress legislates accordingly, it would thereby essentially remove the distinction between member and nonmember banks so far as demand deposit reserve requirements are concerned and would thereby essentially remove the slippage that arises because of this distinction. This source of slippage is structural or institutional, and thus quite different from the other three sources of slippage, which arise from behavior patterns of the public and the commercial banks. An appendix to this chapter provides a brief look at the way that the slippage problem is affected by this structural characteristic. However, in the chapter proper as elsewhere in this book, we assume that all commercial banks are member banks, and within the chapter we limit attention to the three behavioral conditions in the list above.

THREE FACTORS CAUSING SLIPPAGE

Commercial Banks Have Time
As Well As Demand Deposits

In Chapter 2 we raised the question of whether the public had the power to increase or decrease the money supply at its own discretion. As an illustration, it was assumed that John Jones and a million other persons each decides to transfer $1,000 from his time deposit to his demand deposit account at his commercial bank. By the narrow definition of money with which we are working, the result is a $1 billion increase in the supply of money (and a $1 billion decrease in the amount of near-moneys). We asserted, however, in Chapter 2 that the ability to do this at any time it likes does not give the public the ability to change the money supply other than temporarily, because the monetary authorities can, if they feel it is called for, take the action necessary to offset this. Let us now see how this might work out.

First, however, we must note that the Federal Reserve authorities impose minimum percentage reserve requirements on time deposits as well as on demand deposits, though at a much lower level on the former than on the latter. As was mentioned in Chapter 4, the actual percentage requirement applicable to demand deposits is not uniform for all banks. The effective percentage varies directly with the amount of a bank's deposits. As of October 1974, for demand deposits the requirement was 8 percent on the first $2 million, 10 1/2 percent from $2 to $10 million, 12 1/2 percent from $10 to $100 million, 13 1/2 percent from $100 to $400 million, and 18 percent on all demand deposits over $400 million. For time deposits, there is a uniform percentage on savings deposits regardless of the amount held by a bank, but on other time deposits the percentage varies with the amount of these deposits. As of October 1974, the requirement on savings deposits was 3 percent, and on other time deposits, 3 percent on the first $5 million and 5 percent on all over $5 million. Although their existence should be noted, there is no need to take these complications into account in the illustrations we now turn to—therefore, we assume for simplicity that the percentage on all time deposits is 5 and on all demand deposits is 15.

The transfer by the public of $1,000 million from time to demand deposits is shown by the (a) entries in Table 5–1 for the commercial banks. Other things being equal, this transaction in itself means a $1,000 million increase in the money supply. But if the commercial banks had zero excess reserves before this switch occurred, they now have a reserve deficiency of $100 million because there has been an increase in required reserves of that amount and no change in the total of legal reserves. If the Federal Reserve authorities do not want to see the stock of money expand, they are not likely to act in a way to provide the commercial banks with additional legal reserves. This leaves the commercial banks as a group with no way to remove their reserve deficiency but a reduction in their deposit liabilities. The banks will reduce loans and investments by $666.6 million, and the public, in paying off loans at the banks and in purchasing securities sold by the banks, will reduce its demand deposits by $666.6 million. This is shown by the (b) entries. At this point, we have on the asset side a decrease of $666.6 million in loans and investments and, on the liabilities side, a decrease in time deposits of $1 billion, a net increase in demand

TABLE 5–1

COMMERCIAL BANKS

Assets			Liabilities	
			Time deposits	−$1,000.00 (a)
			Demand deposits	+$1,000.00 (a)
Loans and investments	−$666.66	(b)	Demand deposits	−$666.66 (b)
Deposits at Federal Reserve Banks	−$50.00	(c)	Demand deposits	−$50.00 (c)
Loans and investments	−$283.33	(d)	Demand deposits	−$283.33 (d)

Net Changes		Net Changes	
Deposits at Federal Reserve Banks	−$50.00	Time deposits	−$1,000.00
Loans and investments	−$950.00		
	−$1,000.00		−$1,000.00

FEDERAL RESERVE BANKS

Assets			Liabilities	
U.S. Government securities	−$50.00	(c)	Deposits of commercial banks	−$50.00 (c)

deposits of $333.3 million, or a decrease in the total of deposits of $666.6 million, which matches the decrease in loans and investments on the asset side. Also at this point, the banks' unchanged total for legal reserves once again is equal to required reserves, since the $50 million released from required reserves by the $1,000 million reduction in time deposits is just sufficient to cover the $50 million increase in required reserves that results from the $333.3 million net rise in demand deposits. So far as the money supply goes, the original increase of $1,000 million has been reduced to a $333.3 million increase.

If the Federal Reserve authorities don't want any increase at all, they may wipe out this remaining $333.3 million increase by selling $50 million of securities in the open market, which will give us the results shown in the two T-accounts by the (c) entries. The commercial banks lose $50 million of legal reserves as the Federal Reserve Banks charge their accounts for the $50 million in checks drawn against the commercial banks by the purchasers of the securities. Required reserves decrease by $7.5 million when demand deposits decrease by $50, so the commercial banks now have a reserve deficiency of $42.50 million. Since the Federal Reserve authorities are taking away and not supplying reserves, the commercial banks, as before, have no way out other than a reduction in loans and investments. The (d) entries show a decrease of $283.33 million in their loan and investment assets accompanied by a decrease of $283.33 million in their demand deposit liabilities. The $283.33 million decrease in demand deposits reduces required reserves by $42.50 million, which eliminates the reserve deficiency of that amount.

If we add up the (a), (b), (c), and (d) entries in the commercial banks' T-account, we get the net changes shown at the bottom of that account. The commercial banks' legal reserves equal their required reserves, since their time deposits are down by $1,000 million and their legal reserves are down by $50 million. (We initially assumed that excess reserves were zero.) Because of the action taken by the Federal Reserve authorities, there has been no change in the money supply or in the sum of the public's demand deposits and currency holdings. Demand deposits are back to the level at which they were initially, and (by assumption) currency in the hands of the public has remained unchanged as these other changes took place.

If we were to reverse the preceding by assuming a shift by the public out of demand deposits and into time deposits, we could just as readily show how the Federal Reserve authorities could, if they so desired, prevent what would otherwise be a $1 billion decrease in the money supply. The entries in the T-accounts remain exactly as given above; as is always the case, the only difference is that the signs attached to each entry are reversed, minuses becoming pluses and vice versa.

This specific illustration has been designed to show only the basic mechanics of one possible process by which the authorities might prevent unwanted increases or decreases in the money supply that would result from shifts by the public between demand deposits and time deposits at the commercial banks. Except under very special conditions, the authorities, of course, seek not to prevent all increases in the money supply over time but rather to bring about per quarter and per year that particular amount of increase which seems most appropriate in the interests of economic stabilization. As the public's holdings of money grow over time, so too do the public's holdings of time deposits at the commercial banks, for the public as we have seen has an unrestricted ability to switch from money to time deposits and vice versa and in practice tends to allocate any *increase* in the *total* of its holdings of money and time deposits in part to each.

To the extent that the public varies the way it distributes any increase in the total of its holdings of money and time deposits between the two, it follows that the monetary authorities cannot know in advance how much of an increase in legal reserves they have to provide to the banks in order to bring about some desired increase in the money supply. The larger the increase in time deposits that results indirectly from the increase in bank lending and investing made possible by the increase in legal reserves, the larger will be the increase in the amount of legal reserves needed to produce any desired increase in the money supply. For example, we can no longer say that a 15 percent legal reserve requirement against demand deposits means that $100 million of additional legal reserves will result in $666.66 million of additional demand deposits, given that some portion of this increase in legal reserves will find itself tied up in meeting the reserve requirement against the increase in time deposits that also occurs.

Let us work through an illustration to see what increase in demand deposits will follow from $100 million of additional legal reserves on certain assumptions. We recognize now that the public has time deposits as well as demand deposits at the commercial banks, and we assume specifically that the public chooses to hold $1 in time deposits for every $3 it holds in demand deposits. As before the legal reserve requirement against demand deposits is taken to be 15 percent and against time deposits, 5 percent. For simplicity, we assume here that the public holds all increases in the money stock in the form of demand deposits, or, in other words, it holds an unchanged amount of currency. We will drop this assumption in the next section.

Suppose now that the Federal Reserve Bank of New York purchases $100 million of securities from the public. As indicated by the (a) entries in Table 5–2, the public shows initially a $100 million increase in its demand deposit balances, and the commercial banks show a $100 million increase in legal reserves, $15 million of which is needed to cover the required reserve against the $100 million increase in demand deposits and $85 million of which is excess reserves. This excess reserve figure is, however, changed as we find the public shifting $25 million of its additional $100 million of demand deposits into time deposits in line with its desire to hold time deposits equal to 1/3 of demand deposits. This shift, shown by the (b) entries, decreases required reserves against demand deposits by $3.75 million, or 15 percent of $25 million, and increases required reserves against time deposits by

TABLE 5–2

COMMERCIAL BANKS

Assets			Liabilities		
Legal reserves	+$100	(a)	Demand deposits	+$100	(a)
			Demand deposits	−$25	(b)
			Time deposits	+$25	(b)
Loans and investments	+$700	(c)	Demand deposits	+$700	(c)
			Demand deposits	−$175	(d)
			Time deposits	+$175	(d)

Net Changes		Net Changes	
Legal reserves	+$100	Demand deposits	+$600
Loans and investments	+$700	Time deposits	+$200
	+$800		+$800

FEDERAL RESERVE BANKS

Assets			Liabilities		
U.S. Government securities	+$100	(a)	Deposits of commercial banks	+$100	(a)

$1.25 million, or 5 percent of $25 million. After the shift, the banks thus have $87.50 million instead of the initial $85.00 million of excess reserves.

The question now raised is by how much can the banks as a group increase their loans and investments and their demand deposits on the basis of this amount of excess reserves. With the assumed reserve requirements and the assumed ratio of time deposits to demand deposits, the answer whose calculation we will turn to below is the $700 million figure shown by the (c) entries. If the banks expand loans and investments by $700 million, they initially create additional demand deposits of an equal amount in favor of the borrowers and the sellers of the securities. As these new demand deposits are disbursed by their owners and distributed throughout the economy, our assumption is that \$175 million of the \$700 million will be switched from demand to time deposits as indicated by the (d) entries.

If we now sum the (a), (b), (c), and (d) entries on each side, we find the figures for "Net Changes" shown at the bottom of the T-account. Demand deposits have increased by \$600 million, which, on the assumption of unchanged currency holdings, means that the public's money stock is up by this amount. Time deposits have increased by \$200 million, or by 1/3 of the increase in demand deposits. The public's desired ratio of \$1 of additional time deposits per \$3 of additional demand deposits is satisfied. Required reserves have increased against demand deposits by \$90 million and against time deposits by \$10 million, or a total just equal to the \$100 million increase in the amount of the banks' legal reserves.

If we had here started with the *sale* of \$100 million of securities to the public by the Federal Reserve Bank, we would have found the four (a) entries as given but with signs all reversed. The figures in all of the following entries would also remain as given but again with the change of each sign.

This approach through the T-account shows explicitly several steps in the process by which the system generates the net changes summarized at the bottom of the T-account. It does not, however, determine what these net changes will be. These are found by writing an appropriate equation and solving it for the assumed values. We saw in Chapter 3's simplest case, which assumed away time deposits and all other complications, that the amount of demand deposits a dollar of reserves could support with, for example, an 18 percent legal reserve requirement was found by solving $\$1 = 0.18(x)$ in which x equals \$5.55. If \$1 of legal reserves will support \$5.55 of demand deposits, it follows that an *increase* in legal reserves of \$1 will support an *increase* in demand deposits of \$5.55. In the present case we want to find what increase in demand deposits and what increase in time deposits a given increase in legal reserves will support on the assumptions that the percentage reserve requirement is 15 against demand deposits and 5 against time deposits, and that the public chooses to hold time deposits equal in amount to 1/3 of its demand deposits. Given the assumption that the increase in legal reserves is \$100 million, we want, in other words, to find the change in demand deposits, ΔDD, and the change in time deposits, ΔTD, in the following equation in which Δ means "change in":

$$\$100 \text{ million} = 0.15\Delta DD + 0.05\Delta TD$$

Given that $TD = 0.333DD$, which also gives us that $\Delta TD = 0.333\Delta DD$, by substitution we have:

$$\$100 \text{ million} = 0.15\Delta DD + 0.05(0.333\Delta DD) = 0.166\Delta DD$$

and ΔDD = \$600 million and ΔTD = 0.333ΔDD or \$200 million, the figures which appear as the net changes in the T-account for the commercial banks in Table 5–2.

Instead of the values assumed here, one may, of course, start off with a different change in the dollar amount of reserves, different percentage reserve requirements against either or both kinds of deposits, and a different ratio of time deposits to demand deposits, and solve for the changes in the amount of demand deposits and time deposits that follow from these alternative values. Or, in general, if we let ΔR stand for the change in the dollar amount of legal reserves, r for the percentage reserve requirement against demand deposits, r' for the percentage reserve requirement against time deposits, and a for the ratio of time deposits to demand deposits, we may write:

$$\Delta R = r\Delta DD + r'\Delta TD$$

Given that $\Delta TD = a\Delta DD$, by substitution we have:

$$\Delta R = r\Delta DD + r'(a\Delta DD)$$

$$\Delta R = (r + r'a)\Delta DD$$

$$\Delta DD = \frac{1}{r + r'a} \Delta R$$

and

$$\frac{\Delta DD}{\Delta R} = \frac{1}{r + r'a}$$

which may be described as the *demand deposit multiplier*. Substituting the values we assumed above into $\frac{1}{r + r'a}$ gives us $\frac{1}{0.15 + 0.05 \times 0.333} = \frac{1}{0.166} =$ 6 for the demand deposit multiplier. DD will change by six times any given change in R, or any change in R will change DD by a multiple of 6.

If the public's currency holdings remain unchanged as its demand deposits change, the change in demand deposits is equal to the change in the money supply, working as we are with the narrow definition of money that limits money to these two items. Since we are at the moment specifically assuming that currency holdings remain constant, the demand deposit multiplier is the same as what may be called the *money supply multiplier*. In the illustration, we may, therefore, also say that any given change in R will change both DD and the money supply, M, by six times the change in R.

Since a demand deposit multiplier of 6 means that the commercial banking system can support \$6 of demand deposits per dollar of legal reserves, values in the (c) entries in Table 5–2 may appear to be incorrect. Following the transactions covered by the (a) and (b) entries, the banks found themselves with \$87.50 million of excess reserves and in the (c) entry proceeded to create $700 million of additional demand deposits. The multiplier of 6 would indicate that only $525 million of additional demand deposits (6 × $87.50 million) can be created on the basis of that amount of excess reserves. What appears to be a discrepancy here is explained by the fact that the $700 million figure for additional demand deposits is the figure before the public converts part of that amount into time deposits. The (d) entries show that $175 million of this amount is so converted; this leaves $525 million of the $700 million as the addition to demand deposits, just the amount expected on the basis of the demand deposit multiplier of 6. It will also be noted that the $175 million increase in time deposits is equal to 1/3 of the $525 million increase in demand deposits in accordance with the public's desired ratio of 1 to 3. In general in the present model, before the public adjusts its TD in response to any change in its DD, the temporary increase in DD possible on the basis of any given amount of excess reserves will be $(1 + a)$ times the amount of DD that will remain after the public has converted the amount of DD into TD needed to maintain the indicated ratio between the two types of deposits. If all we want to find is the final amount of DD remaining after this adjustment, we avoid this aspect; the equation incorporating the demand deposit multiplier developed above gives us that answer directly.

Since this equation will tell us this, it will also tell us the amount by which the Federal Reserve authorities must increase legal reserves to bring about a particular increase in demand deposits. Suppose that amount is $1,500 million. With the percentage reserve requirements and other values as given above, the necessary increase in legal reserves is $\Delta R = \frac{\$1,500 \text{ million}}{6}$, or $250 million, of which $225 million is needed to cover the 15 percent legal reserve requirement against the $1,500 million increase in demand deposits and $25 million is needed to cover the legal reserve requirement against the $500 million increase in time deposits that will be generated as the public acts to maintain its time and demand deposits in the indicated ratio.

Whether we want to find what increase in demand deposits will result from some specific increase in legal reserves or what increase in legal reserves is necessary to produce some specific increase in demand deposits, we can find the answer from the equation above only on the assumption that all of the other things that may affect the answer but are not explicitly allowed for in the equation itself remain constant. One of these is the amount of currency held by the public, and, as seen in Chapter 1, this amount does not remain constant as the amount of demand deposits varies over time. To allow for this, we next drop the assumption that the public's currency holdings remain unchanged and trace certain effects that follow from so doing.

The Public Varies Its Currency Holdings

As in the preceding section, we will work here through a T-account illustration to show the changes that result, given certain assumptions, from a $100 million increase in legal reserves. The percentage reserve requirements is taken to be 15 against demand deposits and 5 against time deposits, with the ratio of time deposits to demand deposits equal to 1/3, the same values assumed above. We now add the assumption that the public chooses to maintain a ratio of currency to demand deposits of 1/4. In other words, given the narrow definition of money with which we are working, the public chooses to hold 1/5 of its money in currency form and 4/5 in demand deposit form. This gives us an easy ratio to work with and also one that is not far from the actual ratio, as may be seen from the figures in Table 3–3.

We will designate currency by the letter C and write $C = 0.25\ DD$ in line with our present assumption. For changes in demand deposits, the public adjusts its currency holdings so that $\Delta C = 0.25 \Delta DD$.

We start off as before by having the Federal Reserve Bank of New York purchase $100 million of securities from the public, which, at least initially, adds $100 million to the demand deposit liabilities of the commercial banks and an equal amount to their assets in the form of legal reserves as shown by the (a) entries in Table 5–3 below for the commercial banks. The public holds $100 million in additional demand deposits, and we assume that it promptly carries out the adjustments needed to give it the desired ratios of time deposits to demand deposits and of currency to demand deposits. As the millions of people involved effect the necessary transactions, we get the results given by the (b) and (c) entries. The specific figures in these entries are found by first solving the equation $\Delta DD + 0.333 \Delta DD + 0.25 \Delta DD = \$100$ million. This equation enables us to find how a change of $100 million is to be divided into three parts, ΔDD, ΔTD, and ΔC, in a way that makes $\Delta TD = 0.333 \Delta DD$ and $\Delta C = 0.25 \Delta DD$. Solving for ΔDD gives us $63.17 million, and from this it follows that $\Delta TD = \$21.06$ million and $\Delta C = \$15.77$ million, as shown in the (b) and (c) entries.

After the transactions indicated by these entries have taken place, the commercial banking system finds itself with $84.23 million of additional reserves, $15.77 of the original $100 having been lost through the withdrawal of that amount of currency. The change in demand deposits at this point is ($100 million − $21.06 million − $15.77 million) or $63.17 million, on which the legal reserve requirement is $9.48 million. The change in time deposits is $21.06 million, on which the legal reserve requirement is $1.05 million. Subtracting this

TABLE 5–3

COMMERCIAL BANKS

Assets			Liabilities		
Legal reserves	+$100.00	(a)	Demand deposits	+$100.00	(a)
			Time deposits	+$21.06	(b)
			Demand deposits	−$21.06	(b)
Legal reserves	−$15.77	(c)	Demand deposits	−$15.77	(c)
Loans and investments	+$280.00	(d)	Demand deposits	+$280.00	(d)
			Time deposits	+$58.96	(e)
			Demand deposits	−$58.96	(e)
Legal reserves	−$44.22	(f)	Demand deposits	−$44.22	(f)
Net Changes			**Net Changes**		
Legal reserves	+$40.00		Demand deposits	+$240.00	
Loans and investments	+$280.00		Time deposits	+$80.00	
	+$320.00			+$320.00	

FEDERAL RESERVE BANKS

Assets			Liabilities		
U.S. Government securities	+$100.00	(a)	Deposits of Commercial banks	+$100.00	(a)

$10.53 million increase in required reserves from the $84.23 million increase in legal reserves indicates excess reserves of $73.70.

By how much can the commercial banking system initially expand its loans and investments and its demand deposits on the basis of this amount of excess reserves? The answer, whose derivation we will return to below, is the $280 million figure shown by the (d) entries. Additional loans and investments of $280 million result initially in additional demand deposits of $280 million, but then the public carries out the transactions needed to convert some of its increase in demand deposits into time deposits and currency with the results shown by the (e) and (f) entries. If now we sum the changes in demand deposits shown by the entries (a) through (f), we find the net change of $240 million shown under that heading at the bottom of the commercial banks' T-account. In the same way, we find a net change of $80 million for time deposits. On the assets side, the net change in legal reserves is found to be $40 million, $60 million of the original $100 million having been lost to the banks via currency withdrawals. This change of $40 million, it will be seen, is just the amount needed to meet the change in required reserves resulting from the change in deposits.

If one were to start off with the sale of $100 million of securities to the public by the Federal Reserve Bank but with all other assumptions as given above, every entry would be exactly as given except that each would now carry the opposite sign. For example, under "Net Changes," there would be a $240 million decrease in demand deposits and an $80 million decrease in time deposits instead of the increases of those amounts now shown.

Whether we take the case of an increase or a decrease in legal reserves, the entries in the T-account for the commercial banks can indicate only some of the steps in the process by which that change in legal reserves leads to changes in deposits and other items. To determine what the actual net changes will be for each of the items at the end of the process, we must start off by recognizing the following fact: the $100 million increase in legal reserves will be absorbed *in part* in meeting the required reserve against the increase in demand deposits that results as the banks expand loans and investments on the basis of their increased reserves, *in part* in meeting the required reserve against the increase in time deposits that results as the public converts some of its increase in demand deposits into time deposits, and *in part* in meeting the public's demand for currency as the public converts some of its increase in demand deposits into currency. Given the percentage reserve requirements with which we are working, we may sum up all of this by saying that the $100 million will be distributed into three parts in a way that satisfies the following equation:

$$\$100 \text{ million} = 0.15\Delta DD + 0.05\Delta TD + \Delta C$$

From our assumptions that $\Delta TD = 0.333\Delta DD$ and $\Delta C = 0.25\Delta DD$, by substitution we have:

$$\$100 \text{ million} = 0.15\Delta DD + 0.05(0.333\Delta DD) + 0.25\Delta DD$$

$$\$100 \text{ million} = 0.4167\Delta DD$$

$$\$100 \text{ million} \left(\frac{1}{0.4167}\right) = \Delta DD$$

$100 million $\times$ 2.4 = $240 million

When ΔDD equals $240 million, ΔC equals 0.25($240 million), or $60 million, and this is the amount of the $100 million increase in reserves absorbed in meeting the drain of currency into the hands of the public. When ΔDD equals $240 million, ΔTD equals 0.333($240 million), or $80 million; and 0.05($80 million), or $4 million, is the amount of the $100 million increase in reserves that is absorbed in meeting the required reserve against the increase in time deposits. Finally, when ΔDD equals $240 million, the amount of the $100 million increase in reserves absorbed in meeting the required reserve against the increase in demand deposits is 0.15 ($240 million), or $36 million, and this is just the amount of the $100 million remaining after allowance for the amounts absorbed in meeting the currency withdrawals and in meeting the reserve requirement against the increase in time deposits.

In the same way, we could find the change in demand deposits for any other required ratio of legal reserves to demand deposits, for any other required ratio of legal reserves to time deposits, for any other ratio the public chooses for its time deposits to its demand deposits and for its currency holdings to its demand deposits, and for any other dollar amount of change in the banking system's legal reserves. If we let c stand for the ratio of currency to demand deposits, we may write as a general equation:

$$\Delta R = r\Delta DD + r'(a\Delta DD) + c\Delta DD$$

$$\Delta R = (r + r'a + c)\Delta DD$$

$$\Delta DD = \frac{1}{r + r'a + c}\, \Delta R$$

and

$$\frac{\Delta DD}{\Delta R} = \frac{1}{r + r'a + c}$$

which is the demand deposit multiplier.

Substituting the values we assumed above, this multiplier has a value of

$$\frac{1}{0.15 + (0.05 \times 0.333) + 0.25} = \frac{1}{0.4167} = 2.4$$

so that our $100 million increase in legal reserves produces the $240 million increase in demand deposits we derived above. A rise or fall in the sum of the four coefficients in the denominator of the multiplier will, of course, decrease or increase the size of the multiplier and will thus indicate a smaller or larger change in demand deposits for any given change in the banking system's legal reserves.

If we assume, as we did in the first section of this chapter, that the public's holdings of currency remain unchanged, then the change in demand deposits that results from any change in legal reserves is equal to the change in the money supply. As noted on p. 92, the demand deposit multiplier is then equal to what may be called the money supply multiplier. However, in the more realistic case of the present section, allowance is made for the fact that the public's currency holdings change with its demand deposits, so changes in demand deposits alone do not indicate the change in the money supply. The demand deposit multiplier of 2.4 derived above states that *demand deposits* will change by 2.4 times any change in legal reserves, not that the *money supply* will change by 2.4 times any change in legal reserves. For the values we are working with, the money supply will change by 3 times any change in legal reserves, because the money supply multiplier is equal to the demand deposit multiplier times $(1 + c)$ or in the present case $2.4(1 + 0.25) = 3.0$. This relationship is derived in the following way.

Since any change in the money supply, ΔM, is the sum of ΔDD and ΔC, we may add ΔC to both sides of the equation

$$\Delta DD = \frac{1}{r + r'a + c}\Delta R$$

which gives us

$$\Delta M = \Delta DD + \Delta C = \frac{1}{r + r'a + c}\Delta R + \Delta C$$

Since $\Delta C = c\Delta DD$ and since ΔDD is as above given, we now have

$$c\Delta DD = \frac{c}{r + r'a + c}\Delta R$$

Therefore,

$$\Delta M = \frac{1}{r + r'a + c}\Delta R + \frac{c}{r + r'a + c}\Delta R$$

or

$$\Delta M = \frac{1 + c}{r + r'a + c}\Delta R$$

which gives us

$$\frac{\Delta M}{\Delta R} = \frac{1 + c}{r + r'a + c}$$

as the money supply multiplier in the present case. Substituting the numerical values assumed earlier, we get

$$\frac{1 + 0.25}{0.4167} = 3.0$$

The demand deposit multiplier was found to be

$$\frac{1}{0.4167} = 2.4$$

On our assumptions in this section, we thus find that the money supply multiplier is $(1 + c)$ times the demand deposit multiplier. If we had assumed a value for c of 0.333, the demand deposit multiplier would have been 1/(0.50) or 2.0, and the money supply multiplier would have been 1.33/(0.50) or 2.67, in which 2.67 = 2(1 + 0.333).

Since the multipliers developed here indicate the change in demand deposits and the change in the money supply that follow, on certain assumptions, from any given change in legal reserves, they may also be used to indicate how much of a change in legal reserves the Federal Reserve authorities must bring about in order to produce any particular change in demand deposits or in the money supply. Because the change in demand deposits is not equal to the change in the money supply, the equation showing the change in demand deposits for any given change in legal reserves is not of special interest to the monetary authorities. The authorities' concern is primarily with the change in the money supply and not with the change in demand deposits, which is only part of that change. If the authorities seek a change in the money supply of $1,500 million, a money supply multiplier of 3.0 means that $1,500/3, or $500 million, in additional reserves is necessary to bring about that change. This same $500 million will bring about a change in demand deposits of $1,200 million as given by the demand deposit multiplier times the change in legal reserves, or 2.4 × $500 million. The change in the public's currency holdings is $300 million, or 1/4 of the change in demand deposits.

The multipliers give us the net change in money supply and in demand deposits for any given change in legal reserves, but they do not show any of the steps in the process by which the public and the banks bring about these net changes. Several of these steps were shown in Table 5–3. However, the numerical values shown there for one of the steps in the T-account may appear to be inconsistent with those expected from the demand deposit multiplier, and it is necessary to show that there is actually no inconsistency. The problem here is nothing more than an extension of that encountered in a similar context in the preceding section of this chapter.

The T-account showed the commercial banks with $73.70 million of excess reserves after the completion of the transactions covered by the (a), (b), and (c) entries. The demand deposit multiplier of 2.4

would indicate that the banks as a group should be able to expand loans and investments and create additional demand deposits in the amount of 2.4 × $73.70 million, or $176.8 million. However, what we find under the (d) entries is $280 million rather than $176.8 million. This discrepancy is accounted for by the fact that the $280 million is the temporary figure that exists before the conversion of part of this amount into currency and part into time deposits. As shown by the (e) and (f) entries, $58.96 million is converted into time deposits and $44.22 million is withdrawn in currency, so $176.8 million of the $280 million remains as the net increase in demand deposits at this stage in the process. And this is the figure we would expect from the demand deposit multiplier of 2.4 and excess reserves of $73.70 million. It may also be seen that the $58.96 million increase in time deposits and the $44.22 million increase in currency in the hands of the public are equal to 1/3 and 1/4, respectively, of this figure. In general, for any given values of a and c, we find that before the public adjusts its TD and C holdings in response to any change in DD, the temporary increase in DD will be $(1 + a + c)$ times the amount of DD that will remain after the TD and C adjustments have been made.

The Banks Choose To Hold Excess Reserves

It was said earlier that although bankers abhor nonearning assets, they have no choice but to hold nonearning assets in the form of legal reserves sufficient to meet the percentage reserve requirements against their deposits. This abhorrence of nonearning assets implies that they will not hold legal reserves greater than the required amount, or, in other words, that they will not choose to hold excess reserves. Expressed in positive terms, this implies that they are ordinarily in a fully "loaned up" position. Actually, however, we find that some banks, especially smaller banks in rural areas, pursue a deliberate policy of holding some amount of excess reserves. Although this means sacrificing the income that could be earned on these funds if they were put into loans and investments, it does provide the nonmonetary advantage of greater liquidity, which for some bankers apparently more than offsets the income foregone.

It might seem that holding reserves equal to the amount legally required gives any bank adequate liquidity, but, contrary to the popular belief, banks can count only to a very limited extent on required reserves to provide liquidity. Only a small fraction of the total of a bank's deposits at the Federal Reserve Bank and its holdings of currency are available to meet customer withdrawals of currency or to pay balances due to other banks, since the great bulk of these assets are immobilized in meeting the legal reserve requirements. Some latitude, however, is provided by the way the reserve requirements are calculated. For one thing, each bank must meet its legal reserve requirement on a weekly and not a daily basis. Furthermore, while the amount of its required reserves depends on the amount of its deposits and the percentage reserve requirement, the amount of legal reserves on hand during any week does not have to meet the requirement on that same week's deposits. That week's deposits have to be covered by reserves of the second following week, and so forth for the deposits of every other week, so a bank always operates with two weeks' notice as to the amount of legal reserves it must have on hand for any one week to cover its requirements. These two provisions mean that required reserves provide a degree of liquidity, although not as much as some bankers would like. To avoid the possibility of having to borrow or to liquidate assets to prevent what otherwise would be a deficiency of reserves, some banks, therefore, follow a policy of maintaining a protective margin in the form of excess reserves. Various factors will influence how large this amount will be, but a major factor in each case will be the level of the bank's demand deposits.

Because extra liquidity can be gained only by the sacrifice of extra income, it follows that bankers will lean more toward greater liquidity and lesser income, the lower are interest rates on their earning assets. The level of these interest rates is a measure of the price paid for liquidity, and banks will buy more liquidity at a lower than at a higher price, other things being equal. Thus, the banks that hold excess reserves will gear the amount so held not only to the amount of their deposit liabilities but also to the cost of holding those excess reserves as measured by the level of interest rates. In periods of very high interest rates, despite the continuing desirability of extra liquidity, few bankers will not be tempted to adjust their holdings of excess reserves sharply downward. By the same argument, in periods of very low interest rates that accompany severe recessions, bankers will adjust their holdings of excess reserves upward, sometimes almost involuntarily. In such periods, the banks enjoy relatively small demand for loans at the same time that the risk on the average loan rises. They also have little incentive to purchase short-term securities at the very low rates of return then available. Under these conditions, the banks cut the interest rates paid on time deposits to successively lower levels and at least temporarily suspend what is ordinarily a vigorous competitive struggle to attract more deposits.

We could note here still other factors affecting bankers' decisions to hold larger or smaller amounts of excess reserves, but all that is immediately relevant is the fact that the banks as a group (but not necessarily every bank in the group) do indeed choose to carry some amount of excess reserves. Although this amount depends on the level of interest rates and other factors in addition to the level of deposits, for simplicity in the illustration that follows we will assume that the banks, on the average, choose to hold excess reserves equal to some given percentage of demand deposits, specifically 3.33 percent. We could also show the banks holding excess reserves equal to a smaller percentage of time deposits, but they are not very likely to do this. As was mentioned, under ordinary circumstances excess reserves are held to provide greater liquidity, and the need for liquidity arises predominantly from the volatility of the banks' demand deposits, not from their more stable time deposits.

In now examining how the banks' holdings of excess reserves affect the amount of their demand deposits and other variables, we again follow the procedure of the preceding two sections. As before, our illustration begins with the purchase of $100 million of securities from the public by the Federal Reserve Bank of New York, a transaction that produces the results shown by the (a) entries in Table 5—4. As before, we assume that the public chooses to hold time deposits ɛqual to 1/3 of demand deposits and currency equal to 1/4 of demand deposits, and we have added the assumption here that the banks choose to hold excess reserves equal to 1/30, or 3.33 percent, of demand deposits. The (a), (b) and (c) entries here are identical with those in Table 5—3.

Given the transactions covered by those entries, the banks as a group find that $73.70 million of the original increment of $100 million in legal reserves remains as excess reserves. (Of the other $26.40, $15.77 was lost through currency withdrawals, and $10.53 was allocated as required reserves against the increase in demand and time deposits.) However, the banks do not view all of this $73.70 million as the basis for an expansion of earning assets and deposits; part of it, specifically $2.09 million (or an amount equal to 3.33 percent of the additional demand deposits of $63.17 million), is the amount of legal reserves the banks wish to hold over and above the required reserves against this specific addition to demand deposits. This means that only $71.61 becomes the basis for an expansion in loans and investments, and it turns out that the expansion possible on the basis of this amount, given our various assumptions, is the $251.89 million shown by the (d) entries.

We will turn to the exact calculation of this figure below, but it may be seen here that this preliminary addition to demand deposits will, after all adjustments, leave the banks as a group holding additional excess reserves equal to 1/30 of the final addition to demand deposits that remains after an amount equal to 1/3 of that final addition has

TABLE 5–4

COMMERCIAL BANKS

Assets			Liabilities		
Legal reserves	+$100.00	(a)	Demand deposits	+$100.00	(a)
			Time deposits	+$21.06	(b)
			Demand deposits	−$21.06	(b)
Legal reserves	−$15.77	(c)	Demand deposits	−$15.77	(c)
Loans and investments	+$251.89	(d)	Demand deposits	+$251.89	(d)
			Time deposits	+$53.04	(e)
			Demand deposits	−$53.04	(e)
Legal reserves	−$39.78	(f)	Demand deposits	−$39.78	(f)

Net Changes		Net Changes	
Legal reserves	+$44.45	Demand deposits	+$222.22
Loans and investments	+$251.89	Time deposits	+$74.10
	+$296.34		+$296.34

FEDERAL RESERVE BANKS

Assets			Liabilities		
U.S. Governments securities	+$100.00	(a)	Deposits of commercial banks	+$100.00	(a)

been converted into time deposits and an amount equal to 1/4 of that final addition has been withdrawn in currency. Expressed in another way: after allowing for the portion of the $71.61 of excess reserves lost by the banks in meeting the currency withdrawals and in meeting the required reserves against the increase in both demand deposits and time deposits that result from the expansion of loans and investments, the portion that is left should be equal to 1/30 of the final increase in demand deposits. On the basis of the figures given in the T-account, the calculations may be made to show that this is the case. The final increase in demand deposits resulting specifically from the transactions covered by the (d), (e) and (f) entries turns out to be $159.07 million; the amount of the $71.61 million remaining as excess reserves after the same transactions turns out to be $5.30 million, or the desired 1/30 of the increase in demand deposits.

If we now sum the entries (a) through (f), we get the results shown as "Net Changes" at the bottom of the commercial banks' T-account. The banks show a net increase in legal reserves of $44.45 million, of which $37.04 million is the amount needed to cover required reserves on the increase in demand and in time deposits and $7.41 million is the increase in the amount of excess reserves the banks wish to hold. The other $55.55 million of the original $100 million increase in legal reserves was lost through currency withdrawals by the public, $55.55 million being 1/4 of $222.22 million. Last, the increase in time deposits (apart from a rounding discrepancy) is equal to 1/3 of the increase in demand deposits. The public has distributed its total holdings of demand deposits, time deposits, and currency in the way it wants; the banks have expanded their loans and investments to the level consistent with legal reserve requirements and their own preferences for excess reserves.

As always, our results would be unchanged other than in sign if we were to begin this same illustration with the assumption that the Federal Reserve Bank of New York sells $100 million in securities to the public.

The $222.22 million figure for the net change in demand deposits (and from this the figures for the other net changes) that will result under present assumptions from a $100 million change in legal reserves is found directly through an appropriate extension of the equation employed in the preceding section of this chapter. The equation must now be written to allow for the fact that the $100 million increase in legal reserves will be absorbed in four uses: the three covered in the preceding section—namely, required reserves against the increase in demand deposits, required reserves against the increase in time deposits, and currency withdrawals—plus a fourth use, an amount of excess reserves that the banks desire to hold. We may express this as follows:

$$\$100 \text{ million} = 0.15\Delta DD + 0.05\Delta TD + \Delta C + \Delta ER$$

in which ER indicates the amount of excess reserves the banks wish to hold. Given the assumption that this amount is 0.033 of their demand deposits, we have $ER = 0.033\ DD$ and, in terms of changes, $\Delta ER = 0.033\ \Delta DD$. Recalling the other assumption we made earlier, we have by substitution:

$100 million = $0.15\Delta DD + 0.05(0.33\Delta DD) + 0.25\Delta DD + 0.033\Delta DD$

$100 million = $0.45\Delta DD$

$100 million $\left(\dfrac{1}{0.45}\right) = \Delta DD$

$100 million $\times 2.222 = $222.22 million

If we now let e stand for the ratio of desired excess reserves to demand deposits—i.e., $ER = e(DD)$ and $\Delta ER = e(\Delta DD)$—we may write as a general equation for the present case:

$$\Delta R = r\Delta DD + r'(a\Delta DD) + c\Delta DD + e\Delta DD$$

$$\Delta R = (r + r'a + c + e)\Delta DD$$

$$\Delta DD = \frac{1}{r + r'a + c + e}\Delta R$$

and

$$\frac{\Delta DD}{\Delta R} = \frac{1}{r + r'a + c + e}$$

is the demand deposit multiplier. The result here differs from that in the preceding section only by the addition of e to the denominator of the ratio that is the demand deposit multiplier. In our illustration, this multiplier is

$$\frac{1}{0.15 + 0.05 \times 0.333 + 0.25 + 0.033} = \frac{1}{0.45} = 2.222$$

so ΔR of $100 million gives rise to ΔDD of $222.22 million.

As a next step, the money supply multiplier in the present case may be found in the same way shown in the preceding section. Working through those steps will show that

$$\Delta M = \frac{1 + c}{r + r'a + c + e}\Delta R$$

and

$$\frac{\Delta M}{\Delta R} = \frac{1 + c}{r + r'a + c + e}$$

is the money supply multiplier. The money supply multiplier as before is equal to $(1 + c)$ times the demand deposit multiplier. In the present illustration,

$$\frac{\Delta M}{\Delta R} = \frac{1.25}{45} = 2.7777$$

or the money supply multiplier is 1.25 times the demand deposit multiplier of 2.2222.

To ask the same question asked in the previous sections: How much of a change in legal reserves must the Federal Reserve authorities bring about to produce a $1,500 million change in the money supply? From the money supply multiplier of 2.7777, we have $1,500/2.7777 = $540 million as the necessary change in legal reserves. This $540 million change in reserves also brings about a $1,200 million change in demand deposits as given by the demand deposit multiplier, 2.2222, times that change in reserves. The change in the public's currency holdings is $300 million, or 1/4 of the change in demand deposits.

In the present case, this $540 million change in reserves would be absorbed as follows: $300 million through withdrawals of currency from the banks by the public, which means that $240 million is the part of the initial change that remains as a change in the commercial banks' legal reserves, an amount in turn divided into a change of $180 million in required reserves to cover the $1,200 million change in demand deposits, a change of $20 million in required reserves to cover the $400 million change in time deposits, and $40 million, which is the change in the amount of excess reserves the banks choose to hold.

Having derived the multipliers for the present case, we return to a now familiar type of question raised but left unanswered in the T-account. The (d) entry in the T-account shows that the banks, on the basis of $71.61 million of excess reserves they hold over and above the amount they choose to hold, are able to expand loans and investments and create new demand deposits in the amount of $251.89 million. According to the multiplier just derived, this amount of excess reserves would be able to support 2.222 $\times$ $71.61 million, or $159.12 million, in additional demand deposits. The discrepancy here is of the same kind encountered at the corresponding point in the previous section. The $251.89 figure is found from $159.12 (1 + 0.333 + 0.25) = $159.12 (1.583), in which 0.333 is the value of a and 0.25 is the value of c. The $251.89 is the temporary figure that exists before the conversion of part of this amount into time deposits and part into currency. The demand deposit multiplier times excess reserves gives us the figure that exists after these adjustments have taken place; the figure we want at this point in the T-account, however, is the one we have—that before these adjustments have taken place.

As we saw earlier, the demand deposit figure at the bottom of the T-account under the heading of "Net Changes" is one that may be derived directly from the demand deposit multiplier. The $222.22 million is equal to the initial change in reserves of $100 million times the demand deposit multiplier of 2.22.

THE MULTIPLIERS: VARIATIONS IN THE a, c, AND e RATIOS
AS A LIMITATION ON THE CONTROL OF THE MONEY SUPPLY

The series of multipliers developed in three steps in the first part of this chapter may be brought together at this point. In Table 5–5 are listed the demand deposit multipliers and money supply multipliers for four cases, the first of which is the one that underlies the analysis in Chapter 3, where all complications were avoided by assuming that the public does not hold any time deposits, that it does not vary its currency holdings, and that the banks do not choose to hold any excess reserves. In brief, there the assumptions were that a, c, and e were all zero. The next three multipliers in each column are those that follow from dropping these assumptions one by one as we did in the three sections of the preceding part of this chapter. As long as c is assumed to be zero, the public's currency holdings do not change as its demand deposits change, and the demand deposit multiplier and the money supply multiplier are therefore the same. In the

TABLE 5–5

ASSUMPTIONS	DEMAND DEPOSIT MULTIPLIERS	MONEY SUPPLY MULTIPLIERS
$r = 0.15$; a, c, and e are all zero	$\dfrac{1}{r} = \dfrac{1}{0.15} = 6.66$	Same as demand deposit multiplier
$r = 0.15$; $r' = 0.05$; $a = 0.333$; c and e are both zero	$\dfrac{1}{r + r'a} = \dfrac{1}{0.166} = 6.00$	Same as demand deposit multiplier
$r = 0.15$; $r' = 0.05$; $a = 0.333$; $c = 0.25$; and e is zero	$\dfrac{1}{r + r'a + c} = \dfrac{1}{0.4166} = 2.4$	$\dfrac{1 + c}{r + r'a + c} = \dfrac{1.25}{0.4166} = 3.0$
$r = 0.15$; $r' = 0.05$; $a = 0.333$; $c = 0.25$; and $e = 0.033$	$\dfrac{1}{r + r'a + c + e} = \dfrac{1}{0.45} = 2.22$	$\dfrac{1 + c}{r + r'a + c + e} = \dfrac{1.25}{0.45} = 2.77$

last two cases, c is no longer assumed to be zero, and the money supply multiplier is no longer the same as the demand deposit multiplier.

To what extent do variations in these three coefficients restrict the ability of the Federal Reserve authorities to control the money supply? The final money supply equation developed above provides a helpful framework within which the dimensions of this question can be outlined.

$$\Delta M = \frac{1 + c}{r + r'a + c + e} \Delta R$$

From a purely mechanical point of view, it should be clear that ΔM is rigidly linked to ΔR as long as the value of the multiplier remains fixed. If such were actually the case, the Federal Reserve authorities' control over ΔM would be as exact or precise as its control over ΔR, and its control over ΔR is in fact fairly precise. However, fairly precise control over ΔR will be accompanied by a control over ΔM which is less precise to the degree that the values of the terms in the multiplier show frequent, sizable, erratic, and therefore unpredictable changes.

Of these terms, the Federal Reserve authorities have complete direct control over r and r' in the sense that they can set these percentage reserve requirements at any specific level within the limits imposed by Congress and neither the public nor the commercial banks have any power to change them. As for the other three terms in the multiplier, the Federal Reserve authorities have no direct control at all. For any time period, the public decides the ratio it will maintain between its time deposits and its demand deposits—i.e., the value of a; and for any time period the public also decides the ratio it will maintain between its currency holdings and its demand deposits—i.e., the value of c; finally, the commercial banks decide the ratio they will in any time period maintain between their desired holdings of excess reserves and their demand deposit liabilities—i.e., the value of e. Actions taken by the Federal Reserve authorities can affect indirectly the values of a, c, and e, but the public and the commercial banks still have the power to maintain larger or smaller values for a, c, and e from one time period to the next quite independently of actions taken by the Federal Reserve authorities.

It then follows that, despite their complete control over r and r', the authorities will be unable to make ΔM the amount they want it to be in any particular month if the public and the commercial banks behave in a way that causes frequent, large, and erratic variations in the values of a, c, and e. Suppose the Federal Reserve authorities want to see an increase in the money supply of $500 million over the next month. With unchanged percentage reserve requirements, the amount of increase in legal reserves needed depends on the values of a, c, and e;

but if these vary significantly and unpredictably from month to month, the increase in legal reserves provided by the authorities may produce an increase in the money supply possibly twice as large or half as large as the one aimed for during that month. As the data on the change in the money supply become available, the error, if there is indeed one, will be revealed. If the authorities still have an unchanged money supply goal, say an increase of $500 million, they then take the necessary corrective action by providing still more legal reserves if the error was too little an increase in the money supply or by taking away some legal reserves if the error was too large an increase in the money supply. It is, of course, possible that this action, intended to be corrective, will turn out to be perverse if there are now changes in a, c, and e in the opposite direction to the earlier changes. This in turn calls for corrective action in the opposite direction by the Federal Reserve authorities. Even under these most adverse hypothetical circumstances, however, control by the authorities does not become completely impossible. Through what in effect may be a continuing process of adjustment, the authorities over a longer period of time can still make ΔM come out close to the magnitude that was intended for that longer period of time.

The time period is critical here: the longer the time period under consideration, the closer the authorities can come to their objective as the short-term errors in one direction or the other are averaged out. If we take the very short-term period of a week, the authorities might take actions during a week with the expectation that the actions will result in some particular increase in the money supply during the next week, but they would not be surprised to find that there is an actual decrease in the money supply in that next week. Once we stretch the time period under consideration out to a month, errors in direction of change become less likely. On a quarterly basis, the magnitude of the change in the money supply may still be off target but probably not the direction of change. Over a still longer period of time, the magnitude of the change in the money supply can probably be brought within a fraction of 1 percent of the intended figure.

Just how precisely the authorities can control the money supply is a question on which there is no small disagreement among economists. This was not the case a decade or so ago; the question had not then received the intensive study it has received since, and a very close degree of control was then almost taken for granted. For example, it was then accepted virtually without question that the commercial banks would follow a policy of being fully "loaned up"—i.e., that the e ratio had a normal value of zero. When this element of slippage between ΔR and ΔM is thus removed bodily from the money supply equation, there appears to be a much closer tie between ΔR and ΔM, other things being equal. Today all agree that e is not zero and that it is therefore a necessary element in that equation.

It has always been recognized that a and c are positive values and necessary elements in the money supply equation, but it was not commonly believed earlier that either of these values weakened seriously the linkage between ΔR and ΔM. To pursue this would go far beyond the introductory nature of this book, but as another illustration of the change from the earlier view, in the mid-sixties there was advanced what has been called the Gramley-Chase thesis. This seems to say that under certain conditions the monetary authorities may simply be unable to control the money supply because of the way that time deposits respond to certain interest rate differentials which appear over the course of the business cycle. In terms of our simple money supply equation, this argument suggests that the a ratio may behave in such a way that the Federal Reserve authorities are at times powerless to offset its effects on ΔM through their control over ΔR.

A CONCLUDING NOTE

We will not pursue these matters further. Our major purpose in this chapter has been to introduce the a, c, and e ratios and to see how variations in them complicate the Federal Reserve authorities' task of controlling the money supply through their control over the commercial banks' legal reserves. Whether the task is complicated to a degree that vitiates Federal Reserve control of the money supply, as some seem to suggest, is a controversial matter. What we can say without controversy is that the variations in a, c, and e loosen the linkage between ΔR and ΔM and that the Federal Reserve authorities cannot adjust precisely for this slippage in a period of a month or perhaps several months. As a last word we may also say without too much controversy what has been said several times before: the Federal Reserve authorities can operate with sufficient precision to bring the money supply figure within a fraction of 1 percent of the figure aimed at over a period of approximately a quarter year.

APPENDIX TO CHAPTER 5
THE QUESTION OF SLIPPAGE: MEMBER AND NONMEMBER BANKS

Of the 14,200 commercial banks in the United States, about 60 percent are not members of the Federal Reserve System. However, the 40 percent that are members include most of the larger banks in the country, so about 75 percent of the total assets and total deposits of all commercial banks are in fact in member banks. Banks that are members enjoy such advantages of membership as direct access to loans at the Federal Reserve Banks, but they also suffer such disadvantages as more stringent reserve requirements on their deposits. Because these more stringent reserve requirements mean that, other things being equal, a member bank can have a smaller fraction of its total assets in the form of earning assets, this disadvantage directly affects profitability and in so doing offsets for many banks the various advantages of membership. Primarily because of the weight of this disadvantage, membership has become increasingly less attractive. From 1960 to 1974, about 750 banks gave up membership by withdrawal or merger. Of 1,900 newly chartered state banks, less than 100 elected to become members. Over the same period, about 870 new national banks were chartered, and these automatically became members as all nationally chartered banks are legally required to be members.

To enable them to exercise closer control over the money supply, the Federal Reserve authorities have asked the Congress for the power to impose the same demand deposit reserve requirements on nonmember banks that are imposed on member banks, and it is to be expected that the Congress will grant this power. However, during the long-existing situation of member banks and nonmember banks being subject to different reserve requirements, to what degree has the Federal Reserve for that reason been unable to control the money supply through the use of its major tools—reserve requirements, discount rate, and open market operations?

The fact that the Federal Reserve has not been able to set the minimum reserve requirements for nonmember banks has not, of course, meant that these banks had complete discretion over variations in the amount of their assets and deposits. They have been subject to lower reserve requirements set by the states, not to no reserve requirements at all. These requirements vary widely among the fifty states in terms of the assets that qualify as legal reserves and in terms of the minimum ratio that must be maintained between these assets and a bank's deposits. Cash in vault qualifies in all cases as such an asset, but beyond this many states permit banks to count as legal reserves the deposits they carry with other commercial banks and some states even accept earning assets such as holdings of U.S. Government securities or the securities issued by the state government of the state in which the banks operate.

We have seen that if the Federal Reserve authorities raise the percentage reserve requirement that member banks must meet, this will exert pressure toward a contraction of the loans and investments and the deposits of the member banks by reducing the amount of excess reserves held by these banks. Does a rise in the percentage reserve requirement for member banks impose anything approaching an equal amount of pressure toward contraction on the banks not subject to those requirements? Such a rise changes neither the amount of their assets that qualify as legal reserves nor the level of the state-regulated percentage requirements they must meet. The answer is, therefore, basically, no: the banks not subject to Federal Reserve reserve requirements are essentially immune to changes in the percentage reserve requirements ordered by the Federal Reserve authorities. And it may be added that there is no tendency for the states to change the form or the level of the reserve requirements they impose to keep these at all in line with those imposed by the Federal Reserve authorities. These requirements are set at a given level by state legislatures and tend to remain unchanged indefinitely or for very long periods of time.

What about the other two principal tools in the hands of the Federal Reserve authorities? If the Federal Reserve Banks raise the discount rate charged on the loans it makes, does the impact of this on a bank vary according to whether it is a member bank or a nonmember bank? Because nonmember banks are not permitted to borrow from the Federal Reserve Banks (except under certain emergency conditions), it might seem that the rate charged by the Federal Reserve Banks, whether high or low, is of no consequence to the nonmember banks. However, higher rates charged by the Federal Reserve Banks to member bank borrowers will be accompanied by higher rates charged by those who make loans to nonmember bank borrowers, so that any change in the rate charged by the Federal Reserve Banks is of considerable consequence to any bank that finds it necessary to borrow.

Given the fact that in some states nonmember banks may meet their legal reserve requirements, at least in part, with deposits carried in certain other commercial banks, such nonmember banks may be able to obtain additional legal reserves when needed by borrowing from another commercial bank that qualifies and having the amount of the loan credited to its deposit balance at that bank. Although this transaction may be concealed by the many other transactions that are occurring at the same time, it is possible that a nonmember bank's borrowing from another commercial bank may *in effect* amount to borrowing by that nonmember bank from a Federal Reserve Bank. Suppose a nonmember bank short of legal reserves gets a $1 million loan from a bank at which its deposits count as legal reserves. This transaction is shown by the (a) entries in the T-accounts below. If the lending bank (which we will assume is a member bank) in turn finds itself without enough legal reserves to meet the now higher required reserves that result from the rise in deposits created by this and other loans it has made, it may

NONMEMBER BANK

Assets			Liabilities		
Deposits at member bank	+$1	(a)	Borrowings from member bank	+$1	(a)

MEMBER BANK

Assets			Liabilities		
Loans to nonmember bank	+$1	(a)	Deposits of nonmember bank	+$1	(a)
Deposits at Federal Reserve Bank	+ 1	(b)	Borrowing from Federal Reserve Bank	+$1	(b)

FEDERAL RESERVE BANK

Assets			Liabilities		
Loans	+$1	(b)	Deposits of member banks	+$1	(b)

apply for and secure a loan of $1 million from its Federal Reserve Bank. The result of this is shown by the (b) entries. It may be said that the nonmember bank in this indirect way has what amounts to access to the discount window at the Federal Reserve Bank. If the·banks that have direct access to the discount window must pay higher rates, it is to be expected through this link that they in turn will charge higher rates to those nonmember banks that come to their loan windows to borrow. Furthermore, it follows that whatever effectiveness changes in the discount rate may have as a device to influence the amount of member bank reserves, these changes in the discount rate will have a similar effectiveness in their application to nonmember bank reserves as the rate paid by nonmember bank borrowers to whomever they borrow from tends to rise and fall in line with the rate paid by member bank borrowers at the Federal Reserve Banks.

To conclude, we may say that nonmember banks feel indirectly the effects the member banks feel directly as the Federal Reserve Banks raise and lower the rate charged on loans made to their member banks. This conclusion stands in contrast to that reached for changes in percentage reserve requirements, for there we found that banks not subject to Federal Reserve reserve requirements do not feel any appreciable effects from changes in the percentage reserve requirements that the Federal Reserve authorities order.

To turn to the third major tool, we may ask whether purchases and sales of securities in the open market by the Federal Reserve Bank of New York will be basically the same in their effect on member and nonmember banks. Here the answer is essentially, yes, since there is no significant difference in effect whether the ultimate purchasers of securities sold by the Federal Reserve Bank or the ultimate sellers of securities purchased by the Federal Reserve Bank are *depositors* of member or of nonmember banks. (This answer would be subject to some qualification in the event that the ultimate purchasers or sellers are member or nonmember banks, but we will not here pursue this aspect.)

In Chapter 4 we traced the effect of purchases and sales of securities by the Federal Reserve Bank to the public on the assumption that all of the commercial banks were member banks so that all of the public's demand deposits were by assumption in member banks. In this case, the purchases by the public of securities sold by the Federal Reserve Bank involves an equal decrease in the amount of the member bank's deposit liabilities and in member banks' legal reserve assets. If we now allow for the fact that there are nonmember banks also and assume that the purchasers of some given amount of securities sold by the Federal Reserve Bank are investors who have their demand deposits at nonmember banks, we still find the same basic result: an equal decrease in the amount of the nonmember banks' deposit liabilities and in the nonmember banks' legal reserve assets. The difference between the two cases arises from the way in which the Federal Reserve Bank collects the checks received from the investors who purchased the securities it sold.

Unlike member banks who can pay the Federal Reserve Bank by having the Federal Reserve Bank charge the deposit balance each member bank has at the Federal Reserve Bank, nonmember banks would ordinarily pay the Federal Reserve Bank for the checks presented against it by writing a check against the deposit balances they carry with other banks that are member banks. These deposits in many states count as legal reserves, so the nonmember banks lose legal reserves equal in amount to the decrease in their deposit liabilities. If this particular method of settlement were followed, the entries in the T-accounts would be as shown below for the case of the sale of $100 million of U.S. Government securities by the Federal Reserve Bank of New York to purchasers who have their demand deposits at nonmember banks. Note that in this case the member banks as well as the nonmember banks lose $100 million in legal reserves, a result that follows from the fact that the demand deposit balances carried by the nonmember banks at the member banks count as legal reserves and are here drawn down as a means of paying the Federal Reserve Banks the $100 million owed to them. If the nonmember banks were to pay this $100 million by sending that amount of cash from their vaults to the

Federal Reserve Banks, it may be seen that the reserve position as well as the deposits of the member banks would remain unchanged.

FEDERAL RESERVE BANKS

Assets		Liabilities	
U.S. Government securities	−$100	Deposits of member banks	−$100

MEMBER BANKS

Assets		Liabilities	
Deposits at Federal Reserve Banks	−$100	Deposits of nonmember banks	−$100

NONMEMBER BANKS

Assets		Liabilities	
Deposits at member banks	−$100	Deposits of security purchasers	−$100

If we now compare the tool of open market operations with the other two major tools of the Federal Reserve authorities, we find in the present context that being a nonmember bank in itself makes no significant difference so far as the impact of open market operations is concerned. If the Federal Reserve Bank of New York sells securities that are purchased by the public, whether it is nonmember banks or member banks or both that lose reserves depends on which banks hold the deposits of the investors who are the ultimate purchasers of the securities. A change in the Federal Reserve Banks' discount rate, on the other hand, has its direct impact only on member banks or on the banks to which it makes loans. However, as we saw above, a higher discount rate to member banks will tend to be accompanied by higher rates that nonmember banks must pay on their borrowing, so changes in the discount rate exert their impact indirectly on the price of borrowed funds for nonmember as well as for member banks. It is only in the case of changes in the percentage reserve requirement that banks not subject to Federal Reserve reserve requirements are essentially isolated from the effects of the action taken by the Federal Reserve authorities.

The Federal Reserve authorities have made infrequent use of their power to change the percentage reserve requirements. In the last twenty years, the requirements on demand deposits were raised only twice, in 1968–69 and in 1973; they have, however, been reduced a number of times over this period. One reason for avoiding increases in the percentage follows from the differences just noted between the impact of this tool and the two other major tools. If the authorities choose to use higher percentage requirements as a means of contracting the earning assets and the deposit liabilities of the commercial banks, they place the burden of the contraction almost completely on the member banks over whose reserve requirements they have control. This puts those banks at a competitive disadvantage with nonmember banks and will cause some member banks to sacrifice the advantages of membership in favor of the advantage of the less onerous reserve requirements that go with nonmembership. To the extent that this occurs, the use of this tool by the Federal Reserve authorities to force a contraction may be self-defeating. For the smaller the fraction of total deposits held by member banks, the larger must be the rise in the percentage reserve requirement to produce any desired contractionary effect, but the larger the rise in this percentage, the greater the tendency for banks to become nonmembers and the smaller the fraction of total deposits held by member banks. All of this will, of course, be altered if the Federal Reserve is given the power it has requested to impose the same demand deposit reserve requirements on nonmember banks that it imposes on member banks.

As long as the Federal Reserve does not have this power, it follows that the monetary control powers available for its use in an essentially unrestricted way are those of the open market operation and the discount rate. However, for reasons different from those noted for increases in reserve requirements, the authorities also make little use of discount rate changes other than as a means of supporting the effects brought about through the use of open market operations. The upshot of this is that the Federal Reserve authorities place major reliance on open market operations or on that one of the three major tools of monetary control whose immediate impact does not in itself depend on what fraction of total commercial banks assets or deposits are held by member and by nonmember banks.

Although the final conclusion to which this now brings us is subject to various qualifications, we may say in general that the fact that about 25 percent of the total deposits of all commercial banks are held by nonmember banks does not mean that 25 percent of the commercial banking system escapes the effects of actions taken by the Federal Reserve authorities to contract or expand the deposits of that system. If the authorities worked only through changes in percentage reserve requirements and had control over reserve requirements for only 75 percent of all demand deposits, this statement quite definitely could not be made. It is the fact that they do work predominantly, even though not exclusively, through buying and selling of securities in the open market which does permit this statement to be made.

six

CONTROLLING THE MONEY SUPPLY: THE CHOICE OF TOOLS

Whatever the degree of control the Federal Reserve may exercise over the money supply in any time period, it operates basically through the authorities' control over the amount of legal reserves held by the commercial banks. As this is the case, it would seem that the implementation of a decision by the authorities to work toward any particular change in the money supply calls for nothing more than an appropriate change in the Federal Reserve Banks' loans outstanding or in their holdings of government securities or in the percentage reserve requirements imposed on commercial bank deposits. Each of these presumably can be used to alter the reserve position of the commercial banks in a way that will tend to produce the desired change in the money supply.

At first glance, it seems fair to say that an extra dollar of reserves from one source looks very much like an extra dollar from another source. Therefore, if the authorities' intent is, for example, to increase the money-creating capacity of the commercial banks, it would not appear to matter whether the authorities do this by cutting the discount rate by the amount needed to induce the banks to borrow the appropriate amount of reserves or, alternatively, by purchasing the amount of securities in the open market needed to supply that amount of reserves or, alternatively, by reducing the percentage reserve requirements by the amount necessary to reclassify the appropriate amount of existing legal reserves from required to excess or, alternatively, by any combination of the preceding.

From a purely mechanical point of view, which of these alternatives is followed would appear to be a matter of indifference, but as a practical matter it makes considerable difference whether the Federal Reserve authorities use one or another of these tools. For example, an increase in the excess reserves of the commercial banking system provided through lending by the Federal Reserve Banks involves an increase in the indebtedness of the commercial banks to the Federal Reserve Banks (on which the particular debtor banks pay interest), while an equal increase provided in either of the other two ways does not. Reserves obtained by borrowing imply a temporariness that is not characteristic of reserves obtained otherwise, since the latter do not involve an obligation to repay. And beyond this, although an increase of excess reserves provided by open market operations is like an increase provided by a change in percentage reserve requirements in that neither adds to the indebtedness of the commercial banks, they in turn differ in other ways such as the geographical distribution of the initial impact of each on the money supply. Because open market operations are carried out in New York City, the additional excess reserves supplied via such operations accrue at first primarily to the money market banks and then over the following days are diffused gradually through the country. On the other hand, because an equal amount of excess reserves provided through a reduction in percentage reserve requirements will be distributed throughout the nation's banks in proportion to the deposits of each, the immediate effect on the money supply will be more widespread geographically than in the case of open market operations.

These are only two of the dozens of differences found in the way that the major tools of monetary control operate in practice. Some of the differences appear as an advantage of one tool or a disadvantage of another. It is, of course, only after a careful weighing of all the advantages and disadvantages, of all the strengths and weaknesses, that the Federal Reserve authorities can decide rationally what tool or combination of tools appears to be the most appropriate in any existing set of circumstances.

All things considered, over the last twenty-some years the authorities have found that open market operations enable them to produce desired changes in the banks' reserve position with a minimum of unfavorable other effects, and it is this tool on which they have come to place major reliance. However, looking back a half-century to the early years of the Federal Reserve System, from 1914 through the 1920's, one finds that open market operations were not even generally recognized as tools of control, and the discount rate was the only tool then employed by the authorities. The discount mechanism has never since played nearly as important a role, although there are some specialists who favor a modification of present practices that would considerably enlarge its role once again. There are, as might be guessed, other specialists who oppose any such modification and support the status quo and a few at the extreme who would do away altogether with lending by the Federal Reserve Banks.

In this disagreement, as in any other of this kind, different specialists come up with different evaluations as to the balance of advantages and disadvantages of one instrument in comparison with another. There is almost no question today among these experts that open market operations should continue to be the Federal Reserve authorities' primary weapon of monetary management, but this still leaves open the possibility of expanded use of the discount rate and perhaps greater use also of changes in percentage reserve requirements. Beyond this is another set of tools known as selective credit controls. This includes the regulation of margin requirements on the purchase of securities and of down payments and repayment periods on the purchase of consumer durable goods. This by no means exhausts the possibilities. The Federal Reserve in recent years has used as a tool of credit control its power to regulate the maximum rate of interest commercial banks can pay on time deposits. And there are various other instruments which economists have proposed but which have never been adopted in this country.

All of this adds up to a major area of study and one that is much more complex than might appear at first glance. In this chapter we will attempt no more than a brief introduction to this large subject, indicating some of the advantages and disadvantages, strengths and weaknesses of each of the three major tools. Each of these three tools is a so-called general tool of monetary control. The last section of the chapter provides a brief discussion of the selective controls.

THE DISCOUNT RATE

Of the various instruments of monetary control, the discount rate is surely the one most familiar to the general public and probably also the one most misunderstood by the general public. The popular conception is that the discount rate is the basic device used by the Federal Reserve to control other interest rates—i.e., that a rise in the discount rate means that before long a rise will follow in other interest rates, especially rates charged by the commercial banks on the various types of loans they make. This conclusion is drawn from what the general public views as a self-evident fact: if the commercial banks must pay higher rates on the loans they secure from the Federal Reserve Banks, they will charge higher rates on the loans they make to their customers and other lenders will also raise their rates in line.

The Discount Rate and Other Interest Rates

Although there is at times some truth in this common view, there is usually more of the opposite in it. It implies that the amount and cost of credit extended by all those financial institutions that deal with the public is closely geared to the amount and cost of the loans made by the Federal Reserve Banks. So far as amount is concerned, the largest 12-month increase in Federal Reserve Bank loans in recent years was $1.9 billion, which occurred from July 1972 to July 1973. During this same period, outstanding debt in the form known as consumer credit went up by $23.9 billion, in the form of loans on real estate went up by $72 billion, and in the form of commercial and industrial loans by banks went up by $30.0 billion. There are a number of other categories of loans with similarly large amounts involved, but the amounts in the few categories noted are sufficient to suggest that the change in the amount of credit extended to the public in the form of loans is of a magnitude many times too large to be accounted for by the change in the amount borrowed by the commercial banks from the Federal Reserve Banks. Nor is this conclusion essentially altered after making allowance for the fact that the amount so borrowed is multiplied into a larger amount of bank deposits and money supply. Changes in the amount of loans made by the Federal Reserve Banks play a role at the margin, but this is only a marginal role and not one that begins to warrant the conclusion that the cost and availability of loans secured by the general public depends on the cost and availability of loans secured by the commercial banks from the Federal Reserve Banks.

This, it must be noted, does not amount to saying that the cost and availability of loans to the public is only marginally influenced by the actions of the Federal Reserve authorities. Their actions are of appreciable influence, but this influence is exerted primarily through open market operations rather than through variations in the discount rate. If the intent is to restrict the lending capacity of the commercial banks, the indicated open market action is, of course, a sale of some of the securities held by the Federal Reserve Banks. With no decrease in the demand for loans by the customers of the commercial banks, the decrease in the capacity of those banks to make loans will usually mean that some prospective borrowers are turned away altogether, that others are permitted to borrow less than they might otherwise, and that most of those who are accommodated in part or in full are required to pay a higher interest rate on the loans obtained.

How does the discount rate fit into this operating procedure? It may be apparent that if the discount rate charged by the Federal Reserve Banks remains unchanged as these other rates rise, there is plainly a greater profit incentive than before for the commercial banks to turn to the discount window to secure additional reserves with which to accommodate their customers' demands at the now higher interest rates that may be gotten. If the Federal Reserve Banks raise their discount rate under these circumstances, the rise may be no more than a technical adjustment designed to bring the rate they charge more closely in line with other interest rates, which have already risen, and to thereby limit the commercial banks' resort to the discount window as a way of escaping the pressure that has been applied to them through restrictive open market operations. Contrary to the newspaper headlines announcing that most other interest rates will soon be higher, the rise in the discount rate in this situation is not a harbinger of such higher interest rates but a recognition of the fact that a rise in these other interest rates has already occurred.

This sequence does not, however, preclude the possibility that other interest rates may indeed rise following a rise in the discount rate. It is possible that a rise in the discount rate, which is no more than a technical adjustment, may still generate expectations among the general public that causes them to act in a way that forces other interest rates upward. However, in most cases the cause of a further rise in other interest rates is more likely to be a *further* tightening of the commercial banks' reserve position through other Federal Reserve actions than it is likely to be a response to a higher discount rate. As we have noted, recent experience suggests that the discount rate typically follows other interest rates as they move upward and downward, and that changes in the discount rate in most cases indicate essentially passive adjustments to altered conditions in the money market rather than being the means by which the Federal Reserve authorities seek to initiate altered conditions in that market.

Although we thus find that the discount rate does tend to follow other interest rates upward, it is nonetheless ordinarily held at a level appreciably below other interest rates. For instance in April 1974 the discount rate continued a series of increases that began in January 1973 by reaching a level of 8 percent, the highest level since the Federal Reserve System was established. Still, at the same time the interest rate that could be earned on risk-free, short-term U.S. Government securities was about 8 1/2 percent and on virtually risk-free commercial paper (the promissory notes of leading corporations with 4 to 6 month maturity) about 10 percent. For commercial banks across the country, the average rate on short-term business loans was well above 11 percent—or actually several percentage points above this if allowance is made for certain indirect charges like compensating balances.

When other interest rates are falling, there is similarly a lag in the downward adjustment of the discount rate, which at times leaves the discount rate higher than the rate on short-term U.S. Government securities and commercial paper. However, the problem that arises as a result of a differential in this direction is far less serious than its opposite, to whose implications we now turn.

The Bases for Borrowing

A differential of this kind raises the question of how the actual upward adjustment of the discount rate can serve to limit the commercial banks' resort to the discount window when the discount rate still remains far below the rate the banks are able to earn by making ordinary short-term business loans to their customers and even appreciably below the rates they can earn on practically risk-free securities. Given a situation in which the Federal Reserve has acted to reduce the ability of the commercial banks to expand their loans by the amount that would meet the demands of their customers, and given the desire of each commercial bank to somehow accommodate fully its regular customers as a means of assuring their continued patronage, the indicated relationship between the discount rate and other interest rates would appear to provide the banks with a ready answer to the situation. As individual banks feel the pressure exerted by the restrictive open market operations carried out by the Federal Reserve, all they need do is turn to the discount window to replenish their reserves and do this at a discount rate which, although higher than before, is higher by no more and probably by less than are the interest rates they can secure on the loans they make to their customers.

If the commercial banks could and did act in this way, it is apparent that the discount window would be a wide-open escape hatch through which they could offset whatever tightening of their reserve position the Federal Reserve might have brought about in other ways. The discount window is not, however, an unobstructed escape hatch. Although the relationship between the discount rate and other interest rates ordinarily provides the banks with a profit incentive to borrow whenever they have insufficient reserves to meet loan demands, the amount of lending the Federal Reserve stands ready to provide at the discount window in any time period is not left to be determined by the commercial banks purely on a profit basis. If this were the sole basis, that amount would likely have been many times larger than it actually was in years like 1969 and 1973–74, when the Federal Reserve tried to hold the banks' lending capacity substantially below what was needed to accommodate the loan demand they faced.

There are various situations encountered by individual banks that are recognized as proper bases on which to borrow from the Federal Reserve Banks, but the simple fact that a bank may be able to earn a higher rate on the use of such borrowings than the rate it has to pay for them is not a proper basis. A bank that attempted to borrow from the Federal Reserve Bank continuously with no motive other than an improvement in the appearance of its profit and loss statement would before long find the discount window shut in its face. The Federal Reserve Banks hardly ever find it necessary to turn down a loan application because hardly ever does a commercial bank cross over that vaguely defined but reasonably well-understood line between what is a proper and an improper basis on which a commercial bank may borrow from them. Also reinforcing this is a tradition against borrowing from the Federal Reserve Banks that goes back to the 1920's, although the reluctance of some banks to be in debt to the Federal Reserve Banks is probably not as strong today as it was in the past.

To the extent that one can state in a few words what constitute acceptable bases for borrowing, those words are that a bank should borrow from its Federal Reserve Bank only to cover needs that could not reasonably be foreseen or against which preparation could not reasonably be made. This is the idea conveyed by Regulation A, issued by the Board of Governors of the Federal Reserve System in 1955.

> Federal Reserve credit is generally extended on a short-term basis to a member bank in order to enable it to adjust its asset position when necessary because of developments such as a sudden withdrawal of deposits or seasonal requirements for credit beyond those which can reasonably be met by use of

the bank's own resources. Federal Reserve credit is also available for longer periods when necessary in order to assist member banks in meeting unusual situations, such as may result from national, regional, or local difficulties or from exceptional circumstances involving only particular member banks. Under ordinary conditions, the continuous use of Federal Reserve credit by a member bank over a considerable period of time is not regarded as appropriate.

The first sentence of this statement does not preclude borrowing by a bank for the purpose of expanding its earning assets and thus does not preclude borrowing because it is profitable for the bank to do so. However, such borrowing must be to meet "seasonal requirements for credit beyond those which can reasonably be met by use of the bank's own resources," a provision that limits both the amount a bank may borrow and the period for which it may borrow. The use of the discount window as a steady source of whatever amount of additional reserves a bank might profitably put to use is, of course, clearly ruled out by the last sentence in the statement.

A less restrictive regulation, other things being equal, would probably have meant a substantially higher level of borrowing at various times over the last two decades than was actually experienced. During this period, purchases of U.S. Government securities were the major means by which the Federal Reserve increased the legal reserves of the banks. Over these years the amount of legal reserves obtained by the banks through borrowing ordinarily amounted to something between a fraction of 1 percent and 2 percent and only on rare occasions exceeded 5 percent of their total legal reserves. During the 1920's, when loans were used by the Federal Reserve as the major means of supplying and varying the amount of reserves held by the banks, this percentage averaged about 30 and at times was as high as 40. Although loans in the last two decades would not have approached these percentages of earlier years even if there had been a less restrictive regulation on borrowing, it is safe to say they would then have accounted for a higher percentage of bank reserves than they actually did.

The Discount Window: An Escape Hatch?

Despite the limited role that borrowing has played in recent years, some economists believe that it should be suppressed even more. To these critics, the discount window still looms as an escape hatch which seriously blunts the effectiveness of Federal Reserve sales of securities in the open market. As we have noted, the commercial banks cannot borrow at will from the Federal Reserve Banks, but whatever may be the additional amount of reserves obtained in this way in any time period, that amount neutralizes what otherwise would have been the restrictive effect imposed by an equal amount of securities sold by the Federal Reserve Bank.

In terms of T-accounts, this result may readily be seen by combining these two transactions (each of which was traced out separately in Chapter 4). Assuming the Federal Reserve Bank sells $100 million in securities to the public for the purpose of reducing commercial bank reserves by a like amount, the effect on the banks' legal reserves is shown by the (a) entries in the T-accounts below. However, for the commercial banking system as a whole, there will be no *net* change in reserve position if some banks in the system apply for and receive $100 million of additional loans at the Federal Reserve Banks. This transaction is shown by the (b) entries. The reserves lost by the system in one way are recovered in another, and on balance the total of loans and securities and the total of deposits remains unchanged.

FEDERAL RESERVE BANKS

Assets			Liabilities		
U.S. Government securities	−$100	(a)	Deposits of commercial banks	−$100	(a)
Loans	+$100	(b)	Deposits of commercial banks	+$100	(b)

COMMERCIAL BANKS

Assets			Liabilities		
Deposits with Federal Reserve Banks	−$100	(a)	Demand deposits of public	−$100	(a)
Deposits with Federal Reserve Banks	+$100	(b)	Borrowings from Federal Reserve Banks	+$100	(b)

One might argue that the Federal Reserve can compensate for the effect of any borrowing by selling whatever larger amount of securities is necessary to produce the desired restrictive effect. But the answer to this argument is that the adjustment of these two flows to produce the desired effect is not as easy as the adjustment of a pair of water valves. It it not very difficult to effect some specific decrease in the level of water in a tank by opening wider the outflow valve to compensate for the fact that there now is an open inflow valve. It is far more difficult, if possible at all, to effect some specific decrease in the level of the banks' legal reserves by expanding the reserve outflow via open market sales to compensate for the fact that there is now a reserve inflow via loans.

The short-run control that the Federal Reserve has over the amount of legal reserves is assuredly weakened by the fact that the banks may fall back on loans from the Federal Reserve Banks. In terms of the physical analogy, the problem is especially complicated by the fact that the Federal Reserve controls fully only the size of the opening of the U.S. Government securities valve, while the commercial banks have some control over the size of the opening of the loans valve. It is true that the Federal Reserve has complete control over the discount rate, but it has far less control over the amount of loans the banks seek and secure at any given discount rate. With two sets of hands on the controls, despite the far greater strength of the Federal Reserve's hands, adjustments clearly cannot be made as precisely as would be the case if the commercial banks were required to remove their hands from the controls.

Because the availability of loans at the Federal Reserve Banks reduces the closeness with which the Federal Reserve can control the amount of legal reserves, one step removed it also reduces the closeness with which the Federal Reserve can control the money supply. In the preceding chapter we examined a series of slippages that are found between changes in legal reserves and changes in the money supply. In terms of the equation $\Delta M = \frac{1 + c}{r + r'a + c + e} \Delta R$, we saw that short-run unpredictable changes in a, c, and e will produce short-run changes in the money supply different from those expected at the time the Federal Reserve effects particular changes in legal reserves. Because of these slippages, it followed that the Federal Reserve's control over ΔM was less close than its control over ΔR.

At the present point in this chapter we have met a slippage of a different kind but one with a similar effect—a slippage between the intended change in reserves and the actual change in reserves that results from the fact that open market operations may be followed by a larger or smaller change in borrowings at the Federal Reserve Banks than had been expected by the Federal Reserve. Other things being equal, the degree of control the Federal Reserve is able to maintain over the money supply in the short run depends on the degree of control it is able to maintain over the commercial banks' reserve position. The unpredictable short-run changes in loans outstanding at the Federal Reserve Banks introduces a slippage into the Federal Reserve's short-run control over these reserves and so into its control over the money supply.

There are economists like Milton Friedman who believe that close control over the rate of growth of the money supply is essential to the economy's health (for reasons to be considered in detail in Part III) and who accordingly favor certain legal, institutional, and procedural changes that would help prevent or at least reduce variations in this rate. Simply from the viewpoint of the mechanics involved, one way to enable the Federal Reserve to control the money supply more closely is through the elimination or limitation of the present slippage, and toward this end Friedman has long favored ending the commercial banks' present privilege of securing reserves by borrowing from the Federal Reserve Banks, a privilege whose exercise he regards as more than a negligible slippage in the monetary machinery.

The Discount Window: A Safety Valve?

It can hardly be denied that the closing of the discount window would give the Federal Reserve the means to exercise a closer short-run control over the money supply. For example, there would be no question as to how much of any given reduction in the banking system's reserves effected by the Federal Reserve through a sale of securities would be returned to the banks through loans obtained at the Federal Reserve Banks—the answer is simply none. Under such an arrangement, individual banks in the system that at any time found themselves with a deficiency of reserves would have to adjust by reducing the amount of their loans or security holdings or by borrowing from other banks in the system that might have excess reserves. If the Federal Reserve had already squeezed all excess reserves out of the system, any further sale of securities by the Federal Reserve, other things being equal, would mean that the banks would have no way of adjusting except through a decrease in their earning assets.

Many economists see the need for reform of the discount mechanism, and not only because of the slippage it produces, but few are in favor of going to Freidman's extreme of an outright scrapping of the mechanism. In the judgment of most, there are sufficiently strong arguments to warrant maintaining the system in some form. One, which stands in sharp contrast to the argument that discounting serves as an escape hatch for the banks, is that discounting serves as a "safety valve" or "shock absorber." It provides a means by which the Federal Reserve can at times come to the temporary aid of particular banks that might otherwise be forced into abrupt liquidation of sizable amounts of assets with consequent losses to themselves and possible disruption to financial markets. This argument for discounting, expressed in one way or another, is as old as the Federal Reserve System itself; a major reason for the establishment of the System was to provide a "lender of last resort," a place to which commercial banks could turn in times of need as an alternative to the forced liquidation of assets that had so often in the past led to financial panics.

The banking system has undergone various structural changes since the 1930's that make the maintenance of the discount window no longer a necessity to avert panics of the kind experienced many years ago. However, it has been argued that maintaining the discount window is still essential in the contemporary setting for the quite different reason that it enables the Federal Reserve to move more freely and deliberately in effecting changes in the banks' reserve position than would otherwise be the case. The existence of the "safety valve" gives the authorities time to react to changes in conditions, whether these are of their own making or due to other forces. Those banks that first feel the impact of such a change—e.g., an unexpected large withdrawal of currency by the public—are the first to react, and they make their reaction known at the discount window. If some temporary expansion in reserves seems appropriate in the face of this change in conditions, these extra reserves can be passed out through the discount window with no action by the Federal Reserve in the open market. But without the discount window, the burden placed on open market operations would be just that much greater. If the discount window were permanently closed, the Federal Reserve would have to learn to react more quickly than they now do, despite the danger that a quick reaction is more likely to be an overreaction or underreaction than one that follows only after a more careful study of conditions.

From this same viewpoint, not only does the discount window give the Federal Reserve more time to decide what change in the reserve position of the banking system as a whole is called for in view of some change in conditions, but it gives the Federal Reserve more maneuverability in its use of open market operations to try to bring about the indicated change in that position. The discount mechanism has already been likened to a safety valve or a shock absorber; in the present context it has been likened to a set of brakes. The speed with which a vehicle may be driven safely is obviously much greater if that vehicle is equipped with brakes. The extent to which the Federal Reserve can safely carry restrictive open market operations is similarly greater if there is a discount window to which the banks may turn. The damage that otherwise would follow if the authorities were to carry such operations too far would be prevented as those banks that were hit especially hard temporarily met their problem by turning to the discount window. As all agree, the open market operation is the Federal Reserve's primary instrument of monetary control; the present argument is that this highly effective instrument has even greater effectiveness when given the freedom in use which is made possible by the availability of the discount window to absorb the impact of errors which are more likely with that greater freedom of use.

A Floating Discount Rate

The two questions posed above — "The Discount Window: An Escape Hatch? and "The Discount Window: A Safety Valve?" — are not mutually contradictory. In acting as a safety valve, discounting also to some extent operates as an escape hatch. However, the consensus of expert opinion probably is that discounting is more beneficial in its provision of a safety valve than it is harmful in its provision of an escape hatch. Therefore, the question as seen by most specialists is not whether the discount mechanism should be discarded or retained but in what form it should be retained. The objective, of course, is a form that preserves its advantages and eliminates or minimizes its disadvantages. The disadvantage of a degree of slippage introduced into the Federal Reserve's control of the money supply is inherent in the discount mechanism and cannot be eliminated except by the elimination of the discount window itself. There are, however, other disadvantages in the present operation of the discount mechanism that can be eliminated by appropriate reform.

A reform measure many economists feel would go far toward meeting this objective is the use of a system of "floating discount rates," which would change from week to week or over some other short time period. Although changes do occur under the present system, they are irregular and relatively infrequent, and each such change involves a specific discretionary action by the Federal Reserve authorities. In the floating system, changes would be automatic. The discount rate would rise or fall from one week to the next in line with the change in some selected market interest rate. The rate most often suggested for this purpose is that on Treasury bills, which are short-term U.S. Government obligations actively traded in huge amounts among financial institutions every day. Each Monday the Treasury sells by auction some amount of new Treasury bills to make payment on the issue maturing that week and sometimes also sells some amount to raise new funds; the prices established in the auction determine the yield as of that date. The discount rate for the week would then be set at whatever level is needed to maintain some predetermined constant differential of the discount rate over the Treasury bill rate.

Under this system, the discount rate not only would necessarily be above the rate the banks earn on any holdings of Treasury bills but, depending on how large a differential were imposed, would also be above the rates they earn on some other assets in their portfolios. With the discount rate adjusted weekly, the disadvantage inherent in the "escape hatch" feature of the discount window would become less serious, while the advantage provided by the "safety valve" feature would be available much as it is today. Banks could borrow on the same basis as now, but a smaller portion of their borrowing would likely be induced by the profit incentive than is now the case. At present, the Federal Reserve does not ordinarily adjust the discount rate upward until the differential between market rates and the discount rate has become appreciable and has persisted for some time. But the larger this differential and the longer it persists, the greater is likely to be the expansion of borrowing induced by the profit incentive that this situation presents to the banks. We noted earlier that borrowing from the Federal Reserve Banks motivated solely by the fact that the rate charged there is lower than the rate the banks can earn is not regarded by the Federal Reserve as a legitimate basis for borrowing. However, the larger this differential, the greater the profit incentive, and the greater the amount of this kind of borrowing that is likely to occur, despite the close surveillance by the Federal Reserve Banks over the borrowing behavior of the commercial banks.

Under the floating discount rate system, the automatic periodic adjustment of the discount rate means that this differential remains practically constant, and the swings in the amount of borrowing that now occur because the profit incentive to borrow varies would in large part be removed. The discount window would continue to be used as a safety valve or shock absorber, although it would be available on somewhat less favorable terms to the banks than is now the case. The discount window would, however, be less likely to be abused than it is under the present system.

Another shortcoming of the present system that a floating discount rate system would help eliminate is the frequent misunderstanding by the general public of the meaning of the discretionary changes made from time to time by the Federal Reserve. As noted at the beginning of this section on the discount rate, these changes are frequently no more than technical adjustments designed to bring the discount rate closer into line with other interest rates—actually most of the changes that occur over periods during which interest rates are gradually rising or falling are of this kind. It is important to see that changes like these are clearly not indicative of a change in Federal Reserve policy toward tighter or easier credit. There are, however, other changes in the discount rate, particularly at turning points in the business cycle, that are independent of preceding changes in other interest rates and may be indicative of a change in Federal Reserve policy. The difficulty under the present system is that a large segment of the public looks at each and every change in the discount rate as an indicator of a change by the Federal Reserve toward a tighter or easier policy.

If this involved nothing more than a misinformed public, it would not matter especially. What makes it matter is that the public's response to what it takes the change in the discount rate to mean may have destabilizing effects on the national economy. Suppose, as is usually the case, that a rise in the discount rate is generally interpreted by the public as a signal that the Federal Reserve is moving toward a tighter policy, which will mean coming higher levels of other interest rates. Although, as we have seen, the discount rate action is most probably merely a technical adjustment, the public, apparently including much of the press, tends to believe that the action was taken because the Federal Reserve feels that the economy is moving ahead too vigorously or is getting too close to an outbreak of inflation. Beyond this, if the public not only believes that this action was deliberately taken to slow down the economy but also believes that the Federal Reserve authorities have the determination to take whatever further action may be needed for this purpose, they may well become afraid that what is intended as a healthy economic slowing may develop into an actual economic downturn. This is sufficient to lead some more cautious business firms and consumers to cancel or postpone certain spending plans. If this reaction to the Federal Reserve's action is at all widespread, the impact may be great enough to lead to the very slowdown that was feared. In terms of the present illustration, it may be called destabilizing because no slowdown of the economy was called for and none was intended by the Federal Reserve in raising the discount rate. The trouble arose from the public's misinterpretation of the meaning of the Federal Reserve action.

Suppose again, as but one of several other possibilities, that the public interprets the rise in the discount rate as an "official" forecast of inflation ahead. If the public takes this as a forecast and believes it is a correct forecast but does not believe that the Federal Reserve will have the determination to carry its restrictive policy as far as would be needed to meet the problem, their reaction would be the opposite of that in the previous illustration. A certain amount of spending that would not have occurred during the current period will be carried out before the expected higher prices become a reality. Again, if this reaction is at all widespread, the impact on the economy may be significant and in this case destabilizing in the upward direction in contrast to the other case, which was destabilizing in the downward direction.

This brings us to a conclusion: with the system of floating discount rates, the possibility of destabilizing effects of this kind is sharply reduced. There would no longer be the present system of occasional, discrete rate changes of 1/4 percentage point or more, each invariably accompanied by newspaper headlines here and there announcing that the Federal Reserve is changing its policy in one way or another. Changes would occur weekly, would be of much smaller size, and, more basically, would be of a nondiscretionary type. Before long the story on each weekly change would be buried somewhere in a corner of the financial pages.

The prospect of so basic a reform in the discount mechanism as the adoption of a floating discount rate is quite remote. It has, how-ever, deserved mention here as a device that would help to correct the several major disadvantages of the present system which have been discussed in these few pages. In summary, this alternative arrangement would permit the maintenance of the discount window basically un-changed in its role as a shock absorber but severely restricted in its undesirable but unavoidable role as an escape hatch. And, by ending purely discretionary changes in the discount rate, it would end the misinterpretation the public often places on these changes and thereby avoid what are sometimes the destabilizing actions the public takes in response to these changes.

PERCENTAGE RESERVE REQUIREMENTS

As we saw in Chapter 4, $1 of legal reserves enables the commercial banks to carry a maximum of $5 of demand deposits if the minimum reserve requirement is 20 percent, a maximum of $10 of demand deposits if the minimum reserve require-ment is 10 percent, and so forth. It follows from this that whoever has the power to raise or lower the minimum percentage reserve require-ment the banks must maintain has the power to lower or raise the maximum amount of demand deposits the banks may carry on the basis of any given amount of reserves. It follows in turn that whoever has this power also has the power to increase or decrease the maximum money supply consistent with any given amount of legal reserves held by the banks.

From the inception of the Federal Reserve System in 1914 until 1935, no such power had been granted by the Congress. Although the Congress itself could, of course, at any time change the minimum percentage reserve requirements it had set forth in the original Federal Reserve Act, it actually left them essentially unchanged through these years. It first granted power to vary these requirements to the Federal Reserve in 1935. Continuously since that date the Federal Reserve has had the authority to raise and lower the percentage reserve requirements at its discretion, but the highest and lowest levels at which it may set them must fall within the upper and lower limits set by the Congress in the Federal Reserve Act as amended.

A major reason underlying this grant of power by the Congress to the Federal Reserve specifically in 1935 was that such power had come to be sorely needed as of that time. Changes in reserve requirements are well adapted to effect large changes in the banks' reserve position, changes of a magnitude that cannot always be brought about practically via loans or open market operations. As of 1935 the commercial banks had accumulated several billion dollars of excess reserves, a huge amount even by today's standards and an amount the Federal Reserve Banks could not have offset by reducing their loans to zero or even by selling all the government securities they held at that time. The power to raise percentage reserve requirements was needed by the Federal Reserve to meet this special situation and was granted by the Congress. It may be noted that this situation, a massive accumulation of excess reserves over a period of several years, was primarily the result of a vast inflow of gold, which followed from the devaluation of the dollar in 1934, an action that raised the U.S. buying price of gold from $20.67 to $35.00 per ounce.

In several steps during 1936 and 1937 the Federal Reserve raised the percentage reserve requirements to double their original level, the full limit to which they could go under the new law. This action cut the demand deposit multiplier in half—each dollar of reserves was now able to support only half as many dollars of demand deposits as before. This action, however, did not necessarily force a contraction of the loans and security holdings of the banks and therefore of their deposits. The higher reserve percentages, even though twice the previous percentages, did no more than reclassify what had been excess reserves into required reserves; they did not raise required reserves above actual reserves, an action that would necessarily have forced a contraction of banks' deposits unless otherwise offset. The intent of the Federal Reserve at the time was not to decrease the volume of earning assets and deposit liabilities of the banks; it was to prevent what later could have been a dangerously large and rapid expansion in the assets and deposits of the banks if loan demand, which had been badly depressed for five years, were to show a sudden and sharp revival. Of course, to the extent that the large excess reserve holdings were no more than was necessary to meet what may have been an unusually high desired ratio of excess reserves to deposits by the banks (the *e* ratio of the preceding chapter), the action of the Federal Reserve was in fact decidedly contractionary. As we will see in Chapter 14, some economists who see it this way regard this action as a major factor in the sharp recession of 1937–38.

Over the almost forty years that the Federal Reserve has had this particular power, they have used it several dozen times. It has, however, never again been used on a scale as in 1936—38 for nothing like the circumstances of those years has since been faced. Through appropriate open market operations, the Federal Reserve has been able to keep the excess reserves of the banks under close control, preventing large swings in either direction. For example, just as the large gold inflow of the thirties tended to build up the banks' legal reserves, the large gold outflows during the sixties tended to draw down their legal reserves. However, whereas substantial increases in reserve requirements had to be employed during 1936—38 to absorb the build-up of excess reserves, no substantial decreases in reserve requirements were employed during the sixties to compensate for the effect of gold outflow on legal reserves. Instead the legal reserves lost as a result of gold outflows were offset by open market purchases of securities by the Federal Reserve. Again, the open market operation is the instrument the Federal Reserve finds best adapted to meet almost all situations nowadays.

This major reliance on open market operations is due in part to a constraint on the greater use of changes in reserve requirements that the Federal Reserve has imposed on itself. The Federal Reserve has chosen to make changes in percentage reserve requirements no smaller than 1/2 of 1 percentage point. And this percentage change, small as it may seem, still involves a dollar change in the reserve position of the banks so large as to limit its use to those infrequent occasions when a large change is deemed necessary by the Federal Reserve. For example, if deposits total $200 billion, if the average reserve requirement is 10 percent, and if actual legal reserves are $20 billion, the banks as a group have neither an excess nor a deficiency of reserves. A decrease in the average reserve requirement of just 1/2 percentage point would reduce required reserves by $1 billion, create excess reserves of this amount, and permit an expansion of bank earning assets and deposits of over $10 billion, neglecting currency drains and other complications. In the reverse case, an increase in the average reserve requirement of 1/2 percentage point, the result is an increase in required reserves of $1 billion, a reserve deficiency of $1 billion, and a contraction of bank earning assets and deposits of almost $10 billion, again neglecting currency inflows and other complications. An expansion or contraction of deposits on anything like this scale over any short period of time is bound to be destabilizing to the economy and not a result the Federal Reserve would deliberately bring about.

Because of the sizable impact of even a 1/2 of 1 percentage point reserve requirement change, the Federal Reserve has at times found it necessary to supplement a change in percentage reserve requirements with open market operations. For example, if a 1/2 of 1 percentage point reduction in reserve requirements against demand deposits were to add, say, $500 million to excess reserves at a time when the Federal

Reserve wanted to add no more than $300 million to excess reserves, the authorities could sell securities in the open market to offset the other $200 million of excess reserves. This sort of coordination of reserve requirement changes and open market operations permits the Federal Reserve to change the percentage reserve requirement by 1/2 or even 1 percentage point, even though they do not want to produce the full change in excess reserves that will accompany these changes.

It may be apparent that this sort of offsetting operation could be avoided altogether if the Federal Reserve were simply to employ changes of 1/4 or even smaller fractions of a percentage point. There is nothing to stand in the way of making such small changes and of doing this on a frequent basis other than the difficulties it would create for the banking system. This objection would not be controlling, however, if it could be shown that the Federal Reserve could better accomplish its objectives by such small frequent changes in reserve requirements than by effecting the same changes in the banks' reserve position through open market operations. So far as the mere mechanics of effecting some desired change in the reserve position of the banks is concerned, the Federal Reserve today can do through open market operations practically anything it can do through changes in reserve requirements. However, as we noted in the introduction to this chapter, an additional dollar of reserves from one source is not identical in its impact with an additional dollar from another source—in the present context, providing a given number of dollars of excess reserves via a cut in percentage reserve requirements will not have the same effects as providing the same number of dollars of reserves via open market operations. The differences in these effects are such that some economists find advantages in the use of changes in reserve requirements over open market operations as a means of effecting specific changes in the banks' reserve position.

One advantage, it is argued, is that changes in reserve requirements enable the Federal Reserve to achieve the desired goal of altering the banks' reserve position without intervening in the market in the way it must when it buys and sells securities. This, it is held, enables the Federal Reserve to maintain a high degree of neutrality—it takes actions to increase or decrease the money supply as it sees fit without at the same time directly influencing the prices of securities, either short term or long term, and thereby without directly influencing interest rates, either short term or long term. In this way, the Federal Reserve limits itself to what some economists hold is its proper role, controlling the money supply, without simultaneously affecting the structure of interest rates and the allocation of credit. The latter are left to the forces of the market place. The Federal Reserve cannot limit its role in this way when it engages in open market operations.

According to some economists, another advantage of changes in reserve requirements over open market operations is the one we mentioned incidentally in the introduction to this chapter: the effects of the former are felt at the same time by banks throughout the country. Changes in reserve requirements are, therefore, likely to affect conditions in the economy more promptly than are open market operations, whose effects are at first felt chiefly by the banks in New York City, where the open market operations are carried out. Thus, if the intent is to slow spending through a restriction of the availability of credit, that purpose may be more promptly achieved if the banks throughout the country rather than primarily the New York banks find their lending power cut back. A change in percentage reserve requirements can at any one time exert a generalized geographical effect; restrictive open market operations cannot.

There are several other lesser arguments one could list in support of changes in reserve requirements, but to each of these as well as the preceding there are also counterarguments. For example, with regard to the two noted above there is disagreement as to how important it is for the Federal Reserve to be neutral in the sense indicated and as to whether there is a significant difference in the time taken by the two instruments to make their effects felt nationally. On balance, the case for making smaller fractional changes in the percentage reserve requirements and thus more frequent use of such changes does not appear to be very strong, at least not as long as we limit attention to the present basic system of percentage reserve requirements. This apparently is the view of the Federal Reserve, for it shows no sign of moving toward the smaller percentage changes that would make changes in reserve requirements a more flexible tool than it now is. The likelihood is that, apart from their use to effect certain technical adjustments, changes in reserve requirements will continue to be used only to bring about substantial changes in the banks' reserve position, which means that they will only be used on the infrequent occasions when such substantial changes appear to be needed.

Following more frequent changes in earlier years, from 1960 to 1968 the Federal Reserve left the reserve requirements against demand deposits completely unchanged and from 1968 to 1974 made only 3 changes, each of 1/2 of 1 percentage point. Over these years, the number of changes made in the percentage against time deposits has not been much larger. This overall record for recent years thus does not suggest that changes in reserve requirements have been a major tool used by the Federal Reserve to affect the banks' reserve position—it surely does not begin to compare with the Federal Reserve's use of open market operations in this regard.

It should be pointed out before we leave this subject that, although it will remain a far less important tool than open market

operations, changes in reserve requirements may become more important and more frequently used in the years ahead. We noted in the
preceding chapter that, after living quietly with the existing awkward
arrangement for twenty-five years, the Board of Governors of the
Federal Reserve System has specifically and formally asked the Congress for a change in that arrangement to make demand deposits in all
banks subject to the reserve requirements set by the Federal Reserve for
demand deposits. At present about 25 percent of the total demand
deposits of commercial banks are held in banks that are not member
banks of the Federal Reserve System and whose reserve requirements
are set by the various state governments. This means that if reserve
requirements imposed by the Federal Reserve on member banks become much more stringent than those imposed by the states on nonmember banks, there tends to be an exodus of banks from membership
in the Federal Reserve System to take advantage of the lighter reserve
requirements that go with nonmembership. This has long been a factor
the Federal Reserve has had to consider in contemplating an increase in
reserve requirements. However, if demand deposits in all banks were
subject to the Federal Reserve's reserve requirements on such deposits,
this would cease to be such a factor and upward changes in reserve
requirements on demand deposits which might be ruled out under the
present arrangement could be put into effect without fear of their
effect on membership in the system. This structural change may be
ordered by the Congress before long, and with it could come a somewhat more important role for change in reserve requirements as a tool
of monetary control.

OPEN MARKET OPERATIONS

It is interesting that what for many
years now has been the most important tool of monetary control was
not even recognized as such a tool in the early years of the Federal
Reserve System. In those days each of the 12 Federal Reserve Banks in
the system purchased securities merely in order to obtain the interest
income needed to cover its expenses and produce a minimum profit.
However, before long it was recognized that the buying and selling of
securities by the reserve banks affected commercial bank reserves in the
manner shown by the mechanics traced out in Chapter 4. As a result,
by 1922 the 12 Federal Reserve Banks informally began to coordinate
their buying and selling so as not to produce undesirable variations in
commercial bank reserves. In 1935 federal legislation formally created
the Federal Open Market Committee within the Federal Reserve Sys-

tem, which from that time to the present has exercised full control over the open market operations of the system.

At several points in the preceding pages open market operations have been described as the most important and by implication the "best" of the tools the Federal Reserve has available to regulate the banks' reserve position. Although we have not prepared specific lists of the advantages and disadvantages of each tool, in discussing above changes in percentage reserve requirements several possible disadvantages of open market operations were incidentally indicated—their lack of neutrality and their initial geographic impact in one place. But these shortcomings of open market operations are relatively insignificant in comparison to some desirable characteristics unique to this tool. Neither changes in reserve requirements nor changes in discount rates can begin to approach open market operations in terms of flexibility and precision, and these are two extremely valuable properties. Open market operations can be varied from day to day or even within the same day—the ultimate in flexibility—and they can be carried out in virtually any dollar amount—the ultimate in precision. Let us look at these two features a little more closely.

In line with the directive issued to him by the Federal Open Market Committee as a result of its regular tri-weekly meeting, the manager of the so-called open market account in the Federal Reserve Bank of New York carries out purchases and sales of government securities whose aim is to produce the degree of pressure or ease in the banks' reserve position consistent with the objective set forth in that directive. Because there are numerous other factors affecting the banks' reserve position from day to day (for example, short-run inflows to and outflows of currency from the banks), the manager sometimes finds it necessary to buy securities on balance in one week, sell in the next, and then buy again the following week in an effort to maintain the degree of ease or tightness called for by the directive. Without the use of open market operations, this kind of adjustment would not be possible.

Clearly the banks' reserve position could not be managed in this way by means of variations in the discount rate. It is true that the Federal Reserve has the power to raise or lower the discount rate by whatever amount may be necessary to discourage or encourage the commercial banks to borrow, but the amount of change in loans that will follow from any given change in the discount rate is not something the Federal Reserve can predict with any accuracy. Borrowing occurs at the initiative of the commercial banks, and its amount does not depend completely on the spread between the discount rate and the rates the banks can earn on loans and securities. It may be argued that the Federal Reserve, if its purpose is to increase the banks' reserves by some given amount, may put through successive cuts in the discount rate until borrowing increases by the desired amount. In the opposite case, it could put through successive increases in the discount rate until borrowing decreased by the desired amount (although here the maximum decrease would be the amount of discounts and advances initially outstanding). However, such a use of the discount rate would mean a discount rate that changed with considerable frequency and over a rather wide range. This would tend to produce similar instability in other short-term interest rates and possibly disorderliness in financial markets. The problem created by the announcement effects of the present infrequent changes in discount rates would be compounded under such an arrangement with its frequent and perhaps sizable discretionary changes in the rate.

For similar reasons, the banks' reserve position could not be managed through changes in reserve requirements as flexibly and precisely as is possible through open market operations. Unlike discount rate changes, whose effect on the banks' reserve position depends on the responsiveness of the commercial banks to the rate change, changes in reserve requirements affect the banks' reserve position in a way essentially beyond their control and independent of any response by them. The Federal Reserve can tell in advance with some precision the effect of any change in percentage reserve requirements on the banks' reserve position, although complete precision is ruled out by the shifting about of deposits between different sized banks and between demand and time deposits, both of which involve differences in the minimum reserve requirement per dollar of deposits. This, however, is a minor obstacle in comparison to another: to try to do through changes in reserve requirements what it now does through open market operations, the Federal Reserve would have to change legal reserve requirements with great frequency and with practically no notice, raising them one week and perhaps lowering them the next and then again raising them. Even if deposits of all banks were to be made subject to the Federal Reserve reserve requirements by act of Congress so that escape would not be possible by giving up membership, such an arrangement would still be completely impractical. It would call on thousands of individual commercial banks to make almost day-to-day adjustments in their portfolios of loans and securities in order to meet the frequently changing percentage reserve requirement. The disorderliness in this case would probably be even greater than that resulting from the attempt to accomplish the same thing by continuous changes in the discount rate.

It is generally conceded that only through open market operations can the Federal Reserve hope to maintain finger-tip control over the reserve position of the banks. But beyond this, there is even an argument in support of open market operations over changes in reserve requirements in the specific situation for which changes in reserve requirements are presumably ideally suited—namely, to bring about large changes in the banks' reserve position. This argument runs along these lines. If the Federal Reserve seeks to remove a substantial amount of excess reserves by raising reserve requirements, it is all banks and not only those banks with excess reserves that feel the impact of this increase. The banks without excess reserves will be forced to reduce their earning assets or else borrow in order to meet the higher requirements. In this case, they have no problem in identifying who is to blame for their having to take this unpleasant action. On the other hand, if the Federal Reserve brings about the same change in the banks' reserve position via open market operations, again some banks without excess reserves will be forced to sell securities, contract loans, or borrow in order to adjust for the reserves lost as their depositors draw checks in payment for the securities purchased, via dealers, from the Federal Reserve. In this case, however, these banks lose reserves in the course of what are routine transactions, and they cannot identify the Federal Reserve as the proximate cause of their predicament. One may, of course, say that the Federal Reserve officials should do what needs to be done without regard for the feelings of the bankers, but if the same objective can be achieved without incurring their ill feelings, nothing is lost and something is gained.

The emphasis we have placed here on the advantages of open market operations does not mean that this tool is free of disadvantages; several, indeed, were noted earlier. But when all of the advantages and disadvantages of each of the three principal tools are carefully weighed, some economists conclude that open market operations are not only far and away the best single tool in the hands of the Federal Reserve but even that the other two tools are virtually unnecessary. We noted in discussing the discount rate that Milton Friedman would do away with that instrument altogether, and we may note here that he would do the same with changes in reserve requirements. They would be set at a particular level and then left there permanently. The Federal Reserve would, in other words, control the reserve position of the banks solely through open market operations. This extreme position follows in part from the fact that Friedman would have the Federal Reserve abandon its efforts to vary the money supply so as to counteract the business cycle and would have it simply increase the money supply year in and year out at a stable rate, a proposal to be examined in detail in Chapter 15. But other leading monetary economists who strongly disagree with this proposal still come close to agreeing with Friedman on the role of changes in reserve requirements. The late Warren Smith of the University of Michigan saw no need for the Federal Reserve to resort to such changes except under the most unusual circumstances. Since Smith would also have retained the discount rate only in a very minor role, he came close to Friedman in that he would have had the Federal Reserve rely almost entirely on open market operations to effect changes in the reserve position of the commercial banks.

Although there are economists who would go over completely or almost completely to a one-tool arrangement, it is likely that all three of the major tools will remain in use for the foreseeable future. The Federal Reserve authorities feel that the use of all three tools is at times a more effective way to bring about changes in the banks' reserve position than would be open market operations alone. But again, as has been emphasized more than once, the Federal Reserve in its actual operations has for many years relied overwhelmingly on open market operations, and the primacy, if not the exclusivity, of this tool seems assured in the futre.

SELECTIVE CREDIT CONTROLS

If the Federal Reserve sought only to control the overall availability of credit and the total supply of money, the three major tools discussed above would be adequate, or, as some have argued, open market operations alone might be adequate. Through the use of these tools, the Federal Reserve controls the banks' reserve position, which is the medium through which it exercises whatever degree of control it has over the money supply. And it is through control over the money supply that it directly or indirectly exercises whatever degree of control it has over the economy's total spending or aggregate demand for goods and services, with all this means to the economy's total income, employment, and price level.

To the extent that the Federal Reserve seeks to influence spending in particular sectors of the economy rather than the economy as a whole, it may be apparent that general tools like open market operations, discount rates, and reserve requirements are not adequate. By controlling the overall reserve position of the banks, these tools can be used to influence the *total* amount of funds provided by the banks and thus to some degree to influence the *total* amount of the public's spending, but they cannot be used to vary the amount of credit provided in particular markets and thus to influence the amount of spending in particular markets. The allocation of their available lending power among different groups of borrowers or different credit markets is determined by the decisions of the commercial banks, not by the Federal Reserve through any possible manipulation of its general credit controls. If the Federal Reserve seeks to affect specific or selected markets, it must rely on so-called selective controls.

To see the use for and the mode of operation of a selective credit control, let us assume a situation in which the economy's spending on goods and services is at a level that provides both reasonably full employment and reasonably stable prices in the economy. The Federal Reserve would aim to maintain growth in the money supply at a rate consistent with the perpetuation of this happy state of affairs. Assume next that this ideal situation is threatened by the development of a speculative boom in the stock market, a boom nurtured by the banks' lending heavily to customers to finance the purchase of securities. If the Federal Reserve attempts to restrain the expansion of this kind of bank credit by the use of open market sales of securities or its other general controls, it may succeed, but it will almost surely at the same time restrain what is a healthy or nonexcessive expansion of other kinds of credit. In order to meet one problem, it may thus create another problem, for restraining the amount of credit available for ordinary commercial needs could slow the economy as a whole with the consequence of unemployment, possibly falling prices, and eventually a recession.

This hypothetical situation actually corresponds closely to the situation of the U.S. economy in early 1929. In the area of credit, it was only the expansion of credit to finance the purchase of securities that was out of line at the time, but the Federal Reserve had no really effective way to affect this credit market specifically. At first it tried "moral suasion," which is the attempt to have the banks do other than what may be in their self-interest through an appeal to their regard for what is in the public's best interest. The Federal Reserve also later tried to meet the problem by raising the discount rate from 5 to 6 percent, a larger increase apparently being ruled out by the fear of cutting down the flow of credit needed to meet ordinary business requirements. Such moderate measures were far from sufficient, and the stock market boom went on until ended by the ultimate collapse in October of that year. If the Federal Reserve had had in 1929 the selective credit control over loans to finance the purchase of securities that it was given by the Congress in 1934, the history of that period might have turned out much differently.

This particular control operates by setting the minimum percentage of the purchase price of securities a buyer must pay for in cash, which amounts to setting the maximum percentage of the purchase price that he may borrow. A margin requirement of 60 percent means that a minimum of 60 percent must be in cash, or that a maximum of 40 percent may be borrowed. At the limit, a 100 percent margin requirement means all cash and no borrowing. Before the Federal Reserve was given the power to set the minimum percentage that had to be paid in cash, this percentage was agreed on between lender and borrower, and 15 percent margin was quite common during the speculative fervor of 1929. If the Federal Reserve had then had the power and if it had used it to push the margin requirement to the 100 percent limit, it would most likely have had a significant dampening effect on the demand for securities. It is not likely that it could have altogether eliminated the speculative excesses of the time, but it would at least have held back the unsustainable rise in the market to some degree and made the subsequent collapse less severe than it was.

In the years since it received this power, the Federal Reserve has varied the margin requirement 19 times. For example, it held it unchanged at the low level of 40 percent during the depressed stock market of the years 1937–45 and raised it all the way to 100 percent in 1946 during the postwar bull market. Over the past decade the percentage has been changed 6 times and has varied between 50 and 80 percent. It is very difficult to assess the effectiveness of this control in accomplishing its intended purpose; the studies made are not uniform in their conclusions. The Federal Reserve, however, apparently believes it is of some value, for it has chosen over time to raise and lower the percentage in line with the state of the market rather than to set it at some level and simply leave it there.

The regulation of margin requirements is the only selective control that the Federal Reserve has exercised on a continuing basis since the power was first granted. During certain time periods, all of which were war years with the single exception of 1948–49, the Federal Reserve has been given temporary power to set minimum down payments and maximum maturities for loans to consumers to finance the purchase of durable goods. This selective control over consumer credit was last employed during the Korean War.

Like other selective controls, the control over consumer credit aims to affect the amount of credit extended in a specific market, in this case the market for consumer durable goods. By varying the percentage of the purchase price that must be covered in the down payment and/or varying the time period over which the balance—i.e. the amount borrowed—must be repaid, the Federal Reserve is able to influence the amount of spending by consumers for durable goods.

It has been argued that the Federal Reserve is unable to exert much influence on this kind of spending through its use of the general controls, even if conditions were such that it was free to use its general controls toward this end. Suppose that aggregate demand is expanding too rapidly in all sectors so that the Federal Reserve finds it appropriate to use its general controls in a restrictive way. Among other effects, this will tend to raise interest rates and discourage that kind of spending which is responsive to higher interest rates, but credit-financed consumer spending for durable goods is, according to some, largely immune to higher interest rates. And it not only is that the average consumer is not scared off by higher finance costs alone but that the banks themselves will cut back on almost all other kinds of loans before reducing loans to consumers. This type of loan is among the more profitable and accordingly is least likely to be reduced by the banks to the extent that they have a choice. The result is that the attempt by the Federal Reserve to contract consumer credit via general monetary controls puts a disproportionate burden on other types of credit and the types of spending that such credit finances, especially spending by business for plant and equipment. One answer to this deficiency of the general controls is a selective credit control that subjects consumer credit to regulations which do not depend on higher interest rates or lenders' preferences for their effectiveness.

This is but one of a list of arguments that have been made in support of the use of a consumer credit control on a more or less continuing basis. To most of these arguments there are, of course, counterarguments, and it is not clear that either side has an overwhelming case. We will not take time to review these many arguments here. As a practical matter, it has been twenty years since this control was last employed, and it may well be another twenty years before it is employed again.

In the U.S. experience there has been only one other selective credit control employed, a control over mortgage loans to finance the purchase of new housing much like that over consumer loans to finance the purchase of autos, refrigerators, and durable goods of this kind. This control was in effect only during the Korean War, and the experience with it was such that there has been little support for its use again.

A CONCLUDING NOTE

Some writers refer to the Federal Reserve's "arsenal" because for some years now it has had a respectable collection of weapons with which to combat monetary developments to which it is opposed. At first it possessed only the discount rate; in the twenties it discovered and began to use open market operations; in the thirties it received the power to vary percentage reserve requirements and to set margin requirements.

With the exception of changes in margin requirements, the other controls noted all work on the banks' reserve position. An increase in loans or an open market purchase by the Federal Reserve enlarges the amount of the banks' legal reserves and the amount of their excess reserves; a reduction in percentage reserve requirements leaves their legal reserves unchanged but increases their excess reserves. To bring about any desired change in the reserve position of the banks, the Federal Reserve thus has some choice as to which tool or combination of tools it will use. However, we have seen in this chapter that the choice is limited, for in changing the banks' reserve position the Federal Reserve must consider more than the mere mechanics of producing that change. It is when these further considerations are taken into account that we get into the advantages and disadvantages and strengths and weaknesses of the various tools that the Federal Reserve has at its disposal.

Through the remainder of this book we will be referring frequently to the banks' reserve position and to the economy's money supply, which is tied to that reserve position. However, the subject matter touched on in this chapter will not be examined further. When we refer to Federal Reserve action to add to or subtract from the banks' reserves or to add to or subtract from the existing money supply, we will not concern ourselves with what tool or tools would be most appropriate to use under the existing set of circumstances. Although we will for simplicity look at such actions as if they were purely a mechanical matter, we will know from our work in this chapter that they are actually more complex than that.

seven

TREASURY OPERATIONS, BANK RESERVES, AND THE MONEY SUPPLY, I

By appropriate use of the various tools it has available, the Federal Reserve is able to increase or decrease the legal reserves of the commercial banks by any desired amount. And by so manipulating the banks' reserve position, it is able to expand or contract the money supply as it sees fit. While this general statement is not basically incorrect, it is not without qualifications, a number of which have been considered in earlier chapters. Thus, in Chapter 5 we examined some of the major slippages between changes in legal reserves and changes in the money supply whose existence means that control over legal reserves, however close it may be, does not provide an equally close control over the money supply. Variations in the public's desired ratio of currency to demand deposits, in its desired ratio of time deposits to demand deposits, and in the banks' desired ratio of excess reserves to demand deposits make the link between legal reserves and the money supply a good deal less than rigid.

In this and the following chapter we will look into the way that certain operations of the U.S. Treasury, operations that were by-passed earlier in order to simplify the analysis, tend to influence the money supply. As we will see, fitting them into the framework now does not require any major qualifications of conclusions earlier reached. For example, the Treasury may cause significant changes in the amount of the banks' legal reserves simply through the way it manages its demand deposit balances. This, however, does not mean that the Federal Reserve thereby loses control over reserves to that very same degree. It means simply that there is one more complicating factor whose influence the Federal Reserve must at times try to offset in order to achieve the result it seeks. This is less difficult than it might otherwise be, since the Treasury ordinarily but not invariably works hand in hand with the Federal Reserve to minimize the extent to which certain Treasury operations complicate the Federal Reserve's task. However, it is still true that the Federal Reserve could come closer to realizing its target with respect to the banks' reserve position and the economy's money supply if such complicating factors were completely absent.

TREASURY PAPER CURRENCY AND COIN
AND THE MONEY SUPPLY

If a layman were asked how the Treasury could increase the money supply, he would most likely say "by printing and issuing more currency." However plausible this may sound, it is not, strictly speaking, really correct: an increase in the amount of Treasury currency outstanding does not *in itself* mean an increase in the money supply. It must be recalled that the money supply is conventionally defined as the sum of paper currency, coin (which we will here want to distinguish from currency in the form of paper), and demand deposits *in the hands of the public*, and that the public in turn is defined to exclude the Federal Reserve Banks, the commercial banks, and the U.S. Treasury. When the Treasury prints and issues more currency, this currency does not pass directly into the hands of the public because the Treasury pays its bills not with currency but with checks drawn against deposit balances it maintains at the Federal Reserve Banks for this purpose. Thus, the mere issuance of Treasury currency per se does not change the money supply. One can best see what it does change directly and the way in which this occurs by turning to the relevant T-accounts.

Treasury Paper Currency

Although the Treasury has not been permitted to do so except under very unusual circumstances, we will assume that the Treasury may at its discretion print and issue practically any number of pieces of green paper on which are engraved "This is $1," "This is $5," and so forth, each carrying the identification of the U.S. Treasury as the issuer. These pieces of paper, however, do not contain any kind of promise, express or implied, by the Treasury to convert at the bearer's demand each dollar's worth into anything else like gold or silver at some specified rate. Until 1934 the Treasury had issued to the public pieces of paper known as gold certificates, which contained such a promise; they were convertible into gold, $20.67 of gold certificates being exchangeable at the Treasury at the bearer's demand for one ounce of gold. Similarly, until 1968 the Treasury had issued other pieces of paper known as silver certificates, which were convertible into silver, $1.29 of silver certificates being exchangeable at the Treasury for one ounce of silver. Unlike gold and silver certificates, pieces of paper, like the kind first mentioned above, that are not specifically exchangeable at the Treasury for anything else are usually described as *inconvertible currency* or fiat money. During the Civil War the Treasury issued what was at the time a huge amount of this kind of currency to help cover the government's heavy expenses. Popularly known as "greenbacks" and officially as United States Notes, a little over $300 million worth of this kind of currency has been left in the circulation on a permanent basis by decision of Congress.

The truly unique feature of this kind of currency is, of course, the fact that the quantity of it that potentially may be issued by the Treasury is limited only by the availability of paper, ink, and printing presses, which as a practical matter means that its quantity is potentially unlimited. Its direct cost to the issuer is nothing more than the cost of running it off the presses. However, the fact that its cost of production is negligible in no sense means that the ability of each unit of this kind of currency to command goods and services in the marketplace is correspondingly negligible. To repeat a basic point first introduced in Chapter 1, the value of a unit of currency—i.e., how much or how little in goods and services one can get for it—will become negligible only if the quantity of it that is issued is expanded without limit.

By the same token, its value will remain reasonably stable if the quantity issued is restrained to the degree needed to achieve this result. The fact that a currency unit is not convertible into gold or silver or anything else at some fixed rate at the Treasury is not *in itself* a critical factor in establishing how much the currency unit will purchase in the domestic marketplace.

Returning now to our assumption that the Treasury is permitted to issue inconvertible currency, let us suppose that the Treasury runs off $1 billion worth. As has been noted, the Treasury does not pay any of the federal government's employees, suppliers, or other creditors with currency—it pays with checks drawn against its deposit accounts with the Federal Reserve Banks. Thus, to put the $1 billion of currency into disbursable or "spendable" form, the Treasury delivers it physically to the Federal Reserve Banks and receives payment in the form of a $1 billion credit to its deposit accounts at these banks. This is similar, of course, to what any individual does when he takes currency to his commercial bank and has his checking account credited for the amount in question, but there is a major difference. The currency he delivers to the bank does not change the total amount of currency that exists in the system, while the newly printed currency the Treasury has turned over to the Federal Reserve Banks is that much of a net increase in the amount of currency that exists in the system. However, to repeat, it is *not* part of the money supply at this point because it is currency held by the Federal Reserve Banks and not by the public.

Let us call this currency Treasury Notes, the word Treasury indicating their issuer in the same way that "Federal Reserve" in the term "Federal Reserve Notes" indicates their issuer. (These notes, which are hand-to-hand money, must be distinguished from the Treasury's interest-bearing obligations of intermediate maturity known as Treasury Notes.) The T-account entries for the transactions described above are then the ones labeled (a) in Table 7–1. It should be noted immediately that the inviolable rule for a T-account appears to have been violated in the Treasury's account: The +$1 for the asset "Deposits with the Federal Reserve Banks" is not offset by an equal decrease in another asset or an equal increase in some liability. Purely for bookkeeping purposes, one could enter on the liability side of this T-account "Treasury Notes outstanding +$1" and thereby make the account balance. This, however, should be recognized as a fictional sort of liability—these Treasury Notes as a final kind of currency are not something that bearers can legally present "for payment" in any other form whatsoever. The Treasury assumes no responsibility to "redeem" and incurs no liability in the ordinary sense of the word by issuing this kind of note.

The entries for this transaction in the Federal Reserve Banks'

TABLE 7–1

FEDERAL RESERVE BANKS

Assets			Liabilities		
Treasury Notes	+$1	(a)	Deposits of the Treasury	+$1	(a)
			Deposits of the Treasury	−$1	(b)
			Deposits of the commercial banks	+$1	(b)
Net Change			Net Change		
Treasury Notes	+$1		Deposits of the commercial banks	+$1	

COMMERCIAL BANKS

Assets			Liabilities		
Deposits with Federal Reserve Banks	+$1	(b)	Demand deposits of the public	+$1	(b)
Net Change			Net Change		
Above entry			Above entry		

U.S. TREASURY

Assets			Liabilities
Deposits with Federal Reserve Banks	+$1	(a)	
Net Change			
Above entry			

PUBLIC

Assets			Liabilities
Accounts receivable from Treasury	−$1	(b)	
Demand deposits	+$1	(b)	
Net Change			
Above two entries			

T-account present no complication. The Federal Reserve Banks acquire the Treasury Notes, which are clearly assets to the Federal Reserve Banks, and pay for them by incurring an increase in their deposits, which are, of course, liabilities.

Let us assume that the Treasury now proceeds to draw checks totaling $1 billion in payment of various accounts payable. As is typically the case, the recipients of the checks deposit them to the credit of their checking accounts at the commercial banks. The commercial banks in turn send the checks on to the Federal Reserve Banks, where they are credited to the accounts of the commercial banks in question. These transactions are covered by the (b) entries in the T-accounts. *At this point, the money supply has increased by $1 billion in the form of that amount of additional demand deposits held by the public, and the commercial banks' legal reserves have also increased by $1 billion in the form of that amount of additional deposits in their accounts with the Federal Reserve Banks.* So far as the change in the money supply goes, the public may, of course, choose to switch part of the addition into time deposits, but at the moment there is an increase in the money supply equal to the increase in Treasury Notes outstanding, even though these notes remain for the time being in the vaults of the Federal Reserve Banks.

As indicated earlier, the Treasury is not authorized to issue inconvertible pieces of paper of the kind described above. Actually, so far as the nation's paper currency is concerned, the Treasury has practically ceased to be a supplier at all. As of the end of 1973, paper currency outstanding totaled about $68.8 billion, $68.2 of which was made up of Federal Reserve Notes. The remaining $600 million is classified as Treasury currency, but of this about $300 million is in the process of retirement, and about $300 million is the unchanging amount of United States Notes, or "greenbacks," that the Congress has decided to leave in circulation.

Treasury Coin

As a supplier of hand-to-hand money, the Treasury's role today is limited essentially to one it has played from the time of the first Coinage Act of 1792: through the Bureau of the Mint, it is the sole issuer of coin. But this role too has changed drastically over the years. In earlier times the Treasury issued gold coins that were worth fully as much for the metal they contained as they were worth as money, but in 1933 gold was removed completely from the coinage. On the other hand, from the 1870's to the 1960's, silver coins (dimes, quarters, half-dollars, and dollars) had been worth much less for the metal they contained than they were worth as money. But in 1961, because its stock of silver was running low, the Treasury suspended the sale of silver to domestic industrial users at the price of 90.5 cents per ounce, which was then well below the price on the world market. The price of silver in the United States accordingly began a sharp rise. Once it passed $1.2929 per ounce, the actual silver contained in the silver dollar become worth more than a dollar. Once the price passed $1.3824 per ounce, which it did in 1967, the same was true for the actual silver in the subsidiary silver coins—half-dollars, quarters, and dimes. As these coins became worth more for their silver content than they were as money, they disappeared from circulation or from use as money. For the Treasury to have tried to replace these coins by issuing still more coins with the same silver content clearly would have been futile. The Coinage Act of 1965 was the solution adopted. It reduced the silver content of newly minted half-dollars from 90 to 40 percent. New dimes and quarters, although identical in design and size to the former 90 percent silver coins, were made silverless—each is cupronickel clad on a copper core. Later legislation ended the minting of the 40 percent silver half-dollar and thus made this coin silverless like the others.

The market value of the metal in each of these coins is now far less than the value of each as money. As of 1974 the value of the metallic content of the cupronickel Eisenhower dollar was 6.8 cents and of the cupronickel half-dollar was 3.4 cents. However, with the market value of silver over $5.00 per ounce in 1974, the value of the metal in the old silver dollar and half-dollar that had been minted up to 1965 became $4.16 and $2.08, respectively. Correspondingly the values of the old silver quarters and dimes became $1.04 and 41.6 cents. With its 40 percent silver content, the value of the metal in the silver-clad Kennedy half-dollars, which had been minted from 1966 through 1970, was 87 cents in 1974.

During 1974 it appeared that even the lowly penny might become worth more for its metallic content than as money. The price of copper doubled from 68 cents per pound in 1973 to $1.34 per pound in the spring of 1974. At a price of $1.535 per pound, the copper in a penny would be worth 1 cent, so at a price somewhat above this a profit could be made by melting down pennies. Despite a hastily passed act of Congress making the melting down of pennies illegal, the expectation of a further large rise in the market value of copper led to hoarding of pennies on so large a scale as to produce a penny shortage in the spring of 1974. The mint was unable to produce pennies as rapidly as needed to meet the demands of hoarders and the needs of trade, despite producing at its maximum rate of output of about 10 billion pennies ($100 million) per year.

Apart from special situations like this, the Treasury regularly issues coin of each denomination in whatever amounts are required to meet the demands of the public. Just as in the case of a paper money issue by the Treasury, the coin is delivered to the Federal Reserve Banks, which show an increase in the asset "Cash" and in the liability "Deposits of the Treasury." The Treasury may draw checks against this addition to its deposit balance just as it draws against an addition effected in any other way. As described above, these checks, when deposited by their recipients in their demand deposit accounts at the commercial banks, involve an equal addition to the money supply and to the commercial banks' legal reserves. The actual coin delivered by the Treasury to the Federal Reserve Banks, like actual Treasury paper currency, remains in the vaults of those banks until needed to meet in turn the requests of their customers for more of these kinds of money.*

Although Treasury issues of inconvertible paper currency and coin are similar in this regard, it may be apparent that there is, at least potentially, a major difference between the two: the former's cost of production is negligible, whereas the latter's cost may run from a few percent to 100 percent of the face value of the coins produced. With newly issued coins now completely silverless, the cost of production of a dollar's worth of dimes, quarters, halves, and dollars is only a small fraction of the dollar that results. With the sharp drop in the price of copper to about 75 cents per pound by late fall of 1974, the production cost of a dollar's worth of pennies was again much less than the dollar's worth of money that resulted. The Treasury shows a substantial "profit," technically known as seigniorage, on each dollar's worth of coin produced, although that profit remains smallest on pennies. On paper currency, each dollar is almost completely profit.

Although people historically drew a sharp distinction between inconvertible paper currency and coin in terms of the intrinsic value of each, the difference between them today is more one of degree than of kind. For example, the intrinsic value of a dollar's worth of quarters is only a few cents. This is clearly greater than the practically zero intrinsic value of a dollar's worth of paper currency but still nowhere near the value of the coins as money. One does not ordinarily speak of

---

*It is worth noting that any request for coin by the commercial banks is necessarily met by the Federal Reserve Banks through an equal reduction in the asset "Cash," or specifically "Coin," and in the liability "Deposits of commercial banks," but a request for paper currency may, within limits, be met in either of two ways. If the Federal Reserve Banks have any Treasury paper currency on hand, they may meet requests by a reduction in this asset matched by a reduction in the liability "Deposits of commercial banks." Alternatively, they can meet requests by issuing more Federal Reserve Notes—in this case there is an increase in the liability "Federal Reserve Notes outstanding," matched as before by a decrease in the liability "Deposits of commercial banks." Because the Treasury is no longer increasing the amount of its paper currency issue, the Federal Reserve Banks typically have little Treasury paper currency on hand and meet almost all requests for paper currency by expanding their issue of Federal Reserve Notes.

"inconvertible coin," but viewed in this way the adjective is today almost as applicable to most of the coins struck as it is to paper. Thus, while the Treasury is not legally authorized to issue inconvertible paper currency, it is authorized to issue what is very similar to this in the form of coin whose intrinsic value is nominal relative to its monetary value.

The congressionally imposed ban on the Treasury issuance of inconvertible paper currency is designed to prevent the Treasury from "resorting to the printing press" in times of stress to get the money to pay its bills. It might be argued from the forgoing that there is a danger that the Treasury may "resort to the mint" for the same purpose. After all, it can potentially raise any number of additional dollars needed by stamping out that much coin, the cost of production being only a fraction of the amount of dollars so secured. For example, if it needs another $10 billion and if the cost of the metal, labor, machine time, and everything else involved runs 5¢ per $1 of coin produced, it can get the $10 billion *net* that it wants simply by producing $10,526 million of additional coin and delivering this to the Federal Reserve Banks.

Although there has been any number of experiences with debasement and overissue of coin and paper currency in the remote and also in the not so remote past, in countries with advanced central banking systems, like the United States with its Federal Reserve System, resort by the Treasury to the direct issue of huge amounts of hand-to-hand money is not to be expected, even when there is no ban imposed on such issues by powers beyond the Treasury. This does not say that the Treasury may not act in a way that results in the issue of huge amounts of new money; what it does say is that the Treasury resorts to a more sophisticated and roundabout way of doing this than the direct issue of hand-to-hand money. Without itself printing a single additional dollar of currency, the Treasury can borrow in such a way that each dollar borrowed in effect amounts to the creation of an additional dollar of currency. We will see in detail how this occurs later in this chapter.

TREASURY SPENDING AND THE MONEY SUPPLY: TAX-FINANCED AND DEFICIT-FINANCED SPENDING

If the Treasury were to finance an increase in its spending by printing more paper currency or stamping out additional coin, it would clearly bring about an increase in the money supply. It may also bring about an increase in the money supply by borrowing to finance an increase in spending, and the major purpose of the balance of this chapter is to see under what conditions and by what process this takes place. First, however, it will be helpful to look into the question of whether an increase in Treasury spending that is financed by additional taxation brings about a change in the money supply. This question can be handled quickly. The case is straightforward: an increase in Treasury spending financed by an equal increase in tax collections has no effect on bank reserves or on the money supply. However, there are some people who believe that the Treasury, as it collects taxes and spends the amount so raised, somehow makes money disappear in the process, perhaps the consequence of the tendency to attribute all sorts of undesirable effects to the activities of the tax collectors. It will not be too difficult to see that there is no truth in this belief.

Treasury Spending Financed by Taxation

Let us assume that the Federal government seeks to raise an additional $1 billion to cover a like amount of additional spending. One possibility is to secure this amount by imposing new taxes or by raising rates on existing taxes to the degree needed to generate the extra revenue. What is the effect of the collection *and* expenditure of this $1 billion (or of any other dollar of tax receipts and expenditures) on the commercial banks' legal reserves and the economy's money supply?

In Table 7–2, the (a) entries in the T-account for the public show a $1 billion decrease in tax liabilities and a $1 billion decrease in the asset "Demand deposits," the result of the public's writing checks of this amount in favor of the Treasury. The (a) entries in the other T-accounts show the changes that follow as the Treasury deposits these checks to the credit of its accounts in the Federal Reserve Banks, as the Federal Reserve Banks charge the $1 billion amount against the deposit accounts of the commercial banks, and as the commercial banks, of course, charge this amount against the deposit accounts of the taxpayers who drew the checks in favor of the Treasury. At this step, there is temporarily a reduction of $1 billion in the money supply and in the commercial banks' legal reserves. This, however, is reversed at the next step—the expenditure of the $1 billion by the Treasury has the effects shown by the (b) entries. As the Treasury makes payments of $1 billion, it draws down its deposit balances at the Federal Reserve Banks by an equal amount. The public, which includes, for example, firms receiving payment for goods supplied and persons receiving payment for salaries due, deposits these checks in the commercial banks, which sets into motion the sequence of changes indicated by the (b) entries. What we then find is that there is no *net* change in the items with which we are concerned here as a result of the (a) and (b) entries *combined*.

TABLE 7–2

FEDERAL RESERVE BANKS

Assets	Liabilities		
	Deposits of the commercial banks	−$1	(a)
	Deposits of the Treasury	+$1	(a)
	Deposits of the commercial banks	+$1	(b)
	Deposits of the Treasury	−$1	(b)
	Net Change		
	None		

COMMERCIAL BANKS

Assets			Liabilities		
Deposits with Federal Reserve Banks	−$1	(a)	Demand deposits of the public	−$1	(a)
Deposits with Federal Reserve Banks	+$1	(b)	Demand deposits of the public	+$1	(b)
Net Change			Net Change		
None			None		

TREASURY

Assets			Liabilities		
Taxes receivable	−$1	(a)			
Deposits with Federal Reserve Banks	+$1	(a)			
Deposits with Federal Reserve Banks	−$1	(b)	Accounts payable	−$1	(b)
Net Change			Net Change		
Taxes receivable	−$1		Accounts payable	−$1	

TABLE 7–2, continued

PUBLIC

Assets			Liabilities		
Demand deposits	−$1	(a)	Taxes payable	−$1	(a)
Accounts receivable					
from Treasury	−$1	(b)			
Demand deposits	+$1	(b)			
Net Change			Net Change		
Accounts receivable					
from Treasury	−$1		Taxes payable	−$1	

Thus, the banks' legal reserves go down by $1 billion in (a) and go up by $1 billion in (b), so there is no net change in their reserves. Similarly, the public's holdings of demand deposits go down by $1 billion in (a) and up by $1 billion in (b), so there is no net change in their demand deposits. Since there is no reason to assume any change in such things as the public's ratio of currency to demand deposits or in its ratio of time deposits to demand deposits or in the banks' ratio of excess reserves to demand deposits as a result of the Treasury's taxing and spending this $1 billion, and since there is no change in the amount of legal reserves held by the banks, there is no reason to expect any change in the economy's money supply.

The act of collecting taxes and spending these receipts thus does not in itself affect the money supply one way or the other. A dollar of federal tax collections means the public holds $1 less of money, since it gives up a dollar of either demand deposits or currency, both of which are part of the money supply. The U.S. Treasury gains a dollar of demand deposits or currency, but this dollar is not counted as part of the money supply. Expenditure of the dollar by the Treasury returns the dollar to the public's money holdings and returns the money supply to its level before the dollar was taken in taxes.

As a last word here, we should note that if the money supply were defined so as not to exclude the checking account balances and currency held by the U.S. Treasury, there would not even be a temporary reduction of the money supply. Collection of taxes would not in itself affect the money supply; it would affect only the distribution of the existing total between the governments' holdings and the public's holdings. Some economists have argued in favor of this alternative definition, but the definition with which we continue to work is the conventional one that excludes the U.S. Treasury's demand deposits and currency holdings as part of the money supply.

Treasury Spending Financed by Borrowing

Most people recognize that the Treasury does not change the amount of money the public holds as it collects taxes and spends that same amount. However, most people fail to recognize that the Treasury does not necessarily change the amount of money the public holds in the not uncommon event that the government spends more in a time period than it raises in taxes. One of the most pervasive public misconceptions in the field of money is that a U.S. Treasury deficit of any amount in a given year means that the Treasury has added that amount to the economy's money supply during that year. Net borrowing of $10 billion by the federal government in a year is viewed as tantamount to "putting $10 billion more money into the hands of the public." It is possible to defend this sort of statement if one defines money in so loose a fashion as to rob it of any meaning. However, if money is meaningfully defined, for example, as the sum of currency and demand deposits held by the public, then the fact of the matter—and it is a crucially important fact—is that the Treasury may incur a deficit of $10 billion or any other amount in any year (i.e., it may borrow net any particular amount) without adding a single dollar to the money supply in the process. Despite the deficit and the accompanying rise in the federal debt, the public will be found to hold the same amount of money at the end of the year that it held at the start of the year.

The same is true in the rare event of a surplus. If the Treasury were to show a surplus of $10 billion in any year and use this surplus to buy back or retire that amount of its outstanding securities, it need not subtract a single dollar from the money supply in the process. Despite the surplus and the accompanying decrease in the federal debt, the public will be found to hold the same amount of money at the end of the year that it held at the start.

This is not the invariable or even the usual result of Treasury borrowing or debt repayment, but it is one possible result and a result that the Treasury can achieve if it chooses to do so. In the deficit case, the more common result is the one that a large portion of the public believes to be the invariable result: an increase in the money supply. Which result actually follows from each act of new borrowing depends on from whom the Treasury borrows—i.e., to whom it sells its securities. Three groups of purchasers must be distinguished: the public, the commercial banks, and the Federal Reserve Banks. The effects on legal reserves and the money supply of the issue of securities by the Treasury to each of these three groups will be examined in turn by tracing the mechanics of each case through the appropriate T-accounts. Following this, in the next chapter, the same will be done for the retirement of securities by the Treasury.

The case of debt retirement is of much less practical interest than the case of debt issue. For one thing, in the 46 fiscal years from 1929 through 1974, there have been only 9 years in which the federal government showed a budget surplus, the prerequisite to debt retirement. Even this number of years loses much of the weight it might otherwise carry when it is noted that the cumulated total for the 9 years is a surplus of only about $22 billion, less than the deficit in such recent single years as 1968, 1971, and 1972. The cumulated deficits exceeded the cumulated surpluses for the full span of years by enough to raise the national debt from $17 billion in 1929 to $480 billion in 1974. Our major focus is, therefore, appropriately on the effects of deficits.

BORROWING FROM THE PUBLIC   If government expenditures exceed tax receipts, the difference necessarily must be covered by borrowing, since for present purposes we are ruling out the case in which the Treasury simply runs off whatever amount of hand-to-hand money it needs to cover this difference. If the federal government increases its expenditures by $1 billion but does not increase its tax receipts at all, it will increase the size of any pre-existing deficit by $1 billion. In this situation, the Treasury must necessarily issue an extra $1 billion of new securities to obtain the $1 billion needed to cover the increase in expenditures. We want to determine in this section the effects on legal reserves and the money supply when the Treasury sells the securities in question *exclusively to the public.* Recall that the term "public" excludes the Federal Reserve Banks and the commercial banks but includes all other financial institutions such as insurance companies, savings banks, and savings and loan associations, as well as nonfinancial businesses and, of course, individuals. The T-accounts of Table 7–3 trace out the changes that occur as a result of such security sales and the expenditure of the sum so raised by the Treasury.

The effects of the sale of the securities on each of the T-accounts are shown by the (a) entries, and the effects of the expenditure of the sum are shown by the (b) entries. Specifically, the (a) entries in the public's T-account show that the public has drawn checks totaling $1 billion in favor of the Treasury to pay for the securities purchased. The (a) entries in the other accounts show the changes that follow as the Treasury deposits the public's checks in the Federal Reserve Banks and

TABLE 7-3

FEDERAL RESERVE BANKS

Assets	Liabilities		
	Deposits of the commercial banks	-$1	(a)
	Deposits of the Treasury	+$1	(a)
	Deposits of the commercial banks	+$1	(b)
	Deposits of the Treasury	-$1	(b)
	Net Change		
	None		

COMMERCIAL BANKS

Assets			Liabilities		
Deposits with Federal Reserve Banks	-$1	(a)	Demand deposits of the public	-$1	(a)
Deposits with Federal Reserve Banks	+$1	(b)	Demand deposits of the public	+$1	(b)
Net Change			Net Change		
None			None		

TREASURY

Assets			Liabilities		
Deposits with Federal Reserve Banks	+$1	(a)	U.S. Government securities outstanding	+$1	(a)
Deposits with Federal Reserve Banks	-$1	(b)	Accounts payable	-$1	(b)
Net Change			Net Change		
None			Above two entries		

TABLE 7–3, continued

PUBLIC

Assets			Liabilities
Demand deposits	–$1	(a)	
U.S. Government securities	+$1	(a)	
Accounts receivable from			
Treasury	–$1	(b)	
Demand deposits	+$1	(b)	
Net Change			
U.S. Government securities	+$1		
Accounts receivable from			
Treasury	–$1		

as the Federal Reserve Banks return them to the commercial banks against which they were drawn. As in the tax case, the (a) entries alone show a temporary reduction of $1 billion in the public's demand deposits and thus, its currency holdings being unchanged, a $1 billion reduction in the money supply; the (a) entries also show a $1 billion reduction in the banks' legal reserves. The (b) entries, which cover the expenditure of the $1 billion by the Treasury, show a restoration of $1 billion to the public's demand deposits and so to the money supply and a restoration of $1 billion to the banks' legal reserves. For the (a) and (b) entries combined, or for both the borrowing of the $1 billion by the Treasury from the public and the expenditure of this $1 billion by the Treasury, there is no net effect on the money supply or on the banks' legal reserves. This is the same result we found in the preceding section in which the Treasury raised the additional $1 billion by taxation.

So far as the T-accounts of the Federal Reserve Banks and the commercial banks are concerned, there is no difference whatsoever between the tax case of Table 7–2 and the borrowing-from-the-public case of Table 7–3. What differences there are appear in the accounts for the Treasury and the public.

In the Treasury's T-account in Table 7–3 the net changes are seen to be a decrease of $1 billion in the Treasury's accounts payable matched by an increase of $1 billion in the amount of its securities outstanding. The Treasury has thus paid off $1 billion of the amount owed, for example, to various suppliers by increasing the amount owed to those who have purchased its securities. In the tax case, it paid off $1 billion of the amounts owed to suppliers not by switching to another form of debt but by raising tax collections. The Treasury, in a word, there financed the $1 billion by issuing $1 billion in "receipts" for tax payments rather than $1 billion in interest-bearing securities as here.

In the public's T-account in Table 7—3 there is a switch from one asset to another that corresponds with the Treasury's switch from one liability to another. The public increases its holdings of U.S. Government securities by $1 billion and decreases its receivables by $1 billion. In the tax case of Table 7—2, against the decrease in the asset item "Accounts receivable," there was a decrease in the liability item "Taxes payable." In exchange for $1 billion of receivables, it there received $1 billion of "tax receipts" issued by the Treasury rather than $1 billion of interest-bearing securities as in the present case.

Are there any other differences between the tax case and the borrowing-from-the-public case that are relevant here? Our immediate concern is with the effects on bank reserves and the money supply, and we have found that these are not at all affected by whether the Treasury finances additional spending by taxation or by borrowing from the public. However, if we take a step beyond the narrow definition of money, we find what may be an important difference between the two cases: Treasury financing via borrowing from the public will not increase the money supply narrowly defined, but it will increase the money supply more broadly defined, whereas Treasury financing via taxation will not increase the money supply by either definition.

If the Treasury borrows by selling the public U.S. Savings Bonds or Treasury bills or any other kind of Treasury interest-bearing obligation that its owners are able to convert into currency or demand deposits quickly and with little or no loss, the Treasury thereby adds that amount to the public's holdings of near-moneys. In this case, the net effect of the Treasury's borrowing and spending this amount is to leave the stock of money unchanged but to increase the public's holdings of near-money by the amount of the borrowing. If instead the Treasury finances by taxing, which means that it issues only tax receipts to the public, it thereby gives the public nothing that can be counted as near-money in even the broadest possible definition of that term. In this case, the net effect is to leave both the stock of money and the public's holdings of near-money unchanged. Thus, it is technically correct to say that borrowing from the public is indistinguishable from taxing the public in terms of the effect of each on the money supply when that term is narrowly defined to include only the public's holdings of currency and demand deposits; but there is the difference we have noted if the money supply is more broadly defined to include certain holdings that are otherwise considered near-monies.

This difference has a number of implications, the most important probably being the difference between the inflationary impact of borrowing from the public and the noninflationary impact of taxing the public. It is generally agreed that the problem of controlling inflation can better be met by Treasury financing through taxation than through borrowing from the public, even though neither one affects the money supply narrowly defined. The fact that the latter leaves the public with assets that may be quickly and easily converted into the spendable form we call money carries with it a potential inflationary threat clearly absent in the former, which leaves the public with nothing but tax receipts.

This difference helps bring out the economic questionableness of focusing *exclusively* on the narrow definition of money. However, in order to keep the framework within which we are presently working as simple as possible, we will limit attention to money narrowly defined. Within this admittedly imperfect but readily manageable framework, we are able to conclude that federal spending financed by borrowing from the public leaves the money supply unaffected just as does federal spending financed by taxation.

BORROWING FROM THE COMMERCIAL BANKS   In contrast to the absence of a money-supply effect in the above two cases of Treasury financing by taxation and by borrowing from the public, in borrowing from the commercial banks the effect is an increase in the money supply equal to the amount of borrowing from (or to the amount of newly issued securities sold by the Treasury to) the commercial banks. This is shown by Table 7–4, which sets forth the T-account entries for the sale of $1 billion of securities by the Treasury to the commercial banks and the expenditure by the Treasury of the $1 billion it receives.

The (a) entries show that the commercial banks pay the Treasury for the securities through a transfer of $1 billion from their deposit accounts at the Federal Reserve Banks to the Treasury deposit accounts at those banks. As shown by the (b) entries, the disbursement of this $1 billion by the Treasury in payment of various bills of the federal government adds $1 billion to the commercial bank liability "Demand deposits of the public" and $1 billion to their asset "Deposits at the Federal Reserve Banks." This $1 billion rise in the commercial banks' balance at the Federal Reserve Banks restores this balance to what it was before the commercial banks paid for the $1 billion of securities purchased from the Treasury. The $1 billion addition to the demand deposit liabilities of the commercial banks is, however, a net addition to the public's demand deposits; corresponding to the purchase of $1

TABLE 7–4

FEDERAL RESERVE BANKS

Assets	Liabilities		
	Deposits of the commercial banks	−$1	(a)
	Deposits of the Treasury	+$1	(a)
	Deposits of the commercial banks	+$1	(b)
	Deposits of the Treasury	−$1	(b)
	Net Change		
	None		

COMMERCIAL BANKS

Assets			Liabilities		
U.S. Government securities	+$1	(a)			
Deposits with Federal Reserve Banks	−$1	(a)			
Deposits with Federal Reserve Banks	+$1	(b)	Demand deposits of the public	+$1	(b)
Net Change			Net Change		
U.S. Government securities	+$1		Demand deposits of the public	+$1	(b)

TREASURY

Assets			Liabilities		
Deposits with Federal Reserve Banks	+$1	(a)	U.S. Government securities	+$1	(a)
Deposits with Federal Reserve Banks	−$1	(b)	Accounts payable	−$1	(b)
Net Change			Net Change		
None			Above two entries		

TABLE 7—4, continued

PUBLIC

Assets			Liabilities
Accounts receivable	−$1	(b)	
Demand deposits	+$1	(b)	
Net Change			
Above two entries			

billion in government securities by the commercial banks is the creation of $1 billion of demand deposits by the commercial banks. This is the result we see in the T-account for the commercial banks under the heading of "Net Change."

The fact that the public now holds $1 billion more in demand deposits than before must, of course, appear in the T-account for the public. There we do indeed see that the public has received payment in the form of $1 billion of newly created demand deposits for $1 billion owed to it for various goods and services it supplied to the government. This illustration shows quite explicitly that this way of meeting $1 billion of the government's bills involves the creation of an equal amount of new money.

In tracing just above the effects of Treasury borrowing from the public through the T-accounts of Table 7—3, we saw in that table's T-account for the public that the Treasury made payment of $1 billion owed to the public, in effect, with $1 billion of U.S. Government securities. It borrowed $1 billion from the public in order to pay the public the $1 billion owed it. The public ended up with an increase in its holdings of government securities but no increase in its holdings of money. And earlier in Table 7—2—the case of tax-financed government expenditures—we saw that the Treasury, in effect, gave the public only "tax receipts" in payment for the amount it owed to the public. In this case, it taxed the public $1 billion to pay the public the $1 billion owed it. The public's holdings of money in this case also remained unaffected. We find now, the case in which the Treasury resorts to the sale of securities to the commercial banks, that the Treasury action does result in an increase in the supply of money.

There should be nothing surprising in this last conclusion. We saw in some detail back in Chapter 3 that the purchase of securities by the commercial banks, just as the making of loans by the banks, typically gives rise, at least initially, to an equal increase in the public's holding of demand deposits. This is true whether the banks buy newly issued securities directly from the Treasury or existing securities from investors who seek to sell. In other words, so far as the mechanics of the money-creating process go, there is nothing unique about the case in which the commercial banks buy $1 billion of securities directly from the Treasury. Actually, in this regard, there is no basic difference between the banks making $1 billion of personal loans to John Jones and other individuals or providing the U.S. Treasury with $1 billion by purchasing its securities. It acquires in the one case the IOUs of these thousands of individuals and in the other the IOUs of the federal government, but again in both cases the result is a $1 billion increase in the money supply.

In terms of its effect on the money supply, is there any difference then between, on the one hand, the commercial banks' purchases of newly issued securities from the Treasury and, on the other hand, their purchase of securities from others or their making of loans to others? We know that a prerequisite to an expansion in the combined volume of the commercial banks' loans and security holdings is the availability of excess reserves (over and above any amount the banks desire to hold) to meet the increase in required reserves that will result from the increase in deposits this expansion of earning assets generates. We also know that, with any existing amount of legal reserves fully absorbed as required reserves or desired excess reserves, the banks as a group may at any time expand their loans by reducing their security holdings and vice versa, if they so choose, but they cannot under these conditions expand the total of both. Because of the higher average return on loans and because, from the individual bank's point of view, borrowers are also typically depositors, banks will not reduce their loan volume in order to free up the reserves needed to purchase additional U.S. Government securities that the Treasury may be seeking to sell to them. In other words, under conditions where the banks are fully "loaned up," the Treasury will not be able to sell additional securities to the commercial banks unless the Federal Reserve takes the steps necessary to provide the banks with the additional legal reserves they must first have. The Federal Reserve ordinarily cooperates with the Treasury in this way, the alternative being a failure of the Treasury to sell its new securities at the terms offered. This eventuality will not be allowed to occur. However, the Federal Reserve does not cooperate in this way with all other borrowers—i.e., with state and local governments and the whole private sector. If these groups are unable to sell more securities or obtain more loans in the amounts desired, the Federal Reserve does not automatically respond by putting as much more reserves into the commercial banking system as are needed to accommodate all of their demands. The banks' available funds are instead rationed among the borrowers, and interest rates are allowed to rise to squeeze out some prospective borrowers.

We now have from all this one factor in the answer to the question raised above. The commercial banks' purchase of newly issued securities from the Treasury and the expenditure of the proceeds by the Treasury produce an increase in the money supply in the same way that their purchase of other securities or their making of loans does, but the Federal Reserve will ordinarily provide the reserves necessary to effect the former at times when it would not provide the reserves to effect the latter. In other words, at times when the Federal Reserve feels that an expansion in the money supply is not in the best interest of the economy, it may, however reluctantly, still find it necessary to permit such an expansion as the unavoidable by-product of assuring a market for the sale of newly issued Treasury securities. It feels no similar necessity to provide reserves to accommodate any other sector of the economy.

This in part explains the common practice of likening Treasury borrowing from the commercial banks to Treasury resort to the printing press. It is not that private borrowing from the banks, in its effect on the total money supply, does not also resemble a running of the printing press; it is that the latter will be checked by the Federal Reserve when the money supply is growing at what it believes to be an excessive rate, while the former perhaps will not. This is not to say that there are not indeed times when the Federal Reserve attempts to impose the same discipline on the U.S. Treasury that it imposes on other borrowers. At some of these times real conflict between the executive branch of the federal government and the semi-independent Federal Reserve authorities arises. If the Federal Reserve is to meet its responsibility of regulating the money supply in a way that, in its judgment, will contribute most to the stabilization of the economy, such conflict is clearly unavoidable when the judgment of the administration and that of the Federal Reserve do not coincide.

In the event of a conflict of this kind, what the Federal Reserve would do is limit any addition to the commercial banks' reserves to less than the amount that would enable them to purchase all the securities the Treasury seeks to sell them, thereby forcing the Treasury to finance a larger part of its requirements by either or both of the other two methods already discussed: higher taxes or the sale of more securities to the public. The reluctance of the administration and the Congress to raise taxes at almost any time is readily understandable—often one need look no further than the political considerations. The reluctance to increase the amount of borrowing from the public involves some technical considerations, the foremost of which is that it requires that the Treasury offer higher interest rates in order to attract a larger portion of the flow of the public's current saving away from alternative investments. The Federal Reserve at times forces the administration to these alternatives, especially the latter. However, it also at times under pressure accedes to the Treasury's wishes and pumps more reserves into the commercial banks than it would otherwise. It is specifically at times like this that the money supply effects of Treasury borrowing from the commercial banks exhibit a distinct difference from the money supply effects of banks' purchases of other securities or extension of loans, the total of the latter being an amount that the Federal Reserve will limit with little hesitation whenever it feels that the increase in the money supply that will otherwise follow must be prevented.

BORROWING FROM THE FEDERAL RESERVE BANKS   In this final case, the immediate effect of the sale of $1 billion of securities by the Treasury directly to the Federal Reserve Banks and the expenditure of that amount by the Treasury is not only an increase in the money supply of $1 billion as in the preceding case but an increase in the commercial banks' legal reserves of $1 billion. The T-account entries for this case are given in Table 7–5. Our purpose in this table is limited to tracing the immediate effects on these two variables, which are an increase in both legal reserves and the money supply of $1 billion—the entries stop at this point. However, as should be familiar by now, on the assumption of a 20 percent legal reserve requirement against demand deposits (and, for the sake of simplicity, on the assumption that the a, c, and e ratios are all zero), the *ultimate* increase in the money supply will be $5 billion rather than $1 billion. The commercial banks will expand their loans and security holdings by $4 billion on the basis

TABLE 7–5

FEDERAL RESERVE BANKS

Assets			Liabilities		
U.S. Government securities	+$1	(a)	Deposits of the Treasury	+$1	(a)
			Deposits of the Treasury	–$1	(b)
			Deposits of the commercial banks	+$1	(b)
Net Change			Net Change		
U.S. Government securities	+$1		Deposits of the commercial banks	+$1	

TABLE 7–5, continued

COMMERCIAL BANKS

Assets			Liabilities		
Deposits with Federal Reserve Banks	+$1	(b)	Demand deposits of the public	+$1	(b)
Net Change			Net Change		
Above entry			Above entry		

TREASURY

Assets			Liabilities		
Deposits with Federal Reserve Banks	+$1	(a)	U.S. Government securities	+$1	(a)
Deposits with Federal Reserve Banks	–$1	(b)	Accounts payable	–$1	(b)
Net Change			Net Change		
None			Above two entries		

PUBLIC

Assets			Liabilities		
Accounts receivable	–$1	(b)			
Demand deposits	+$1	(b)			
Net Change					
Above two entries					

of the $0.8 billion addition to excess reserves that comes into being as a result of the specific transactions traced through in Table 7–5.

Looking at that table, we find the (a) entries indicate that the Treasury receives payment for the securities delivered with a $1 billion credit to its deposit balances at the Federal Reserve Banks. The Federal Reserve Banks add $1 billion to their asset "U.S. Government securities" and $1 billion to their deposit liabilities; the Treasury adds $1 billion to its asset "Deposits with the Federal Reserve Banks" and $1 billion to its liability "U.S. Government securities outstanding." The (b) entries then show that the expenditure of this $1 billion by the Treasury adds $1 billion to the public's demand deposits as the $1 billion in checks issued by the Treasury to the public is deposited in the commercial banks. And as the commercial banks send these checks to the Federal Reserve Banks, they gain the same amount in additional legal reserves through a transfer of $1 billion from the Treasury's deposit account to the commercial banks' deposit accounts.

For the preceding case, in which the commercial banks rather than the Federal Reserve Banks were the purchasers of the securities issued by the Treasury, the banks first lost $1 billion in legal reserves as they paid for the securities so purchased and regained the same $1 billion as the Treasury expended it. This left the total of legal reserves unchanged on balance. In the present case, the commercial banks gain $1 billion in legal reserves on balance because the Federal Reserve Banks are the purchasers of the securities sold by the Treasury.

It may be apparent that the effects on both the money supply and the banks' legal reserves revealed by Table 7–5 are precisely those that follow from an open market purchase of $1 billion of U.S. Government securities by the Federal Reserve Banks from the public, which were shown in the T-accounts on page 70. A comparison will reveal that the entries in the first two accounts there correspond exactly to the net changes shown in the first two accounts of Table 7–5. Therefore, there should be nothing surprising in the fact that government spending financed by borrowing from the Federal Reserve Banks adds an equal amount to the commercial banks' legal reserves. So far as the effect on these reserves is concerned, the only thing relevant here is the fact of the purchase of the securities by the Federal Reserve Banks and not from whom these securities are purchased. To make the point even more emphatic, not only is the reserve-creating effect of a purchase by the Federal Reserve Banks the same regardless of from whom the purchase is made, but it is the same regardless of what the Federal Reserve Banks purchase. For example, if the Federal Reserve Banks were to purchase a thousand new typewriters at a cost of a half-million dollars, other things being equal, this too would by the same principle add that amount to the legal reserves of the commercial banks. All that is involved is the fact that the Federal Reserve Banks pay for whatever they purchase by creating reserves (and, it may be added, collect for whatever they sell by destroying reserves).

If the purchase of some amount of U.S. Government securities directly from the Treasury and the Treasury's expenditures of that amount has the very same effect on the legal reserves of the commercial banks as would the purchase of the same amount of these securities in the open market, is there any reason to distinguish between them in this regard? The Congress is presumably aware of the fact that Federal Reserve Bank purchases of both kinds are identical in their reserve-creating effect. However, it has imposed the restriction that the Federal Reserve Banks at no time may hold more than $5 billion of U.S. Government securities that they have purchased directly from the Treasury, but it has imposed no restriction on the amount of the very same type of securities the Federal Reserve Banks may hold as long as they are purchased in the open market. What lies behind this seemingly inconsistent rule is a variant of an issue encountered at a different level in the preceding section.

A major reason that the Congress established the Federal Reserve outside the executive branch, making it formally answerable only to the Congress and not to the Chief Executive, was to prevent its possible abuse by the Treasury Department, which is a part of the executive branch. When the Treasury is paying out more than is coming in through taxation or through borrowing from the public, it must turn to the banking system for the balance (again ruling out the direct issue of hand-to-hand money). Other considerations completely apart, its easiest way out is the sale of the required amount of securities to the Federal Reserve Banks. As we saw above, in order for the Treasury to sell to the commercial banks, the latter's reserve position must be such that they are able and willing to buy. In contrast, the ability of the Federal Reserve Banks to expand their assets is subject to no reserve restraint at all. There is no legal limit on the amount of outstanding U.S. Government securities they can purchase—the only limit is the self-imposed one of not purchasing more such securities in any period than the amount deemed necessary to bring about some desired increase in the commercial banks' reserves and in the economy's money supply.

If faced with only this barrier, under certain conditions a determined Treasury might be able to pressure the Federal Reserve into the direct purchase of sizable amounts of its newly issued securities. It is on transactions of this kind that the Congress has imposed the further barrier of a legal limit. With its access to the Federal Reserve Banks so restricted, the Treasury is compelled to turn to the commercial banks to secure some part of any amount it seeks to borrow from the banking system. To some degree, this subjects the Treasury to the discipline of the free financial markets. Its securities must compete there with state and local securities that the banks might also buy and, to some degree, with commercial, consumer, and other classes of borrowers whose promissory notes the banks might also buy. As we have seen, when the Treasury finds it necessary to sell securities to the commercial banks, the Federal Reserve will ordinarily act in a way to assure the "successful" marketing of the Treasury issue. Nonetheless, the Federal Reserve does not act so as to set aside completely the discipline of the market. But in direct sales to the Federal Reserve Banks the Treasury faces no such discipline, and it might on occasion seek this easiest way out if there were not the legal limit imposed by Congress on its ability to do so.

It is not intended here to leave the impression that the Treasury cares only about finding the easiest way to handle its financing. The easiest way may be a seriously inflationary or otherwise destabilizing way, and the Treasury is usually as concerned in the management of its affairs with the stability of the economy as are the Federal Reserve authorities. The problem is, of course, in the fact that they may at times differ as to what policy is most likely the best from this point of view.

eight

TREASURY OPERATIONS, BANK RESERVES, AND THE MONEY SUPPLY, II

If federal spending exceeds tax receipts, the difference is financed by borrowing, and the amount of such borrowing for the time period is the measure of that period's deficit. The national debt increases during that period by the amount of the deficit. On the other hand, if federal spending is less than tax receipts, the difference is the measure of that period's surplus. The Treasury may use the surplus to purchase and retire some of its outstanding interest-bearing obligations. The national debt then decreases during that time period by the amount of the surplus.

TREASURY SURPLUS AND DEBT RETIREMENT

Although a surplus will be used for debt retirement, it appears initially as an increase in the Treasury's bank balance. If during a year the federal government's expenditures are $200 billion and its tax receipts $201 billion, it shows a surplus of $1 billion and initially a rise of $1 billion in its bank balance. As we saw in Table 7–2, an increase in the Treasury's bank balance that results from tax collections means at first an equal decrease in bank reserves and the money supply. This much is true whether the Treasury shows a deficit, a balanced budget, or a surplus for the year as a whole. But as long as expenditures are equal to or greater than tax receipts, every dollar raised through taxation is returned to the public through spending, so the specific process of taxing and spending what is collected in taxes does not in itself affect the money supply or bank reserves in one direction or the other. However, when expenditures are less than tax receipts, not every dollar raised through taxation is returned to the public through spending, with the effect being a possibly lasting decrease in bank reserves and the money supply equal to the difference, or to the amount of the budget surplus.

This definitely would be the result if the surplus continued to be held as an increase in the Treasury's bank balance, but it is not necessarily the result if the Treasury uses the amount of the surplus to reduce the size of the national debt by an equal amount. The first thing we want to do in this chapter is to trace in brief form the effects on bank reserves and the money supply that follow from the overall process of collecting taxes in excess of expenditures and using the resulting surplus for debt retirement.

As in tracing the effects of deficits, we must distinguish the same three cases here, the effects varying according to whether the securities purchased by the Treasury are purchased from the public, the commercial banks, or the Federal Reserve Banks. Just as a deficit financed by the sale of securities to the public leaves bank reserves and the money supply unchanged, so a surplus used to retire securities held by the public also leaves these variables unchanged. In the second case, a deficit financed by the sale of securities to the commercial banks leaves bank reserves unchanged but *increases* the money supply, whereas a surplus used to retire securities held by the commercial banks leaves reserves unaffected but *decreases* the money supply. In the third and final case, a deficit financed by the sale of securities to the Federal

Reserve Banks *increases* both bank reserves and the money supply, while a surplus used to retire securities held by the Federal Reserve Banks *decreases* both bank reserves and the money supply.

In the following three tables, which set forth the mechanics of the three surplus cases, it must be understood that the (a) entry in the Treasury's T-account "Deposits with the Federal Reserve Banks +$1" indicates the Treasury's surplus for the time period and not an amount that otherwise would be returned to the public in the ordinary course of government spending. This must be stated in so many words because the tables themselves do not explicitly say as much. The (a) entries in all of these tables, it may be noted, are identical with the (a) entries in Table 7–2, which were designed to show the effect of an additional $1 billion of tax receipts, but in that table there was no particular reference to whether the budget was in balance or in surplus or in deficit.

The (b) entries in the following three tables then show the changes that occur as the Treasury uses the $1 billion surplus to purchase $1 billion of its securities. In Table 8–1 the purchases are of securities held by the public. The public in the (a) entries gives up $1 billion of demand deposits in paying taxes, but it does not get this $1 billion back through government spending. However, it does get the $1 billion back in another way, since the Treasury uses that amount to buy U.S. Government securities held by the public. This puts the money supply back where it was before the Treasury generated the $1 billion surplus. As may be seen in the T-account for the commercial banks, their legal reserves, which were temporarily drawn down $1 billion by the public's payment of taxes, are also restored to their original level with the retirement of $1 billion of the federal securities held by the public. The major conclusion that follows from this case is that the Treasury will not cause any change in the money supply if it uses a surplus to purchase securities from the public. The same does not follow in the other two cases.

In the (b) entries of Table 8–2, the Treasury uses the $1 billion surplus to purchase securities held by the commercial banks. This removes $1 billion of the commercial bank asset "U.S. Government securities" and adds $1 billion to the commercial bank asset "Deposits with the Federal Reserve Banks." The decrease of $1 billion in the money supply that occurred as the public paid this amount in taxes thus turns out to be a permanent decrease—it is wiped out of existence as the Treasury uses the $1 billion to retire securities held by the commercial banks. However, legal reserves, which were first drawn down by $1 billion, are restored to their previous level as the commercial banks swap $1 billion of their federal security holdings for this amount of deposits at the Federal Reserve Banks. Thus, the major

TABLE 8–1

FEDERAL RESERVE BANKS

Assets	Liabilities		
	Deposits of the Treasury	+$1	(a)
	Deposits of the commercial banks	−$1	(a)
	Deposits of the Treasury	−$1	(b)
	Deposits of the commercial banks	+$1	(b)
	Net Change		
	None		

COMMERCIAL BANKS

Assets			Liabilities		
Deposits with Federal Reserve Banks	−$1	(a)	Demand deposits of the public	−$1	(a)
Deposits with Federal Reserve Banks	+$1	(b)	Demand deposits of the public	+$1	(b)
Net Change			Net Change		
None			None		

TREASURY

Assets			Liabilities		
Deposits with Federal Reserve Banks	+$1	(a)			
Taxes receivable	−$1	(a)			
Deposits with Federal Reserve Banks	−$1	(b)	U.S. Government securities	−$1	(b)
Net Change			Net Change		
Taxes receivable	−$1		U.S. Government securities	−$1	

PUBLIC

Assets			Liabilities		
Demand deposits	−$1	(a)	Taxes payable	−$1	(a)
U.S. Government securities	−$1	(b)			
Demand deposits	+$1	(b)			
Net Change			Net Change		
U.S. Government securities	−$1		Taxes payable	−$1	

TABLE 8–2

FEDERAL RESERVE BANKS

Assets	Liabilities		
	Deposits of the Treasury	+$1	(a)
	Deposits of the commercial banks	−$1	(a)
	Deposits of the Treasury	−$1	(b)
	Deposits of the commercial banks	+$1	(b)
	Net Change		
	None		

COMMERCIAL BANKS

Assets			Liabilities		
Deposits with Federal Reserve Banks	−$1	(a)	Demand deposits of the public	−$1	(a)
U.S. Government securities	−$1	(b)			
Deposits with Federal Reserve Banks	+$1	(b)			
Net Change			Net Change		
U.S. Government securities	−$1		Demand deposits of the public	−$1	

TREASURY

Assets			Liabilities		
Deposits with Federal Reserve Banks	+$1	(a)			
Taxes receivable	−$1	(a)			
Deposits with Federal Reserve Banks	−$1	(b)	U.S. Government securities	−$1	(b)
Net Change			Net Change		
Taxes receivable	−$1		U.S. Government securities	−$1	

PUBLIC

Assets			Liabilities		
Demand deposits	−$1	(a)	Taxes payable	−$1	(a)
Net Change			Net Change		
Above entry			Above entry		

TABLE 8–3

FEDERAL RESERVE BANKS

Assets			Liabilities		
			Deposits of the Treasury	+$1	(a)
			Deposits of the commercial banks	−$1	(a)
U.S. Government securities	−$1	(b)	Deposits of the Treasury	−$1	(b)
Net Change			Net Change		
U.S. Government securities	−$1		Deposits of the commercial banks	−$1	

COMMERCIAL BANKS

Assets			Liabilities		
Deposits with Federal Reserve Banks	−$1	(a)	Demand deposits of the public	−$1	(a)
Net Change			Net Change		
Above entry			Above entry		

TREASURY

Assets			Liabilities		
Deposits with Federal Reserve Banks	+$1	(a)			
Taxes receivable	−$1	(a)			
Deposits with Federal Reserve Banks	−$1	(b)	U.S. Government securities	−$1	(b)
Net Change			Net Change		
Taxes receivable	−$1		U.S. Government securities	−$1	

PUBLIC

Assets			Liabilities		
Demand deposits	−$1	(a)	Taxes payable	−$1	(a)
Net Change			Net Change		
Above entry			Above entry		

conclusion in this case is that the Treasury will tend to cause a reduction in the money supply but no change in bank reserves if it uses a surplus to retire securities held by the commercial banks.

Finally, in the (B) entries of Table 8–3 the Treasury uses the $1 billion surplus to purchase securities held by the Federal Reserve Banks. Following through the entries reveals that not only is $1 billion of the money supply wiped out of existence as in the preceding case but the same happens to an equal amount of bank reserves. Thus the conclusion here is that the Treasury will tend to cause a reduction in both bank reserves and the money supply if it uses a surplus to retire securities held by the Federal Reserve Banks.

In view of these conclusions, whose security holdings should be reduced in the event of an actual surplus in the budget? As an initial general statement, we may say the following: just as the Treasury should not borrow by selling newly issued securities to the Federal Reserve Banks if economic conditions are such that bank reserves and the money supply should not both be enlarged, so it should not do the reverse of using a surplus to purchase its outstanding securities from the Federal Reserve Banks if economic conditions are such that bank reserves and the money supply should not both be contracted. Appropriately adjusted statements like this could be made for the other two cases. However, considerations other than the effect on bank reserves and the money supply have to be taken into account in any actual debt retirement. The policy that appears most advantageous under the existing economic conditions, all things considered, is something worked out jointly by the Treasury and the Federal Reserve. The complex questions of debt retirement policy have not been our concern in these pages—that concern has only been to see the way in which debt retirement affects bank reserves and the money supply according to the group from whom the retired securities are purchased. This much has now been done in brief form, and we will not here go beyond this.

TREASURY DEPOSIT BALANCES, BANK RESERVES, AND THE MONEY SUPPLY

The standard definition of money excludes currency and demand deposits held by the U.S. Treasury. Therefore, any time any person or business firm that is part of the public makes payment to the Treasury for taxes due or for securities purchased, the result of this specific transaction is by definition a decrease in the money supply equal to the amount of that payment. By the same token, any time the Treasury makes payment to any person or business that is part of the public, the result of this specific transaction is just the reverse, an increase in the money supply of that amount.

Control of the money supply is recognized by all, including the U.S. Treasury, to be the function primarily of the Federal Reserve authorities, although we saw earlier that on some occasions the Treasury may act in a way that produces changes in the money supply contrary to the Federal Reserve authorities' desires. In this section, we will find a quite different situation in which the Treasury produces some changes in the money supply that cannot be avoided despite its best efforts to do so. This follows from the fact that it is not possible for the Treasury (or almost anyone else, for that matter) to synchronize perfectly its receipts and its expenditures. To the degree that these diverge, the Treasury's deposit balance rises and falls, and to this degree the money supply falls and rises, other things being equal.

Changes in the Treasury's balance sometimes run as much as $5 billion from one week to the next. Changes of this magnitude or even much smaller changes are by no means inconsequential for short-run changes in the money supply, but they could be far more consequential if the Treasury did not deliberately act to prevent these changes from producing still larger changes in the money supply. To see what is involved here, let us start off with a buildup of the Treasury's deposit balance by, say, $100 million. This, as we have noted, will mean a reduction in the money supply of this amount, but what must now be seen is that this change in the money supply is consistent with a $100 million decrease in the commercial banks' legal reserves or no change in those reserves or any amount in between these. The particular result we find in any one case depends on nothing more than the Treasury's decision as to *where it will carry its additional balance*, in deposit accounts with the commercial banks or with the Federal Reserve Banks or with both. If the additional balance is carried with the commercial banks, it does not involve any decrease in their legal reserves; if it is carried with the Federal Reserve Banks, it involves a decrease in legal reserves equal to that additional balance.

Only in the former case will the decrease in the money supply be no larger than the increase in the Treasury balance. In the latter case, not only is there an initial decrease in the money supply equal to the amount of the transfer of demand deposits from the public's accounts to the Treasury's accounts, but there is a further decrease, and a much larger one, that makes the total decrease in the money supply equal to the decrease in legal reserves times the money supply multiplier. For example, a $100 million increase in the Treasury's balance at the Federal Reserve Banks, which means a $100 million decrease in legal reserves, would potentially lead to a $500 million total decrease in the money supply if the multiplier were 5 and if other things remained equal as the multiplier process worked itself out. In the simplest possible case with the a, c, and e ratios all equal to zero and r equal to 20 percent, the $500 million decrease in the money supply would be the sum of the initial decrease of $100 million and a further decrease of $400 million, which would result as the commercial banks contracted demand deposits by this $400 million due to a reserve deficiency of $80 million.

It is evident that even fairly small variations in the Treasury's deposit balances could be magnified into fairly sizable variations in the money supply if the Treasury consistently deposited all of its receipts directly in its accounts with the Federal Reserve Banks. It is to avoid this outcome that the Treasury carries demand deposits balances in "Tax and Loan Accounts" with over 10,000 of the nation's more than 14,000 commercial banks. These are banks that want such accounts and meet the requirements the Treasury imposes, one of which is to guarantee the safety of the Treasury's balances. (Each participating bank is required to set aside or pledge an amount of its U.S. Government security holdings equal in value to the Treasury's deposit balance with it; in the event that a bank is unable to meet its total liabilities, the Treasury is assured that this particular liability will be met by the sale of the pledged securities.) As the Treasury receives checks from the public in payment of taxes or other amounts due, it ordinarily deposits these checks to the credit of its Tax and Loan Accounts in the same banks against which these checks were drawn, thereby leaving these banks' reserve positions individually unaffected. Thus, if on April 15 John Smith in New York City draws a check for $1,000 against his account with Chase Manhattan Bank payable to the Internal Revenue Service in settlement of the amount of tax due on his preceding year's income, the Treasury Department makes note of this receipt and routes the check back to Chase, where the Treasury will receive a credit for $1,000 in its Tax and Loan Account. John Smith's account will naturally be charged for the $1,000. Chase's reserve position, however, is unchanged.

This $1,000 as well as other amounts received by the Treasury will remain in Tax and Loan Accounts only temporarily. Since the Treasury makes payments to the public by drawing checks against its deposit balances with the Federal Reserve Banks, it is continuously drawing down these accounts. As this occurs, the Treasury continuously replenishes these balances by the transfer of some of its balances from Tax and Loan Accounts at the commercial banks. Of course, in drawing checks against its balances at the Federal Reserve Banks, the Treasury is continuously returning funds to the public, which deposits them to the credit of their accounts in Chase and the thousands of other commercial banks. This makes the circle complete. All of these steps are shown

TABLE 8–4

FEDERAL RESERVE BANKS

Assets	Liabilities		
	Deposits of the commercial banks	−$1	(b)
	Deposits of the Treasury	+$1	(b)
	Deposits of the Treasury	−$1	(c)
	Deposits of the commercial banks	+$1	(c)
	Net Change		
	None		

COMMERCIAL BANKS

Assets			Liabilities		
			Deposits of the public	−$1	(a)
Deposits with Federal Reserve Banks	−$1	(b)	Deposits of the Treasury	+$1	(a)
			Deposits of the Treasury	−$1	(b)
Deposits with Federal Reserve Banks	+$1	(c)	Deposits of the public	+$1	(c)
Net Change			**Net Change**		
None			None		

TREASURY

Assets			Liabilities		
Deposits with commercial banks	+$1	(a)			
Taxes receivable	−$1	(a)			
Deposits with commercial banks	−$1	(b)			
Deposits with Federal Reserve Banks	+$1	(b)			
Deposits with Federal Reserve Banks	−$1	(c)	Accounts payable	−$1	(c)
Net Change			**Net Change**		
Taxes receivable	−$1		Accounts payable	−$1	

TABLE 8–4, continued

PUBLIC

Assets			Liabilities		
Demand deposits	–$1	(a)	Taxes payable	–$1	(a)
Demand deposits	+$1	(c)			
Accounts receivable from					
U.S. Government	–$1	(c)			
Net Change			Net Change		
Accounts receivable from					
U.S. Government	–$1		Taxes payable	–$1	

by the entries in the T-accounts of Table 8–4. We arbitrarily assume here, as before, changes of $1 billion.

The (a) entries show the transfer of $1 billion from the public's demand deposits to the Treasury's demand deposits *at the commercial banks*—the money supply is down by $1 billion, but legal reserves are unchanged at this point. The T-account of the Federal Reserve Banks is so far unaffected. The (a) entries in the Treasury T-account indicate a rise in its deposit balance of $1 billion and a decrease in taxes receivable of this amount; the (a) entries in the public's T-account show a decrease in its deposit balances of $1 billion and a decrease in taxes payable of this amount.

The (b) entries show the effects of the transfer of $1 billion of the Treasury's deposits from the commercial banks to the Federal Reserve Banks. This does not *in itself* further affect the money supply, but it does reduce the commercial banks' legal reserves by $1 billion. Finally, the (c) entries indicate the changes that follow from the expenditure of the $1 billion by the Treasury – namely, a $1 billion rise in the public's deposits balances, which puts them back where they were before the tax payment, and a $1 billion rise in the banks' legal reserves, which puts them back where they were before the Treasury transferred the $1 billion from its accounts with the commercial banks to its accounts with the Federal Reserve Banks.

Actually, the transactions covered by entries (a), (b), and (c) do not have to occur in the exact sequence suggested in the description above. The Treasury seeks to manage its balances to produce the minimum effect on the banks' reserve position. Toward this end, it is possible in Table 8-4's illustration that the commercial banks as a group will not actually lose reserves as shown by the (b) entries. If the (c) entries are timed to coincide with the (b) entries, we could find that the banks receive from their customers on a particular day $1 billion in Treasury checks (via (c) entries), which when forwarded to the Federal Reserve Banks exactly offset what otherwise would have been a loss of $1 billion in reserves due to a transfer of this amount by the Treasury from its commercial bank balances to its Federal Reserve Bank balances (via (b) entries). This would then leave the banks' legal reserves completely unchanged as the transactions behind the (a), (b), and (c) entries took place.

To produce this sort of result is essentially what the Treasury seeks. Although a precise offsetting like the one just described can occur only by chance, the Treasury is able to coordinate the transfer of balances from the commercial banks to the Federal Reserve Banks with its scheduled disbursement of funds closely enough to prevent a large impact on the reserve position of the commercial banks. It would, of course, be possible for the Treasury to manage the distribution of its deposit balances in just the other way: to effect deliberate changes in the banks' reserve position. When one notes the size of the Treasury balances—during 1973 its monthly balance in Tax and Loan Accounts averaged $8.1 billion and in the Federal Reserve Banks $2.5 billion—its potential impact in this direction is seen to be huge. In practice, however, shifting of Treasury balances has rarely been employed for the purpose of deliberately causing changes in the banks' reserve position. Such deliberate changes are left to the Federal Reserve authorities to effect with their regular tools, primarily open market operations. The Treasury in practice seeks to minimize the impact on reserves that accompanies the management of its deposit balances; it tries to ease the Federal Reserve's task, not to complicate it unnecessarily.

A CONCLUDING NOTE

There are various Treasury operations that affect bank reserves and the money supply. The one people think of first, probably because it does this in the most direct manner, is the outright issuance of currency and coin by the Treasury. This has come to be of decreasing importance, quantitatively, over the years as the Federal Reserve Banks have assumed the task of supplying practically all of the paper money and the Treasury has limited itself to supplying coin. However, even in the earlier years of the Federal Reserve System, a time when the Treasury was more important as an issuer of hand-to-hand money than it is now, its operations with the greatest impact on bank reserves and the money supply were still the indirect ones associated with its sale and retirement of federal government securities. This chapter and a major part of the preceding chapter have been devoted to tracing the mechanics of the way in which variations in the size of the national debt produce variations in bank reserves and the money supply.

Although it is now thirty years behind us, there is no better actual illustration of the way this works than the experience during World War II. In this longer-than-average concluding note, we will look briefly at these aspects of that war-financing experience.

The scope of the financing problem is the first matter of interest. Federal expenditures were running at less than $10 billion annually before the defense effort began about mid-1940, but four years later they were running at almost $100 billion annually. The war ended in the summer of 1945, and government expenditures for the 1946 fiscal year fell back sharply to $66 billion. During the six years from July 1, 1940, through June 30, 1946, the Treasury spent $383 billion. To appreciate what this figure meant at the time, we have only to note that it was ten times as much as the federal government had spent during World War I and twice as much as it had spent during all of the preceding 150 years.

During these six years, income tax rates were raised sharply—for example, the top marginal rate on the personal income tax was lifted to an all-time high of 91 percent—and special war-time taxes like one on excess profits were introduced. These changes, combined with the tremendous enlargement of the tax base, produced a massive expansion of federal tax receipts—from less than $10 billion in fiscal 1941 to over $50 billion in fiscal 1945. For the six-year period, federal tax receipts totaled $197 billion. This, however, covered just over half (about 51 percent) of the $383 billion of expenditures, meaning that the balance of $186 billion, or 49 percent, of federal expenditures for those years had to be otherwise covered.

The possibilities open to the Treasury in this direction are those discussed in the section of the preceding chapter on borrowing. For one, it could have sought to borrow this whole amount from the public, thereby leaving the money supply unaffected by its financing. Alternatively, it could have borrowed all or some part of this amount from the Federal Reserve Banks and the commercial banks, thereby increasing the money supply, at least initially, by the amount of its borrowing from them. Finally, instead of interest-bearing obligations, the outright issuance by the Treasury of this amount of inconvertible paper currency was, in a sense, yet another alternative. However, we have seen that in modern times treasuries refrain from the use of this device, which is so abhorrent to the public, although by borrowing from their central banks they may produce results that are in certain ways indistinguishable from the results of the outright expansion of Treasury paper currency outstanding.

Which alternative should have been adopted? This is anything but an easy question. Actually one may even argue that the Treasury could have avoided the need to choose among these alternatives by collecting taxes equal to its expenditures—in a word, by maintaining a balanced budget—despite the fact that its budget had unavoidably risen by leaps and bounds over these years to meet the seemingly insatiable demands of the military. Still, tax collections could have been expanded to produce this result—every last dollar the Treasury spent for tanks, guns, planes, and everything else increased the economy's income by a dollar, so this same number of dollars could have then been scooped up by the Treasury with sufficiently high tax rates. But the required tax rates would have been so high relative to prewar rates as to have discouraged many people from working as hard as was needed if the economy was to produce the vast quantities of matériel being absorbed by the war. The existence of an unprecedentedly high degree of public support for the war would probably not have been enough to overcome the incentive-discouraging effects of tax rates at the level required. Perhaps taxation was pushed about as far as was feasible without moving toward the type of completely controlled home economy that was found in wartime Germany.

If then some amount of borrowing was the only practical alternative, which of the alternative lenders or combination of lenders should the Treasury have turned to? Here the major consideration was the economy's health, present and future. To prevent its serious deterioration both during and after the war called for a scheme of government borrowing during the war that would have the minimum inflationary impact then and later. This objective could best be met by borrowing in a way that would not expand the money supply. And, the mechanics of the borrowing process being what they are, the way to do this is to borrow from the public.

What one might expect to have happened was for the Treasury to have met its borrowing requirements entirely in this way. The public was able to buy the necessary amount of securities. Each dollar the Treasury spent for tanks, guns, planes, and everything else increased the economy's income by a dollar, so those dollars not scooped up by the Treasury through taxes were there to be borrowed by the Treasury. However, to have gotten the public to voluntarily buy this vast amount of Treasury securities over these years would likely have required a rise in the interest rate substantially above anything that ever had been paid in the past. To avoid what would have been the huge annual interest charge produced by a very high interest rate on what was sure by war's end to be a very large debt and to bypass some possibly insoluble technical problems that would accompany this approach, the Treasury from the beginning of the war followed a policy of selling as much of its securities as it could to the public at a relatively low fixed interest rate and then filling the balance of its requirements at an even lower interest rate by turning to the banking system.

During the six-year period the Treasury covered $109 billion, or approximately 55 percent of its net borrowing, by sales to the public. (Again keep in mind that the public encompasses all purchasers other than the commercial banks and Federal Reserve Banks).* About $46.1 billion of this amount was in the form of sales of U.S. Savings Bonds to individuals. Patriotic appeals by war heroes and movie stars, Savings Bond campaigns, payroll savings plans, savings stamps for children, and every other device that showed promise (other than higher interest rates) was employed to produce this result.

The balance of the Treasury's borrowing had to be financed through the banking system. Subtracting the $109 billion borrowed from the public from its total net borrowing of $199 billion indicates that $90 billion was borrowed from the banks. If the purpose was to minimize the potential effect of this borrowing on the money supply, the monetary mechanics of the borrowing process suggest that this whole $90 billion should have been borrowed from the commercial banks. This, it is true, would have tended to add $90 billion to the money supply over this time period, but no more than that. On the other hand, to have borrowed the whole $90 billion from the Federal Reserve Banks would not only have tended to add $90 billion to the money supply as in the case of borrowing from the commercial banks, but it would in addition have added $90 billion to the commercial banks' legal reserves and, under the then existing reserve requirements, something like $75 billion to their excess reserves. In view of the fact that the total legal reserves of the member banks at the beginning of the war were less than $13 billion, the potential of any such addition to reserves is apparent: it would have given the commercial banks a practically unlimited capacity to expand private credit as soon as sufficient demand appeared with the return to a peacetime economy. Adding the huge increase in the money supply that would accompany

---

*The Treasury's actual net borrowing over the six-year period was $199 billion rather than $186 billion, and the 55 percent figure is based on this larger amount. In addition to the $186 billion total deficits of these six years, there was a buildup in the Treasury's deposit balances with the Federal Reserve Banks and the commercial banks of about $13 billion. That is, as of mid-1946 the sum of its balances in the banks was $13 billion higher than it had been six years earlier. This amount was allowed to run down to a more normal level once hostilities ended—in mid-1945 it had been almost $23 billion higher than five years earlier.

any such actual expansion of credit to the already greatly swollen war-time money supply would almost inevitably have led to an even more disastrous inflation than was actually suffered in the early post-war period.

The actual outcome was that the commercial bank holdings of U.S. Government securities increased by approximately $68 billion and the Federal Reserve Banks' holdings by approximately $22 billion during the six-year period. The total of $90 billion could not have been absorbed by the commercial banks alone unless there had been a sufficiently drastic cut in percentage reserve requirements to enable the existing amount of legal reserves held by the banks to meet the percentage reserve requirements against a vastly increased volume of deposits. Nothing like this was even considered by the authorities. What was done was to have the Federal Reserve Banks purchase, in part directly from the Treasury but mostly in the open market, an amount of U.S. Government securities that would provide the commercial banks with the additional legal reserves they needed to enable them to purchase the amount of securities the Treasury found it necessary to place with them. It turns out that $22 billion was the amount purchased by the Federal Reserve Banks to meet this need and to allow for other reserve-absorbing factors like the increase in the amount of currency in the hands of the public.

Although there were any number of other factors involved in the Treasury's wartime borrowing policy, the factors we have touched on here should give some understanding of why the $199 billion of Treasury net borrowing during the six-year period was divided as it was—$109, $68, and $22 billion among the public, commercial banks, and Federal Reserve Banks, respectively. Although other factors were at work here too, it turned out that this pattern of Treasury financing was accompanied by an increase in the money supply from about $39 billion in 1940 to $105 billion in 1946, more than a 2 1/2-fold expansion. In terms of growth rates, this six-year period may be compared with the following 25 years, ending in 1971, during which the money supply did little more than double. The rise in the money supply during the war years could have been held well below the $66 billion figure noted, or it could have been allowed to rise well above this. Treasury policies designed to lead to other distributions of its total borrowing among the three groups of borrowers could have produced these alternative results. To understand the mechanics of Treasury borrowing, bank reserves, and the money supply developed in this and the preceding chapter is to understand what the preceding statement says.

nine

THE CREATION AND CONTROL
OF MONEY: AN OVERVIEW

Our concern over the preceding
eight chapters has been limited to the definition of money and the
process by which money is created and its quantity controlled. This
final short chapter of Part II adds nothing really new to what has
preceded; it is designed primarily to provide an overview of the essentials of the process already covered in some detail. However, it does
take a different approach to these essentials, and in so doing it may
shed some additional light on that process. In any event, it does offer a
form of summary statement and some such statement is very desirable
to wrap up what has so far been covered.

With respect to a definition of money, there is a choice ranging from the narrow definition to successively broader definitions that include more and more of the things which, from the viewpoint of the narrow definition, are designated as near-moneys. But however money may be defined, it is easy enough for anyone to understand that the definition must include demand deposits as well as currency. Demand deposits clearly meet the requirement of general acceptability and, no matter how narrowly one may want to define money, he will not deny the label of money to anything that so qualifies. Nonetheless there are many people, both young and old, who can easily understand the preceding but still find it difficult to understand that the bulk of our money supply can exist as something no more tangible than bookkeeping entries in the records of commercial banks. There is the understandable feeling that something as powerful as money must have more substance than this.

Be this as it may, the fact is that not only is the bulk of our money supply made up of demand deposits but the very creation and destruction of money in our economy as in every other advanced economy is, in the main, a process reflected in nothing more substantial than increases and decreases in the total amount recorded to the credit of the public in those bank bookkeeping entries that we call demand deposits. As a practical matter, to control the money supply over time thus becomes essentially a matter of controlling the total amount the banks show in these entries.

Of course, the total money supply, by any definition, includes also the paper currency and coin that the public holds. This is an amount that grows larger over time in line with the growth of the public's demand deposit holdings as the public chooses to convert part of the increases in its demand deposit holdings into currency. There are, it is true, increases and decreases in the public's currency holdings from one week to the next, and even from one month to the next, that are nothing more than reflections of short-term, irregular withdrawals from and additions to the public's demand deposit balances. However, over the longer time period the public's currency holdings show change in only one direction, increase, and this long-term increase occurs not at the expense of but rather in combination with and as a result of the long-term increase in demand deposits.

Although there is, as always, more than one factor at work, the total number of dollars credited to the public in those bookkeeping entries we call demand deposits increases as it does primarily because the volume of the commercial banks' loans and security holdings increases as it does. When we look at the commercial banks as a group, we can say that it is lending and investing by the banks that gives rise to demand deposits; if we want to be at all correct, we should not say that it is demand deposits that give rise to the banks' lending and investing. Or, expressing it somewhat differently, we may say that an increase in deposits for the commercial banks as a group is derived from an increase in commercial bank credit, and not the other way around.

This is what lies behind one of the most basic ideas in the field of money and banking: *the commercial banks monetize debt.* The word "monetize" means to turn something that is not money into money. As the banks make loans and buy securities, they acquire the promises to pay of individuals, businesses, and governmental units. These IOUs are not in themselves money, as anyone would quickly learn if he tried to pay his phone bill by scribbling out a promissory note or if he tried to buy an automobile with U.S. Government securities—these things simply are not generally acceptable in payment. But even though one cannot pay his phone bill or buy a car with these IOUs, he can buy or pay for demand deposits with them. Anyone who is an acceptable credit risk can exchange his promise to pay $1,000 plus interest at some future date for a bank's promise to pay $1,000 immediately in the form of a demand deposit of that amount. His promise to pay, which is not money, has, so to speak, been transformed into the bank's promise to pay, which is money. The bank has monetized, or turned into money, the individual's debt. The same process occurs as the banks exchange their promises to pay in the form of demand deposits for the promises to pay in the form of securities issued by the federal government and others.

The reason that banks are not only willing but anxious to monetize credit in this way is probably clear: they acquire the promises to pay of others on which they collect interest income at rates as high as 18 percent per year. They give in exchange their promises to pay in the form of demand deposits on which they provide a limited amount of "free" services such as processing depositors' checks, providing depositors with monthly statements, and so forth, but on which they pay no interest explicitly. The spread between the average annual cost of the services provided per dollar of demand deposits and the average annual interest income earned per dollar of loans and security holdings is, in a very rough way, a measure of the gross profit earned per dollar of these earning assets during the year.

The banks, like any other type of business, are plainly there to make profits. And their profits tend to grow larger as the volume of their earning assets and their gross interest income grow larger. To secure an additional dollar of interest income is ordinarily to incur some addition to costs, but the addition to costs will generally be less than the addition to income, so there is a net addition to the total of profits. The profit motive is sufficiently strong to permit us to say that the banks will, in order to get those additional dollars of interest income, expand the total of their loans and security holdings to the limit that they can.

What sets this limit? As the banks increase their loans and security holdings, they increase their deposits. The larger the amount of deposits, the larger must be the banks' holdings of those assets they can use to meet the requests of depositors who may at any time choose to convert some or all of their deposits into currency. The only assets that fully qualify for this use are currency itself or its complete equivalent— namely, any asset that, if need be, all banks can simultaneously, immediately, and unconditionally convert into currency without any loss whatsoever. The amount of currency and such equivalent assets held by the banks thus sets an upper limit to the amount of deposits the banks are able to carry. Because additions to loans and security holdings mean additions to deposits, one may therefore also say that indirectly it is the amount of currency and equivalent assets which the banks hold that sets an upper limit to the amount of earning assets they are able to own.

If the commercial banks as a group were today able to secure additional currency or its equivalent without delay, without loss, and without limit in exchange for earning assets they hold, the above noted limit to their ability to acquire more earning assets would cease to exist. They could make loans and buy securities at will, create deposits in parallel fashion, and then, if that became necessary, convert some part of these earning assets into currency to meet the requests of any of those depositors who at any time chose to convert to currency.

However, the fact is that they are unable to do this. The only source of additional currency to the commercial banks as a group is the Federal Reserve Banks, and these banks are specifically obligated to issue paper money only in exchange for deposits the commercial banks have at the Federal Reserve Banks. This makes this specific asset the one and only commercial bank asset that is in the fullest sense the equivalent of currency for the banks as a group. This single fact—that the commercial banks as a group have no absolutely assured sources of additional currency beyond their deposit balances at the Federal Reserve Banks—is *in itself* sufficient to set a limit of kinds on the ability of the commercial banks to expand their earning assets. In such a world, each bank would voluntarily choose to maintain what it regarded as a "safe" ratio between the sum held in currency plus its equivalent and the total of its deposits simply as a matter of self-preservation or self-interest. Not to do so would be to face the certainty of having to close its doors and discontinue its operations the first time a few customers asked for currency in exchange for their demand deposits. To avoid such a calamity, each bank would limit the expansion of its loans and security holdings to the level permitted by the existing sum of its cash and equivalent assets and by the ratio it regarded as a safe ratio between such assets and deposits. Different banks would choose different ratios, and the limit to the amount of earning assets the banks as a group would hold on the basis of any given amount of currency and equivalent assets would be a somewhat variable thing; but there would still quite definitely be a limit.

What we have in actual practice, of course, is a system of legal reserve requirements that makes this limit a much less variable thing than it otherwise would be. The Federal Reserve specifies the minimum ratio the banks must maintain between legal reserves and deposits, and it counts as legal reserves only bank-held currency and the one other bank asset which we have seen is fully the equivalent of currency for the commercial banks as a group. By controlling the total amount of the banks' holdings of these two assets, the Federal Reserve is able to set a reasonably specific upper limit to the amount of deposits the banks may have entered on their books at any time. To set this upper limit is in turn to set an upper limit to the amount of earning assets the banks may own, since, again, increases in their earning assets involve increases in deposits, which call for increases in the amount of legal reserves the banks are required to hold.

How do the Federal Reserve Banks control the amount of legal reserves held by the commercial banks? Basically, the answer is by controlling the total of their own assets. Much as commercial banks create additional deposit liabilities by expanding their earning assets, so the Federal Reserve Banks create additional deposit liabilities and also Federal Reserve Notes (these being interchangeable liabilities for the Federal Reserve Banks) by expanding their assets. A similar parallel follows in the case of a decrease in the total of their assets.

Although the Federal Reserve Banks can increase or decrease the sum of their deposit liabilities and Federal Reserve Notes outstanding by increasing or decreasing the amount of any of the assets they hold, the asset best adapted for such use on either a large or small scale and on a continuing basis is their holdings of U.S. Government securities. Open market operations thus become the major tool through which the Federal Reserve Banks produce desired changes in the sum of their deposit and Federal Reserve Note liabilities.

Other tools exist, but they are less important. Thus, the Federal Reserve Banks also allow changes in the total of their deposit and Federal Reserve Note liabilities to come about at the initiative of the commercial banks. Under certain conditions, particular banks in need of additional reserves are able to secure them on a temporary basis by obtaining loans directly from the Federal Reserve Banks. Unlike lending, open market operations, when used to expand reserves, do not in any way tend to put the additional reserves into those banks whose reserve positions are such as to lead them to borrow, so the initial distribution among the banks of any addition to reserves varies according to the way in which it is brought about. However, the quantitative effect of the addition of $1 million to the Federal Reserve Banks' assets is the same whether that addition is in the form of loans or U.S. Government security holdings; other things being equal, each will add $1 million to the legal reserves of the commercial banks.

Finally, the Federal Reserve can directly influence the reserve position of the commercial banks without having the Federal Reserve Banks buy or sell assets and without changing the amount of their deposit and Federal Reserve Note liabilities. By raising or lowering percentage reserve requirements, the Federal Reserve can reclassify what were excess reserves into required reserves and vice versa without in the process changing the total of legal reserves held by the commercial banks. The limit to the amount of deposits the commercial banks may carry on their books depends not only on the dollar amount of legal reserves held but on the ratio that must be maintained between legal reserves and deposits. If the banks as a group are just meeting this ratio, a rise in percentage reserve requirements will force them to decrease the amount of their earning assets in order to decrease the amount of their deposits in order to make the existing amount of their legal reserves equal to the higher required percentage that such assets must then bear to deposits. However, apart from the exception presented by the case of changes in percentage reserve requirements, it is basically correct to say as we did above that the Federal Reserve Banks control the total of the earning assets and deposit liabilities of the commercial banks by controlling the amount of their own assets; in this way they control the total of their deposit liabilities and Federal Reserve Note liabilities, the two liabilities that to the commercial banks are two assets and (with a minor exception) the only assets that qualify as legal reserves.

Although it is basically correct to say this much, it is not correct to go on and say that the Federal Reserve can, for example, add $100 million to or subtract $100 million from the commercial banks' legal reserves by simply increasing or decreasing the assets of the Federal Reserve Banks by $100 million. This one-to-one ratio obtains only if all other things remain equal, and all other things do not remain equal. However, it is still permissible to say that over time the Federal Reserve Banks can add to or subtract from the commercial banks' reserves in whatever amount is desired by varying their total assets in whichever direction and by whatever amount is needed to offset or compensate for the other things that do not remain equal.

As we saw in the preceding chapter, one of these other things is the size of the Treasury balance at the Federal Reserve Banks. If the

Federal Reserve Banks increase their asset "U.S. Government securities" by $100 million at the same time that the Treasury balances at the Federal Reserve Banks are increased by a transfer of $100 million of Treasury deposits from commercial banks, the $100 million increase in Federal Reserve Bank assets, which would have added $100 million to commercial bank reserves if still other things had remained equal, will be exactly offset by the Treasury action and will leave commercial bank reserves unchanged. If the Federal Reserve's intention is to add $100 million to legal reserves, the Federal Reserve Banks would have to add $200 million to their assets under these circumstances. If on another occasion the Federal Reserve's intention had been to reduce commercial bank reserves by $100 million, the same Treasury transfer noted here would have produced that result in itself, other things remaining equal; the Federal Reserve could have achieved the desired result without the need for the Federal Reserve Banks to vary the total of their assets at all.

Another of the things that does not remain equal is the amount of currency held by the public. If the Federal Reserve Banks increase their asset "U.S. Government securities" by $100 million at the same time that the public is withdrawing $100 million in currency from the commercial banks, the $100 million increase in Federal Reserve Banks assets, which would have added $100 million to commercial bank reserves if still other things had remained equal, will be exactly offset by this action of the public and will leave commercial bank reserves unchanged. The balance of this paragraph parallels the preceding: it will take a $200 million addition to Federal Reserve Bank assets to effect a $100 million addition to commercial bank reserves under these specific circumstances.

There are still other factors that operate on commercial bank reserves in the same way as shifts in Treasury balances and deposits or withdrawals of currency by the public. The existence of these factors considerably complicates the Federal Reserve's task of controlling the amount of the commercial banks' reserves but does not vitiate that control. The complications are such that the Federal Reserve is not able to maintain anything like pinpoint control over the amount of the commercial banks' reserves from week to week, but they are not such as to deny the Federal Reserve the ability to assert its will over a longer period of time.

This brings us back to the question of why control over the commercial banks' legal reserves is so important: by controlling the legal reserves of the commercial banks, the Federal Reserve is able to control their profit-induced urge to make more loans and buy more securities or, in other words, to monetize more and more assets, a process that involves, at least initially, the addition of a dollar to the money supply for each dollar of assets monetized. However, unless the commercial banks have the legal reserves needed to meet the reserve requirement against the demand deposits they create as they monetize assets, the banks simply cannot monetize assets, much as they would like to do so.

Although this means that the Federal Reserve's ability to maintain control over the commercial banks' legal reserves gives them control over the money supply, it does not mean that the Federal Reserve can control the money supply as closely as it can control the banks' legal reserves. There are the slippages resulting from such factors as changes in the way that the public chooses to divide its holdings of deposits at commercial banks between demand and time deposits. By the narrow definition of money, a switch by the public from time to demand deposits involves that much of an increase in the money supply, even though it involves no change in the amount of the bank's legal reserves and no monetization of additional assets by the banks. Another factor of this kind is the changes in the amount of excess reserves the banks desire to hold. If they choose to operate with a lower ratio of excess reserves to deposits, they can monetize more assets, the previously desired excess reserves now being used to meet the reserve requirement against the deposits newly created as a result of the monetization of assets. Such newly created demand deposits constitute newly created money, and this newly created money comes into being without the banks' first securing additional legal reserves.

Slippages like these mean that even if the Federal Reserve could maintain pinpoint control over the commercial banks' reserve position, it still could not maintain an equally precise control over the money supply. The question of how closely the Federal Reserve is actually able to control the money supply is one to which not all monetary economists give the same answer. One source of difficulty in answering this question flows from the fact that the Federal Reserve does not by any means devote itself single-mindedly to maintaining some prescribed rate of growth in the money supply. For example, the fact that the money supply may grow at an unusually rapid rate at times is not necessarily indicative of an inability on the part of the Federal Reserve to prevent such a result—in deciding whether to ease or tighten the commercial banks' reserve position, the Federal Reserve considers much more than the effect of this change in reserve position on the money supply. As we will see in detail in Part III, before 1970 the effect on the money supply was definitely a secondary consideration; the major consideration was the effect of changes in the banks' reserve position on money market conditions, especially interest rates. Thus, if the Federal Reserve believed that a rise in interest rates which was under way should be checked, they would ease the banks' reserve position to the degree necessary to permit whatever increase in the money supply was needed to accomplish this objective. If in the process the money supply rose for a few months at an exceedingly fast rate, it indicated, not a loss of control over the money supply, but a voluntary relaxation of that control for the purpose of restraining the rise in interest rates, an objective the Federal Reserve presumably thought would contribute more to the stability of the economy than would a less rapid rate of growth in the money supply and a greater rise in interest rates.

Whether the Federal Reserve can better contribute to the stability of the economy by preventing sizable swings in interest rates or by permitting the money supply to grow at a steady rate over time has become a central, if not *the* central, question of monetary policy in recent years and is yet another question to which we will be giving attention in Part III. What is relevant in this overview is that the Federal Reserve authorities take whatever actions they do because they believe that these are the actions best designed to achieve the stabilization objective.

Since the actions themselves are undertaken to vary the commercial banks' reserve position and through this the economy's money supply, the justification for devoting chapter after chapter to the matter of the creation and control of the money supply may now be more apparent. Of course, if variations in the money supply did not actually affect the stability of the economy in one way or another, there would be little more interest in the supply of money than there is in the supply of tea. It is, however, because too much money may cause instability in the form of rising prices and because too little money may cause instability in the form of rising unemployment that the supply of money is a matter of unique importance. Although there are again considerable differences among economists' assessments of the way in which money exerts its impact and the degree of that impact, they all agree that the amount of money in the system is of some importance—a few say of overriding importance—to the stability of the system. It is to this very important question of the way in which, and the degree to which, changes in the supply of money affect income, output, employment, and the price level that Part III is devoted.

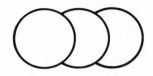

part three
THE INFLUENCE
OF MONEY
ON NATIONAL INCOME

ten

HOW MUCH
DOES MONEY MATTER?
A PREVIEW

The idea that variations in the money supply affect the economy's income, output, employment, and price level has been around in one form or another for at least a couple of hundred years. During most of this long span, changes in the money supply were regarded as a major determinant, if not *the* major determinant, of changes in the level of overall economic activity. At the extreme were those who blamed each instance of instability in the form of a rise in prices on too much money and each instance of instability in the form of recession or depression on too little money. However, during very recent history, the years from roughly the late thirties to the early sixties, changes in the money supply had come to be viewed as much less important in this regard than changes in things like the level of government expenditures and taxation and the government surplus or deficit. Most economists had come to focus on these fiscal variables to the almost complete disregard of the monetary variable. Then over the past decade money staged an impressive comeback—a good number of economists came around to the belief that money is by no means so unimportant as they had generally believed over the preceding several decades. Some others held fast to what was essentially the earlier view, and still others found themselves somewhere in the middle ground.

As this debate broke wide open in the late sixties, it came to be expressed in terms of the question: "How much does money matter?" And various economists found themselves taking positions along a spectrum from "money doesn't matter" to "money matters some" to "money matters much" to "money matters most" to "money alone matters." Few economists today have such singleminded convictions on this question as to maintain an unrelaxed grip on positions they may have once held at one extreme or the other, but the positions in between the extremes are still divergent enough to provide the basis for what probably has been the liveliest and at times the most heated debate in economics in the last twenty years. Although this debate has so far generated more heat than light, the heat is by no means out of proportion to the importance of the issue. The question here involves nothing less than the usefulness of fiscal and monetary policy in the effort to maintain stability in the economy, and there is probably no more practical issue in the whole area of public policy economics. While economists will continue to grapple with and disagree vehemently over just how much money matters, they will also continue to agree just as strongly that *it matters very much how much money matters.*

TWO VIEWS OF MONEY

Most people have never even heard of monetarism and Keynesianism, terms commonly used to designate the opposing sides in this debate over how much money matters. However, whether or not he has ever read a single page on the subject, everyone feels that he knows something about money, and from what he knows, a debate over whether money matters makes no more sense than a debate over whether breathing matters. Obviously money matters, and it matters a great deal—just try to get along for very long in this world without any! From this particular point of view, there is indeed hardly room for debate, but this is the narrow point of view, which sees money as nothing more than the thing in terms of which everyday buying and selling transactions are mediated by each of us. This is the view taken in Chapter 1, where the focus was on money as a medium of exchange, as the lubricant that keeps the wheels of business and commerce turning smoothly. On the other hand, when one raises the question of how much money matters, his point of view is a much broader one. It accepts without debate that money is not merely important but indispensable in its role as a medium of exchange, but it then passes on to consider how important money is as a determinant of the level at which the economy as a whole operates—in other words, on the extent to which the amount of money in the economy affects the aggregate amount of goods and services produced, the level of employment, interest rates, prices, and other basic variables whose values are indicative of the overall performance of the economy.

An economist who once took the extreme position that money doesn't matter (and there seem to be almost none at this extreme any more) was in no sense suggesting that the economy could get along without money. Neither he nor anybody else denies the conclusion we reached in Chapter 1, that the wheels of business would surely grind to an almost complete halt if there were no money. Essentially what this economist was saying is that the changes in the supply of money from quarter to quarter and year to year do not matter so far as such things as the economy's level of output or of employment are concerned. Money does not matter in the sense that its amount is held to be without influence on basic variables such as these.

An economist who takes the extreme position that only money matters (and there may be a few of these today) says the very opposite, of course. His position is that, within the limits of the economy's productive capacity, it is the behavior of the money supply that determines whether the economy produces at that capacity level or falls short of it. More precisely, as the economy's productive capacity grows over time through growth of its labor force and capital stock and improvements in technology, it is the rate of growth of the money supply, according to this economist, that will determine whether actual employment grows in line with the growth in the labor force and whether actual output grows in line with the growth in capacity output.

It is not hard to see that an economist may back some distance away from one extreme and still find plenty of room to disagree with another economist who has backed some distance away from the opposite extreme. It is between the extremes that we find most today— they are located at positions designated by signs reading "money matters some," "money matters much," and "money matters most." Each has arrived at the position he supports through more or less intensive study of the considerable body of theoretical and empirical evidence that has accumulated on the issue over the years, especially recent years.

From the layman's point of view, a considerable body of evidence should be all that is required to resolve the question one way or the other once and for all. If all the evidence pointed in one direction or the other, this might be possible. But, as we will see later, there is some evidence that points in one direction, some in the other; and the balance, which probably makes up the largest part, seems to point in one direction or the other depending on how the individual investigator interprets it. The evidence does not speak unambiguously for itself, and there is no way, at least so far, of deciding which of the alternative interpretations of the evidence is the correct one and thus no way of thereby resolving the question. Nor is it likely, given the present and prospective states of our knowledge, that the basic differences that now exist among economists on this question will disappear in the very near future. Continuing research may remove some of the sharpness from the differences, but the underlying differences are likely to be with us for years to come.

MONEY AND SPENDING

While these differences may persist, agreements also are found, but they are at a rather superficial level. It is agreed that how little or how much money matters depends on how little or how much the economy's *spending for goods and services* is affected by changes in the supply of money. Unless changes in the money supply in some way, directly or indirectly, affect the flow of spending for goods and services, there would appear to be no way for changes in the money supply to affect in turn the level of output, employment, and prices, and, as we have seen, it is the extent to which changes in the money supply affect these variables that determines how much or how little money matters. One can, of course, visualize exceptions to this statement. For example, it is conceivable that a mere announcement by the Federal Reserve that the money supply has been increasing at an unusually rapid rate over the last few months may lead some businessmen operating with abnormally low inventories to hire more workers and increase the level of their output in the expectation that an increase in the money supply at this rate will soon mean an increase in their sales, even though no actual increase has yet occurred. However, if the increase in the money supply does not lead to an actual increase in spending, the expected increase in sales will not be realized, and these businessmen will find themselves cutting back output and employment to the previous level or perhaps temporarily below that level in order to work off what they now view as abnormally high inventories. If changes in the money supply are to exert a lasting effect on output, employment, and prices, it is thus essentially correct to say that this effect will be realized only to the extent that changes in the money supply actually generate changes in spending.

Most economists today will agree with this as a basically correct but also rather trivial observation. The substantive issue is one of ascertaining the way in which changes in the money supply may give rise to changes in spending and whether there is anything like a systematic relationship exhibited by the changes in the money supply and the changes in spending that occur over time. The first is a question of economic theory, for it seeks to explain why increases or decreases in the public's money balances may bring about changes in the public's spending; the second is a question of the empirical record, for it looks at the actual figures on changes in the money supply and changes in spending in the effort to detect whether a significant relationship actually exists and, if it does, whether it is one in which the changes in the money supply appear to have been the cause of the changes in spending or whether the changes in spending appear to have been the cause of the changes in the money supply.

With regard to the most basic question of the way in which changes in the money supply may affect the level of spending, the answer is not nearly as apparent as some people seem to believe. It certainly cannot be meaningfully answered, as some journalists and businessmen try to do, by merely saying that "people will spend more if they have more money." Actually, some of those who say precisely this do not really mean what they are saying. Frequently what they mean is that people will spend more if they have more *income.* Because income is received in the form of money, there is a quite general and understandable tendency to say that people have more money to spend when income rises, even though a look at the record will show that there is at times a decline in the amount of money held at the same time that there is a rise in the level of income. For example, from 1959 to 1960, disposable personal income increased from $337.3 to $350.0 billion, and personal consumption spending increased from $311.2 to $325.2 billion; but the amount of money held by households decreased from $66.2 to $65.0 billion. Therefore, anyone who says that personal consumption spending rose in 1960 over 1959 because households had more money to spend would be absolutely wrong, assuming he employs the conventional definition of money as holdings of demand deposits and currency. On the other hand, he would not necessarily be right but he would not be clearly wrong if he says that personal consumption spending rose in 1960 over 1959 because people had more disposable income in 1960 than in 1959.

Although the 1959–60 experience shows that there is no "law" that changes in the money supply and in spending must be in the same direction, the overall record of experience actually shows few year-to-year changes and not even very many quarter-to-quarter changes in which the money supply and spending changed in opposite directions. This is true whether we take only a part of the economy as in the illustration (that is, spending by persons and the amount of money held by them) or whether we take the economy as a whole (that is, spending by all sectors and the amount of money held by all sectors, which equals the economy's total money supply). However, to recognize the fact that the level of spending and the supply of money do ordinarily change in the same direction does not permit us to accept as a fact that "people will *ordinarily* spend more if they have more money," a qualified version of the stronger statement noted above. The observation that there is typically a parallel movement in the two variables does not by itself tell us that it is more money which is the cause of more spending. It may be just the other way around: more money may be the result of more spending, and more spending in turn may be the result of other forces whose magnitudes are essentially unaffected even indirectly by changes in the money supply.

CAUSE AND EFFECT

If the idea that more money will cause more spending strikes one as eminently reasonable, the idea that more spending will cause more money is likely to strike him in the opposite way. However, anyone who has some understanding of the way that changes in the money supply actually come about can see that the money supply may indeed vary as it does, at least in part, as a result of variations in spending.

As we saw in Part I, if the commercial banks have excess reserves (over and above the amount they wish to hold), they will stand ready to expand the amount of their loans to credit-worthy business and other types of borrowers. Suppose, for the sake of illustration, that consumers step up their spending sharply, perhaps due to a decided improvement in the economic outlook that ends the fear many consumers may have had for the security of their jobs and their incomes. Goods start to move off the shelves of the stores more rapidly, larger orders are placed with manufacturers, and many of the unemployed are able to find jobs. As the overall tempo of business activity picks up, the banks are faced with an increase in the demand for loans. Consumers may borrow directly from the banks to finance the purchase of major items like automobiles and may run up their charge account balances at stores to purchase other items. To carry these balances and perhaps to finance an increase in inventories, retailers too will seek to borrow more from the banks. In a similar way, additional loan demand can be expected to appear at earlier stages in the production process—wholesalers, manufacturers, raw material producers. However, what is specifically relevant here is the fact that there is an increase in the money supply to the extent that the banks satisfy the additional loan demand by drawing down their excess reserves. The same result will follow if the banks do not initially have excess reserves but the Federal Reserve authorities conclude that an increase in the money supply is warranted under the circumstances and accordingly provide the banks with the additional reserves needed to meet the expanded loan demand.

Whether the banks already have the necessary reserves or the Federal Reserve provides them, the supply of money will increase in this case as a result of an increase in the level of spending. The rise in spending came first; the rise in the money supply followed. Consumers and businesses initially decided to spend more in the absence of any change at all in the amount of money they held; the case was not one in which an increase in the amount of money they were holding led them to increase their spending.

One may, of course, argue, as do the monetarists, that in the absence of an expansion of the money supply such an increase in spending, however initiated, would be pulled up short before it had gone very far. A greater stock of money, they say, is needed to mediate the larger dollar volume of transactions involved in the higher level of spending—an inability of the banks to provide this larger stock of money would mean that an expansion of spending of a scope that otherwise could have occurred will be ruled out by a shortage of money.

From this argument of the monetarists, it is a short step to the reinstatement of the supply of money as the prime mover in the system. In other words, the monetarists may grant that increases in spending may at times be initiated by forces unrelated to the size of the money supply. However, by holding that such rises in spending cannot be sustained without an appropriate expansion of the money supply, they in effect reassert the primacy of the stock of money. They thus seem to have it both ways. An increase in spending initiated by an increase in the money supply carries with it the wherewithal to mediate the greater volume of transactions that are involved; on the other hand, an increase in spending initiated by any other force can be sustained only if it is followed by the increase in the supply of money required to mediate the greater volume of transactions.

The Keynesians will not accept this in such bald form. As they put it, an increase in spending initiated, for example, by the more optimistic expectations of consumers does not necessarily require for its maintenance an expansion of the money supply. The existing money supply may well be adequate to the task. One of the arguments that lies behind this is that the existing money supply can be made to work harder, which is to say that each dollar of the money supply can be made to mediate a larger number of dollars of transactions per quarter and per year than was previously the case. One way to bring this about is to give holders of money an incentive to be more economical in their use of money balances—that is, to cause them to seek ways to handle any given amount of transactions with smaller money balances, which means that, overall, an existing total of money balances can be made to handle a greater amount of transactions.

Such an incentive is provided by the general rise in interest rates that will occur as the increase in loan demand induced by the higher level of spending comes up against the inability of the commercial banks to increase their total earning assets and deposits because the level is already at the upper limit set by the existing amount of their legal reserves. The public's holdings of demand deposits and currency always involve a cost to the public in the form of the interest that could have been earned by switching from money to some interest-bearing asset. The higher are interest rates, the greater is the cost per dollar of money held; therefore, the higher are interest rates, the stronger is the incentive for holders of money to pare down their balances. Thus, a firm that previously maintained an average balance of $1 million in its checking account may now find it worthwhile to reduce this to $0.95 million, despite the inconvenience and even some extra cost involved in the more careful management of cash flow that this requires; doing this releases $0.05 million on which the higher interest rate that can now be earned more than compensates for the headaches and slight extra cost. The firm's lending of this $0.05 million does not increase the money supply by a single dollar, but it does mean that the original $1 million now does more work or mediates more transactions than it did before. If the firm now manages to handle the same volume of transactions with $0.95 million that it previously was using $1.0 million to handle, and if the $0.05 million it releases is used as efficiently as the $0.95 million it retains, the $1 million is now doing about 5 1/4 percent more work than previously.

If in general holders of sizable money balances respond in this way, it follows that an increase in spending unaccompanied by an increase in the money supply does not have to be choked off by a lack of money to mediate the higher level of transactions. The extra money needed is *in effect* provided by the existing money supply's more rapid turnover, which is induced by the rise in interest rates. There presumably is a limit to how far this process can go—no matter how high interest rates may rise and no matter how strong the incentive to economize on the size of one's money balance may become, it remains that $1 of money cannot be transferred from one holder to another fast enough to handle an unlimited dollar volume of transactions per year. There are also other aspects of this process that demand attention. For one, rising interest rates can provide an incentive for more economical use of existing money balances, which in turn can provide the means for handling the higher level of spending, but rising interest may also have an adverse effect on spending itself by discouraging some firms and individuals from borrowing to finance additional spending. We will return to aspects like these in later chapters, examining in detail what has been merely mentioned here.

However, at this point we have introduced the minimum needed for the purposes of the present preview—namely, the identification of the basis for the monetarist argument that it is changes in the money supply which underlie appreciable expansions in the economy's spending and the basis for the Keynesian argument that an existing money supply is capable of supporting an appreciable expansion of the economy's spending initiated by other forces. The closer the monetarist position is to being the correct position, the more does money matter; the closer the Keynesian position is to being the correct position, the less does money matter. The question of overriding importance is which side is closer to being correct, and this is merely another way of asking the same question with which we started: How much does money matter?

Although this preview has now provided some understanding of the meaning of this question, it has done nothing toward providing an answer. This question is as difficult as it is important, and there is no answer that is both brief and meaningful at the same time. The remaining chapters of Part III will be concerned either directly or indirectly with working toward an answer to this most basic question of monetary economics.

eleven

INCOME AND SPENDING

How much money matters depends on how much it affects the economy's spending, because it is through spending that money affects the level of income, output, employment, and prices. In contrast to the sharp controversy between Keynesians and monetarists over what causes changes in spending, there is a good deal of agreement among them as to the way that changes in spending, once they occur, lead to changes in income, output, employment, and the price level. But while this is a less controversial area among economists, it is one that can be perplexing to laymen. One source of trouble is that laymen use these terms in loose and contradictory ways and do not fit them into the kind of consistent framework that is used by all economists.

In this chapter we will establish the briefest possible kind of framework through which we can approach the way that money may influence the levels of spending, income, and output. We will see that in the way these terms are used in such a framework, income, output, and spending (with qualifications to be noted) are all equal-sized dollar amounts in any time period: for every dollar of spending, there is a dollar of income, and for every dollar of spending or every dollar of income, there is a dollar's worth of output. We will look at the way a change in the dollar value of output may be divided between a change in physical output and in the price per unit at which that output sells. We will look at why rising prices mean corresponding rises in income and dispose of the fallacy that buyers as a group can be priced out of the market by inflation. Last, we will look at the relationship between changes in output and changes in employment. Then in the following chapter we will be ready to begin to see the way that money affects spending, income, and output in terms of the basic framework put together in this chapter.

INCOME, OUTPUT, AND SPENDING

Consider first these three terms, the first and last of which are familiar to almost everyone through firsthand experience. According to the common meaning of these words, almost everyone has some income from one or more sources—for example, wage or salary income from his labor, interest income from his savings account, Social Security income from the government, dividend income from his stock holdings; and almost everyone does some spending for various things ranging from the commonplace, like food and clothing, to the exotic, like a South Pacific cruise. For the nation as a whole, total income then appears to most people to be merely the sum of the separate incomes of each of us from all sources, and total spending appears to be a similar collective total for all of us. In the case of output, one of the common meanings is that it is the production that flows out of factories, mines, farms, and offices. For the nation as a whole, output then appears to most people as the total value of everything produced in these places.

Assume that someone unversed in these matters were to set out on his own to estimate the economy's income, output, and spending for a particular time period. He would very quickly find that such loose meanings as those given above are virtually worthless to him and that he must define each term with great care if the resulting totals are to have meaning in themselves and to have meaning to others. Because these terms can be defined in any number of ways, some of what one person may choose to include as income another may choose to exclude. The same problem arises in the case of the nation's total output and in the case of its total spending. Precise definitions are the first order of business.

Once the content of these terms has been clearly specified, our accountant would be able to turn to the task of estimating the dollar amount of each for the U.S. economy. Sooner or later in the course of laboring over what would quickly begin to look like an impossible task, he would make a very important discovery: his estimate for the value of the economy's output in any time period can be obtained most effectively by estimating for that time period the total amount of spending for all those goods and services that are by his definition counted as part of that output. He will find that the value of the amount of these goods produced during the period and the amount of spending for them will differ only by the value of any change in inventories. If there is an increase in inventories during any time period, this means that spending has fallen short of the value of output; the addition to inventories must be added to spending to get the correct figure for the value of output. If there is a decrease in inventories during any time period, spending has exceeded the value of output; the decrease in inventories must be subtracted from spending to get the correct figure for the value of output. The accountant would also discover in time that the figure obtained in this way for the value of the economy's output may be obtained alternatively by estimating the total amount of income generated specifically in the course of producing that total output. He would, in other words, find that he can arrive at his objective, an estimate of the value of the economy's output, through an approach either from the side of spending or from the side of income.

He could then write the relationship that exists among the values for income, output, and spending in any time period as the following identity:

| Amount of income generated by the production of goods and services | $\equiv$ | Market value of the economy's output of goods and services | $\equiv$ | Amount of spending on goods and services plus change in business inventories |

A simple illustration will bring out the logic of this identity. From the huge total for the market value of the economy's output of goods and services in any time period, let us pick out the amount of 50 cents, which is the value of a shoe shine provided by a boy working on the street. Corresponding to this unit of output will be spending of 50 cents by the person who had his shoes shined—this, of course, is looking at the value of the unit of output from the spending side. Also corresponding to this unit of output will be income of 50 cents to the shoe shine boy, which, of course, is looking at this unit of output from the income side. Thus, in a very loose way, we may say that corresponding to output with a market value of 50 cents is found spending of that amount and income of that amount. However, even in this simplest possible illustration, it is not quite correct to say that all of the 50 cents is income to the shoe shine boy in the sense of wages earned by his labor or profit earned by his entrepreneurship. Perhaps 2 cents will be needed to cover the shoe polish and other materials used up, but this then passes on to his supplier and back through the production process to become eventually 2 cents of wage, profit, and related income to others. Perhaps the shoe shine boy must pay sales tax equal to 4 percent of his sales to the state; then 2 cents of the 50 cents passes on to become a receipt (income) of government. If he has business debt, maybe he needs something like 1 cent of every 50 cents of receipts at his existing business volume to cover the interest on his debt; this 1 cent then passes on to become income of his creditor. He also should make allowance for wear and tear on his brushes and shoe shine stand, say equal to 1 cent per unit of output; this is a part of his gross income that he retains and sets aside in a depreciation reserve to replace his capital equipment when it wears out. However, after allowance for all such factors, we still find that the output of one shoe shine at a market value of 50 cents generates 50 cents of income as that term is defined in this accounting system.

In general, what is true of this one isolated unit of output is true for the economy's total output. As defined by the Department of Commerce, this total, known as *gross national product*, or GNP, was $1,294.9 billion for 1973. For every dollar in this economy-wide total we find a dollar of income in one or another of the forms listed on the left-hand side of Table 11–1. For every dollar in this total, we also find a dollar of inventory change or a dollar of spending in one or another of the forms listed on the right-hand side of the table. The totals on the two sides are the same, as they both measure the same thing: the value of the economy's output. On the left is a breakdown of all the income generated in the course of producing that output, and on the right is a breakdown of all of the spending for that output plus the change in inventories that picks up the output to which there corresponds no sale to a final purchaser. Where it will cause no confusion we will hereafter simplify in referring to the total on the right by describing it merely as

TABLE 11–1

GROSS NATIONAL INCOME AND GROSS NATIONAL SPENDING
1973 (in billions of dollars)

Compensation of employees			Personal consumption expenditures	805.2
Wages and salaries	691.6			
Supplements to wages and salaries	94.4		Gross private domestic investment	209.4
			Structures and producers'	
Proprietors' income		96.1	durable equipment	194.0
			Change in business inventories	15.4
Rental income of persons		26.1		
			Government purchases of goods and services	276.4
Net interest		52.3		
			Net exports of goods and services	3.9
Corporate profits		105.1	Exports of goods and services	100.4
			Imports of goods and services	96.4
National Income		1,065.6		
Indirect business taxes		119.2		
Capital consumption allowances		110.8		
Other items		−0.7	Gross National Spending plus	
			Change in Inventories	1,294.9
Gross National Income		1,294.9		

the total of spending without noting in every case that it is actually this total adjusted upward or downward as needed to allow for the change in inventories.

We next look briefly at the content of the major components on the spending side and then do the same on the income side.

SPENDING FLOWS

"Personal consumption expenditures" include all spending by persons on currently produced goods, ranging from durables like automobiles, eyeglasses, and television sets to nondurables like shirts, wine, magazines, bread, and toothpaste. Also included are expenditures for all kinds of services including those provided by taxi drivers, lawyers, electric and gas utilities, auto repair shops, and shoe shine boys. It is standard practice to designate the total of these expenditures as C.

"Gross private domestic investment" is the term used for that part of the total accounted for by business. Here is included business spending for currently produced machinery, equipment, and tools and also for all new construction. Business spending for such things is spending to acquire durable assets that are used up over the years in the course of production. However, in the usual sense we do not think of these as purchases of things that business resells, despite the fact that they are over time incorporated in the things that business produces and sells. On the other hand, there is also a huge amount of spending by business for things that are currently incorporated into whatever the firm produces and in this way are thought of as spending by business for things that it resells. All such spending by business is excluded from the total described as gross private domestic investment. Thus, we do not count the spending by a winery for grapes or for any other "raw material" as part of total spending. We do want to count whatever part of the year's production of grapes that goes into wine as part of that year's output, but we will do so when we include spending by persons for wine. Therefore, to count this as part of spending by the winery would be to count the same product twice. In the same way, we do not count a department store's purchase of shirts as part of the spending total. This portion of the economy's production will be counted when we include spending by persons as they purchase these shirts from the store. However, at this point comes in the need to take account of inventory changes. If the winery has more wine, grapes, or other materials on hand at the end of this year than at the end of last year, that is an amount of this year's output that will not be included in spending by consumers and must be included under the heading of a change in inventories or it will not be included at all. In the same way, if the department store has more shirts on hand at the end of this year than at the end of last year, that reflects an amount of the year's goods produced but not sold to consumers and therefore an amount that has to be shown as a change in inventories in order that it be shown at all. The total for investment, which is the sum of business spending for durable equipment and construction and the change in inventories, is designated by the letter I.

"Government purchases of goods and services" include all expenditures by federal, state, and local government in exchange for which a currently produced good or service is supplied. Spending for goods ranging from Skylab to paper clips, for services of those ranging from state governors to street cleaners are included, the value of the output corresponding to each such expenditure being measured by the amount spent for it. However, not included in this government spending total are all government transfer payments—e.g., unemployment compensation, Medicare payments, and Social Security benefits. Because no current production matches payments of these kinds, they cannot be included in a spending total that is designed to be a measure of the value of the economy's output of goods and services. To designate the total of government spending that is included—namely, purchases of goods and services—the letter G is used.

The above three components include all spending originating with domestic purchasers. All such purchasers may be classified as either persons, businesses, or governmental units. However, in a country that has commerce with other countries, the sum of $C + I + G$ will not be equal to the value of the economy's output. If the economy has exported more goods and services than it has imported, the sum of $C + I + G$ will understate its total output; in the opposite case, it will overstate its total output. Accordingly, to allow for the influence of imports and exports requires that we add to the other three spending streams the difference between exports and imports, or net exports, which may be designated as X_n. This will, of course, be negative if imports exceed exports. We now have the fourth component found on the spending side of Table 11–1. In terms of symbols, we have $C + I + G + X_n$ as equal to total spending plus the change in inventories, or, what is the same thing, as equal to GNP.

INCOME FLOWS

Turning to the income side, we find the first five items have a common characteristic: they are returns for productive services supplied or returns to the so-called factors of production. The first, "Compensation of employees," which year after year makes up in the neighborhood of two-thirds of the gross national income, includes all wages and salaries paid by business and government as well as supplements like contributions for social insurance and for private pension and health programs. "Proprietors' income" is income of self-employed persons. This is largely a return to the labor provided by these persons within their own businesses, but it also includes a return on real assets held within these businesses and a profit element. As it is defined by the Department of Commerce, "Rental income of persons" is made up mostly of an estimate of the rental value of the housing that persons own. "Net interest" is the amount of interest paid by business after deducting the amount of interest received by business; it is an amount that flows to persons and is a return to them for the provision of money capital to business so that business can acquire plant and equipment. "Corporate profits" are the net earnings of all corporations before taxes. Since all payments by corporations of wages and salaries, interest, and other charges have already been allowed for, this remaining amount is altogether profits and is viewed simply as the return to entrepreneurship. The sum of these first five items is equal to *national income*, according to the formal definition of that term. To move from national income to the gross national income total at the bottom requires the addition of the several other items listed.

All the goods and services included on the spending side are valued at the prices actually paid for them by purchasers. An automobile that otherwise would sell for $4,000 is included not at $4,000 but at $4,200 if it is subject to a 5 percent sales tax. This and all the other taxes included indirectly in the prices of goods and services are picked up under the heading of "Indirect business taxes."

"Capital consumption allowances" are as much a cost to business of producing goods and services as are business payments of wages and salaries, interest, or indirect taxes. Business does not pay this amount out to persons or to government as it does wages and salaries, interest, or taxes, but in effect sets it aside to be used for replacement of plant and equipment that are gradually consumed in the course of producing goods and services.

Some minor items have been combined here under the heading "Other items" and involve details that may be skipped over for purposes of this rough sketch.

The shoe shine illustration above showed on the spending side 50 cents, which we now note would appear as part of *C*, and 50 cents on the income side, which would in large part be made up of proprietors' income, with the balance perhaps made up of indirect taxes, net interest, and capital consumption allowances. The $1,294.9 billion on the spending side of the account for the whole United States for the year 1973 includes shoe shines and all other consumer purchases under

C plus other purchases under I, G, and X_n; the \$1,294.9 billion on the income side would include the income generated by all the shoe shines during the year and by the production of all the other goods found under C, I, G, and X_n.

THE FOSTER-CATCHINGS FALLACY

Because the national income statisticians find the same total on the spending side and on the income side (apart from a small statistical discrepancy) does not mean that they have discovered any economic principle; what they have is nothing more than an identity. Like any other identity—for example, the balance sheet identity first introduced in Chapter 2, Assets $\equiv$ Liabilities + Net worth—it is something that is true by the definitions given to the terms and as such is beyond refutation; it is unlike an economic theory, which, by the fact that it is a theory, is not necessarily true and is at least potentially subject to refutation. Furthermore, just as the balance sheet identity holds true for every possible date—March 15, 1972, December 31, 1973, etc.—for which a balance sheet might be prepared, so the present identity holds true for every possible time period—the first quarter of 1971, the whole year of 1972, the last half of 1973, etc.—for which one might measure the flow of income and the flow of spending.

No matter how high or low the actual total of income and no matter how high or low the actual total of spending may be in any period, we know that these two sides (apart from estimating errors) must display the identical total. To know this, however, is not to know why the total for any time period was what it was or why the total changes as it does from one period to the next. For this we need theory, and it is here that we find the rival explanations described as Keynesianism and monetarism.

Although the identity in itself is completely powerless to explain the period by period changes in the magnitude found on either side, it is still important in this connection because to understand the identity is sufficient to prevent one from accepting explanations that are basically fallacious at the outset. This idea has now been put to rest, perhaps permanently, but various economists in the past, especially two Americans, W. T. Foster and W. Catchings, during the 1920s, argued that fluctuations in the economy's level of output were due to an inherent or built-in "flaw in our price system." They held that the system at times fails to generate sufficient income to enable income recipients to purchase the full amount of goods produced at prices that provide firms with the minimum profit margins needed to keep them producing.

In essence, the flaw is supposedly found in the undeniable fact that profits on any given amount of output are not paid out in the process of producing that output. Profits are not paid until realized, and they cannot be realized as goods are in the process of production, only when goods reach the end of the process and pass into the hands of buyers. On the other hand, other types of income, the most important of which are wages and salaries, are paid out in the very process of producing output. Therefore, it would appear that the amount of income generated in the process of production falls short of the cost of production, here including as part of the cost of production the minimum profit margin required to make it worthwhile for firms to maintain production.

This argument has a grain of truth if one looks at output for only one short period of time. However, since the process goes on period after period, it may be seen that the incomes earned in a current period include incomes like wages and salaries, which arise from goods in process of production during that period, as well as profits, which are realized in that period on goods that were in the process of production in the preceding period. In the simplest case, if we think of the economy operating at an unchanged level of output period after period, it may be apparent that the sum of incomes earned, including profits, in each period will be equal to the cost of production of the period's output, although the profits realized in each period, whether paid out as dividends or retained within firms, may be profits actually derived from goods in process of production in the preceding period but not finished and sold until the current period. This precise matching of income earned in the course of production for each period with the cost of production of the economy's output for that period is subject to some qualification in the more involved and more realistic case in which the economy's level of output is expanding from one period to the next, but it is a minor qualification and not so serious as to be called a "flaw" in the system.

If we pass over this minor qualification, we may say with virtually complete accuracy that an expanding economy generates sufficient income to enable the recipients of this income to purchase the economy's expanding output at prices that afford profit margins adequate to make firms go on producing more output. The fact that the level of output drops off at times cannot be explained adequately in terms of the Foster-Catchings alleged "flaw" in the system. The explanation, in other words, is not to be found in any internal inconsistency or contradiction in the system that somehow leads to a production of goods without a corresponding generation of income.

In their attempts to explain the fluctuations in the economy's output, all economists today, whether Keynesian or monetarist, take as their point of departure that the amount of income generated in each time period is equal to the value of the economy's output for that time period, recognizing at the same time that this is subject to minor qualification. Doing this amounts in effect to the rejection of the Foster-Catchings thesis and the acceptance of the income-output branch of the three-part identity set forth above. All economists also take as their point of departure the other branch of the same three-part identity, that between the amount of the economy's spending and the value of its output. It is only in going beyond this identity—in their explanations of why the aggregate amount of goods and services produced varies as it does over time—that the Keynesians and monetarists go their different ways. We will be pursuing those differences later, but we have tried in this section to make clear a matter over which there is no difference today: the identity between the flow of income and the flow of output and between the flow of output and the flow of spending.

OUTPUT AND PRICES

From the identity that exists between income, output, and spending in any time period, it follows that from one time period to the next all these items will undergo the same change in amount. However, when one speaks of changes from one time period to the next, it is important to keep in mind that "output" is merely a short form for the more exact form, "market value of output." If spending has risen by 10 percent from one year to the next, the value of output must also have risen by 10 percent, and so too the level of income must have risen by 10 percent. However, the *physical* amount of goods and services produced will have risen by 10 percent only if the average of the prices of all these goods and services has remained unchanged between the two years in question. Because this rarely occurs, what we typically find is a difference between the percentage increase in the market value of the economy's output and the percentage increase in the physical amount of that output, and typically the former percentage exceeds the latter. Every year from 1949 to 1974 has shown a positive percentage change in the market value of output, but in every one of these years the percentage change in the physical amount of output has been smaller than the percentage change in the market value of output. This is nothing more than another way of saying that in every one of these years the price level of the goods and services included in GNP has risen.

In some years a positive percentage change in the value of output will be accompanied by a negative percentage change in the physical amount of output. For example, total spending for GNP rose from $930.3 billion in 1969 to $976.4 billion in 1970, or 5 percent, while the index number that measures the average change in prices of all the goods and services in GNP rose by 5.5 percent. If a person increases his spending for beer from $100 in one year to $105 in the following year, or by 5 percent, he will, of course, get less beer in the second year than in the first if the price of beer rises by anything more than 5 percent. And this is what happened, on the average, in the case of all goods and services from 1969 to 1970: the increase in the value of output of 5 percent was accompanied by a decrease in the physical amount of output as the average price per unit of this output showed an increase of 5.5 percent. In an even more recent example, total spending for GNP at an annual rate rose from $1,337.5 billion in the fourth quarter of 1973 to $1,352.2 billion in the first quarter of 1974, or at a 4.4 percent annual rate, while the price index for GNP rose at a 10.4 percent annual rate. The increase in the value of output was here again accompanied by a decrease in the physical amount of output.

In very rare instances one also finds the opposite case of a negative percentage change in the value of output being accompanied by a positive percentage change in the physical amount of output. From 1948 to 1949 the value of output declined from $257.6 billion to $256.5 billion, or by less than 1/2 of 1 percent. However, at the same time, the price level fell by a little more than 1/2 of 1 percent, which means that there was a slight positive percentage increase in the physical amount of output.

These are plainly infrequent cases. The typical case is one in which there is a rise in spending and therefore in the value of output and in which this rise is accompanied by a smaller relative rise in the physical amount of output. The practical question then asked is this: To what extent will a given increase in spending and in the value of output be accompanied by an increase in output and to what extent by an increase in the price level? The short answer to what is actually a very large question is that it depends on whether that increase in spending occurs with the economy operating far below its productive capacity, at this capacity, or somewhere in between these extremes. The fact that the 7.7 percent increase in spending which occurred from 1961 to 1962 was accompanied by a 6.6 percent increase in physical output and only a 1.1 percent increase in prices is in part explained by the fact that the economy was then operating well below capacity. In the same way, the fact that the 7.6 percent increase in spending from 1968 to 1969 was accompanied by a 4.8 percent increase in prices and only a 2.7 percent increase in physical output is in part explained by the fact that the economy was then operating close to capacity in terms of both men and equipment. The closer to capacity the economy is operating, the more difficult it becomes for employers to secure experienced workers of the kind required to expand their production; employment of marginal workers forces up labor cost per unit of output and, with this, prices of output. Also, the closer to capacity, the more frequent and severe become the problems faced by firms in securing all of the materials and supplies needed to maintain an uninterrupted flow of production; disruption in production raises cost per unit and, with this, prices. The same is true for other factors, all of which tend to exert upward pressure on prices that grows greater with each step closer to capacity production.

That the degree of capacity utilization is a primary determinant of how a change in spending is distributed between a change in physical output and a change in the price level of output is a well-established proposition in economics. This, however, should not be misinterpreted as a general explanation of the behavior of the price level. It tells us something about how we may expect the price level to respond to an increase in spending in an economy operating with a great deal of slack and in one that is taut. But an economy operating under either of these conditions or one in between may exhibit a rising price level in the absence of any appreciable increase in spending. Instead of prices being pulled up by a rise in spending, a process generally described as "demand-pull inflation," they may be pushed up with unchanged spending through a force such as excessive increases in money wage rates, a process described as "wage-push inflation."

Although it is appropriate at this point to mention the fact that increases in spending are not the only source of a rise in the price level, our purpose here is not to enter into any explanation of inflation. It is the very modest one of merely making clear that changes in spending and in the value of output may be and typically are accompanied by changes in both physical output and prices. Still in merely doing this we see that we have one very important relationship that must be taken into account in any coverage of the causes of inflation.

INCOME AND PRICES

During times when the rate of inflation becomes unusually high—for example, years like 1973 and 1974—we hear through the land the argument that the American people are no longer able to buy the goods that they are producing, that the public in general is being priced out of the market by inflation. This has a ring of truth to it because a dollar will obviously buy much less as prices rise rapidly. Nonetheless, it is basically fallacious, and the fallacy in it is readily revealed by the identity between income, value of output, and spending. Let us take two extreme cases to explain: a year-to-year 10 percent increase in the value of output made up of a 10 percent increase in the physical amount of output and a zero increase in the price level, and a year-to-year 10 percent increase in the value of output made up of a zero percent increase in the physical amount of output and a 10 percent increase in the price level of output. In both the high inflation and the zero inflation case, the rise in income will be the same. If the value of output rises by 10 percent, income will rise by 10 percent, regardless of whether the increase in the value of product is due entirely or not at all to inflation. If a shoe shine boy produces no more shoe shines this year than last year but the price per shine rises by 10 percent, there will be a 10 percent increase in the flow of income corresponding to the 10 percent increase in the value of an unchanged physical amount of output.

As long as it is true that income expands as rapidly as the value of output, it cannot be argued that the recipients of income are collectively unable to increase their spending on goods and services as fast as the value of goods and services increases. In the face of a rise in prices, it is true that they will have to spend more per unit of output, but to secure the same amount of goods and services obtained in the earlier period, they need only spend the same fraction of their total income that they spent in the earlier period. When we look at the system *as a whole*, we thus see that inflation does not price buyers out of the market, nor does it force them to dip into savings or go into debt to secure the same goods and services they got at the lower price level. If increases in the value of output brought about by increases in prices somehow did not produce the same rise in income brought about by increases in physical output, this would not be true. But as has been emphasized, there is the same increase in income from an increase in the value of output brought about in either of these two ways.

While the proposition that the public as a whole is priced out of the market by inflation is clearly a fallacy, that certain groups which make up the whole may be priced out is anything but a fallacy. We can say flatly that income of the public as a whole will rise to match any increase in the value of output caused by inflation, but we cannot say that the income of each separate group will rise in this matching way. On the contrary, we know that groups like retired persons living on pensions fixed in dollar amount or on interest from savings will fall behind. We also find that other groups, like persons whose income is tied closely to business profits, will manage to get ahead because business profits will tend to rise more rapidly than prices, at least for awhile. And groups in between, like wage-earners whose wage rate is adjusted quarterly to reflect changes in the price level, may stay approximately even.

One of the worst things about inflation is the way it redistributes income from one group to another according to whether each group is able to get more or less than its share of the income total that grows as fast as inflation. In the absence of such redistribution, each group would remain in the same relative position, and no group would be priced out of the market by inflation, but of course such redistribution does in fact occur. However, it remains true that the identity between any rise in the value of output and in the level of income makes a fallacy out of the argument that the public as a whole can be priced out of the market by inflation. It is recognition of this that is important to an understanding of the analysis of the economy as a whole, and this is the kind of analysis we need in order to consider the impact of money on the economy.

OUTPUT AND EMPLOYMENT

Will a change in the economy's total spending mean a change in the number of persons employed? We have seen that a change in spending is accompanied by an equal change in the value of output and that the change in the value of output typically is composed of some change in the physical amount of output and some change in the price level of output. Although changes in the price level may indirectly affect employment, the basic determinant of how many people firms will provide jobs for is how much output firms are producing. Employment tends to increase as output expands and tends to contract in the opposite case. To the degree that changes in spending are not entirely absorbed by higher prices, the answer to our question is, therefore, that changes in spending mean changes in employment in the same direction.

Just as price changes mean that the changes in output that follow from changes in spending are not proportional with the changes in spending, there are reasons why changes in employment do not show a proportional or any other kind of fixed relationship with changes in output. An illustration used above shows what is involved here. We noted that the 7.7 percent increase in spending from 1961 to 1962 was accompanied by a 6.6 percent increase in output and a 1.1 percent increase in prices. The record shows also that the number of persons employed increased by 1.5 percent from 1961 to 1962, or at a rate less than one-fourth the rate of increase in output. In contrast, the 7.6 percent increase in spending from 1968 to 1969 was accompanied by a

2.7 percent increase in output and a 4.8 percent increase in prices. In this case the percentage increase in employment was 2.6, or almost proportional with the increase in output. In both cases, we find employment changing in the same direction with output. But the rate of increase in output from 1968 to 1969 was much less than half the rate from 1961 to 1962, while the rate of increase in employment from 1968 was almost twice the rate from 1961 to 1962.

A major part of the explanation for this is found in the fact that the economy in 1961–62 was just coming out of the 1960–61 recession and was operating well below capacity. Unemployment then averaged over 6 percent, and the utilization rate of manufacturing capacity averaged under 80 percent. From 1961 to 1962 there was a great increase in output produced per man—i.e., in labor productivity. This typically occurs during the early part of the expansion phase of the business cycle. Because employers do not cut their personnel to the minimum possible during recession, as recovery begins they are able to achieve some expansion of output with their existing personnel. Furthermore, as it becomes necessary to hire more workers, the possibility of finding just the kind of workers needed is good with a large number of persons unemployed.

In comparison, during 1968–69 the economy was reaching capacity operation under the stimulus of the Vietnam war. Unemployment was at 3.5 percent, its lowest level since the early fifties, and the utilization rate of manufacturing capacity was at a relatively high 87 percent. Under these conditions, expansion of output could not be realized by getting greater output per man. Firms were using their existing personnel fully, so more output could not be gotten without hiring more people. But with the tight labor markets then existing, firms often could not find the kind of people they preferred. In such a situation, it often becomes necessary to take on 6 new men to do the job that 5 better suited men could do. Because of forces like these, in an economy operating near capacity the rate at which employment grows will be equal to or even greater than the rate at which output grows.

Another important part of the explanation for the variation in the relationship between output changes and employment changes is found in the way that changes in spending are distributed among different goods and services. A rise in spending concentrated on relatively labor-intensive output will mean a greater increase in employment for a given increase in output than will a rise in spending that calls forth the very same increase in output from industries whose production is less labor intensive. For example, the 2.7 percent increase in output would have involved more than a 2.6 percent overall increase in employment if more of that output had been in the form of services and less in the form of manufactured goods. Actually, in the present instance, the increase in real GNP originating in manufacturing was 4.3 percent, and the increase originating in service industries was 2.9 percent.

While a given increase in output in the service industries will increase employment more than the same increase in manufacturing, transportation, mining, and still other industries, it is interesting to note that how much of an increase in employment results in service industries for a given increase in the output of those industries also depends on the distribution of output among different services. The output of services includes those provided by laundry workers and those provided by surgeons, but we count both the employment of one more laundry worker or one more surgeon as an increase in employment of one person. However, because the services provided by a surgeon in two weeks will count as an amount of output equal to that of a dozen or more laundry workers, the amount of employment corresponding to a given increase in the output of services can vary considerably with the kind of services people seek to obtain.

These illustrations are sufficient to make clear why we cannot expect a proportional or any other kind of fixed relationship between changes in output and changes in employment over time. We will have little more to say about this relationship in later chapters as we return to the central question of what determines the economy's total spending—but one must keep in mind that lying behind the focus on this question is always the question of how changes in total spending affect prices, output, and employment.

A CONCLUDING NOTE

The disagreement between Keynesians and monetarists over how much money affects spending is a disagreement on a matter of the greatest economic importance. But the effect of money on spending is of importance, not because of the importance of spending in and of itself, but because it is only through spending that money affects how much income people receive, how much output is produced, how many people have jobs, and how high the price level of goods may be. While it may be self-evident that income, output, employment, and prices are the important quantities, the relationship of these quantities to the level of spending is not self-evident. In this chapter we have built a minimum framework that shows these relationships in the simplest possible manner. And this framework provides the background for chapters that follow, where we explore the question of how much spending is affected by money.

○

twelve

SIMPLE KEYNESIANISM
AND MONETARISM:
THE EXTREMES

To argue that money does not mat-
ter is to argue that the observed changes in the level of spending in the
economy are due to something other than changes in the money
supply. From this point of view, a rise in spending is not impeded by an
unchanged money supply. If the determinants of spending are such as
to bring about a rise in total spending from one time period to the next,
the existing money supply, according to this point of view, will simply
turn over a larger number of times in the latter period to carry out the
greater dollar volume of transactions accompanying the higher level of

spending during that period. In other words, all that is needed to handle a 10 percent increase in spending from one time period to the next is a 10 percent increase in the rate at which an unchanged stock of money turns over, and it is maintained that this increase will occur as required. Also from this point of view, if the determinants of spending are *not* such as to bring about a rise in total spending, a rise in the money supply will not make any difference. Total spending will remain unchanged, and the larger money supply will simply turn over a smaller number of times per time period to carry out the unchanged volume of transactions that take place at the unchanged level of income. A 10 percent increase in the money supply that is not accompanied by a change in total spending means that the rate of turnover of this larger money supply will have decreased by 10 percent from one time period to the next.

THE KEYNESIAN EXTREME

There is a simple model constructed on the basis of this point of view. In it income, output, and spending are determined without assigning any role at all to how much money there is in the economic system. Over the past twenty-five years this is the first model every student of economics has faced in his introductory course. It is the best known of the models described as Keynesian, although it is not the same model that Keynes developed in his major work. As suggested by the title of that work, *The General Theory of Employment, Interest, and Money*, Keynes did not rule out money in developing his theory of what determines the economy's income, output, and employment. Our focus in this book is specifically on the role played by money in determining these variables, and a full treatment of that first model without money is not needed for this purpose. However, some understanding of the basic principle that underlies it is helpful, and this much can be secured through a simple approach that by-passes its inherent complications. The point of departure for the approach we will take is the identity considered in the preceding chapter.

| Amount of income generated by the production of goods and services | $\equiv$ | Market value of the economy's output of goods and services | $\equiv$ | Amount of spending on goods and services plus change in business inventories |

We saw there that the largest part of the total on the income side is made up of compensation of employees, corporate profits, proprietors' income, and other earnings that also amount to returns to factors of production. Most of the balance is made up of two other items: indirect taxes, which reflect the portion of the value of output that government takes in through sales and excise taxes on goods and services, and capital consumption allowances or depreciation, which reflect the portion of the proceeds from the sale of the economy's output that business sets aside for future replacement of capital goods that wear out in the course of producing output.

The same total on the income side may also be broken down in other ways, one of which is of particular interest for present purposes. This is a breakdown that shows how much of the gross income flow is absorbed at all levels of government in taxation, including other kinds of taxation as well as indirect taxation, the total for which is designated by T; how much is devoted to private saving, or the sum of saving by persons and business, an amount designated by S; and the remainder, or how much goes into personal consumption expenditures, designated by C. Without getting into the considerable detail that would be necessary to understand this breakdown fully, we may still see the principle through a simple illustration.

Suppose that we have the sets of figures given in Part A of Table 12–1 for the income and spending sides of the identity. If we assume certain behavior on the part of the recipients of income and certain structural characteristics of the system like the level of tax rates, the gross income flow of $100 broken down as shown in Part A may also be broken down as shown in Part B. We trace this in the following paragraphs.

Starting off with the gross income flow of $100, we find that $75 becomes income of persons. This is equal to $57 of compensation of employees, $9 of proprietors' income, $4 of dividends, $3 of net interest, and $2 of rental income of persons. Looking at it in the opposite way, we find that $25 of the gross income flow does not become income of persons. This includes $6 of corporate profits, specifically the $4 that goes to government as corporate income taxes and the $2 that is held back by corporations as undistributed profits; the $10 of indirect business taxes, which goes to government; and the $9 of capital consumption allowances, which is an amount saved by business for later use in replacing capital goods. Of the $75 that becomes income of persons, persons pay out a portion to government in personal income taxes, an amount here assumed to be $10. Subtracting $10 from personal income of $75 leaves disposable personal income of $65. This is the amount of income available to persons during the time period to dispose of as they please, and the initial division of this total goes into the amount they choose to spend for goods and services (personal consumption expenditures) and the amount they choose to

TABLE 12–1

A

Compensation of employees		$57	Personal consumption expenditures		$60
Proprietors' income		9	Gross private domestic investment		14
			Structures and durable equipment	$12	
Corporate profits		10	Change in inventories	2	
Corporate profits taxes	$4				
Dividends	4		Government purchases of goods and services		25
Undistributed profits	2				
			Net exports of goods and services		1
Net interest		3			
Rental income of persons		2			
Indirect business taxes		10			
Capital consumption allowances		9	Gross National Spending plus		
			Change in Inventories, or		
Gross National Income		**$100**	**Gross National Product**		**$100**

B

Personal consumption expenditures		$60	Personal consumption expenditures		$60
Saving		16	Gross private domestic investment		14
By persons	$ 5		Structures and durable equipment	$12	
By business	11		Change in inventories	2	
Taxes		24	Government purchases of goods and services		25
Indirect business taxes	$10				
Corporate profits taxes	4		Net exports of goods and services		1
Personal income taxes	10				
			Gross National Spending plus		
			Change in Inventories, or		
Gross National Income		**$100**	**Gross National Product**		**$100**

save (personal saving). We assume that personal consumption expenditures total $60 of the $65, which leaves a residual of $5 as personal saving for the time period.

We can back up and find how much of the gross income flow of

$100 is absorbed by government in taxation: indirect business taxes of $10, corporate income taxes of $4, and personal income taxes of $10, for a total of $24. Next we can find how much of the gross income flow is devoted to saving. The amounts retained by business, $9 of capital consumption allowances and $2 of undistributed corporate profits, gives us a total of business saving of $11. Personal saving is $5 as noted just above. The sum of these, $16, is the economy's total for private saving during the time period. Subtracting from the gross income flow of $100 the $24 that is collected by government in taxes and the $16 that is saved by business and persons leaves $60 as the amount of this $100 that is spent by persons on goods and services. We have omitted certain aspects in the interest of simplifying, but the principle is this: whatever the gross income flow in any time period, whether it remains at $100 or rises to $110 or falls to $90 or shows any other change in the following and in still later time periods, that total can always be broken down into these three components.

For the time period in question, $60 of the $100 of gross income goes into the component of personal consumption expenditures, or C. The right-hand side of the account shows this same $60 as one of the four spending flows for goods and services. On the income side, this amount is viewed as one of the uses to which the gross income flow is put; on the spending side this amount is viewed as one of four streams that make up total spending for goods and services. If we subtract C from both sides of the account, what remains on the income side is the sum of $40 made up of S and T and on the spending side is the sum of $40 made up of I, G, and X_n. Because of the identity between the totals on the two sides, it is always true by definition that there is a dollar of saving or a dollar of taxes for every dollar of investment, government purchases, and net exports, or it is always true that there is a dollar of investment, government purchases, and net exports for every dollar of saving and taxes. For every time period the identity holds: $S + T \equiv I + G + X_n$. There is no necessary identity between any one item on one side and an item on the other side; the identity exists between the sums of the indicated items on each side.

What is shown in Part B of the table can also be shown graphically, as in Figure 12-1. The three streams on the left show the breakdown of the $100 of gross income into $C + S + T$. C of $60 as a use of income on the left side of the figure is matched by C of $60 as spending for goods and services on the right side of the figure. Similarly, $S + T$ of $40 on the left side is matched by $I + G + X_n$ of $40 on the right.

It cannot be emphasized too strongly that all of what we have brought out to this point follows strictly as a matter of accounting definitions. What we have is the definitional matching between the sums on the two sides. Our interest in the accounting is only to provide

FIGURE 12–1

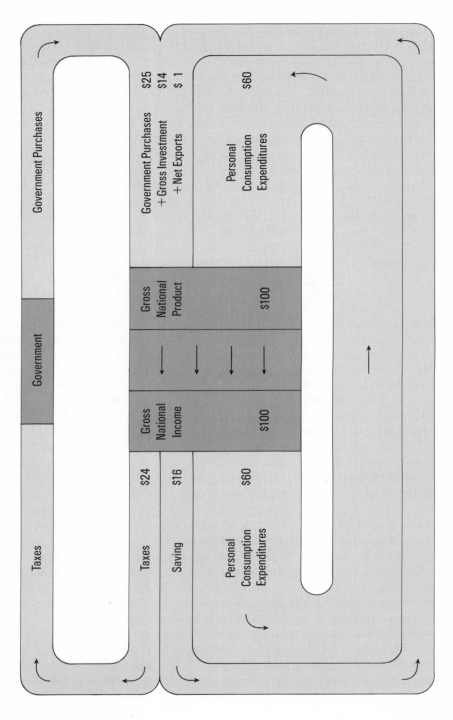

a framework through which we can get into the economics, and with what we now have before us we can do this.

There are various economic questions that might be asked, but the major one is whether or not the existing level of output, valued at $100 at the current price level, will remain unchanged in the following time period or will rise or fall. Recall from the preceding chapter that a rise in the value of output that is not accompanied by a proportional rise in the price level will mean a rise in the physical amount of output and in the level of employment; a fall in the value of output not accompanied by a proportional fall in the price level will mean a fall in real output and employment. Therefore, the answer to this question says something about the very important matter of the amount of goods that will be available per person and the number of persons who will have jobs.

The key to the answer is found in whether the total spending for goods and services is sufficient at the existing price level to take off the market the amount of goods that firms expect to sell. They collectively produce the amount they do because they expect that sales will be at a level to buy up the amount produced. This, however, is subject to an important qualification: firms at times will produce less or more than the amount they expect to sell in order to draw down or build up their inventories. For example, they might produce the $100 in our illustration even though they expect that sales will be $102, the purpose being to cover $2 of sales out of inventories and thereby reduce the level of inventories during the time period by $2. This, of course, is something they would seek to do only if existing inventories were $2 above the desired level. Alternatively they might produce the $100 even though they expect that sales will be only $98, the purpose being to add the difference of $2 to inventories and thereby build up inventories by $2 during the time period. In a parallel way, this, of course, is something they would seek to do only if existing inventories were $2 below the desired level.

Suppose that the latter situation prevailed, and firms produce the $100 they do in the expectation that sales will be $98. With the realized results for the time period being those shown by the figures in the account above, we see that their plans are realized. Output at the rate of $100 generates income at the rate of $100 out of which persons have $65 after taxes and out of which amount they spend $60 and save $5. Government spending for goods and services is given as $25, net spending by foreign buyers is given as $1, and spending by business for structures and producers' durable equipment is given as $12, or total spending is $98. With output at $100 and spending at $98, the unsold output is $2, and this is necessarily the amount added to inventories. Firms planned on adding $2 to their inventories, and this turns out to be the amount they actually do add. Actual spending turns out to be just the amount that firms had planned for; the actual change in inventories turns out to be just the amount that firms had planned for. This describes an equilibrium situation in which the aggregate supply of goods and the aggregate demand for goods are in balance for the period.

We may also describe this equilibrium situation in another way. The sum going into saving and taxes on the income side is $16 and $24 respectively, or a total of $40. Each of these dollars is a dollar of the gross income flow that is not spent by persons—i.e., not devoted to the purchase of consumer goods. If the total demand for goods is to be $100, or equal to the total output of goods, this "leakage" of $40 must be offset by an equal amount of demand originating with others than persons. And so it is because there is spending of $25 by government, net spending of $1 by foreign buyers, and spending of $12 for structures and producers' durable equipment by business. Although this adds up to spending of only $38 by these groups, in addition there is demand by business for $2 of output to add to its inventories, and this is as much a demand for output as is spending by persons or any other group. Thus, corresponding to the "leakage" of $40 into saving and taxes on the income side is an offsetting "injection" of spending and planned additions to inventories just equal to that $40.

If firms had produced for the time period at a rate greater or less than $100, the result would have been a disequilibrium, which means that that existing rate of output would change. To illustrate: suppose firms altogether had produced $110 for the period. Corresponding to this higher level of output is a corresponding higher level of gross income, and we may note how that increase in gross income might be divided into saving, taxes, and consumption expenditures. All kinds of considerations enter in here. If that additional $10 is largely in the form of wages and salaries of lower income workers, we can anticipate that a relatively small portion will be taken in personal income taxes or devoted to personal saving and that a relatively large portion accordingly will be used for personal consumption expenditures. In contrast, if that additional $10 is largely in the form of corporate profits, a relatively large portion will be taken off the top by government via the corporate income tax, and some portion of the remainder may be saved by business as undistributed profits. What is left becomes income of persons in the form of dividends; a portion of this goes to government via the personal income tax, and what is finally left, the addition to disposable personal income, is devoted to personal saving and personal consumption expenditures. If the dividend recipients happen to be mostly upper income persons, this split will be more into personal saving and less into consumption expenditures than if they happen to be pensioners and moderate income persons. It is apparent that this extra $10 may be split up in any number of ways. However, to get on with our illustration, let us assume simply that the extra $10 of income is split up as was the original $100. Each of the income components thus increases by 10 percent, consumption from $60 to $66, saving from $16 to $17.6, and taxes from $24 to $26.4, as shown on the income side of Part A of Table 12–2.

We now introduce an assumption that is crucial to the basic Keynesian model. Although the level of output and the level of income

TABLE 12–2

A: DISEQUILIBRIUM: UNPLANNED INCREASE IN INVENTORIES OF $4

Personal consumption expenditures	$66.0	Personal consumption expenditures	$66
Saving	17.6	Gross private domestic investment	18
		Structures and durable equipment $12	
Taxes	26.4	Change in inventories 6	
		Government purchases of goods and services	25
		Net exports of goods and services	1
		Gross National Spending plus Change in Inventories, or	
Gross National Income	$110.0	Gross National Product	$110

B: DISEQUILIBRIUM: UNPLANNED DECREASE IN INVENTORIES OF $4

Personal consumption expenditures	$54.0	Personal consumption expenditures	$54
Saving	14.4	Gross private domestic investment	10
		Structures and durable equipment $12	
Taxes	21.6	Change in inventories −2	
		Government purchases of goods and services	25
		Net exports of goods and services	1
		Gross National Spending plus Change in Inventories, or	
Gross National Income	$90.0	Gross National Product	$90

are higher by $10 for the period because businessmen chose to produce at this higher rate, there are no automatic forces present in the economy to cause an increase in the sum of the amounts that businessmen want to invest or government wants to spend or foreigners want to buy that will just equal the increase in output that is not removed from the market by the increase in personal consumption expenditures. In the present illustration, the rise in income of $10 is accompanied by a rise in consumption expenditures of $6 and a rise in "leakages" of $4, $1.6 into saving and $2.4 into taxes. To have the demand for goods rise by as much as the output of goods, the rise in leakages of $4 must be offset by a rise in injections of $4 in the form of that much more planned investment, government purchases, or net exports. But again the crucial Keynesian contention is that there are no automatic forces at work in the economy to see that this offsetting actually takes place. For simplicity, let us assume that there is no such offsetting at all. Thus, the amount that business wants to invest remains at $14 per time period, the amount that government chooses to spend remains at $25 per time period, and the amount of net foreign demand or net exports remains at $1 per time period. In this event, the distribution of the actual output of $110 for the period must appear as on the spending side of Part A of Table 12–2.

Of the increase in output of $10, $6 has been taken off the market by the $6 increase in personal consumption expenditures that results from the increase in gross national income of $10. But because there has been no increase in the amount of output taken off the market by other groups of purchasers, the remaining $4 of the additional output must end up as an increase in the amount added to inventories. As before, the assumption was that businessmen wanted to add $2 to inventories for the period, but it turns out that the actual result is an addition of $6 to inventories for the time period.

The extra $4 increase in inventories may be variously described as an undesired, involuntary, or unplanned increase. Total inventories are now $4 greater than desired. How do firms react? They will cut back output to a level below expected sales in the effort to work off the excess inventories. However, a cutback in output means a cutback in income, and a cutback in income will mean a cutback in personal consumption expenditures. This means that the reduction in inventories will be less than the reduction desired, and this will lead to a further cutback in output and in income. An adjustment process is under way in which the level of output, income, and spending all contract until an equilibrium is established. In the present illustration, if planned investment spending, government purchases, and net foreign demand do not change, that equilibrium will be the $100 level considered earlier.

A similar analysis follows for the opposite kind of disequilibrium. In brief, if firms for some reason had cut back output from the initial equilibrium level of $100 to $90, gross income would have dropped correspondingly. How this income would be divided between a decline in consumption, saving, and taxes depends on numerous considerations, a few of which were noted above in asking how an increase in income would be divided. Depending on these considerations, it is apparent that the decline may be split up in any number of ways. We will not get into this question but simply assume a straight 10 percent decline in each. Consumption then becomes $54, saving $14.4, and taxes $21.6. If business spending for structures and durable equipment remains at $12, government purchases remain at $25, and net foreign demand remains at $1, total spending will then be $54 + $12 + $25 + $1, or $92. With output at $90, the result must be a decrease in inventories of $2. These results are shown in Part B of Table 12–2.

Given the earlier assumption that business had planned an increase of $2 in inventories, what they find with an actual decrease of $2 is that inventories are $4 below the desired level. How do firms react in this case? In the next time period they will expand output to a level above expected sales in the effort to get inventories back up to the desired level. However, an expansion in output means an expansion in income, and this means an increase in personal consumption expenditures. This increase in consumption expenditures bites into what otherwise would have been the desired addition to inventories and leads to a further expansion of output and income in the next period as firms again try to restore inventories to the desired level. An adjustment process is under way in which the level of output, income, and spending all expand until an equilibrium is established. As before, if planned investment, government purchases, and net foreign demand do not change, that equilibrium will be the $100 level considered earlier.

From this examination of these disequilibrium levels of output, $110 and $90, one can better see why the $100 level is the equilibrium level. One may also perhaps see from this what is needed to bring about a change in the equilibrium level from the existing $100: a change in the amount that businessmen want to add to inventories per period or a change in the amount of business spending per period for structures and durable equipment or a change in government purchases per period or a change in net foreign demand per period or a change in the amount that persons choose to spend out of their existing disposable income per period. Any one of these or any nonoffsetting combination of these will mean a change in the demand for goods and services and a change in the equilibrium level of income. And any of these changes will ordinarily mean a change in the equilibrium level of income greater than that initial change in demand. The ratio of the change in the equilibrium level of income to a change in demand of the kinds noted here is known as the *multiplier*. For example, if conditions are such that a $4 increase in government purchases of goods and services leads to a $10 increase in the equilibrium level of income, the multiplier is 2 1/2. If that same increase in government spending brought about an increase in income of $8, the multiplier would be 2.

Without getting into a formal analysis of the multiplier, we may note merely that the reason that the equilibrium level of income rises by an amount greater than the initial rise in spending, here $4, is that that initial rise in spending, by raising income by an equal amount, induces a further rise in personal consumption spending (and possibly also in other kinds of spending), which in turn brings about a further rise in income, a further rise in spending, and so forth. For example, suppose, as we did above, that an increase in gross national income gives rise to an increase in consumption spending equal to 0.6 times the increase in gross national income. Then an initial increase in G of $4 will, by producing an initial increase in gross national income of $4, lead to a rise in C of 0.6 × $4, or $2.4. For this time period, the rise in spending, value of output, and gross national income is, therefore, not just the increase in G of $4 but this plus the increase in C of $2.4, or a total income increase of $6.4. But the increase in C of $2.4 in turn means that much of an additional increase in gross national income, which will bring about a further increase in C of 0.6 × $2.4, or $1.44. In this next time period, total spending is thus $7.84 above the original level. When the process has fully worked itself out, the new equilibrium level of spending will be $10 above the original level. In this case the multiplier is 2 1/2, so the increase in income is 2 1/2 times the original increase in G of $4, or the increase in income is $10.

Once the multiplier is determined, the basic Keynesian model translates changes in business spending, government spending, and the like into changes in the equilibrium level of income. A striking element of this model is that the change in the equilibrium level of income that results from a change in one of the spending streams is presumed to be uninfluenced by the economy's money stock. For example, a rise in government purchases will produce a rise in the equilibrium level of income that is some multiple of that rise in government purchases, but the size of that multiple does not depend at all on whether there is a change in the money supply at the same time that there is the change in government purchases. This conclusion, it must be emphasized, is the conclusion that follows from a simple Keynesian model that represents an extreme position. From what we have already noted about monetarism, it may be clear that it is conclusions like these that follow from this Keynesian model that are rejected summarily by the monetarists.

THE MONETARIST EXTREME

The monetarists in turn have a simple model that represents an extreme position at the other end of the spectrum. As might be guessed, it is conclusions drawn from this model that are rejected summarily by Keynesians. Our next step is to examine this particular monetarist model. First off, we may note that it is a model that finds no particular usefulness in the kind of framework set forth above, and we will have no occasion to use that framework in this section. As we saw, the Keynesian model approaches the explanation of total spending by dividing that total into spending by particular groups—namely, consumers, businesses, government, and foreign buyers. We did not go into this, apart from noting that consumption spending depends in part on the amount of gross income secured by persons, but what is done in a fuller treatment is to explain what determines the level of each of these kinds of spending and thereby to explain the total. Because they see total spending to be an amount determined by the money supply, the monetarists have no use for this breakdown; they reason directly from the total money supply to total spending.

On any particular day, there is some existing stock of money in the hands of the public. We are ordinarily interested not in the amount for a particular day but in the average amount over a period of time. For the month of January 1973, the average amount (average of daily figures) of M_1 was $255.4 billion, for the month of December $270.4 billion, etc. If we want the figure for the average stock of money for the year 1973, we can average the 12 monthly figures, which gives us $263.6 billion. We can arrive at an average for any other time period in the same way. We can also in this way arrive at an average for the stock of M_2 or for the stock corresponding to any other definition of money.

Given nothing more than the figure for the average stock of money for a time period and one other item of information, the simple monetarist model is prepared to tell us what the economy's equilibrium income level will be for that time period. In Part I we dealt at length with what determines the stock of money; here we must deal with this other item needed to work through the simple monetarist model. Let us start off by assuming that the average stock of money is $20 for a given year. (For purposes of illustration, we can work better with the more manageable small numbers than the actual numbers.) If this is the amount that exists, then by definition it must also be the amount that the public holds. However, this amount that the public actually holds is not necessarily the amount the public wants to hold; in any time period, the public may want to hold a larger or smaller amount of money than it actually does hold.

One of the biggest questions in monetary economics is the question of what determines how much money the public wants to hold. One short answer to this very large question is to say that the public wants to hold whatever amount of money it finds necessary to mediate the volume of transactions accompanying the existing level of income and output. Each person and each firm decides the amount of money he or it needs for this purpose from one week to the next and continually seeks to adjust the amount held to match the amount needed. How can they do this? One way in which a person or firm may build up his or its money balance is by selling securities or other financial assets to acquire money: the seller has dollar for dollar less of other financial assets and more of the financial asset money; the buyer has dollar for dollar less of the financial asset money and more of other financial assets. There is no change in the money supply through this exchange but only shifts in the ownership of the existing money supply.

While individual units may readily make such exchanges, it is critically important to see that, with a given stock of money in existence, not all persons and firms simultaneously can do what individual units can do. In order for any one to increase his money holdings, another must be willing to decrease his money holdings. If all are trying to increase, there is no one trying to decrease, and no one can then succeed in increasing his holdings. It is just as true that, with a given stock of money that exists to be held, not all simultaneously can decrease the amount of money they hold. Any one can always switch from money to other financial assets, but this requires that another stands ready to exchange other such assets for money. If all are trying to get out of money into other financial assets, there is then no one trying to get out of other such assets into money, and no one can succeed in decreasing the amount of money he holds. Of course, as a practical matter not everyone is ordinarily trying to move in the same direction at the same time, so those individuals and firms who want to build up their money balances will be able to find others who want to give up money balances in exchange for the financial assets the former seek to exchange for money balances.

Let us suppose now that the amount of money balance needed to mediate transactions is $1 for every $5 of gross national product or gross national income. That is, to carry out the buying and selling transactions that lie behind each $5 of gross national product requires $1 of money. What this figure will actually be per dollar of product depends on a long list of factors—but factors that do not change appreciably except over time measured in years. For example, an increase in the rapidity with which money can be transferred (faster check clearing) will enable each dollar of money to carry out more transactions or do more work in a given time period and will mean that less money is needed per dollar of product. Another factor working in the same direction is integration of industry. If a steel-producing firm is integrated all the way back to the ore and coal mines, every stage in the production of steel is within the same firm, and money payments are not called for at successive stages of production as they are when production at successive stages is carried out by separate firms. The dollar amount of transactions to be mediated with money per ton of steel produced will clearly be smaller, the greater the degree of integration. Another factor is the availability of credit and the use of credit cards. To the degree that the use of credit enables persons and firms to achieve a closer synchronization between the dates at which they make payments of money and the dates at which they receive money, they are able to carry out a given dollar volume of transactions with a smaller amount of money. In terms of gross national product, a smaller amount of money is needed per dollar of product.

If $1 of money holdings is required to carry out the buying and selling transactions that lie behind each $5 of gross national product, the assumption made above, it may also be said that the public wants to hold an amount of money equal to 1/5 of the gross national product. Thus, if the gross national product is $100 for the year, the average money holdings the public needs to handle all of the transactions that accompany that product will be $20, or $20 = (1/5)$100. If $20 happens to be the actual money stock for the year and if $100 happens to be the actual gross national product for the year, the public is holding the amount of money it wants to hold. This defines an equilibrium in which the supply of money, $20, is equal to the demand for money, (1/5)$100, or the amount of money that exists to be held is just equal to the amount that the public wishes to hold. More important, this establishes the equilibrium level of gross national income or gross national product. This must be $100; any other level is a disequilibrium level. As we did with the simple Keynesian model, let us assume disequilibrium income levels, note why they are disequilibrium levels, and observe why the level of income will tend to return to the equilibrium level.

Suppose that the money supply is given as $20 and, as before, the public wants to hold $1 of money per $5 of gross national income or product. If the level of income were $90, the public would want to hold money balances of (1/5)$90, or $18, but is actually holding $20, or $2 more than they choose to hold. We noted above that persons and firms that find themselves holding larger money balances than are needed may switch out of money into securities and other financial assets, and we may ask if equilibrium cannot be restored in the present case in this way. Within the simple monetarist model, the answer is, no. With the money stock given, some persons and firms can reduce their money holdings only to the degree that others increase theirs. There may be exchanges in which some firms and persons reduce their money balances by purchasing securities, but the other persons and firms who sell the securities must have increased their money balances on a matching basis. Such exchanges will not reduce the total of money held by all. There will still be $20 of money held, more than the $18 the public wishes to hold with gross national product of $90.

However, switching out of money into financial assets is not the only possibility. Holders of surplus money balances can also switch into real assets. In a word, they may buy goods of all kinds, ranging from structures like apartment buildings, to durables like automobiles and television sets, to nondurables like shirts and shoes. They could also use the surplus money balances to buy more services of all kinds. But using money to buy goods and services does not decrease the money supply any more than does the use of money to buy financial assets other than money. In both cases, the existing money supply merely passes from the hands of the buyers into the hands of the sellers. However, when the excess money is used to buy goods, there is an increase in the demand for goods, or an increase in spending as we use that term in economics. There is initially an increase in the value of output and in gross national income equal to the increase in spending.

The process by which equilibrium will be restored in the present model may now be apparent. As long as the public holds an amount of money greater than 1/5 of the gross national income or product and thus an amount greater than it wants to hold, it will attempt to dispose of the surplus by spending it. However, because this does not alter the actual amount of money the public holds, the adjustment process cannot come about by the public's reducing the money supply to the lower amount it wishes to hold. The adjustment process must occur through action by the public that raises the value of output and income to the level at which the unchanged money supply becomes the amount of money the public wants to hold.

In our illustration this occurs as spending expands to lift the income level to $100. Then the $20 of money the public actually holds is the amount it wants to hold. As long as the public wants to hold $1 of money for every $5 of gross national income or product, $90 cannot be the equilibrium level of income unless the money supply is $18. If we have the money supply set at $20 by the monetary authorities and if the public is powerless to change it, the equilibrium level of income, given our other assumptions, is necessarily $100.

To trace through the opposite kind of disequilibrium situation, suppose that the income level was $110. With the money supply again given as $20, the public then wants to hold money balances of $22 but is actually holding $20, or $2 less than the desired amount. If the public had it in its power to raise its money holdings to $22, by so doing it would hold the amount of money desired at the indicated level of income and that level of income would become the equilibrium level. But again the public does not have this power; the monetary authorities determine what the money supply will be, and our assumption is that they have fixed it at $20.

As in the other case, the process by which equilibrium is restored involves adjustments in spending. In the case where the public found itself with excess money holdings, it sought to dispose of the excess by spending that much more, thereby eventually raising the level of income until the unchanged money supply became the amount of money it wanted to hold at that level of income. In the present case, it will try to build up its money holdings by spending that much less. But a reduction in spending does not increase the total amount of money held by the public any more than an increase in spending reduces it. To the degree that some persons and firms succeed in building up their money holdings by reducing their money outlays, others must experience a decrease in their money holdings, given that the total money supply is unchanged. The adjustment process cannot come about by the public's increasing the money supply to the larger amount it wants to hold. The adjustment process will occur through a decrease in the level of spending such that the level of income will eventually fall to $100, at which level the $20 of money the public actually holds becomes the amount of money the public wants to hold. As long as the public wants to hold $1 of money for every $5 of gross national income or product, $110 cannot be the equilibrium level of income unless the money supply is $22. If the money supply is set at $20 by the monetary authorities, the equilibrium level of income, given our other assumptions, is necessarily $100.

As may be apparent from the discussion above, in the simple monetarist model, a change in the equilibrium level of income comes about because there is a change in the total money supply. Refer again to an initial equilibrium in which the income level is $100, the money supply is $20, and the public seeks to hold $1 in money for each $5 of income or to hold in money an amount equal to one-fifth of income. If the Federal Reserve buys securities in the open market in the amount needed to increase the money supply by $2 to $22, the result is a disequilibrium. At the existing income level of $100, the public is holding more money than it wishes to hold. As described above, the adjustment process in a disequilibrium of this kind involves an increase in spending as persons and firms seek to exchange their surplus money balances for goods. In the present illustration, spending will rise until the income level is lifted to $110 per time period. At this income level, the stock of money, the amount of money the public actually holds, $22, is just equal to the amount it wants to hold: one-fifth of the income level. Equilibrium has been restored: $22 = (1/5)$110.

Starting off again with an initial equilibrium in which the income level is $100, the money supply is $20, and the public seeks to hold $1 in money for each $5 of income, if the Federal Reserve sells securities in the open market in the amount needed to reduce the money supply by $2 or from $20 to $18, we have an illustration of the opposite kind of disequilibrium. At the existing income level of $100, the public is holding less money than it wishes to hold. The adjustment process is then one in which persons and firms reduce their money outlays in the attempt to build up their money holdings. With the money stock fixed at $18, they cannot, of course, succeed in this. However, the reduction in spending means a decline in the income level, and spending continues to shrink until the income level has fallen to $90 per time period. At this income level, the $18 of money holdings is equal to one-fifth of the income level and thus equal to the amount the public wants to hold. Equilibrium has been restored: $18 = (1/5)$90.

Although these illustrations are based on an admittedly extreme monetarist model, they bring out in striking form the basis for the monetarist belief in the power of money. It is changes in the money supply that bring about changes in spending and thereby in the level of income, and there is a stable relationship between changes in the money supply and the changes in income that they bring about. Particular changes in the money supply (or, in a more refined statement, in the rate of growth of the money supply) lead to predictable changes in the level of income (or in the rate of growth of income). The extreme monetarist would say that a $2 billion change in the money supply will always lead to a $10 billion (or some other specific) change in the income level.

A CONCLUDING NOTE

There is a simple Keynesian model in which the changes in the level of income that occur in response to such changes as increases in government purchases or decreases in taxes are independent of whether or not these changes are accompanied by changes in the money supply. The key elements in this extreme Keynesian model were considered in the first part of this chapter. There is also a simple monetarist model in which changes such as increases in government purchases or decreases in taxes have no effect on the level of income, and in which changes in the level of income are attributed entirely to changes in the money supply and vary proportionally with money supply changes. The key elements of this extreme monetarist model were considered in the second part of this chapter. Looking at the difference between Keynesianism and monetarism in their extreme forms is helpful as a first step, but it is necessary to go beyond these models to get any understanding of what separates economists who today are referred to as Keynesians and monetarists.

In the following chapter we will move from the extreme Keynesian model to a model in which it is recognized that money does matter, that the effect on income of fiscal actions like a change in government purchases or a change in taxes is influenced importantly by what is happening at the same time to the money supply. We also move from the extreme monetarist model in which a given change in the money supply produces a change in the level of income whose magnitude is based entirely on the assumption that the public seeks to maintain a fixed ratio between its money holdings and the level of income.

thirteen

KEYNESIANISM, MONETARISM, AND THE RATE OF INTEREST

$\bigcirc$nce they looked beyond the Keynesian and monetarist models in their extreme forms, most economists concluded that the basic difference between Keynesianism and monetarism lay in the way that each views the public's demand for money. The central question appeared to be the extent to which the amount of money the public wishes to hold is influenced by the rate of interest. In general, the Keynesians have maintained that the demand for money is interest-sensitive, and the monetarists have denied this. However, in the face of a growing body of empirical evidence that supports the Keynesian position, some monetarists in the last few years have come to accept that the rate of interest has a significant influence on the demand for money. But, for reasons we will see in this chapter, accepting this amounts to accepting the Keynesian conclusion that fiscal actions like a change in government purchases or a change in taxes can bring about changes in the level of real income even though there is no change in the money supply. As this is a denial of a foremost tenet of monetarism, it plainly is something that monetarists cannot accept.

One way to yield on the question of the interest sensitivity of the demand for money without yielding on the assertion that fiscal policy cannot affect the real income level is, strange as it may sound, to remove the level of real income as a variable in the system. In the last few years many monetarists have adopted the pre-Keynesian, or old classical, model based on the assumption of flexible money wages. In that model, if money wages decline freely whenever the number of persons seeking employment at the going wage rate exceeds the number of job vacancies, there is no barrier to the full employment of the labor force. The economy will automatically tend to operate at the level of output that can be produced by a fully employed labor force. How much output is produced at this level of employment depends on the size of the labor force, the size of the economy's capital stock and the state of technology, but it is an amount which, on the assumption of flexible wages, will be produced regardless of whether government spends more or less or taxes more or less. It is also an amount that is independent of whether there is more or less money in the system.

This may sound odd at first, but it merely amounts to saying that fiscal and monetary policies cannot affect the level of real income and output if that level is already the full employment level. One might add that there is nothing at all that can affect the level of real income and output in the short run if that level is already at the maximum attainable with the available resources and their productivity. The only things that can then increase it are more resources or increased productivity of the available resources, and this occurs only over time. Neither changes in government spending or taxes nor changes in the money supply add to the economy's real resources or bring about changes in the productivity of such resources.

This is not to say that monetary and fiscal changes are without any effects at all with output already at its full employment level. An increase in the money supply will affect the level of income in the way described for the extreme monetarist model of the preceding chapter. However, since real output is already at the maximum consistent with available resources, the increase in the income level, an increase proportional to the increase in the money supply, will be made up completely of an increase in the price level and not at all of an increase in output.

Incidentally, just as the assumption of flexible wages leads us back to the pre-Keynesian theory of automatic full employment, it also leads us back to the old quantity theory of money, which held that prices vary proportionally with the money supply.

Fiscal changes also will not be without effect in an economy operating at full employment. While the level of real output and employment will not be affected, the composition of that total will be affected. For example, an increase in government spending financed by borrowing from the public will push up interest rates and cause a decline in investment spending. It will mean a transfer of resources from the private sector to the public sector but no change in the total output of the economy.

The recent maneuver in which some monetarists have returned to a model of automatic full employment has left more than a few economists baffled. Automatic full employment can be expected only in an economy far different from the one we know. The economy we know is dominated by oligopolies and labor unions; the kind of competitive forces that are needed to yield the automatic full employment result are not at work. The economy as it now operates continues periodically to face employment problems.

Therefore, it seems appropriate to work with a model that does not assume that any departure from the full employment level of output is automatically corrected by a return to full employment. In such a model, if the demand for money is interest-sensitive, fiscal policy is capable of increasing the economy's real income and employment; if the demand for money is interest-insensitive, fiscal policy is incapable of increasing the economy's real income and employment. The question of the interest-sensitivity of the demand for money thus remains a basic difference between Keynesians and monetarists or, to be more correct, at least between Keynesians and those monetarists who have not sidestepped the problem by assuming that the economy automatically maintains the full employment level of output. Our purpose in this chapter is to examine the way in which the relation between the rate of interest and the amount of money the public wants to hold influences the level of output and employment.

In this connection, we should recall a relationship noted briefly in Chapter 11: anything that brings about a given increase in spending may cause at one extreme a rise in output proportional to the increase in spending, at the other extreme a rise in prices proportional to the increase in spending, or some combination of both. In an economy operating below the full employment level of output, some part of the increase in spending will be reflected in increased output and employment. Because the model we will work with is that of an economy in this position, we here have that result. For present purposes, there is no need to go beyond this to how much of an increase in spending is absorbed by an increase in output and how much by an increase in prices—it is sufficient to recognize, for example, that fiscal action that raises spending will to some degree also raise the level of output and employment.

THE INTEREST RATE
AND THE DEMAND FOR MONEY

Although monetarists recently have yielded somewhat on the question of the interest-sensitivity of the demand for money, they had for some time before held firmly to the position that the amount of money the public wants to hold does not depend significantly on either the rate of interest or any other influence except the level of income. To the extent that this is correct and to the extent that the amount of money the public wishes to hold per dollar of income is stable over time, there is to that extent no support remaining for the Keynesian position. Changes in government spending and taxation would be powerless to affect the level of income and output. The only way to affect that level would be through variation in the money supply. If the economy was operating below the level of output consistent with its available resources, for example, the appropriate increase in the money supply would move the economy to the full employment position. If, again, the public always sought to maintain a stable ratio of $1 of money per $5 of its income, any time its money holdings became greater than 1/5 of income it would increase spending by the amount that would raise income to the level at which the larger money supply was again equal to 1/5 of income. Depending on how increases in spending were absorbed by increases in the price level and increases in output, there was some increase in the money supply that would provide the increase in spending needed to get the economy to the full employment output position. The Keynesian approach could never do this if the demand for money is insensitive to the rate of interest.

If the demand for money is sensitive to the rate of interest, however, the Keynesian approach will be able to produce an increase in the level of real income and output. Let us see why. Note first something already emphasized: while they recognize that the amount of money the public wants to hold is related closely to the level of income, Keynesians assert that the amount the public wants to hold per dollar of income may still vary significantly over time as a result of other influences. Although we stated repeatedly in the preceding chapter that the public would seek to hold the amount of money that is "necessary" or "needed" to handle the transactions associated with the existing level of income, we must now consider the possibility that this amount might vary at any existing level of income. This is because if persons and firms wish to avoid the inconvenience of the careful management needed to hold this amount down to its very minimum, the amount "needed" in this sense will be larger than this irreducible minimum. A major factor affecting the public's willingness to put up with the inconvenience and difficulty involved in trying to work with minimum money holdings is the rate of return available on other assets.

The amount of his assets that anybody holds in the form of money is an amount on which he receives an implicit return in the form of the convenience and security that goes with having an immediately available stock of purchasing power at hand. On the balance of his assets, there is an explicit return, either actual or expected. Holdings of near-moneys like savings deposits, savings and loan shares, U.S. Savings Bonds, Treasury bills, and the like provide an explicit interest return; holdings of stocks provide a return in dividends and/or expected capital gains; holdings of real property provide a return in the form of rental income. Now the fact that no similar kind of return is available on assets in the form of money suggests that persons and business firms will try to keep the holdings of this asset down to the very minimum amount needed to handle the transactions each engages in. But to economize on money holdings requires that time and energy be devoted to planning and that in some cases expenses be incurred. For a person or business that receives money and pays out money on a day-to-day basis and in amounts that vary considerably from day to day, it may be clear that to hold the amount of money balance to a minimum calls for continuous management. And if one switches what is a temporary surplus money balance into interest-bearing assets like Treasury bills, there is a brokerage cost incurred each time one purchases and sells such securities.

Each person and firm weighs the cost in terms of fees incurred and time and effort required to switch into and out of earning assets against the rate of return provided by such assets. If that rate is relatively low, the cost involved will exceed the return secured, and such switching will not be worthwhile. However, at a little higher rate of interest, it will become worthwhile to try to cut down somewhat on the size of the money balance and switch some part of that balance into earning assets. The higher the rate of interest that can be earned, the more worthwhile it becomes to try to cut down further on the size of one's money balance. Presumably there is some very high rate of interest at which persons and firms will have carried this process to its limit, which means that they will have cut their holdings of money down to the absolute minimum with which, through the most careful planning, it is still possible to mediate the volume of transactions that has to be mediated.

What this enables us to say is that, other things being equal, the amount of money balances the public will wish to hold will vary inversely with the rate of interest. Thus, a rise in the rate of interest means that the public will find it worthwhile to economize on their money balances so as to carry out a given volume of transactions with smaller money balances. Persons and firms who were holding more money than the minimum needed to carry out their transactions may turn this excess over to borrowers under the incentive of the higher interest rate being paid, and this money then becomes available to mediate a greater volume of transactions. The rise in the interest rate provides, in effect, an increase in the amount of money available to handle transactions, although the actual money supply has not changed at all.

According to the Keynesian model sketched in the preceding chapter, an increase in deficit-financed government spending, for example, will bring about an increase in the equilibrium income level, even though the money supply remains unchanged. With no increase in the money supply, it is granted that this fiscal action will tend to push up interest rates, but the rise in interest rates will, in the way outlined here, lead to an economizing by the public in its money balances and provide what amounts, in effect, to an increase in the money supply to carry out the now higher volume of transactions. Looked at in this way, the existing money supply is made to do more work, to turn over a larger number of times per time period, and the fact that the money supply is fixed does not prevent an increase in income that the Keynesians maintain will follow from an increase in government spending.

However, there would also appear to be an upper limit to how much work a fixed money supply can do. Almost all Keynesians accept this, and they therefore grant that there can be conditions under which a fixity of the money supply will rule out an increase in income. But there are a few extreme Keynesians, like Professor Kaldor of Cambridge University in England, who deny that the amount of money can ever limit the growth of income. Apart from what amounts to an increase in the money supply through an increase in its rate of turnover, the public, according to Kaldor, can also in effect create more money in another way if it needs more than is provided by the central bank. What would happen is that private corporations like General Motors and A.T.&T. would issue promissory notes and script currency, which would come to be used as money. Clearing houses to settle net credit and debit balances among issuers of these instruments would be set up just as clearing houses now settle balances between banks. A second money-system and payments-system would be established to operate side by side with the official money system.

Although this cannot be ruled out as a possibility under very extraordinary conditions—something like this occurred in the early thirties in this country with the shortage of official money that then existed—it is not a development that one need consider if he focuses on the kinds of conditions that prevail 99 percent of the time. Under these conditions, we look to a higher rate of turnover of the regular money supply as the means by which a higher level of income can be handled with a fixed official money supply, and we recognize that this can occur to the degree that there is "slack" in the system. Monetarists grant that slack of this kind will be found in times of deep recession with the relatively low interest rates that then prevail, but they point out that this is not the typical position in which the economy finds itself. The economy is more commonly near its full output level and, with the economy in this position, they assert that the public has already economized its money balances almost to the maximum possible and there is accordingly practically no room for the existing money supply to support a still higher level of income than it is already doing. Growth of income cannot then occur without growth in the money supply.

What we have sketched in these introductory paragraphs comes close to what many economists see as the underlying difference between the Keynesian and monetarist views. The Keynesians believe that the typical state of affairs is one with sufficient monetary slack to permit growth in the income level with a fixed money supply. And monetarists believe that the typical state of affairs is one in which slack is clearly not sufficient for this purpose. It is to a more detailed and careful treatment of this difference and some other matters into which it leads that the balance of this chapter is devoted.

FISCAL POLICY, THE INTEREST RATE, AND THE INCOME LEVEL

Keynesianism gave birth to modern fiscal policy—to the deliberate manipulation of government spending and taxing as means of bringing about desired changes in the level of real income. If the economy was in recession, an appropriate increase in government spending and/or an appropriate cut in tax rates would bring about the increase in spending needed to get the economy out of recession. In the face of inflation, the opposite kinds of changes were in order. Monetarists basically reject both sides of this: too little spending as in recession is the result of too little money, and too much spending that leads to inflation is the result of too much money.

We can gain some understanding of the foundation for these opposed conclusions by turning again to the income-spending identity, with its breakdown on the income side into $C + S + T$ and on the spending side into $C + I + G + X_n$.

The monetarists do not deny that it is possible, for example, for an increase in G to occur with no change in the money supply, but they maintain that with no change in the money supply the increase in G will be at the expense of a decrease in one of the other spending streams. The net result will then be no increase in the income level. Similarly, the monetarists do not deny that an increase in C can be brought about via a reduction in personal income taxes with no change in the money supply, but they maintain that with no change in the money supply the increase in C will be at the expense of a decrease in one of the other spending streams. Again the net result will be no increase in the income level. From their viewpoint, only if an increase in government spending or a decrease in taxes is accompanied by an appropriate increase in the money supply will these fiscal actions be followed by a rise in the income level, and they hasten to add that the increase in income that does occur is then the result of the change in the money supply and in no sense the result of the fiscal actions, which are just so much wasted motion. We will look at the basis for the monetarist argument, first, in its application to the case of an increase in government spending and, second, in its application to a cut in taxes; and then we turn to the Keynesian reply to the monetarist argument.

The Monetarist Argument:

Increased Government Spending Is Nonexpansionary

To understand the monetarist argument requires that we start off by examining some aspects of the *financing* of spending that lie behind the income-spending identity. The figures assumed for this identity in Table 12–1 were as follows:

$$C \quad + \quad S \quad + \quad T \quad = \quad C \quad + \quad I \quad + \quad G \quad + \quad X_n$$
$$60 \quad + \quad 16 \quad + \quad 24 \quad = \quad 60 \quad + \quad 14 \quad + \quad 25 \quad + \quad 1$$

Recall that the saving of $16 is the total of private saving and in this illustration is made up of $5 of saving by persons and $11 of saving by business (depreciation or capital consumption allowances and undistributed corporate profits). Suppose that the figures given here remain unchanged over a number of time periods. In each of these periods businessmen have sought to maintain investment of $14. Our earlier assumption was that $12 was for construction and durable equipment and $2 for additional inventories, but every dollar of both kinds of investment requires a dollar of financing. To meet their financing requirements in each period, business may draw on the economy's saving for each time period. Although business generates saving of $11 per time period internally, it must still raise $3 outside. Persons devote $5 of their disposable income in each time period to saving, and it is this flow of saving that business taps for the $3 it needs in external funds.

In each of these periods, government must finance spending of $25. Our assumption is that it draws $24 from the economy's gross income flow through its tax receipts and shows a deficit of $1 for the time period. This $1 of deficit may appropriately be described as governmental or public "dissaving."

Finally, in each time period there are net exports of $1; the rest of the world is buying $1 more of the domestic economy's goods and services than it is selling to the domestic economy. If the domestic economy were importing the same amount that it exports, the rest of the world would be able to finance its purchases of the domestic economy's exports dollar for dollar with its exports to the domestic economy. But with the difference of $1 here assumed, the rest of the world faces the problem of financing that amount in another way. In terms of the identity, this must be viewed as if foreigners tap the domestic economy's flow of saving for $1 per time period. That is, they borrow from the domestic economy's flow of current saving the $1 needed to cover what is not covered by their exports to the domestic economy.

Note the balance that we now have. Gross private domestic investment is $2 less than private saving, and this leaves on the income side the $2 flow for the period available to finance the government's deficit and the economy's net export balance. Any number of other illustrations could be presented, but it will always be true from the identity that there will be a dollar of $S + T$ for every dollar of $I + G + X_n$ and therefore that the sum of the economy's $I + G + X_n$ can be financed in every time period by drawing on the portion of the gross income flow not devoted to personal consumption expenditures, an amount necessarily equal to $I + G + X_n$.

By looking behind the identity between $S + T$ and $I + G + X_n$, we will now begin to see the basis for the monetarist position that an increase, for example, in G that is not accompanied by an increase in the money supply will not bring about a net increase in the economy's spending or income level. We will start off with the same set of figures given in Part B of Table 12–1. Suppose that the existing level of income is estimated to be $10 below that needed for full employment. Furthermore, the government's Keynesian economists estimate that the multiplier is 2 1/2, so an increase in government purchases of $4 will be the increase needed to get the economy to the full employment position. (To minimize complications, we assume a stable price level; if a rise in the price level is expected with any rise in income, a correspondingly larger increase in government purchases would be required to get the required increase in real income.) Suppose that G is increased accordingly from the existing $25 level to $29. Until the impact of the rise in G is felt, everything else remains unchanged: at the existing income level of $100, persons maintain consumption spending at $60, business holds plant and equipment spending at $12 and aims for an increase in inventories of $2, and the net export balance remains at $1. Government tax receipts remain at $24 as before.

Because tax receipts are $24 and government spending is now $29, the government deficit becomes $5, and it must borrow this amount during the time period. Our assumption is that the increase in government spending is not accompanied by an increase in the money supply. As was examined in detail in Chapter 7, this means that the government does not finance any part of the increase in its spending by borrowing from the banking system. It must, in other words, finance the increase by drawing on the economy's existing flow of saving for the time period. From this existing flow of saving we accordingly now have government trying to draw $5, business trying to draw $14, and foreign borrowers trying to draw $1. But the total amount of private saving for the time period is $16, $5 of personal saving and $11 of business saving, or $4 less than the total that borrowers seek to secure.

The result that must follow under these conditions may be apparent. Prior to the increase in government spending, market forces had established a rate of interest—say, 6 percent—that brought the demand for and the supply of the period's saving into balance. That rate will have to be higher now because an additional $4 has been added to the demand side. How much higher will it be? According to the extreme monetarist position, the interest rate will rise by the amount needed to squeeze out an amount of other borrowing equal to the amount of government borrowing. If the government stands ready to pay whatever interest rate is required to enable it to get the amount it needs out of the flow of current saving, it will succeed in getting the amount needed. But if government succeeds, there must then be an offsetting decline in the amount that others are able to secure out of what is an unchanged flow of current saving.

Because we usually think of private investment spending as the kind of spending most sensitive to interest rate changes, the decline in other borrowing may be in borrowing by business. Thus, one possibility is that the rise in the interest rate will squeeze out investment spending of an amount just equal to the increase in government spending to leave the total spending unchanged. The figures before and after the increase in G would then be as follows:

	C	+	S	+	T	=	C	+	I	+	G	+	X_n
Before:	60	+	16	+	24	=	60	+	14	+	25	+	1
After:	60	+	16	+	24	=	60	+	10	+	29	+	1

Because S is made up of saving of $11 by business and $5 by persons, it may appear odd that I would be cut back by the rise in interest rates to $10, or to a level below the amount of saving generated within business, but this is not implausible. What occurs in this case is that $1 of the $11 of business saving is devoted by some firms to the purchase of the securities the government is selling. At the interest rates prevailing at the time, purchase of securities appears more attractive to these firms than the use of their current saving to acquire plant and equipment or to enlarge their inventories.

The Monetarist Argument:
Decreased Taxation Is Nonexpansionary

Through a similar analysis, the monetarists assert that government is also unable to raise the income level by means of tax reductions unaccompanied by an increase in the money supply. Again we can illustrate by starting off with the original identity.

C	+	S	+	T	=	C	+	I	+	G	+	X_n
60	+	16	+	24	=	60	+	14	+	25	+	1

As before, suppose the objective is to bring about a rise in income of $10 as needed to restore the system to the full employment level of output. If the government can bring about an initial increase of $4 in personal consumption spending at the existing income level, this rise in spending will be subject to a multiplier in the same way as an increase of $4 in government spending. An initial increase in consumption spending, in the same way as an increase in government spending, gives rise to an increase in income, which calls forth a further increase in consumption spending, and so forth in successive rounds. With the multiplier equal to 2 1/2, an initial increase in consumption spending of $4 may therefore be expected to eventually raise the income level by the desired $10, according to the Keynesian economists. Skipping over some complications, it appears that the desired initial increase in consumption spending of $4 can be secured by a cut in personal income taxes of approximately $4.30. As was noted earlier, with disposable personal income of $65, consumption was found to be equal to 92.3 percent of disposable personal income. An increase in disposable income of $4.30 may then be expected to increase consumption by 92.3 percent of this amount, or by approximately $4.

Having arrived at what the appropriate figure is, the government takes the steps necessary to cut tax receipts from the existing total of $24 to $19.70 by reducing personal income tax receipts by $4.30. At the existing $100 level of gross national income, disposable personal income rises from $65 to $69.30, and the $69.30 is split by persons into $64 of consumption spending and $5.30 of personal saving. Business saving is $11 as before, but total tax receipts are now down from $24 to $19.70. The existing $100 level of gross national income is thus now split up as follows:

C	+	S	+	T	=	Gross national income
64	+	16.30	+	19.70	=	100

In terms of total spending, the effect of the tax cut would appear to be the desired initial increase of $4 in spending because we do find that consumption spending is up by $4. However, there will be an initial rise in *total* spending of $4 only if the total accounted for by the other spending streams remains unchanged. Monetarists maintain that this will not happen as long as the money supply remains constant, and the reasoning here follows that traced for the case of an increase in government purchases. In the present case, with no change in government spending from its level of $25, the cut in tax receipts from $24 to $19.70 means a deficit of $5.30 for the period. As before, if government seeks to tap the economy's flow of saving for this amount during the current time period, there is then an addition of $4.30 to the demand for the period's flow of saving. The total demand is now $5.30 by government and $14 by business and $1 by foreign borrowers, or a sum of $20.30. The total supply is $16.30, $5.30 of personal saving and $11 of business saving, or $4 less than the total borrowers seek to secure.

The result to be expected in this case is the same as in the case of the increase in government spending. The fact that borrowers seek to secure during the time period an amount $4 greater than the amount provided by the flow of saving for that period will lead to a rise in the rate of interest. Again according to the extreme monetarist position, the rise will be the amount needed to squeeze out of the system an amount of other spending equal to the increase in consumer spending.

Actually, one should allow for the possibility that some of the spending squeezed out will be consumption spending. The increase in disposable personal income resulting from the cut in taxes will stimulate an increase in overall consumption spending, but the rise in the interest rate will discourage consumption spending for autos and other durable goods whose real cost rises with higher costs of financing. This means that, on balance, we may not get the net increase in consumption spending assumed above. However, to keep complications to a minimum, let us again assume that the full brunt of the rise in the interest rate falls on investment. We will then have the following sets of figures for the identity before and after the cut in personal income tax receipts.

	C	+	S	+	T	=	C	+	I	+	G	+	X_n
Before:	60	+	16	+	24	=	60	+	14	+	25	+	1
After:	64	+	16.30	+	19.70	=	64	+	10	+	25	+	1

On the spending side, there is no change in the total, but C is up by \$4 and I is down by \$4. On the income side, T is down by \$4.30, the amount of the tax cut, and this is matched by the increase in C of \$4 and the increase in S of \$0.30.

To sum up to this point: what we have examined in these two illustrations are the two major fiscal policy actions that government can take in the effort to affect the income level—changes in government spending and changes in tax receipts. And we have described the extreme monetarist conclusion that such fiscal actions are powerless to affect the level of income: without a change in the money supply, actions like increased government spending or tax reductions will bring about an increase in one kind of spending only by crowding out an equal amount of other kinds of spending. We turn now to the Keynesian critique of this conclusion.

The Keynesian Reply to the Monetarist Argument

The extreme monetarist conclusion has validity only in the event that the existing money supply is already doing all the work it is capable of doing, only if the amount of buying and selling of goods and services that can be carried out with the existing money supply is already at its limit. There is obviously some limit to the dollar volume of such transactions that each dollar of the money supply can mediate in any time period. Were there not, then the U.S. economy could handle all of the transactions involved in the production and distribution of our approximately \$1,400 billion GNP for the year 1974 with a money supply of only \$1. It is apparent that each of us individually has to have on hand more than \$1, on the average over the year, to handle the relatively small volume of transactions each of us carries out during the year. It should be equally apparent that for the economy as a whole a money supply that runs into many billions of dollars is needed.

While this much is undeniable, it is not the same as saying that the average money stock the public holds is always, or even usually, the absolute minimum needed to handle the existing volume of transactions. As was noted in the introduction to this chapter, if the rate of interest, a major element in the cost of holding money, is relatively low, persons and firms will *not* go to the trouble and inconvenience of conducting their transactions with the very minimum money balance possible. If it is not uncommon to find that they hold more money than the absolute minimum needed for the existing volume of transactions, it follows that that same money supply is capable of handling a larger volume of transactions than it is actually handling. Under such circumstances, the monetarist conclusion that a rise in the income level is ruled out by the inability of the existing money supply to handle the greater volume of transactions is invalid.

Suppose that the average money stock during a period of time is \$20 and the income level for that period is \$100, the same figures used earlier. The public is holding \$1 in money per \$5 of income. Now add to this picture a \$4 rise in government purchases of goods and services designed to raise income toward its full employment level. Assume this creates a deficit, which the government finances by borrowing from the public. As we have seen, one result of this will be a rise in the interest rate as demand for the flow of current saving is increased by the enlarged government borrowing, and a result of the rise in the interest rate will be that some private spending will be choked off. However, another result of the rise in the interest rate will be a reduction in the amount of money the public wants to hold per dollar of income. The release of what are now excess money balances held by some persons and firms means that the *unchanged* money stock will be used to handle a greater volume of transactions than it was handling before the rise in the rate of interest. Putting these two results together gives us another result: the increase in government spending, despite the unchanged money supply, can lead to a rise in the income level.

To identify the rise in the income level, the change in the rate of interest, and the other specific results that will follow from any particular change in government spending financed in this way requires the use of a mathematical model that economists have devised for this purpose. While we cannot enter into such a model here, we may for illustration note several possible sets of results that would be consistent with a new equilibrium. Suppose that the effect of the indicated increase in government spending and of the other changes it brings about is a rise in the interest rate from 6 percent to 7 percent, or 1 percentage point, and that this causes the public to reduce the amount of money it wants to hold from $1 per $5 of income to $0.975 per $5 of income or, expressed as a ratio, from 0.200 of income to 0.195 of income. By the more careful management of its money balances, the public can then handle the transactions accompanying an income level of $100 with $19.50 of money instead of $20.00, and the higher interest rate provides the incentive to do just this. At an income level of $100, this then in effect releases $0.50 of money, and, at the desired ratio of 0.195, this $0.50 of money is adequate to handle the transactions accompanying approximately another $2.50 of income ($0.50/0.195≈ $2.50). In other words, with the reduction in the ratio from 0.20 to 0.195, the existing money supply of $20 is able to support transactions accompanying an income level of $102.50. Suppose that this same 1 percentage point rise in the interest rate causes a reduction in investment spending of $3 so that on balance, given the $4 increase in government spending, there is a net increase in spending of $1. Assuming a multiplier of 2 1/2, the rise in the equilibrium income level is $2.50, or income rises from $100 to $102.50

What we have in this illustration is a rise in the interest rate less than the rise that would choke off an amount of private spending equal to the increase in government spending and thus a rise in the interest rate consistent with an increase in total spending and an increase in the income level. What we also have is a rise in the interest rate of just the magnitude needed to cause the public to reduce the amount of money it wants to hold per dollar of income by the amount needed to enable the existing money supply to handle the greater volume of transactions at the new higher level of income. There is a new equilibrium established in which the supply of and demand for goods are in balance, with goods being produced at the rate of $102.50 per time period and income being generated at the rate of $102.50 per time period and in which the amount of money the public wants to hold at the new income level of $102.50 and the new interest rate of 7 percent is $20, or just equal to the $20 supply of money.

The results we get in any particular case depend on how responsive investment spending is to changes in the interest rate and how responsive the public's desired money holdings per dollar of income are to changes in the interest rate. If investment spending is quite unresponsive and the public's desired money holdings are quite responsive, we will get a larger increase in income as a result of a rise in government spending than in the opposite case. These, it may be noted, are the relationships that Keynes believed existed and are those that underlie his model. For example, given the same rise in government spending of

$4, the following is a possible set of this kind of results. The interest rate rises from the original level of 6 to 6 1/2 percent, and this reduces investment spending by $1. Given the $4 increase in government spending, there is then a net increase in spending of $3. Assuming a multiplier of 2 1/2, the rise in the equilibrium level of income is $7.50, or from $100 to $107.50. The indicated one-half percentage point rise in the interest rate causes the public to reduce the amount of money it wants to hold from $1 per $5 of income to $0.93 per $5 of income, or, expressed as a ratio, from 0.20 to 0.186. At this ratio the existing money supply of $20 is able to handle the transactions accompanying an income level of $107.50, or 0.186 × $107.50 = $20.

It may be seen from these illustrations that a rise in government spending will have some expansionary effect on the level of income, even though there is no increase in the money supply, as long as the amount of money the public wants to hold varies inversely with the rate of interest. If we had worked through illustrations involving a reduction in tax receipts instead of a rise in government spending, the same kind of conclusion would have been derived. Because there is considerable empirical evidence in support of the contention that the amount of money the public wants to hold does vary in this way, there is also support for the Keynesian contention that appropriate fiscal actions are capable of bringing about increases in the income level without having to be accompanied by an increase in the money supply.

At the same time, Keynesians grant that under typical conditions the increase in the income level that will result from an increase in government spending or from a decrease in tax receipts will be larger than otherwise if it is accompanied by an appropriate increase in the money supply. Any increase in the income level involves a proportional increase in the volume of transactions, and, in the absence of an increase in the money supply, a rise in the rate of interest is needed to make the public economize on its holdings of money so as to make the existing money supply handle a greater volume of transactions. We saw in the illustrations above the way in which the rise in the interest rate may be expected to occur. However, this rise in the interest rate need not occur if there is an appropriate increase in the money supply, because then the higher volume of transactions can be handled without forcing the public to economize on its money holdings, which is something market forces cause to happen by forcing up the interest rate. Finally, if there is no rise in the interest rate, there will be no crowding out of private spending—i.e., no offset to the increase in government spending.

For example, with a multiplier of 2 1/2, a rise in government spending of $4 with no decline in private spending will raise the income level by $10. However, not to have a rise in the rate of interest with this rise in income requires an increase in the money supply of $2. At the existing interest rate of 6 percent, our assumption is that the public wants to hold money equal to 0.20 of income; to prevent a rise in the rate of interest as income rises from $100 to $110 then requires an increase in the money supply from $20 to $22.

One needs the formal mathematical model to derive specific results in other cases, but it may be seen from the relationships involved that, on the basis of all of our assumptions, an increase in government spending of $4 and an increase in the money supply of $1 instead of $2 will mean an increase in the equilibrium level of income of less than $10 but of more than would have occurred with no change at all in the money supply, as in the illustrations above. It may also be seen that with an increase in the money supply of $1, the interest rate will not remain unchanged but that its rise will be less than if there were no change in the money supply.

Although we see from this that appropriate increases in the money supply will enlarge the expansionary effect on income of an increase in government spending or a decrease in taxation, our major purpose here has been to see that such fiscal actions also can have an expansionary effect on income in the absence of any increase in the money supply. The rise in the rate of interest, by reducing the amount of money the public wants to hold per dollar of income, enables the existing money supply to handle the larger volume of transactions that accompany an expansion in the level of income. This is a basic conclusion of Keynesian economics and a conclusion that is rejected by economists who accept the extreme monetarist model.

This relationship between the amount of money the public wants to hold per dollar of income and the rate of interest, which provides the basis for the Keynesian conclusion, also provides the basis for the Keynesian denial of the monetarist conclusion that an increase in the money supply will produce a proportional increase in the level of income. As long as the amount of money the public wishes to hold varies with the rate of interest and as long as the rate of interest is affected by the money supply, there cannot be a proportional relationship between changes in the money supply and changes in the income level. We turn next to look at this in some detail.

MONETARY POLICY, THE INTEREST RATE, AND THE INCOME LEVEL

With the tools at their command, the monetary authorities are able to exercise fairly close control over the money supply, and the policy they pursue with regard to the rate at which the money supply grows is known as *monetary policy*. We are not interested at this point in how the monetary authorities decide what this policy should be from time to time—whether monetary policy should be tighter or easier—but in how changes in the money supply that result from any monetary policy work their way through the system to affect the income level. In the preceding chapter, we outlined the extreme monetarist model in which the process is simplicity itself: that model assumes that the public chooses to hold an amount of money equal to a fixed proportion of the income level and therefore in that model changes in the money supply necessarily mean proportional changes in the income level. This result follows, it will be recalled, because any increase or decrease in the money supply is expected to produce the increase or decrease in spending that will bring about that result. The critical question one must ask is what basis there is for expecting total spending to respond in this way to changes in the money supply. It may be that there is a better basis for expecting the change in spending to be relatively large in comparison with the change in the money supply in one period and relatively small in another period without showing any stable relationship over time.

The Portfolio Adjustment Process

To make any headway in this area requires that one start at the beginning—i.e., with a situation in which the public finds itself holding more or less money than it did previously—and to proceed from this to the actions that the public may be expected to take as a result. If we refer to the public's total assets, its holdings of money plus all other assets, as its portfolio, what we want to do is to examine the adjustments the public may make in its portfolio as a result of a change in the amount of money in that portfolio. To understand how a change in the money supply works its way through the system to produce a change in the level of income requires that one trace through the sequence of substitutions that occur among the financial and real assets that make up the public's portfolio. The approach to the question before us through portfolio adjustment has been developed over the past twenty years and is used by both Keynesians and monetarists, although the two see that adjustment process working itself out in somewhat different ways.

One way in which changes in the money supply come about is through purchases and sales of securities by the Federal Reserve. Let us get started by assuming that the Federal Reserve purchases Treasury bills in the open market. How this directly affects bank reserves and the money supply was examined in Chapter 4, but that examination did not enter into an aspect that is fundamental here: these purchases tend to raise the price of Treasury bills and reduce their yield. With yields on other securities unchanged at the moment, a process of arbitrage then begins in which the public shifts into these other relatively higher yielding securities, bids up their prices, and thus pushes down their yields. The result of the Federal Reserve action is, then, a tendency for a decline in yields on securities in general. In addition, the Federal Reserve action has provided additional reserves to the commercial banks, which will lead them to purchase more securities and make more loans. Their purchases of securities will tend to reduce yields even more, and their enlarged supply of loan funds will tend to lower rates on credit of this kind. In the event of a sizable and sustained expansionary action by the Federal Reserve, the lower yields on securities and lower rates on loans will spill over into lower rates paid on savings deposits in banks and share accounts in saving and loan associations.

One of the determinants of the amount of money the public wants to hold is the rate of interest it can earn on alternative assets. Other things being equal, the lower that rate, the larger the amount of money it will choose to hold. As an increase in the money supply tends to reduce the yields that can be earned on financial assets in the way just described, one possible result of the increase in the money supply might be that the interest rates earned on financial assets fall to just the extent to make the public willing to hold the larger amount of money that exists to be held. For example, if the money supply has increased from $20 to $21 and if the interest rate, here to be thought of as the average return on interest-bearing financial assets, had originally been 6 percent, a decline in the interest rate to, say, 5 percent, other things being equal, may cause the public to increase the amount of money it wants to hold at an unchanged level of income from $20 to $21. This suggests that the only effect of the increase in the money supply is a decline in the interest rate sufficient to cause the public to want to hold the larger amount of money that now exists to be held.

While this is a possible adjustment, it is unlikely under ordinary circumstances. What the preceding does not take into account is that there are real as well as financial assets that the public could seek to substitute for money. While the public may at first seek to substitute interest-bearing financial assets for what, at the existing interest rate, have become excess holdings of money, the public will sooner or later also want to substitute real assets. As the yields on financial assets decline, the prospective rates of return on holdings of such real assets as apartment buildings, commercial property, and industrial plant and equipment will look relatively more attractive than before. The public may acquire some real assets like apartment buildings directly, but it acquires other real assets like plant and equipment of General Motors or of Westinghouse indirectly through purchase of ownership claims in the form of the common stock of these corporations. Still, whatever the kind of real assets, increased demand for such assets in general will produce higher prices for them, and this will stimulate producers of these goods to expand the output of them.

Note carefully the point we have now reached. There is increased spending of the kind called investment spending, and, as with a rise in any other spending stream, there will be an increase in the level of the economy's output and income. Thus, the increase in the money supply has set into motion a portfolio adjustment process, one part of which is an increase in the demand for real assets that leads to an increase in the production of these assets and to an increase in the level of income.

An extremely important part of the portfolio adjustment process as it has been sketched here is that the substitution of real assets for financial assets that gives rise to the higher rate of investment spending and to the expanded production of real assets takes place as a result of changes in relative yields on different assets. *It is only because the yields on financial assets have fallen relative to the expected yields on real assets that we find the substitution into real assets.* It is, in other words, this difference in yields that gives rise to the increase in investment spending or to the increase in demand for real assets that produces the rise in the economy's output and income level.

In the judgment of a number of leading economists, this proposition is basic to the difference between the Keynesians and the monetarists. The portfolio adjustment process as it has been sketched here is essentially the process as seen by the Keynesians. Monetarists see the process in the same way up to a point, but they part company with the Keynesians by denying that changes in yields on financial assets are a prerequisite to changes in the demand for real assets. They reject the Keynesian argument that the money supply can work its way through to produce an increase in the demand for goods only by first causing yields on financial assets to fall relative to expected yields on real assets. They maintain that, following an increase in the money supply, there can be a portfolio adjustment in which the movement out of money into real assets is direct and not dependent on a prior decline in the yields on financial assets.

Why is this difference so basic? In a word, if a change in the money supply affects the economy's spending only by first bringing about a change in yields on financial assets or interest rates, the effect on spending of a given change in the money supply can be quite variable, depending on how both the amount of money the public wants to hold and total spending vary with interest rates. The linkage between changes in the money supply and changes in spending and income will not then be as close as the monetarists assert it is.

What this linkage might be can be brought out with some numerical illustrations that parallel those used earlier in this chapter. Let us start off as before with the money supply given at $20, the income level at $100, and the interest rate at 6 percent. Our assumption as before is that there is equilibrium at these figures between the amount of money the public wants to hold and the amount of money that exists. This equilibrium is then upset as the Federal Reserve purchases Treasury bills in the open market in an amount that brings about an increase in the money supply from $20 to $22. Now if the portfolio adjustment process is one in which the public seeks to substitute real assets or goods for money and not other financial assets as well as goods for money, a new equilibrium will be established once the increased demand for real assets or goods has led to an expansion of the rate of output of goods to $110 per time period. At this output level, the $22 of money the public holds is the amount the public wants to hold. This, it will be noted, is the result we showed in the previous chapter in discussing the extreme monetarist model.

The difficulty in accepting this as a plausible portfolio adjustment is that it gives no convincing reason for the public to want to substitute real assets for money to the degree required to achieve the indicated new equilibrium. The public has acquired $2 of new money by giving up securities or incurring bank loans in the amount of $2; the $2 of new money did not come floating down from the heavens. It is crucial to see that, in the present case, the increase in the money supply has not meant an increase in the public's wealth. What the public has done is to change the composition of an unchanged total of wealth. In selling the securities the Federal Reserve and the commercial banks sought to buy and in thereby switching from holding securities to holding money, the public must have sold because it found the price the buyers were offering attractive. The fact that the public has switched from securities to money does not necessarily mean that it in turn wants to switch from money to goods.

The Keynesian position is that there is no reason to expect any increase in the demand for goods or real assets unless there is a decrease in yields on financial assets relative to the expected yield on real assets. If this occurs, real assets become attractive relative to money and other financial assets, and we have reason to expect the public to increase its demand for real assets. However, because an essential element in this adjustment process is a change in yields on financial assets or interest rates and because the amount of money the public wants to hold varies with interest rates, the linkage between a change in the money supply and the level of incomes becomes a much looser thing in the Keynesian scheme than in the monetarist.

Start off with the same numerical illustration used above: money supply equals $20, income level equals $100, interest rate equals 6 percent, and the public wants to hold $20 of money with income at $100 and the interest rate at 6 percent. Now insert the $2 increase in the money supply. As in the case of changes in government spending and taxation examined in the first part of this chapter, here too in order to identify the rise in the income level, the decline in the interest rate, and the other specific results that will follow from a particular change in the money supply requires a formal mathematical model. However, as we did there, we may illustrate here by tracing out several sets of possible results that are consistent with a new equilibrium.

One such possible set is an interest rate of 5 percent and an income level of $104. This assumes that the amount of money the public wants to hold per dollar of income increases from $0.20 to $0.21 when the interest rate falls from 6 to 5 percent. It also assumes that the yields expected on real assets are such relative to the interest rate of 5 percent that there is an increase in demand for real assets that produces an increase in spending of $1.60. Adopting a multiplier of 2 1/2 as in the earlier illustrations, 2 1/2 x $1.60 gives us the indicated increase in income of $4, from $100 to $104. At the new equilibrium rate of interest, the amount of money the public wants to hold is 0.21 x $104, or $22, which is the amount of money the public actually does hold.

If we take another case in which the public's desired money holdings are less responsive to the rate of interest and the public's demand for real assets is more responsive to a decline in the yield on financial assets, the same increase in the money supply will produce a larger increase in the income level. A possible set of figures that reflect this is an interest rate of 5 1/2 percent and an income level of $109. In this case we assume that the public increases the amount of money it wants to hold per dollar of income from $0.200 to $0.202 with a decline in the interest rate from 6 to 5 1/2 percent. We also assume that the increase in spending this decline in the interest rate calls forth is $3.60; this increase times the same multiplier of 2 1/2 means a rise in income of $9, from $100 to $109. At the new equilibrium rate of interest, the amount of money the public want to hold is 0.202 x $109, or $22, which is the amount of money the public actually does hold.

In the first of these two illustrations, the $2 increase in the money supply leads to a $4 increase in the equilibrium level of income, and in the second the same increase in the money supply leads to a $9 increase in the equilibrium level of income. One factor in this difference is the difference assumed in the responsiveness of the public's demand for money holdings to changes in the rate of interest. To the degree that this is variable—i.e., to the degree that a given change in the rate of interest is accompanied from time to time by a larger or smaller change in the amount of money the public wishes to hold per dollar of income—it is possible to get substantially different changes in the level of income as a result of a given change in the money supply.

The Keynesians in general see the relationship in question as a variable one, with a correspondingly variable effect on income of a given change in the money supply. Although the monetarists argue that the relationship itself is not quantitatively important in the first place— i.e., that the amount of money the public wants to hold does not depend importantly on the rate of interest—they maintain as a second line of defense that the relationship, to the degree that it exists, is a stable one. In so doing they may still show a fairly stable relationship between changes in the money supply and changes in income. The relationship will not be the proportional one of the extreme monetarist model because now the amount of money the public wants to hold per dollar of income will be a different amount for each rate of interest. However, if the amount of money the public wants to hold per dollar of income changes in an unvarying or systematic way with the rate of interest, a fairly stable relationship can still be shown to exist between changes in money and changes in the income level.

To the extent that it can be done at all, the only way to resolve the question raised here is through an examination of the empirical record. The difficulty in doing so is a familiar one in economics: it is, at least so far, not possible through the most careful study of the record to arrive at clear and unambiguous answers to these questions. Different investigators often come up with significantly different results from their study of the same body of data. In the relationship under consideration here, economists through multiple regression techniques derive estimates of what is called the "interest elasticity of the demand for money," the ratio of the percentage change in the public's desired money holdings to the percentage change in the interest rate. Using the narrow definition of money, M_1, and using short-term interest rates, virtually all studies find a negative sign for this elasticity, indicating an inverse relationship, but the strength of the relationship varies considerably from one study to another. One based on data for 1919–56 shows an elasticity of −0.33, another for 1919–1960 an elasticity of −0.21, another for 1951–65 an elasticity of −0.41, and another for 1947–58 an elasticity of −0.12. If one uses a different definition of money or uses interest rates other than short-term or works with data for other countries, the elasticities turn out to be quite different from these.* We cannot pursue this technical subject here, but we note it merely to make the point that we cannot get easy, secure answers to the questions involved by "looking at the facts." The facts do not speak

---

*A listing of the elasticities found in various studies is given in F. R. Glahe, *Macroeconomics* (New York: Harcourt Brace Jovanovich, Inc., 1973), pp. 276–77.

out with a clear and unambiguous voice. It is, however, true at the same time that whatever answers economists are able to arrive at can be secured only through this approach.

The answers reached so far do not settle conclusively the differences between the Keynesians and the monetarists on this issue. It seems fair to say at this point that majority opinion leans toward the Keynesian side, toward the conclusion that the way that the public's desired holdings of money respond to the rate of interest is such that changes in the money supply cannot be used to forecast changes in the income level with the degree of precision claimed by monetarists in general.

Changes in Money and Changes in Wealth

As described in the preceding section, the Keynesian view is that a decline in the yield on financial assets relative to the expected yield on real assets is an essential element in the portfolio adjustment process through which an increase in the money supply leads to an increase in the level of income. When they are first confronted with this particular analysis, most noneconomists find little sense in it. To them money need not exert its influence on spending indirectly through changes in relative yields. They see a quite direct and simple relation: more money means more spending.

The foundation for the belief in such a direct relationship seems to be the belief that any increase in the money supply is so much of an increase in the public's wealth. If the public finds that its total wealth is now greater and furthermore that the increment to its wealth is in the form of the most liquid of all assets, it is quite plausible to expect the public to raise the level of its spending directly as a result. However, it is a lack of understanding of the process by which changes in the money supply come about that leads many people to the conclusion that an increase in the total money supply is something the public gets without giving up anything in exchange and is therefore an increase in its wealth. In fact, this is quite incorrect for most of the increases that occur. The public's wealth in most cases is the same after the increase in the money supply as it was before; there has been nothing more than a shift in the composition of the public's portfolio. If the public acquires more money but gives up an equal amount of other assets to get it or incurs an equal increase in its liabilities to get it, the public can hardly be expected to change its spending as it would if the increase in money were so much of a net increase in its financial wealth.

In the preceding section, we dealt with one of these typical cases: an increase in the money supply effected by Federal Reserve purchases of securities in the open market from the public. The result of this is that the public holds more money and less securities; there is a change in the composition of its assets but no change in its total assets or total liabilities. The reason that the people who shifted out of securities into money did so was because of the attractive price at which they could sell the securities. The fact that they now hold money is in itself no reason to expect them to switch out of money into goods. Still, as we saw above, such a switch may follow because of the changes in relative yields that results from the increase in the money supply. The unchanged yields expected on real assets or goods may now be attractive in relation to the lower yields now available on financial assets.

Another typical case is that in which additional money comes into being as a result of borrowing by the public at the commercial banks. Here again the public holds more money than before, but it does not thereby increase its financial wealth. Corresponding to the increase in its assets in the form of money holdings is an equal increase in its liabilities in the form of loans payable to the commercial banks. In terms of its effect on the public's financial wealth, an increase in money brought about in this way is not basically different from an increase brought about by Federal Reserve or commercial bank purchases of securities from the public. The two cases, however, do differ in their probable impact on the public's spending. Persons and firms who were induced to switch out of securities into money by the attractive prices offered for securities are under no special pressure to use the money immediately, whereas persons and firms that obtain additional money by borrowing at the banks are very likely to make prompt use of that money. They surely will not pay interest on the debt incurred to secure the money and then leave the money to sit idly for long in their checking accounts. Some of the money borrowed may be used to finance additional spending. However, here too the reason for the increase in spending is what has occurred to relative yields. In the present case, the reason for the rise in borrowing is a decline in interest rates charged by banks relative to the expected rates of return on the real assets to be acquired with the borrowed funds. From an initial portfolio equilibrium, it is relative rates like these that make advantageous portfolio changes that involve equal increases in the public's assets and liabilities.

It is possible, however, for an increase in the money supply to constitute an actual increase in the public's financial wealth and therefore have a direct effect on the public's spending rather than only the indirect effect that follows from changes in relative yields on different assets. But this will occur only in the event that the U.S. Treasury finances a federal deficit in a manner that increases the money supply. There will then be an increase in the money supply with no offsetting decrease in the public's other assets or increase in its liabilities. As we saw in detail in Chapter 7, deficit financing will result in an increase in the money supply if the Treasury covers the deficit by issuing newly printed currency or by obtaining newly created deposits at the Federal Reserve Banks or at the commercial banks in exchange for interest-bearing Treasury obligations. As the Treasury then transfers these funds to the public in the course of making payments, there will be an increase in the public's holdings of money that, from the public's point of view, is a net increase in its financial assets and in its financial wealth. This increase in wealth in turn may be expected to lead to an increase in spending and in the level of income.

In this particular case, where a change in the money supply is accompanied by a change in the public's financial wealth, Keynesians agree with the monetarists that a change in the money supply may exert a direct effect on spending and on the income level. But in the other cases the Keynesians maintain that the effect is an indirect one, which comes about through portfolio adjustments of the kind described above. However, because the Keynesians grant that an increase in the money supply may affect the income level in each of the cases, it may appear that the difference between the Keynesians and the monetarists is not in *whether* changes in the money supply affect the income level but in the *way* that these changes affect the income level. While there is a degree of truth in this statement, it is not to say that the two sides have come to agreement, for the way in which changes in the money supply work their effect on the income level makes a crucial difference to the closeness and stability of the relationship between changes in the money supply and the income level. The way the monetarists see changes in the money supply working their effect indicates a relation that is close and shows only moderate variation over time; the way Keynesians see this process indicates a relation that is loose and shows considerable variation over time.

The crux of the difference is found in the substitutability of assets. To the Keynesians, other financial assets are close substitutes for money. A rise in the price of one good results in an increase in the demand for another good that is a close substitute for it. Therefore, from the Keynesian viewpoint, an increase in the prices of Treasury bills and other interest-bearing securities that results from, say, Federal Reserve actions that increase the money supply, will lead to an increase in the amount of money the public wishes to hold. But while this means that the public will want to hold more money as a substitute for other financial assets, it will also mean that the public will want to hold more real assets. In the portfolio adjustment process as described earlier, the increase in the demand for real assets leads to an increase in the output of goods and in the level of income. However, what is most significant here is the looseness of the connection between a change in the money supply and a change in the income level. Depending on such things as how responsive the amount of money the public wants to hold is to the rate of interest, a given increase in the money supply can bring about a considerable range of possible changes in the level of income.

It is not this way in the monetarist view, or at least in Professor Friedman's particular monetarist view. He finds that real assets rather than financial assets are the closer substitutes for money. Changes in the prices of interest-bearing financial assets that come about in the course of changing the money supply do not lead the public to seek to substitute money for such assets. Thus, in the case of a rise in the money supply that leads to lower rates of return on other financial assets, the public does not seek to hold more of money and less of other financial assets. How much money the public wants to hold is, in other words, not responsive to the rate of interest, or technically it is interest-inelastic. What the public does seek to do is to hold more real assets or goods and less money. It seeks to substitute real assets for money. This also happens in the Keynesian theory, so the difference is a matter of degree. In Friedmanian theory, the public continues in its attempt to substitute real assets or goods for money until the output of goods and the level of income have expanded to the level at which the amount of money actually held is equal to the fixed proportion of the income level that the public wants its money holdings to equal. When this level is reached, the actual money stock will all be needed to handle the volume of transactions that accompany the higher level of output and income.

Because the Keynesian theory holds that the public seeks to substitute real assets or goods for only a part of the change in the money supply—and a part that may vary from time to time—a change in the money supply does not lead to a change in the output of goods and the level of income such that the money supply is equal to some fixed proportion of output and income. The Friedmanian theory gives us the quantity theory conclusion of a stable relationship between changes in the money supply and changes in the income level; the Keynesian theory rejects the quantity theory conclusion of such a stable relationship.

A CONCLUDING NOTE

Can the government, by appropriate variations in the rate of its spending or in the tax rates it imposes, bring about desired changes in the economy's income level? Or, in short, can fiscal policy be employed to stabilize the economy? The basis for an affirmative answer to this is found in Keynesian theory; the basis for a negative answer is found in monetarist theory. In the first part of this chapter we worked through the monetarist attack on the Keynesian contention that fiscal policy can be employed successfully in the way noted and the Keynesian reply to the monetarist attack.

In asserting that fiscal policy can be used in this way, today's Keynesians do not deny that changes in the money supply also exert an important effect on the income level. However, they do not see that money matters in this regard to anything like the degree the monetarists do. In the second part of this chapter we looked into the basic difference between the Keynesian view and the monetarist view of the portfolio adjustment process by which the system adjusts to changes in the money supply. Because the monetarists see this process as one in which real assets are the closer substitute for money and because the Keynesians see the process as one in which other financial assets are the closer substitutes for money, the monetarists reach the conclusion of a relatively close linkage between changes in the money supply and the level of income and the Keynesians reach the conclusion of a relatively loose linkage.

It may be clear that no amount of theoretical argument will be able to answer the question of the degree to which the observed changes in the income level depend on changes in the money supply. The monetarists submit what they regard as eminently logical arguments to support a very close linkage, and the Keynesians submit what they regard as eminently logical arguments to deny such a linkage. The Keynesians find it especially difficult to find logic in the monetarists' description of the portfolio adjustment process, because the monetarists see wealth-holders engaged in all kinds of substitutions among all kinds of assets in response to changes in the relative yields on these assets with one exception: there is no substitution of money for other financial assets. As Professor Friedman visualizes the role of money in the economy, there is apparently no logical deficiency in this one exception.

It would seem that the question of which side has the better case would by now have been conclusively settled by an appeal to the "facts." However, a careful examination of the historical record does not in itself give the kind of support to either side that will conclusively settle the question. Of course, many monetarists flatly reject the statement that the question is in doubt; to them the empirical evidence has settled it quite conclusively and the only difficulty is the blindness of those who cannot see this. For example, *Money and Markets, A Monetarist View,** a recent nontechnical book by a staunch monetarist,

*New York: Irwin, 1971.

Beryl Sprinkel, has a section "What are the Facts?" that is full of statements like these: " . . . there has been voluminous research work compiled and the answer rings loud and clear—money calls the tune," (p. 107) " . . . the evidence was remarkably consistent and unambiguous, (p. 115): " . . . the research has been prodigious and convincing," (p. 117).

There indeed has been a vast amount of empirical work done on this question and in the following chapter we will look at a sample of it. Although we will see that much of it appears to "ring loud and clear" for the monetarists' side, we will also see that there are some strong arguments advanced by nonmonetarists to support their contention that the ring given off by the evidence is "quiet and ambiguous."

fourteen
HOW MUCH
DOES MONEY MATTER?
THE EMPIRICAL EVIDENCE

The general public usually believes that it is an easy matter to settle conclusively whether or not a hypothesized relationship between several economic variables actually exists: all one has to do is look at the "facts" as provided by the historical record. How close and stable is the relationship between the money supply and the level of income? We have detailed figures on the money supply and on gross national product or other measures of income going back over a long period of years, so an examination of this historical record should show what relationship, if any, exists between them.

FIGURE 14–1   RATE OF CHANGE IN MONEY SUPPLY AND BUSINESS CYCLES, 1920–74.

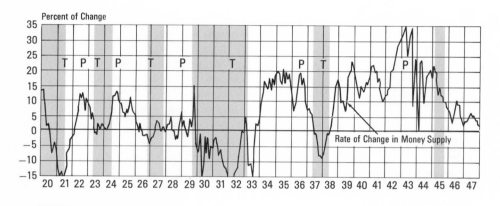

Contraction phase of business cycle

Source: Department of Commerce, Board of Governors of the Federal Reserve Board, National Bureau of Economic Research.

While it is true that study of this record is the only way that we can possibly find what the relationship actually is, this is not to say that such study will tell us definitively what that relationship is. Study of the same record by different people of the highest competence has produced not this definitive answer but considerably different answers to the question before us. In this chapter we want to note a few features of that long and complicated record and enter into some of the problems encountered in trying to get from it a definitive answer to the question: "How much does money matter?"

THE BUSINESS CYCLE TURNING–POINTS APPROACH

When one turns to the historical record, his first problem is to organize the flood of facts provided by that record in a way that will best shed light on the question he seeks to answer. An uncomplicated but revealing presentation is that which shows the rate of change in the money supply in relation to successive expansions and contractions in business activity, as in Figure 14–1. The shaded areas represent contraction or recession periods according to the chronology of the National Bureau of Economic Research, a private

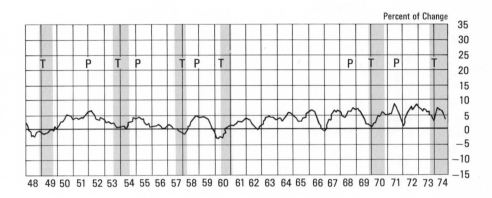

research organization whose business cycle dates are the closest thing we have to an "official" list of such dates. It was quite certain at the time of writing in the fall of 1974 that the downturn that appeared to have started in late 1973 would not only continue through 1974 but through the first half or perhaps all of 1975. The "official" dates of the nation's sixth postwar recession will not be established for some time, but we have here shown it to have started in late 1973. The economy is regarded to be always either in contraction or expansion, so the unshaded areas represent expansion periods.

It should be noted that dating peaks and troughs—the months in which an expansion turns into a contraction and a contraction turns into an expansion—is difficult in any case but especially so in cases where the movement from one phase into the other is very gradual. For example, although the National Bureau set November 1969 to November 1970 as the dates for that contraction, a number of economists in this area believe that expansion did not begin until well into 1971. However, in most cases there is little disagreement on these dates, and they are generally accepted to be as shown in Figure 14–1.

The curve in the figure shows changes in the rate of growth of the money supply, with money supply here defined as M_1, or the sum of currency and demand deposits in the hands of the public. The curve was derived as a six-month moving average of monthly changes expressed at annual rates and based on seasonally adjusted data. A glance at this curve makes clear that the money supply has not grown at anything like a steady rate over the half-century covered. As in the case of general business activity, it is possible to identify peaks and troughs in the rate of growth of the money supply, although deciding what reversals in the curve are to be recognized as peaks and troughs presents very difficult problems as does the dating of peaks and troughs in general business activity. There is no one set of dates on which all will agree, but one of the possible sets is shown in the figure by the letters P and T.

The important thing here is that this or any other realistic set of such dates will reveal something of the greatest importance in the Keynesian-monetarist debate. Over the period of 12 business cycles shown in the figure (counting the 1974 experience as the twelfth), the rate of growth of the money supply turns down before the downturn in general business and turns up before the upturn in general business. Allowing for the fact that it takes time for changes in the money supply to work their way through the system to affect the levels of income, spending, and general business activity, it then seems easy to conclude from Figure 14–1 that the successive business contractions the economy has gone through have been the result of the fact that some months earlier a slowing in the rate of growth of the money supply began. In the same way, it seems easy to conclude that the business expansion that follows every contraction was the result of the fact that some months earlier a rise in the rate of growth of the money supply began. When one finds a relationship that shows such impressive empirical regularity, it seems to cry out loud and clear that "money calls the tune."

This conclusion seems to be reinforced by other evidence not apparent from Figure 14–1, which shows only the duration and not the severity or amplitude of movement of each recession or depression. Of the contractions suffered by the economy during the period covered by the figure, the most severe were those of 1920–21, 1929–33, and 1937–38. As may be seen from an examination of the money growth rate curve, it was also during or just preceding these business contractions that the most severe monetary contractions occurred. Compare these cases with the mild business contraction of 1969–70, during and preceding which the monetary "contraction" was also mild. However "tight" money seemed to be to the public back in 1969, the monetary downturn that then took place actually involved no more than a slowing in the rate of growth of the money supply in contrast to the earlier noted downturns in which the rate of growth of the money supply turned decidedly negative.

In the face of the kind of evidence found in Figure 14–1, no one denies that changes in economic activity have been closely associated with changes in the behavior of the money stock. Figure 14–1 shows that this has been true over the past fifty some years, but the same has been shown to be the case going back as far as the data permit, which is a little over a hundred years. Nor does anyone deny that there is a persistent tendency for the rate of change in the money supply to lead turning points in the level of business activity. However, having acknowledged this much, we must face the crucial question: Does this evidence justify the monetarist conclusion that the changes in business activity are the *result* of changes in the money supply? We will look at a few of the many arguments advanced by the monetarists and their critics.

Although the technical deficiencies of this argument have long been recognized by professional economists, an argument that has been of the greatest importance in winning over laymen to the side of monetarism is the apparent timing relationship in which changes in business activity follow with some lag changes in the money supply. There is a natural inclination on the part of the public to put money in the causal role when the two are related in this way over time. If the historical record had happened to show that changes in the money supply followed changes in business activity with some lag, it would for the same reason be unlikely that monetarism would have won over as many believers as it has from the ranks of the public.

The professional economist learns early in his training to be very wary of concluding that one thing is necessarily the result of another because it follows the other chronologically. It is not unknown for the effect to precede the cause as, for example, in the case where wage rates begin to creep up because prices are expected to do so later. Furthermore, the relationship between the two variables in question may not be one in which the changes in either are the effect of changes in the other; the changes in both may be predominantly the effect of still some other variable.

Beyond this, whatever case might be made for the causality of money on the grounds that money leads business activity is, of course, lost if it is shown that money does not really lead. There is evidence that the lead shown in Figure 14–1 is a result of a biased methodology. The curve in that figure shows the rate of change in the money supply, not the money supply itself. On the other hand, the level of activity is shown simply as expansion or contraction and not as a rate of expansion or contraction. This means that the estimate of the lag that is derived is based on a comparison of the inflection points in *the rate of change of the money supply* with those in *the absolute level of business activity*. Critics have been quick to point out that this will account for a certain lead of money over business activity simply for mathematical reasons, and that the opposite, to plot the rate of change of business activity against the stock of money, would on the same basis result in a lead of business activity over the money supply, a result that would surely weaken the case for monetarism in the eyes of the general public.

Professor Friedman, who originally employed the methodology that gives us the kind of results shown in Figure 14—1, justified his use of the rate of change of the money supply on the practical grounds that the stock of money shows a pronounced trend, which means that it increases in absolute amount with rare interruptions. If the relationship between the money supply series and business activity is to be analyzed by comparing turning points in the money supply with turning points in business activity, it is necessary to make use of some measure of the money supply like its rate of growth that shows reasonably distinct turning points. While the critics grant that Friedman's point is essentially valid, they raise the logical question of why, for the sake of comparability, a similar measure of business activity was not employed. If the percentage change in the money supply is to be used, should it not be compared with the percentage change in business activity? For the latter, gross national product or industrial production is an appropriate series. When this kind of comparison is made, the long leads of money over business activity shown by Figure 14—1 disappear. Over the period since World War II, the peaks and troughs in these two series occur almost simultaneously. On the average, the lead in the peaks and troughs in the rate of growth of the money supply over the peaks and troughs in the rate of growth of GNP are a quarter or less, a lead that has been described as nothing more than an "arithmetic artifact."*

While it is informative to know whether the money supply shows a persistent lead over business activity or whether the two move more or less simultaneously, this in itself still cannot begin to resolve the question of what the causal relationship between the two may be. For this reason, antimonetarists cannot and do not limit their attack to the question of timing. Arguments are advanced which purportedly show that, even if the changes in money do lead the changes in business activity, the direction of causation may still be, not predominantly from the money supply to business, but from business to the money supply. On their side, the monetarists seek to show that the changes in the money supply can be explained in large part by factors not closely related to changes in business activity. If it can be shown that monetary changes have in fact been independent in this sense, it follows that

---

*These are the conclusions reached by John H. Karaken and Robert M. Solow in the Commission on Money and Credit, *Stabilization Policies* (Englewood Cliffs, N.J.: Prentice-Hall, 1963), pp. 15-24.

causation runs from the money supply to business and not from business to the money supply.

In their monumental study, *A Monetary History of the United States, 1867–1960*,* Milton Friedman and Anna Schwartz have provided an amazingly detailed analysis of a near century of monetary and banking developments in this country. With respect to the question now before us, one of their important conclusions is that monetary changes have often had an independent origin and have not been simply a reflection of changes in economic activity. The authors identify six time periods during which the money supply (defined as M_2) showed an absolute decline: 1873–79, 1892–94, 1907–08, 1920–21, 1929–33, and 1937–38. Each of these periods was also a period of major business decline; the last three of these were noted earlier and are shown by the corresponding shaded areas in Figure 14–1. Friedman and Schwartz seek to show that the particular circumstances that produced the decline in the money supply during each of these six periods were of a kind that cannot be explained by the business downturn. Therefore, if there is a causal connection between money and business activity, it is maintained that the direction in these cases cannot be primarily from business activity to money.

To illustrate the nature of their argument, we will look briefly at one of the less involved of these episodes, that of 1937–38. Due primarily to the large inflow of gold following the devaluation of the U.S. dollar in January 1934, excess reserves of the commercial banks increased greatly in the next few years. It was feared by some that these excess reserves might give rise to a runaway expansion of credit. In 1936 Congress granted power to the Federal Reserve to vary reserve requirements of the member banks, and in three steps during 1936 and 1937 the Federal Reserve raised the requirements to the new maximum percentages, which were twice the original. The last of these increases was effective May 1, 1937, and occurred at the same time that the Treasury was engaged in gold sterilization, which was the equivalent of a large-scale restrictive open market operation. Because the higher reserve requirements did no more than absorb the bulk of the excess reserves held by the banks, the authorities did not expect this to lead to a contraction of credit. However, Friedman and Schwartz argue that because of the disastrous experience of 1930–33 the commercial banks wanted to maintain large holdings of excess reserves. In the effort to do this, they responded to the higher percentage reserve requirements by reducing the amount of their outstanding credit and thereby brought about a contraction in the money supply. The money supply had grown

---

*Princeton University Press, 1963.

at a 4.2 percent rate from June 1936 to June 1937, but in the following year it fell at the rate of 2.4 percent.

Friedman and Schwartz contend that this behavior of the money stock cannot be attributed to the contemporaneous course of business. Their view is that it was caused by the deliberate policy measures taken to meet what the authorities regarded as a problem of excess reserves produced by the massive gold inflows to the United States. Therefore, the 1937–38 recession was not causal in the decline of the money stock, but the decline in the money stock was causal of the 1937–38 recession. While the circumstances differ from case to case, the same general conclusion is reached by these writers for all six of the cases noted. To merely mention one other, the post-Civil War episode of 1873–79 was due to the political decision to resume conversion of United States Notes, or "greenbacks," into gold at the prewar rate; this was a development essentially independent of business activity but one that led to a prolonged and severe decline in the money supply and contributed importantly to the decline in business activity. In each case, according to Friedman and Schwartz, the decrease in the money supply cannot be explained by what was simultaneously occurring in the area of business activity, but the decrease in the money supply appears to have been the major factor causing the decline in business activity.

Although this branch of their work has focused on the six major downturns, Friedman and Schwartz see no reason to believe that the behavior of the money supply has not played a significant role in the 21 other recessions that have occurred in the United States between 1854 and 1970. In most of these other recessions, the money supply did not turn down in absolute amount even temporarily. There was, in other words, an almost uninterrupted expansion in the money supply in the face of a decline in business activity. However, as was earlier noted in connection with Figure 14–1, a decline in the rate at which the money supply was growing occurred in advance of the decline in business activity. Friedman and Schwartz do not claim that the minor recessions can be explained by the decrease in the rate of increase in the money supply that preceded them, but they do assert that this in turn had a significant influence on business activity. In these minor recessions, they see influences running both ways—business activity affecting the money supply and the money supply affecting business activity. They see money in these cases more nearly as an equal partner with business activity. However, in the earlier identified major cyclical movements, they see money rather clearly as the senior partner.

On their side, the critics of the monetarists submit a number of reasons to support their belief that the variations in the growth of the money supply have been strongly influenced by business activity.

Consider first an argument that applied during the pre-1914 days of the old-fashioned gold standard. As income and prices rose in one country relative to others, that country would incur a deficit in its balance of payments, which would lead to an outflow of gold. Because the money supply was tied closely to the country's monetary gold stock under that gold standard system, the result would be a shrinkage in the country's money supply. According to the rules of the gold standard game, central banks were to follow a "hands off" policy and allow the money supply to respond freely to these gold movements. As a result of such movements, the money supply could thus contract even as overall business activity continued to expand, but what is relevant here is that the cause of the contraction of the money supply is to be found in what occurred in the sphere of business. One may, of course, argue that the reason for the rise in income and prices in the country in question was an earlier increase in that country's money supply, but this still does not preclude the reverse causation in which the effect of the expansion in business activity on the nation's balance of payments leads to a shrinkage in the country's money supply.

The old-fashioned gold standard has been a thing of the past since the 1930s. Since then central banks have been guided in their regulation of the money supply primarily by the goal of providing domestic stability, and the degree of automatic response of the money supply to international gold movements under the old-fashioned gold standard, however strong or weak it was in its time, was no more at all. What should be noted is this: when central banks, in our case the Federal Reserve, set out to control the money supply in a way that is expected to help stabilize the economy, the result of the actions taken will be a tendency for the rate of growth of the money supply to turn down before a downturn in business activity and to turn up before an upturn in business activity. This is the same relationship just noted under the old-fashioned gold standard, but it is one that does not come about in an automatic way.

To see how this works, assume that a business expansion has begun to move so rapidly and to exert such pressures on prices that the Federal Reserve authorities judge it necessary to take restrictive action. This action will be of a kind that reduces the rate at which the money supply is growing. If a sufficiently restrictive policy is maintained for a sufficiently long period of time, a peak will appear in the money growth series. Business activity, on the other hand, may continue to expand for some time before it reaches a peak. In a similar way, the adoption and maintenance of an easy policy by the Federal Reserve in the face of what appears to be the beginning of a recession would establish a trough in the money growth series while business activity continued to move downward for some time before it reached a trough.

These are changes in the rate of growth of the money supply that come about because of changes in business activity. It is true that they occur as a result of deliberate actions taken by the Federal Reserve, but the basis for these actions is the state of business activity. As we saw in an illustration above, Friedman and Schwartz found the change in the money supply in 1936–37 to be the result of deliberate action taken by the Federal Reserve, the doubling of member bank reserve requirements, but they sought to show that this action was unrelated to business activity at the time. What the critics assert is that in many cases, especially since World War II, the explanation for the lead in the peaks and troughs in business activity is found in the response of monetary policy to business activity and in the response of the money supply to monetary policy. To the degree that this argument is valid, the monetarist contention that business downturns are the result of previous slowdowns in the rate of growth of money or that business upturns are the result of previous speedups in the rate of growth of money is invalid.

The antimonetarists also point out other reasons why we should expect changes in business activity to bring about changes in the rate of growth of the money supply. One of these arises from changes in the composition of the money supply as the level of business activity expands and contracts. The record shows that the public tends to increase the fraction of its money held in the form of currency as the economy moves through the expansion phase of the cycle and to reduce that fraction during the contraction phase. In the early stages of an expansion phase, the money supply may be able to grow substantially because of the increase in bank reserves provided by the central bank in the course of pursuing a contracyclical policy during the preceding recession. But at some point in the expansion, the rise in the currency ratio will cause a decrease in the money supply if additional reserves are not supplied. Recall the process here involved: each additional dollar of currency held by the public is obtained by drawing one dollar of currency out of the commercial banks, and each dollar so withdrawn is a decline in bank reserves of one dollar, which forces a contraction in demand deposits of a multiple of that dollar. Note that the rise in the currency ratio will cause this downturn in the money supply without positive action by the central bank to decrease the total reserves held by the banks; all that it calls for is that the central bank not increase the amount of those reserves. Thus, the way that the currency ratio changes in response to the level of business activity in itself helps to explain how a decrease in the money supply can occur while the level of business activity continues to expand.

Another reason we should expect changes in business activity to bring about changes in the rate of growth of the money supply is found in the behavior of the banks with respect to holdings of excess reserves. Whatever the given total of reserves may be, the commercial banks' holdings of excess reserves are a measure of unused loan-creating power and thus a measure of unused deposit-creating and money-creating power. As the economy comes out of a recession, the banks ordinarily will seek to maintain a relatively high ratio of excess reserves to deposits, but as the expansion moves into high gear, as the pessimism engendered by the recession wears away, and especially as interest rates on loans start to move upward, the banks will move toward a lower excess reserve ratio. Doing this leads to an increase in bank lending and works toward an increase in the money supply. Because the ratio of excess reserves to deposits the banks choose to maintain varies with business activity and because the changes in this ratio tend to cause changes in the money supply, we have in this another way in which changes in business activity exert an influence on the growth of the money supply.

It is apparent from this brief look that the critics of monetarism are no more without arguments to support their position that influence runs from business activity to the money supply than are monetarists without arguments to support the opposite position. With the exception of the six major downturns in which Friedman and Schwartz maintain that the money supply was clearly the senior partner, the differences between them and other monetarists, on the one hand, and the antimonetarists, on the other hand, are a matter of degree. Monetarists recognize an influence running from business activity to money in most cycles, and few of their critics would deny that there is no influence at all running from money to business activity. If it is possible to make a single generalization, it seems that it must be that the monetarists overall see money as the predominant influence on the level of business activity, and the antimonetarists or Keynesians see other factors, so-called real factors, as the predominant influence on the level of business activity, with the money supply varying as it does primarily in response to changes in the level of business activity.

THE ECONOMETRIC APPROACH

A generalization like the one just noted is obviously not very satisfying to anyone. What one would like is some quantitative measure of the importance or unimportance of changes in the money supply as a cause of changes in the level of business activity. Procedures like comparing turning points in the rate of change of the money supply and in business activity over our history, however informative this may be, do not yield the kind of quantitative measure suggested. To get this calls for the use of econometric models, and we will here look briefly at some of the results provided by just a few of these models.

Econometrics itself is the combined use of mathematics and statistics to provide answers to questions in economics. Most of the variables we deal with in economics are quantitative: income, interest rates, money supply, tax receipts, government spending, consumption, and so forth. Theoretical propositions about the way persons and businesses respond to various influences may be expressed in mathematical form. For example, in the preceding chapter some attention was given to the proposition that the amount of money people want to hold depends on the interest rate. Although one does not need more than what was given there to grasp the general proposition that is involved, for use in econometrics a precise formulation in the form of a mathematical expression is required. Once the econometrician has put together an interrelated set of such mathematically expressed theoretical propositions relevant to the question at hand, statistical methods are employed to derive quantitative measures of the mathematically stated relationships from the data covering the actual past experience of the economy. In the illustration noted, a coefficient would be derived; the change in the amount of money the public would choose to hold for a given change in the interest rate, other things being equal, would be indicated by multiplying that change in the interest rate by this coefficient.

In connection with the question of how much money matters, what is of interest is a coefficient that will indicate how much of a change in GNP, or some other measure of the level of aggregate business activity, will occur for a given change in the money supply. We may start off by referring to an econometric study of some years back in which the coefficients obtained were startling enough to produce a major stir in the Keynesian-monetarist debate. This study by two economists of the strongly monetarist Federal Reserve Bank of St. Louis concluded that changes in government expenditures and receipts had virtually no effect on GNP, while changes in the money supply had powerful effects.*

Based on the data for 1952 through mid-1968, the coefficients in their equation, which came to be called the "St. Louis equation," show that a $1 billion increase in the money supply will raise the GNP by $1.5 billion in the same quarter, by just over $3 billion at the end of two quarters, and by about $6 billion at the end of four quarters. In

---

*L. C. Anderson and J. L. Jordan, "Monetary and Fiscal Actions: A Test of Their Relative Importance in Economic Stabilization," in *Review*, Federal Reserve Bank of St. Louis, November 1968.

comparison, a $1 billion increase in government expenditures will raise GNP by a little less than $1 billion at the end of two quarters, but it then causes declines in GNP in the following two quarters that practically offset the increase of the first two quarters. The effect of a $1 billion increase in government expenditures on GNP is less than $100 million at the end of four quarters. A $1 billion decrease in tax receipts does not do much better than an equal increase of government expenditures; at the end of four quarters, the increase in GNP is less than $250 million. In terms of its impact on GNP over the course of one year, a dollar of additional money thus appears to be about eighty times as strong as a dollar of additional government spending and about twenty times as strong as a dollar of tax change! In addition to this startling finding, other statistical measures yielded by this study indicate that the response of economic activity to monetary change is more predictable than its response to fiscal actions and that the main response of economic activity to monetary change occurs in fewer quarters than the main response to fiscal actions. In brief, relative to the effects of changes in government purchases and taxes, the effects of changes in the money supply are "large, predictable, and fast." To the degree that these findings are valid, there can be little question that it is indeed money that really matters, while fiscal actions hardly matter at all.

The critics were quick to jump on these results as suspect for a number of reasons, one of which is alleged deficiencies in the kind of model that was used. In following a technique used earlier in an econometric study by Friedman, these authors rely on the so-called reduced-form approach, which yields a one-equation model. Apart from other difficulties, this equation, which makes the change in GNP a function of changes in the money supply and other variables, can provide unibased estimates of the influence of money on GNP only if the changes in the money supply are independent of the changes in GNP. If in fact the money supply varies in response to variations in GNP, we may find a high coefficient for the money supply, as in the Anderson-Jordan study, not because changes in the money supply cause changes in GNP but for the opposite reason. As may be apparent, we are back to the same problem of reverse causation that we came up against in the preceding section.

Although monetarists who employ this approach have conducted econometric studies whose results purportedly show that the response of the money supply to business activity is quite small and that the money supply therefore technically qualifies as an exogenous variable in the one-equation model, other economists dispute this. As they see it, to separate out the influence of the money supply on business activity from what they find to be the nonnegligible influence of business activity on the money supply requires a detailed structural

model made up of a number of equations that allow the major inter-
dependencies that exist to be appropriately taken into account.

The foremost model of this kind is the Federal Reserve Board-
M.I.T.-Pennsylvania (FMP) model. The first version of this model was
constructed by a group of econometricians at the Board in Washington
and at M.I.T. in Cambridge during 1966—67; it has gone through a
number of versions since then in which a group of econometricians at
the University of Pennsylvania have played a part. This particular model
is one, and not the best known one, of more than a dozen large-scale
models now in use, but it differs from the others in its more detailed
attention to the financial sector of the economy. It permits its user to
learn something about the quantitative effects of monetary policy, to
compare this with the quantitative effects of, say, fiscal policy, and to
do this within the framework of a large-scale model that avoids what
many econometricians believe to be the major shortcomings of the
one-equation St. Louis model.*

What does the large-scale model say will be the response of GNP to
changes in the money supply and in government expenditures and tax
receipts? For the same 1952—68 period on which the St. Louis results
were based, it shows that an increase in the money supply will bring
about an increase in GNP of about $0.4 billion at the end of four
quarters in contrast to the $6 billion claimed by the St. Louis equation.
According to this, the impact of a change in the money supply over the
course of one year is less than one-tenth of that indicated by the St.
Louis model! In the case of fiscal policy, the FMP model shows that a
$1 billion increase in government spending will lead to a $3.4 billion
increase in GNP at the end of four quarters, and that a $1 billion
decrease in tax receipts will lead to an increase in GNP of $3.2 billion
over the same time period. Quantitative results like these are in line
with what most economists had for years believed were to be expected
from these fiscal actions. The results indicated by the St. Louis equation—that fiscal actions have virtually no effect on income—were just
what was to be expected only in the view of the staunchest of the
monetarists.

What is one to make of such conflicting results? The answer would
appear to be that more study is needed. There has been no shortage of
this since 1968, but some of the studies lend support to the monetarist
side, and others do the same for the antimonetarist side. This arises in
part from the fact that the models used in these studies differ in terms
of the explanatory variables included and the behavioral relationships

---

*For a description of the model, see F. De Leeuw and E. M. Gramlich, "The
Federal Reserve-MIT Econometric Model," in *Federal Reserve Bulletin*, January
1968, and "The Channels of Monetary Policy" in the same publication, June 1969.

that are assumed in their construction. Apart from the broad distinction between structural and reduced form models noted above, there is practically no end to the variations that are possible along these lines.

A recent important study by Carl F. Christ* incorporates as a distinctive feature of the model what is known technically as the "federal government budget restraint." The model is otherwise similar to other reduced-form models like the St. Louis model, but its results are, nonetheless, quite different from those given by the St. Louis model. Based on annual data for the period 1891–1970, Christ found that increases in both federal government purchases and the high-powered money supply (the sum of currency in the hands of the public and reserves of the commercial banks) have had substantial stimulative effects on money income. Furthermore, when the long period is broken down into six subperiods, the magnitudes of the effects do not appear to have been stable from period to period. Also, in terms of speed of impact, government purchases exert their effect rather promptly, whereas the speed of response of money income to high-powered money is not clearly established in this study. Anderson and Jordan had concluded in their study that the effects of money supply changes relative to changes in government purchases and tax receipts were "large, predictable, and fast." The Christ study casts much doubt on this.

Having noted this study by Christ that provides little support for the monetarist side, it would only be fair to note next one more study that does provide strong support for that side. However, the point has already been more than adequately made: the results of the econometric studies conflict significantly. At least up to now, we have an abundance of coefficients spewed out by some econometric models to show that changes in the money supply are of extreme importance and an abundance from other models to show a much lesser importance for money.

A CONCLUDING NOTE

The quantitative measurement of the influence of the money supply and fiscal variables on the income level poses problems with which econometricians will continue to grapple, but it is unlikely that they will be able to progress far enough in the next few years to provide a reasonably definitive resolution of

---

*"Monetary and Fiscal Influences on U.S. Money Income, 1891–1970," in *Journal of Money, Credit and Banking,* February 1973, pp. 279–300.

the Keynesian-monetarist debate. As one econometrician recently put it, that debate threatens to outlive us all. In the meantime, we may expect that certain economists who, on the basis of noneconometric evidence, are convinced of the accuracy of their position will continue to accept as the more accurate those econometric studies whose results support their position. Economists who are strongly monetarist and economists who are strongly Keynesian will both find the studies they need in the work that has already been done and that will be done in the years ahead. However, economists who hold neither a strong Keynesian nor a strong monetarist position, and this must include a large fraction of the total, will probably not see their position changed in the near future as the result of what will likely be more mixed results of further econometric studies.

fifteen

THE TARGETS
OF MONETARY POLICY

There are few economists today who hold to the once wide-spread opinion that money doesn't matter. The reverse, in fact, is conceded by practically all, but today's Keynesians insist that fiscal actions also matter and matter much, while monetarists will grant no such significance to fiscal actions. As noted in our brief look at empirical testing, the attempts to identify the relative influence on economic activity of changes in money and changes in fiscal variables have produced anything but uniform results. Because these results do not provide clear evidence to do otherwise, what they say to most economists is that we should continue to assign an important role to both fiscal and monetary policy in our efforts to achieve a more stable economy.

"Monetary policy" refers to the complete set of government actions relating to the behavior of the money supply. In Chapters 4 and 5 we examined the basic mechanics by which certain actions of the Federal Reserve authorities bring about changes in bank reserves and, through this, changes in the money supply. The specific tools the Federal Reserve uses to alter the banks' reserve position were covered in Chapter 6. Thus, these few chapters together showed us how open market operations, changes in the discount rate, and changes in reserve requirments affect the banks' reserve position and how changes in the banks' reserve position affect the money supply. In Chapters 7 and 8 we saw that other governmental actions, specifically those of the Treasury in handling its deposit balance and in borrowing, also affect the money supply, but we noted there that the Federal Reserve authorities can and do take the steps needed to prevent Treasury actions from producing a behavior of the money supply different from what the Federal Reserve is seeking to bring about. However, merely knowing the means by which the Federal Reserve brings about changes in the money supply does not tell us anything about what monetary policy *should* be—whether under any given set of conditions a tighter or easier policy should be followed.

At first glance, the decision as to what appropriate monetary policy should be at any time appears to be an easy one. Because the ultimate purpose of all macroeconomic policy is to attain such goals as full employment, stable prices, a satisfactory rate of growth, and balance of payments equilibrium, we should adjust monetary policy in whatever direction and to whatever degree is needed to provide the maximum contribution to the achievement of these goals. However, as anyone with the slightest acquaintance with economic policy knows, it is quite impossible for monetary policy to do all this. A first and very well-known problem is that of pursuing all of these goals simultaneously. Some of these goals conflict. For example, if we pursue an expansionary monetary policy with the aim of achieving full employment, the expansion of aggregate spending which that policy involves may carry with it a sacrifice of the goal of price stability. Others among these goals do not conflict in this sense but are so related that more than one kind of policy must be used if more than one goal is to be achieved. For example, if we seek to raise the employment level and also reduce a deficit in the balance of payments, the appropriate action may be to rely on an expansionary fiscal policy to meet the domestic employment problem and a contractionary monetary policy to meet the balance of payments problem. The expansionary fiscal policy will bring about an increase in aggregate demand and raise output and employment; the contractionary monetary policy will raise interest rates and replace what may be an existing outflow of capital with an inflow, thus reducing the deficit in the balance of payments.

Even after allowing for the fact that monetary policy may not in certain circumstances be capable of working toward the attainment of more than one goal, the action that should be taken to achieve this single goal is still not as evident as it may seem to be. Take the case of what appears to be the beginning of an economic downturn as reflected by a rise in the unemployment percentage. Suppose also that the single goal chosen for monetary policy is to provide the economy with full employment. Then the obviously appropriate policy is for the monetary authorities to carry out open market operations and/or use its other tools in a way that will increase the rate at which the economy's money supply is growing. If it is clear that the economy is going into a recession, this indeed may be the direction in which to move, but the authorities must also decide how intensively to push the expansionary policy. The problem is that they cannot be properly guided in this decision by the behavior of a variable like the unemployment percentage. A rise in unemployment in a recession will be due, at least in part, to a slowing of total spending, and an increase in the money supply may bring about an expansion of total spending and thus help to reduce unemployment. But unemployment is also being affected continuously by structural and institutional changes throughout the economy. For example, jobs are lost due to relocation of firms with older workers unable to follow them and due to mismatching of jobs and workers as technological change increases the skill and education requirements for many jobs. This kind of unemployment does not yield readily to changes in total spending. Therefore, for the monetary authorities to take a certain unemployment percentage as their target and then simply pump more and more money into the economy as long as the unemployment percentage is above the target level could be disastrous. The result could be a continued state of less than full employment combined with a serious inflation.

Another difficulty in taking a variable like an unemployment percentage as a target is that the impact of monetary policy on total spending occurs only with some lag. It may be six months or more before the additional money created works its way through the system to produce more spending and provide more jobs. To know whether today's monetary policy should be made easier or tighter on the basis of the unemployment percentage would therefore require that we know today what that unemployment percentage will be at that future date when the effect of today's action is felt. We plainly have no such knowledge; we have only a forecast that may turn out to be in serious error.

What is more, even if changes in monetary policy worked their way through to affect employment in very quick order, changes in the unemployment percentage would be deficient as a target for another reason. Changes in the overall position of the economy are reflected by changes in the unemployment percentage or by changes in price levels and growth rates only after some time. For example, if the monetary authorities wait for the unemployment percentage or total output to provide a clear signal that a recession has begun before they alter their policy, the recession may already have built up some steam, and they will find it more difficult to handle than if they had moved sooner. On the other hand, if they move at the first adverse signal given off by such variables, they may do more harm than good. If that first signal was a false signal, a switch to an expansionary policy will have only the undesirable effect of pushing up prices. It will not check a downturn because no downturn is under way.

It is because of problems like these that the monetary authorities cannot select a particular unemployment percentage as a target at which to aim, and the same may be said of other ultimate variables like price indexes and economic growth rates as targets. If they are to get around the problems noted, the authorities must choose as a target a variable whose changes are determined predominantly by changes in monetary policy and whose changes promptly follow changes in monetary policy. It is also plainly imperative that what is chosen as a target variable be closely related to the ultimate goal variables in the sense that a change in the target variable may be expected to affect the ultimate goal variables in a predictable way. Changes in a variable that meet these requirements will provide the monetary authorities with a reliable indicator of the direction in which they are moving and the vigor with which they are moving and will do this promptly. At the same time, because the changes in the target variable will after a lag exert a fairly definite impact on the ultimate goal variables, by seeking to bring about certain changes in the target variable the monetary authorities may succeed in their ultimate objective, which is to bring about desired changes in a goal variable—for example, to bring about full employment.

Unfortunately, there is no variable that fully meets the requirements specified. A variable like the Federal Reserve Banks' holdings of U.S. government securities is determined completely by the monetary authorities, but changes in this variable are so weakly related to changes in the ultimate goal variable that it cannot serve as a target variable. In contrast, a variable like total spending is very closely related to ultimate goal variables like the level of output and employment, but changes in this variable are so much influenced by factors other than monetary factors and are affected with so long a lag that this variable also cannot serve as a target variable. The choice in practice is largely between, on the one hand, interest rates or, more broadly, overall credit conditions and, on the other hand, the money supply or some other related monetary aggregate. Changes in neither interest rates nor the money supply are exclusively the result of Federal Reserve actions, but these variables are closely enough related to Federal Reserve actions to reflect promptly and sensitively changes in such actions. Changes in both of these variables are recognized to have effects on the ultimate goal variables, although there are major differences between Keynesians and monetarists as to the closeness of the linkages.

The use of each of these variables as a target of monetary policy and some of the questions that arise with each will be examined briefly in the balance of this chapter.

INTEREST RATES AS A TARGET

Over the past five years the Federal Reserve authorities have paid much more attention to variations in the rate of growth of the money supply than they did in earlier years. However, they by no means permit their actions to be determined completely by the effect they will have on the rate of growth of the money supply. As was the case through the fifties and the sixties, the behavior of interest rates continues to strongly influence Federal Reserve actions. If conditions are such that a more rapid or less rapid rate of growth in the money supply is needed to prevent very large short-run swings in interest rates, the Federal Reserve authorities will follow a policy that involves substantial short-run fluctuations in the growth rate of the money supply. Large short-run swings in interest rates give rise to uncertainties as to credit conditions in general and reduce the efficiency with which financial markets function. The Federal Reserve authorities believe it important to prevent such swings in interest rates, even though to do this they must permit short-run swings in the money supply of a greater degree than otherwise would be acceptable.

There are, of course, many different interest rates, and they are not all influenced to the same extent by Federal Reserve actions. Because of the nature of Federal Reserve actions in the open market, rates on debt forms like Treasury bills and commercial paper ordinarily respond more quickly and more sensitively to Federal Reserve actions than do rates on debt forms like consumer installment purchase paper and bonds issued by corporations and government. However, it is not necessary for us to make such distinctions; for present purposes it is permissible to lump the various interest rates together and speak of the "level of interest rates," by which we mean an average of all these rates. When we refer to the influence of Federal Reserve actions on interest rates, we will be referring to this average of the many different interest rates.

To serve well as a target of monetary policy, a variable should change primarily as a result of Federal Reserve action. Are Federal Reserve actions the primary force accounting for changes in interest rates? One may approach an answer to this question by first noting that interest rates depend basically on the amounts of funds that borrowers seek to obtain and the amounts of funds that lenders make available. By far the major portion of the total funds available in any period of time is made up of the amount of saving out of current income, but this amount is enlarged by any increase in the money supply during that period or reduced by any decrease in the money supply during that period. Although the amounts accounted for by changes in the money supply are small relative to the amount of saving, they are sufficient as they are applied at the margin to enable the Federal Reserve to bring about the changes in interest rates it wants. By taking the actions necessary to vary the money supply in the appropriate amounts, the Federal Reserve is able, in other words, to make interest rates different from what they would otherwise be or it is able to make them what it wants them to be, at least in the short run.

However, in adopting interest rates as a target and proceeding to take whatever action is needed to achieve the level of interest rates at any time chosen as the target, the Federal Reserve faces the danger of erring and increasing the instability of the system rather than decreasing it. One source of error is found in the fact that interest rates over any time period may change because of a change in market forces—e.g., a decrease in business investment demand—that the Federal Reserve, despite its best efforts, cannot detect at the time it occurs. If this happens, the attainment of the target level of interest rates will turn out to be inconsistent with the attainment of the ultimate goal of full employment. Interest rates are related to this goal in that the amount of borrowing and therefore the amount of spending are affected by interest rates, and the level of output and therefore the level of employment are affected by the amount of spending. If we assume the economy is at a position of less than full employment, the Federal Reserve may be expected to choose as a target a level of interest rates below the one existing. It may then proceed to expand the money supply as required to achieve this target. However, if during the period in which it is carrying out this policy there is a worsening of the business climate and a decline in investment spending, interest rates will tend to fall, and the level they might have moved to in the absence of Federal Reserve policy may be below the target level the Federal Reserve has chosen. What this means is that the Federal Reserve actions designed to bring about a lowering of interest rates to the specified target level may actually bring about a rise in interest rates as this target is attained. The result of this will be a reduction in spending and a worsening rather than an improvement in unemployment.

There is another, closely related source of error. Assume that a given change in interest rates is judged definitely to have arisen from changes in market forces rather than from changes in Federal Reserve actions. In order to take appropriate action the Federal Reserve must still determine the *nature* of the market forces at work, for an action that will be stabilizing in one case will be destabilizing in another. Again an illustration will best bring out the principle. We start off by supposing that the economy is operating at a high level of activity with a low unemployment rate, so any speedup in activity is likely to bring inflation with it. The Federal Reserve therefore seeks to maintain the economy at its existing rate of activity. We assume that in deciding on the rate at which it should permit the money supply to grow the Federal Reserve adopts as its target the maintenance of interest rates at their existing level. But suppose next that interest rates begin to rise, which means that the Federal Reserve will turn to a more rapid rate of monetary expansion in order to bring the interest rate level back down to the target level. What may we expect the consequences of this policy to be?

The answer here depends in part on whether one is a monetarist or a Keynesian. As the monetarist views the world, the Federal Reserve commits grave errors by adopting interest rates as a target of policy. This follows from his belief that the demand for money is a stable function of the income level—i.e., that the public seeks to hold an amount of money equal to an approximately constant fraction of income. In this view, an increase in the amount of money the public wants to hold will not be the result of an increase in liquidity preference—i.e., an increase in the amount of money wanted per dollar of income—but will be the result of an increase in the level of business activity. An increase in business activity unaccompanied by an increase in the money supply will force up interest rates as borrowers seek to obtain a larger amount of funds from a nonexpanding supply. Such a rise in interest rates, however painful it may be to prospective borrowers, should be allowed to run its course without interference by the Federal Reserve. This rise in interest rates is healthy: it is the device by which the market mechanism limits the amount of debt-financed spending to the amount of saving that is forthcoming and thereby prevents the inflationary pressures that would result in a fully employed economy if the former exceeded the latter. If the Federal Reserve provides the reserves to the commercial banks to enable them to expand loans in whatever amount borrowers want at the existing level of interest rates, the increase in the money supply will be clearly inflationary. Therefore, for the Federal Reserve to adopt the level of interest rates as its target means that the actions it takes in trying to hit this target will not contribute to the maintenance of overall economic stability but do just the opposite.

The Keynesians view the world differently. They recognize that increases in the amount of money the public wants to hold do indeed arise from higher levels of business activity, but they do not rule out as some monetarists seem to do that such increases may arise from fluctuations in liquidity preference—i.e., that the public may exhibit appreciable and unforeseen changes in the amount of money it wants to hold relative to the income level. Suppose there were to be such an increase in liquidity preference under the conditions described above. In this case, the Federal Reserve's adoption of an interest rate target for monetary policy will turn out to be healthy for the economy. By expanding the money supply to meet the public's desire to hold more money, the Federal Reserve prevents a rise in interest rates that would be undesirable. Unlike the other case, a rise in interest rates under these circumstances is not called for to check an unhealthy expansion in business activity. In this case, a rise in interest rates, if it were allowed to persist, would force a slowing of business activity and, if severe enough, would bring on a recession.

What this adds up to is that Federal Reserve policy based on interest rates as a target will be appropriate or inappropriate depending on the underlying cause of the change in interest rates. A change in interest rates due to temporary or irregular changes in the demand for money can properly be met with an offsetting change in the money supply. On the other hand, a change in interest rates due to a sustained change in the demand for money that springs from an underlying major change in aggregate spending should not be automatically resisted with an expansion of the money supply. If the Federal Reserve could in each case identify the underlying cause of a rise in interest rates, it would know whether action taken to offset it would be stabilizing or destabilizing and would act accordingly. However, at the time that action is called for, there ordinarily is not sufficient information available to tell the authorities with any certainty whether the cause is of one kind or the other.

Because stability in the demand for money is a hallmark of monetarism, the monetarists do not believe that increases in interest rates are, except in rare cases, due to changes in liquidity preference, and they therefore reject totally the use of interest rates as a target. Milton Friedman has pointed to case after case in which the Federal Reserve's reliance on interest rates as a target has, in his judgment, led them to do just the opposite of what they should have done. He maintains that by not allowing interest rates to move freely in response to market forces the Federal Reserve not only does not contribute to the stabilization of the economy but makes for a more unstable economy than we would have if they were to take no action. The opposite school of thought, which maintains that changes in liquidity preference may be sizable and relatively frequent, finds a strong case for the use of interest rates as a target.

MONEY SUPPLY AS A TARGET

The alternative to interest rates as a target is the rate of growth of the money supply or of a related aggregate like the monetary base (the sum of member bank reserves and currency outside the banks) or the total of bank loans and investments. It makes some difference which monetary aggregate is adopted as a target, but according to the monetarists the important thing is that the target be one of these aggregates and not interest rates.

Why monetarists should hold up a monetary aggregate like the money supply as an appropriate target is readily understandable in view of the key role they have attributed to money. If, as some allege, there is a fast, stable, and predictable relationship between changes in money and changes in GNP, the importance of regulating Federal Reserve actions so as to achieve a money target becomes quite apparent. At the same time, the importance of not regulating these actions to achieve an interest rate target becomes equally apparent. For to pursue an interest rate target means that the rate of growth of the money supply will be altogether different from what it would be if a money supply target were being pursued. With interest rates as the target, the rate of growth of the money supply varies in whatever degree is needed to achieve the level of interest rates being aimed at, and such variations are generally just the opposite of those that would be indicated if the money supply itself were chosen as the target.

Suppose that interest rates are rising sharply and the Federal Reserve is fearful that this may cause a slowdown in business activity at a time when the economy is still operating below capacity. To check the rise in interest rates may require that the Federal Reserve take actions that result in a rapid expansion of the money supply. Although all economists agree that this growth in the money supply will in time exert an expansionary effect on the economy, they do not all believe that the effect is nearly as strong or predictable as the monetarists allege. However, to the monetarists who do see it this way, it is these sometimes relatively large variations in the money supply that occur as a result of Federal Reserve policy actions designed to achieve an interest rate target that are a major cause of the instability in the economy. Therefore, to reverse the practice and take the money supply as a target, permitting interest rates to vary to the degree needed to achieve the money supply target, will, according to the monetarists, remove a major source of instability in the economy.

If then the money supply is to be the target of monetary policy, the question to be faced is: What rate of growth of money should be chosen as this target? At first glance it seems that one can answer the question as follows: whatever the rate of growth of the money supply happens to be at any time, that rate should be raised if the economy appears to be slowing down to an undesirable degree or reduced if the economy appears to be expanding too rapidly. But a moment's thought will reveal that an answer like this does not escape the problems described at the beginning of this chapter. We are using the current state of the economy as indicated by ultimate goal variables like the unemployment percentage, price movements, and the rate of output growth as the basis for deciding the appropriate rate of growth of the money supply. Even if the linkage between changes in the rate of growth of the money supply and changes in these variables was as close as the monetarists assert, in order for the current values of these variables to be used as guide to the rate of monetary growth would require that changes in the rate of monetary growth have a prompt impact on the values of these variables. If there is a lag of six months or more before the impact is felt, then changes in today's rate of money supply growth will affect, not today's economic conditions, but the conditions six months from today.

What all monetarists have in common is the belief that money matters most in determining the level of economic activity. However, on some matters they have their differences, and one of these is over the lag in the impact of monetary policy. We noted in the preceding chapter that the St. Louis equation suggests that the impact of changes in money on GNP are fast and reasonably predictable, at least relative to the impact of fiscal changes. A $1 billion increase in the money supply would raise GNP by $1.5 billion in the very same quarter and by $3 billion in the first two quarters. As was also noted, other studies indicate a much slower response of GNP to changes in the money supply.

Another way of looking at the lag is in terms of the business cycle turning-points approach that was discussed in the preceding chapter.

The ten business cycle peaks since 1920 (1973–74 omitted due to uncertain date) have occurred, on the average, 16 months after the peak in the growth rate of the money supply, and the eleven business cycle troughs since 1921 have occurred, on the average, 8 months after the trough in the growth rate of the money supply. If one believes that the major reason the economy goes into a recession is because of an earlier slowdown in the rate of growth of the money supply and that the major reason the economy comes out of a recession is because of an earlier speedup in the rate of growth of the money supply, these figures suggest that, on the average, it takes 16 months for the slowdown in the growth rate of the money supply to produce the economic downturn and 8 months for the speedup in the growth rate of the money supply to produce the economic recovery. In addition to these fairly long lags, especially at the peaks, it is extremely important to recognize that the individual cases show considerable variability around the average. The lag in business cycle peaks runs from as little as 6 months to as much as 29 months, and the lag in troughs run from as little as 1 month to as much as 12 months.

Milton Friedman, who is as much convinced as any other monetarist of the importance of changes in the money supply growth rate in determining changes in business activity, is also convinced that the target rate of growth for the money supply should not be raised or lowered as changes occur in business activity. To some people this at first sounds like the height of inconsistency. If money matters as much as Friedman believes, one would expect that he would want to raise and lower the money supply target in line with the level of business activity as a means of reducing the instability in activity. However, doing this successfully has certain prerequisites. For one thing, before we can decide what monetary actions should be carried out today, we have to forecast what business conditions will be when the monetary actions carried out today take hold. In the present state of knowledge, forecasts are often far off the mark, and the likelihood of large errors increases with the length of the forecast. The belief that there is a long lag between the taking of monetary action and its impact on business conditions thus becomes a compelling argument against trying to adjust a money supply target upward and downward in a countercyclical fashion. Second, even if forecasting future business conditions could be done with a high degree of accuracy, there would still be a problem presented by the variability of the lag noted just above. If this lag may vary from a few months to a few years and if there is no way to reliably predict its length in any particular case, monetary policy cannot be used effectively to offset undesirable future changes in business activity, even if we could forecast them accurately.

Because of the danger of inaccurately forecasting either future business conditions or the time interval involved between the taking of monetary actions and their impact on business conditions or both, Friedman believes that raising and lowering the money supply growth target from time to time in just the degree needed to provide a more stable economy is at present beyond our ability. There are many who agree with Friedman's view, but there are others who believe that the lags are neither so long nor so variable and that our ability to make fairly accurate short-term forecasts is not so limited as to rule out pursuing a policy that at the minimum "leans against the wind." If the outlook is that business activity will be expanding too rapidly within the coming year, the rate of growth of the money supply should be slowed somewhat and the opposite, of course, if the outlook is that there will be an undesirable slowing in business activity. To many economists leaning against the wind seems to be a wiser policy than steadfastly maintaining the status quo.

In a much quoted statement, Professor Friedman has replied to this contention in the following words:

> We seldom in fact know which way the economic wind is blowing until several months after the event, yet to be effective, we need to know which way the wind is going to be blowing when the measures we take now will be effective, itself a variable date that may be a half-year or two years from now. Leaning against next year's wind is hardly an easy task in the present state of meteorology.*

While this in itself is sufficient grounds to Friedman to reject a policy of varying the money supply growth rate each time the wind changes direction, a more fundamental objection lies hidden behind it. Friedman and monetarists in general believe that the economy is inherently stable, that it has the resiliency to absorb disturbances quite rapidly and return to its long-run growth path in fairly short order. The major reason that it does show marked and sometimes prolonged departures from this path is because the Federal Reserve authorities pursue a policy that involves large swings in the rate of growth of the money supply. Although they undertake this policy with the well-intentioned objective of decreasing the economy's instability, their errors are such as to increase that instability. In Friedman's words:

> Too late and too much has been the general practice. For example, in early 1966, it was the right policy for the Federal Reserve to move in a less expansionary direction—though it should have done so at least a year earlier. But when it moved, it went too far, producing the sharpest change in the rate of monetary growth of the post-war era. Again, having gone too far, it was the right policy for the Fed to reverse course at the end of 1966. But again it

---

*M. Friedman, *A Program For Monetary Stability* (New York: Fordham University Press, 1960), p. 93.

went too far, not only restoring but exceeding the earlier excessive rate of monetary growth. And this episode is no exception. Time and again this has been the course followed—as in 1919 and 1920, in 1937 and 1938, in 1953 and 1954, in 1959 and 1960.*

The picture is one of the Federal Reserve more or less continuously trying to bring stability back into a system that is as unstable as it is only because of the Federal Reserve's earlier attempts to bring stability back into the system. Were it not for this destabilizing kind of intervention by the Federal Reserve, the economy's departures from a stable path of long-term growth that would occur due to such things as bursts of investment spending initiated by innovations and technological changes would be self-correcting and short-lived.

Just as there are those who disagree with Friedman as to the length and variability of the lags between changes in the money supply and changes in business activity, there are those who disagree with him as to the inherent stability of the system. This includes Keynesian economists in general, for a hallmark of Keynesian economics is that there does not exist within the system a self-correction mechanism. Departures from the long-run growth path are not automatically and promptly reversed. However, if one does believe that the economy is not inherently unstable and that neither the Federal Reserve authorities nor anyone else knows enough to determine the variations in the money supply that will reduce whatever instability may arise even in such an economy, he will be able to accept Professor Friedman's elegantly simple prescription for the Federal Reserve: the target of monetary policy should be a steady rate of growth of the money supply. Because the long-term rate of growth of real output under full-employment conditions is approximately 4 percent, the long-term rate of growth of the money supply typically suggested by monetarists is about 4 percent. Barring long-term changes in the rate at which the money supply turns over, growth in the money supply at the same rate as growth in the economy's output may then be expected to contribute to a stable price level for output over the years. Higher or lower rates of growth of the money supply would make for a rising or falling long-term trend in prices.

Although the Federal Reserve has paid considerable attention in the last five years to the rate of growth of the money supply, it has by no means adopted a steady rate of growth of the money supply as a target to replace its traditional interest rate target. Through the fifties and sixties, monetary policy was guided almost completely by interest rates and credit conditions, and these remain a major consideration

---

*M. Friedman, "The Role of Monetary Policy," in *American Economic Review*, March 1968, p. 16.

today. Something about the degree of importance assigned to a money supply target by the Federal Reserve in recent years is revealed by the large variations in the rate of growth of the money supply during those years. To avoid misinterpretation, it must be noted that even if the Federal Reserve were to abandon all else in the interest of attaining a chosen money supply target, it still would not be able to hit the target figure every month or even every quarter. Although the Federal Reserve has ultimate control over the money supply, other forces also are at work, and the money supply in any short period may be different from what the Federal Reserve wants it to be. But if the Federal Reserve were concentrating on hitting a target rate of growth for the money supply, the variability in the money supply would have been smaller than it was in recent years. To illustrate with a couple of extreme cases: the money supply (M_1) increased at an annual rate of 11 percent during the first two quarters of 1971, and then at only an 0.8 percent annual rate during the last two quarters of that year. The money supply grew at a 12.0 percent annual rate during the second quarter of 1973, then at −0.2 percent during the third quarter, and 7.8 percent during the fourth quarter. Movements of this degree are movements that would not occur if the Federal Reserve were to completely subordinate its interest rate target to a money supply target.

Even many of the nonmonetarists who believe the Federal Reserve should lean against the wind object to leaning to the degree that brings on such wide swings in the money supply as those just noted. At the same time that they maintain that the Federal Reserve is correct in trying to offset changes in interest rates that appear to be the result of short-run changes in the demand for money (changes which, it will be recalled, do not occur according to monetarists), they lean far enough toward monetarism to maintain also that the variations in the rate of growth of the money supply that may result from this policy should be limited. Although monetarists favor a narrower band, there has been much overall support for the guideline of a 2 to 6 percent annual rate of growth of the money supply measured on a quarter-by-quarter basis that was recommended by the Joint Economic Committee of the Congress back in 1967.

Requiring that the Federal Reserve operate under this much of a restraint is not the same as dictating to the Federal Reserve how the money supply should respond to any particular economic development. The Federal Reserve may respond as it sees fit, but only within the prescribed limits. As the illustrations given above indicate, these limits are much narrower than the actual range of growth rates shown by the money supply in recent years, and requiring the Federal Reserve to stay within these limits would deny it the wide degree of discretion that it has exercised over the years.

The Federal Reserve in 1970 declared publicly for the first time that, in effect, its adherence to the interest rate target would be relaxed if such adherence appeared to increase or decrease the money supply too much. In its own language, its objective then was to operate "with a view to moving gradually toward somewhat less firm conditions in the money market [lower short-term interest rates]; provided, however, that operations shall be modified promptly to resist any tendency for money and bank credit to deviate significantly from a moderate growth pattern." Although the words "significantly" and "moderate" as used here suggested considerable limitation on the variations in the money supply that would be permitted, they by no means constitute anything like the Joint Economic Committee's proposed guidelines as the basis for determining what increase or decrease in the rate of growth of the money supply would be too much. However, over the next four years the Federal Reserve took several steps in this direction. In 1972 it adopted a policy of trying to keep the annual rate of increase in reserves available to support private nonbank deposits, popularly known as RPDs, within a specified percentage point range. Because the rate of growth of the money supply is closely linked to the rate of growth of RPDs, adopting RPDs as a target is much like taking the money supply as a target. Then in 1974 the Federal Reserve extended this approach to include specifically a percentage point range for the money supply, both narrowly defined, M_1, and more broadly defined, M_2. At the same time it also began to specify a percentage point range for the federal funds rate, the interest rate member banks charge each other on loans of funds on deposit at Federal Reserve banks.

The range for each of these variables is specified by the Federal Reserve authorities in Washington each month for that month and the following month. It is then the task of the manager of open market operations in the Federal Reserve Bank of New York to try to conduct open market operations so as to stay within the prescribed ranges for these variables. For example, if the latest figures show M_1 rising toward the upper limit of its specified range and the federal funds rate falling toward the lower limit of its specified range, he will adjust open market operations in a way to slow the expansion of the money supply, an action that may be expected at the same time to exert upward pressure on the federal funds rate. Because of the complex interplay of forces, it may not be possible for the manager to stay within the specified range for all of the variables. This becomes a problem for the Federal Reserve authorities to meet when they set the ranges for the variables for the next bimonthly period. However, between these changes, the specified ranges serve as guides to the manager in carrying out day-to-day open market operations.

While specifying ranges of tolerance for the monetary aggregates,

M_1, M_2, and RPDs, is a step toward the acceptance of the monetarist position on this subject, it is clear that the Federal Reserve over the last few years has not taken the giant step that some monetarists urge should be taken: the adoption of a specific rate of growth of a monetary aggregate as the exclusive target of Federal Reserve policy. The Federal Reserve has rather adopted a range of growth rates for M_1, M_2, and RPDs as targets and, what is more, changes this range of rates frequently and sizably. It does this in part to prevent what it regards as undesirable movements in interest rates that would result with an unchanged range of growth rates for these monetary aggregates.

For example, despite a rapid growth of the money supply that accompanied the rate at which RPDs grew during the spring and early summer of 1972, the Federal Reserve in August of 1972 still raised the RPD range to 5 to 9 percent from the 3 to 7 percent range it had been. The reason was, in the Federal Reserve's words, that "sharp increases in interest rates in a sensitive market atmosphere . . . should be avoided." The economy had not at the time fully recovered from the 1970 recession, and the Federal Reserve was concerned with the adverse effects a large rise in interest rates might have. Then as the rate of inflation accelerated in late 1972 and the recovery turned into a boom in 1973, the Federal Reserve set a range for RPDs consistent with higher interest rates. For example, in March 1973 it selected an annual growth rate for RPDs with the range of 14 to 16 percent, which it expected "might be associated with some further increase in short-term interest rates and probably also in long term rates." This relatively high range set for RPDs showed a willingness on the part of the Federal Reserve to allow a more rapid rate of growth of the money supply in the interest of preventing a too rapid and potentially destabilizing rise in interest rates, but it was still a range for RPDs consistent with some rise in interest rates. Interest rates thus clearly remained a target of the Federal Reserve at this time—recall that an interest rate target means, not stable interest rates, but interest rates that will not change so rapidly as to be destabilizing to the economy as a whole.

As noted above, the Federal Reserve in 1974 began to specify ranges for two other aggregates and one interest rate in addition to that for RPDs. For example, in February 1974 these were from 6 1/2 to 9 1/2 percent for M_1, 9 1/2 to 12 1/2 percent for M_2, 3 1/2 to 6 1/2 percent for RPDs, and a level for the federal funds rate from 8 1/4 to 9 1/2 percent. The authorities adjust the ranges of one or more of these variables from month to month as appears to be needed to meet their longer run targets for the monetary aggregates and interest rates. Apart from changes in levels, they may also widen or narrow the range of tolerance of any of these variables.

It may be seen that a widening or narrowing in the range of the federal funds rate set by the Federal Reserve authorities says something about whether Federal Reserve policy at the time has primarily interest rates or monetary aggregates as its target. If the rates of growth of the monetary aggregates have diverged from the longer run rates that are the goals for these variables, the rates of growth for these aggregates may be altered more promptly if the range for the federal funds rate is widened. To call upon the manager of open market operations to stay within a very narrow range for the federal funds rate is to limit correspondingly his ability to carry out the kind of open market operations needed to get the growth rate of the aggregates back on the longer term growth path that the Federal Reserve authorities have specified. The larger open market operations needed to do this will involve sizable changes in the commercial banks' reserve position, which is reflected in sizable changes in the federal funds rate and therefore changes in that rate which may exceed the specified range of tolerance. A widening of the range for the federal funds rate, in other words, means that actions may be taken to meet the targets set for growth of the monetary aggregates. On the other hand, a narrowing of the range for the federal funds rate would suggest that the Federal Reserve has as its short-run goal a lesser fluctuation in interest rates. The manager of open market operations may find it necessary to permit greater variations in the monetary aggregates than would be the case if he were not called upon to hold the federal funds rate within the narrow range specified by the Federal Reserve authorities.

When the Federal Reserve in 1972 first specified a range of RPDs as a target of monetary policy, it by no means abandoned interest rates as a target. Interest rates remained a target of policy, but a numerically specified target was not indicated. Since the beginning of 1974, such numerically specified targets for three monetary variables and one interest rate have been indicated. However, very careful study of the changes in the ranges of rates from month to month over a period of months is needed to shed light on the degree to which the actions taken by the Federal Reserve have been influenced by a desire to prevent changes in market interest rates and credit conditions, on the one hand, and, on the other hand, by a desire to prevent fluctuations in the rate at which the monetary aggregates grow.

Whether for good or evil, the Federal Reserve continues to give much attention to interest rates and credit conditions, and, as long as this is the case, considerable variation in the growth rates M_1, M_2, and RPDs may be expected to continue to take place. If in the years ahead the monetarists are able to build a stronger case for giving greater attention to the monetary aggregates, the Federal Reserve will have little choice but to further demote interest rates and credit conditions from their present rank as a target of monetary policy. The Congress after all has the final control and can if it so chooses instruct the Federal Reserve that its function is to control the money supply and not to influence interest rates. However, such action by the Congress would have to be preceded by a reasonably clear-cut victory for monetarism, and that has not yet occurred and does not appear at all imminent. In choosing a target for monetary policy, the Federal Reserve authorities will likely continue to place much emphasis on interest rates but far less than they did before the monetarists forced all economists to recognize that changes in the money supply matter more than most had for years thought was the case.

A CONCLUDING NOTE

If monetary policy were to exert its impact on such ultimate variables as the economy's income, employment, and prices without an appreciable lag, and if the quantitative impact of any given change in monetary policy on these variables were determinable with considerable accuracy, the monetary authorities could be guided in their policy decisions by the movements of these ultimate variables. For example, if confronted with a slowing of income growth, a rise in unemployment, and an absence of inflation, the authorities could with little fear of error speed up the rate at which the money supply was growing. And with the knowledge here assumed they would know the appropriate rate at which to expand the money supply. Of course, neither of the conditions assumed is even approximately realized in practice, so the current values of ultimate variables like income, employment, and price levels are unreliable guides to Federal Reserve policy.

In this chapter we have seen that these facts of economic life force the Federal Reserve officials to back up to intermediate targets, and the choice here is essentially between interest rates, which are price measures, and monetary aggregates such as the money supply, which are quantity measures. Will these men make a greater contribution to the economy's stability if their policy is guided by the objective of controlling interest rates—i.e., the price of money—or by the objective of controlling the supply of money itself? They cannot have it both ways: if they seek to control interest rates, they must allow the money supply to fluctuate, and if they seek to control the money supply, they must allow interest rates to fluctuate. They may, of course, compromise between the two, and in the years since 1970 they have paid much more attention to the money supply as a target than they did earlier. From the monetarist viewpoint, this has been a step in the right direction but far short of the giant step that the monetarists urge.

In the following chapter we will review Federal Reserve policy over the period since the beginning of World War II, and we will have more to say there about interest rates versus money supply as targets of monetary policy. The economy suffered four recessions during the fifties and sixties, and a monetarist interpretation of these years points the finger of blame for each recession at the Federal Reserve to a large degree. The general argument is that its pursuit of an interest rate target caused an ill-timed slowing in the rate of growth of the money supply and that such a slowing caused the economy to go into recession. Without denying that Federal Reserve policy may have been in error in some cases and thus a contributor to one or more of the recessions, a Keynesian interpretation of these same situations points the finger of blame primarily at nonmonetary, or real, developments such as excessive accumulations of inventories that occurred in the economy from time to time over these years.

○

sixteen
MONETARY POLICY
IN THE UNITED STATES
SINCE 1941

Monetary policy in any time period is a success or failure to the degree that it contributes to stabilization or causes destabilization of the economy. Looking back over the years, monetarists see a long string of failures—episode after episode in which the actions taken by the Federal Reserve were destabilizing rather than stabilizing as was intended. Although Keynesians do not find the Federal Reserve failure free, they find that, in general, the actions taken by the Federal Reserve were more often than not the correct actions under the existing conditions and therefore actions that were stabilizing as was intended.

310

One cannot, of course, state with complete certainty whether a given action turned out to be stabilizing or destabilizing without knowing what would have happened in the absence of that action. This is a familiar, unending problem in economics. Thus, the fact that an excessive slowdown or speedup in aggregate spending occurs despite actions taken by the Federal Reserve does not necessarily mean that the actions taken were of the wrong kind or at the wrong time. They may have been of the right kind and at the right time but not of the right degree to offset other forces that were causing an excessive movement in aggregate spending. Therefore, if we observe instability despite the monetary authorities' effort to prevent it, we cannot automatically conclude that the effort has been a failure. It is only a failure if the degree of instability would otherwise have been less; it is a success or at least a partial success if the degree of instability would otherwise have been greater.

The fact that the monetarists believe that the economy is inherently stable helps to explain their finding that Federal Reserve policy has been so frequently destabilizing. If instability follows Federal Reserve actions, it is easy to conclude from this belief that the Federal Reserve actions were responsible. Keynesians do not believe that the economy has any such inherent stability, and thus they do not find it so easy to conclude that cases of instability that follow Federal Reserve actions are due to these actions. They are more ready to admit the possibility that what might have occurred without the Federal Reserve action would have been an even greater destabilizing movement—from which viewpoint, the Federal Reserve action is stabilizing.

The Keynesians are much less critical of Federal Reserve actions for another reason: the Federal Reserve has traditionally employed interest rates as the target at which their actions are aimed, and the adoption of an interest rate target is in certain ways consistent with Keynesian theory. To the degree that changes in the money supply work their way through the system to affect income, output, and prices, Keynesians see these changes doing this by raising or lowering interest rates. The Federal Reserve to be restrictive must act to raise interest rates above what they otherwise would be and to be expansionary must act to lower interest rates below what they otherwise would be. If it takes fairly large swings in the rate of growth of the money supply to achieve the desired changes in interest rates, Keynesians do not get overly concerned. If changes in money affect spending primarily through their effect on interest rates, large swings in the rate of growth of the money supply are not dangerous as long as they are not accompanied by swings in interest rates much larger than they otherwise would be. As we have noted more than once in earlier chapters, all of this is rejected bodily by the monetarists. Whether interest rates change much or little as a result of changes in the money supply is not what is critical according to the monetarists. What is critical is whether the money supply itself changes much or little, because to them it is the changes in the money supply that determine what the eventual changes in spending and economic activity will be.

Given this difference in views, Keynesians and monetarists can examine the same upswings and downswings in economic activity and reach quite different conclusions as to the contribution to these movements made by Federal Reserve policy. The monetarist who finds that a downturn has been preceded by a sharp slowdown in the rate of growth of the money supply will have little hesitation in attributing that economic downturn primarily to the mistaken Federal Reserve policy that brought about the destabilizing slowdown in the money supply growth rate. The Keynesian will not rule this out as possibly the major cause in some cases, but more often he will conclude that the major cause is some real rather than monetary phenomenon. Thus, most of the mild recessions we have gone through since World War II have been explained by Keynesians as the result of inventory liquidations that occurred in response to excessive accumulations of inventories during the preceding expansion.

In this chapter we will look at Federal Reserve policy over the period since 1941 but not in the detail needed to wrestle with the question of whether Federal Reserve policy made the recessions over these years less serious than they otherwise would have been or gave us recessions that otherwise would not have occurred at all. What we will do is provide some data on changes in the money supply, movements of interest rates, and the behavior of output and prices from which some rough conclusions may be drawn.

1941–51: THE PERIOD OF PEGGED INTEREST RATES ON U.S. GOVERNMENT SECURITIES

Federal Reserve policy can be judged a success or failure by its contribution to economic stability in any time period if the actions taken by the Federal Reserve have had economic stabilization as their objective. Although this ordinarily is the objective, there are special circumstances under which this objective is temporarily subordinated to another, and such circumstances existed from the beginning of World War II to the "accord" of March 1951, an event to be discussed shortly. During this period, the customary objective of managing Federal Reserve policy in a way to contribute to a goal such as price stability was sacrificed to meet the real or alleged problems faced by the U.S. Treasury in financing itself during the war years and in managing a greatly swollen national debt in the early postwar years.

A few months after Pearl Harbor the Federal Reserve agreed with the Treasury that yields on U.S. Government securities should be "pegged" for the duration of the war at approximately the levels then in effect. It was foreseen that the war would be long and costly and involve huge amounts of borrowing by the Treasury. The decision was that the pattern of yields would be maintained with a top of 2 1/2 percent on Treasury bonds with 25-year maturities down to 3/8 of 1 percent on 91-day Treasury bills. These exceedingly low rates then in effect had resulted from the nation's worst depression and incomplete recovery during the thirties.

As was reviewed in the concluding note to Chapter 8, the Treasury sought to borrow as much as possible from individuals, life insurance companies, mutual savings banks, and the like, as borrowing from these sources does not increase the money supply and thus minimizes the inflationary impact of borrowing. The balance required had to be borrowed from the commercial banking system, despite the increase in the money supply that this involved. In order for the commercial banks to be able to purchase the amount of securities the Treasury found it necessary to sell to them, they had to be provided with the additional reserves needed for this purpose. This was handled through open market purchases of the appropriate amount of Treasury securities by the Federal Reserve Banks. As long as this was done, there was sufficient demand by the commercial banks to absorb the amount of new issues that the Treasury sought to sell to them and to prevent any decline in the prices of outstanding issues, thus preventing any rise in their yields. The Federal Reserve's role, then, became the purely passive one of conducting open market operations strictly as needed to maintain yields on government securities at the agreed-upon pegged level.

What this meant is that the Federal Reserve Banks completely gave up control over the amount of Treasury securities they held, and with this they completely gave up control over the amount of reserves the commercial banks held, which meant, in turn, that they gave up control over the money supply. The money supply would be permitted to grow at whatever rate was needed to hold interest rates on government obligations at the prescribed level. The destabilizing effects of the very rapid growth of the money supply that would result from this policy was, of course, recognized, but a strong system of wage and price controls was depended on to keep under control the inflationary pressures so generated.

First priority was given to providing the funds needed for the war effort, and to assure that this would be done smoothly called for the policy of stabilizing yields on government securities. For if these yields had been permitted to rise appreciably and the market values of outstanding government securities therefore permitted to fall appreciably over the course of the war years, the Treasury would not have been able to finance as much of the cost of the war as it did by borrowing from the public. It would not have been possible to find investors to purchase new issues of marketable Treasury securities at existing interest rates in the amounts required if investors saw that their values kept falling. Even raising interest rates at each successive borrowing would not be a complete answer, because a higher rate would not be an inducement to the public to buy bonds if it was fairly certain that the rate before long would be still higher. Apart from this problem, an approach like this would also involve a much greater interest charge on the national debt than would be the case with yields stabilized at a low level.

Although there were these compelling arguments in support of the pegging policy during the war years when massive amounts had to be borrowed, it was a policy that carried with it a great inflationary potential for the postwar period. The comprehensive system of direct wartime controls whose need was understood and accepted by business and labor during the war could not be maintained long after the end of the war. Wage controls went first in 1945, and by late 1946 all price controls except those on rents had ended. During the four war years, 1942–45, the money supply (M_1) rose from \$48.2 billion to \$102.4 billion, and the public's holdings of near-moneys, like Savings Bonds and savings deposits, that were readily convertible into money increased at an even more rapid rate. The fuel to fire a huge surge in postwar spending was available, and it was used. During the three years 1946–48, with most controls off, the cost of living rose by 34 percent, or about 11 percent per year; during the four years 1942–45, when all the direct controls had been in effect, the rise had been only 22 percent, or less than half as rapid. It may be noted that the indicated increase for the war years somewhat understates the actual increase as it does not allow for black market prices that resulted under the controls, but even then there remains a pronounced difference in the price experience between the war years and the first few postwar years.

With the war over and with prices rising so rapidly in the early postwar period, one may ask why the Federal Reserve did not abandon its policy of pegging the yields of U.S. Government securities? The whole structure of interest rates, rates on all kinds of private obligations as well as those on U.S. Government securities, was held down by the pegging policy. To have abandoned this policy would have been to permit a rise in the whole structure of interest rates and to have thereby gained whatever stabilizing effect a rise in rates would make by slowing the excessive rate at which aggregate spending was expanding.

A major factor in the answer to this question was the pressure applied by the Treasury against any significant relaxation of the pegging policy. The national debt had risen more than fivefold in five years; it was $45 billion at the end of 1940 and $252 billion at the end of 1945. Apart from Savings Bonds, which have a schedule of fixed redemption values month by month to maturity, the other Treasury bonds that made up the far larger part of the total are so-called "marketable" bonds, or bonds whose market value moves inversely with the level of market interest rates. As the Treasury viewed the situation just after the war, for the Federal Reserve to have departed markedly from the policy of pegging yields on these bonds might have led to a panic among holders of these bonds. If the Federal Reserve were to have permitted these bond prices to fall, banks, insurance companies, and other financial institutions holding huge amounts of these bonds might have begun to dump their holdings before their prices fell further. And any attempt to do this would, of course, have produced the very result that they were seeking to protect themselves against. A large decline in these bond prices would have been disastrous; the solvency of financial institutions would have been threatened as the market value of their bond holdings, which made up a large part of their total portfolios, shrank drastically. Because their liabilities to depositors and policy holders at the same time would remain fixed in dollar terms, a significant decline in the market value of bonds would reduce the value of their assets below liabilities, which, in a word, technically amounts to insolvency. Fears like these were understandable as there had been a minor problem of this kind after World War I when the prices of U.S. Government securities dropped sharply in 1920, and at that time the debt was much smaller in a relative sense.

The Treasury was also concerned, perhaps inordinately, with the interest charge on the debt. With the debt at the end of World War II more than five times what it had been before the war, the interest cost on it would be five times larger at unchanged rates. To compound this increase by letting interest rates rise over their existing level was something the Treasury strenuously sought to avoid. With a debt of given size, the amount of year-to-year increase in the interest charge that results from higher interest rates depends on the maturity distribution of that debt. If the wartime borrowing had been more heavily in the form of very long-term bonds, the major impact of higher rates would not have been felt until those distant dates when these issues matured and had to be refunded by borrowing at whatever rates were then in effect. However, the actual situation for the marketable portion of the debt at the end of 1945 was that 36 percent of it had a maturity date within one year, 20 percent from one to five years, 19 percent from five to ten years, and 25 percent of ten years and over. With this maturity distribution, higher interest costs would not follow too far behind higher interest rates.

Greater than the concern for the adverse effects of falling U.S. Government securities prices on the portfolios of financial institutions and on the Treasury's interest cost was the general concern over the possible adverse effect this might have on overall economic stability. There was fear that rising interest rates would increase the likelihood of the depression that so many economists had predicted would follow from the drastic decline in government expenditures, after the cessation of hostilities. The long, deep depression of the thirties was still fresh in memory, and there was a conviction among many that it had ended only because of the massive increase in government expenditures that the war made necessary. Furthermore, as a result of the experience during the depression, many economists had come to question the effectiveness of monetary policy as a stabilization tool. Keynes had convinced many that the economy suffered from a persistent state of inadequate investment spending, a state summed up at the time by the term "secular stagnation." He maintained that what monetary policy could and should do is to see to it that interest rates were kept low over the long run so as not to throw another barrier in the way of obtaining the amount of investment spending needed to provide a high level of employment without relying on large-scale government spending.

Despite these and other arguments advanced for pegging interest rates at the low wartime level, the Federal Reserve saw the abandonment of this policy as the appropriate step to take in the face of the inflation that existed during 1946–48. However, the pressure from the Treasury for a continuation of the wartime policy with only minor relaxation was unrelenting, the inflation notwithstanding, and the Federal Reserve acceded for the time being. The Federal Reserve's problem then temporarily went away as this first postwar inflation came to an end during the summer of 1948, and the first of the postwar recessions began late in that year. This downturn was not the severe depression that had been feared; it lasted one year and was quite mild. However, it was a downturn, and the Federal Reserve's actions in stabilizing interest rates on the national debt during the period were not inconsistent with overall economic stability. Although this policy still meant that increases in the money supply remained beyond the Federal Reserve's control, the increases that would occur were not a great danger in an economy suffering recession and falling prices.

The problem of inflation returned in the following year with the outbreak of fighting in Korea. There was a great surge in consumer spending starting in June of 1950, and prices rose very sharply. With inflation again under way and with the threat that it might be long and severe under wartime conditions, the Federal Reserve argued strongly that its policy should be conducted to restrain the expansion of money and credit, and thereby prices, and should not be conducted to maintain yields on government securities at their existing low level. With the likelihood that heavy government borrowing might be required to meet expanding military expenditures, the Treasury was as insistent as ever that yields be held unchanged. In the months that followed, the Federal Reserve independently took a number of small steps away from the rigid support policy it had followed for so many years and in early 1951 came into open conflict with the Treasury and with the President himself, who had sided with the Secretary of the Treasury in the dispute. In February the Federal Reserve finally took a large step and flatly informed the Treasury that it would no longer act to maintain the current yields on government securities. With the controversy at a crisis stage, an "accord" was worked out in the next two weeks and announced in March. It was agreed that the Federal Reserve would act to assure the successful financing of the government's borrowing requirements and at the same time would act to minimize the monetization of the public debt.

This was understood to mean that the years of rigid pegging of Treasury securities prices were over. The Federal Reserve would no longer have to buy whatever amount of these securities was necessary to keep their prices from falling and their yields from rising. When the Federal Reserve deemed it advisable to restrict the growth of bank reserves and the expansion of the money supply, it would act accordingly, even though that meant falling prices for government securities and rising yields thereon. Federal Reserve policy was to be conducted to foster overall economic stability, not just the stability of government securities prices.

The Federal Reserve's struggle to free itself of the obligation to maintain interest rates on U.S. Government securities at a fixed level, or, what is the same thing, its struggle to regain control over bank reserves and the money supply, may at first glance look almost like giving up an interest rate target in favor of a money supply target. As we saw in the preceding chapter, the Federal Reserve has traditionally followed an interest rate target, but there is no conflict between this and its rejection of fixed yields on U.S. Government securities as a target. To pursue an interest rate target is not necessarily to try to hold interest rates unchanged, although that is what the Federal Reserve was doing, completely for U.S. Government securities and to a large degree for other securities, as long as it adhered to its pegging policy. Increases and decreases in interest rates are consistent with interest rates as a target as long as such changes appear to be consistent with overall stability of the economy. Thus, the Federal Reserve will at times take steps to force interest rates above or below the level they would otherwise be at in order to slow or stimulate economic activity. However, for the Federal Reserve to hold interest rates at a fixed level as was done during the years of pegging is not consistent with interest rates as a target, because such a policy would not, except by chance, be consistent for any length of time with the overall stability of the economy. Thus, although the Federal Reserve once again secured control over the money supply as a result of the accord, this by no means says that the Federal Reserve adopted the money supply as a target. It is fair to say that for a period of almost twenty years following the date of the accord, interest rates were the target of Federal Reserve policy.

1951–61: THREE EXPANSIONS AND THREE RECESSIONS

The accord of March 1951 gave the Federal Reserve a freedom of movement it had not enjoyed for years. It still had the obligation of "maintaining an orderly market" for U.S. Government securities, which meant it had to buy in the open market if declines in the prices of Treasury obligations threatened to become disorderly, but this did not begin to limit its freedom to pursue a restrictive monetary policy in the way that its earlier commitment to peg government securities prices had. It was now in a position to restrict the amount of bank reserves and bank credit when it felt that such restriction would promote the stability of the economy, as long as the ensuing rise in interest rates was not so rapid as to cause disorder in the government securities market. This position, it may be noted, was not one with which many Federal Reserve officials had had previous experience. During the forties Federal Reserve actions had been dictated by its commitment to peg government securities prices, and during the preceding decade of the depressed thirties there had been little call for the Federal Reserve to adopt a restrictive policy.

Having attained the position in which it could once again use monetary policy in an effort to keep the economy moving along a stable growth path, did the Federal Reserve succeed in making the economic path smoother than it otherwise would have been? During the first ten years after the accord, the record shows three departures from a stable path or, in other words, three recessions: July 1953 to August 1954, July 1957 to April 1958, and May 1960 to February 1961. One extreme view is that these recessions would not have occurred were it not for the mistaken actions taken by the Federal

Reserve; the opposite extreme is that these recessions would have been much longer and much more severe were it not for the enlightened actions taken by the Federal Reserve. This is not to suggest that anybody holds either of these extreme views; between them are any number of others that one may hold, and one need not hold the same for each recession.

The 1953–54 Recession

Recall that it was the resurgence of inflation following the outbreak of the Korean conflict in 1950 that brought the controversy between the Treasury and the Federal Reserve to the crisis that was resolved by the accord. Once freed from its earlier commitment by the accord, the Federal Reserve permitted interest rates on government securities to drift upward. By the end of 1951 short-term interest rates were double the level of two years earlier, and long-term Treasury bond rates were above 2 1/2 percent for the first time since World War II. By the first half of 1953 rates had risen still more, and the Treasury for the first time since the twenties found it necessary to pay over 3 percent on a new issue of long-term obligations. To the Federal Reserve authorities who evaluated their policy in terms of the movement of interest rates, policy had been restrictive from 1951 into early 1953. However, those who maintain that the rise in interest rates would have been even greater under the boom conditions prevailing by early 1953 conclude that the actual rise in interest rates does not indicate a restrictive monetary policy. To the degree that Federal Reserve policy actually kept them lower than they otherwise would have been, policy was expansionary and not restrictive. Furthermore they maintain that this is born out by the behavior of the money supply: from late 1951 to early 1952 the rate of growth of the money supply was one of the highest during the fifties.

Overall monetary policy during the Korean expansion could not be called vigorously countercyclical. A lesser rate of growth of the money supply and greater rises in interest rates would have been necessary to warrant such a conclusion. Still, in view of the fact that this was the first attempt since the thirties to use monetary policy for economic stabilization purposes, the policy followed was perhaps as good as could have been expected. One thing seems quite certain: the money supply would have grown even faster if the Federal Reserve had still been tied to its earlier pegging policy, and with such growth the results would have been worse than they were.

The Korean expansion came to an end as the economy slid into recession in the summer of 1953. Did Federal Reserve policy contribute to or possibly even cause this recession, or did it shorten and reduce the severity of a recession whose cause is to be found elsewhere? The record clearly shows a move toward more restrictive monetary policy in early 1953, a move precipitated by the Federal Reserve's fear at the time of a resumption of inflation. The inflation that began in mid-1950 with the outbreak of the Korean conflict was sharp but short-lived; the rapid rise of prices ended in the spring of 1951, and prices increased little in the following two years, in part due to the system of price and wage controls that was in effect from 1951 to 1953. But beyond this, the underlying pressures on prices from 1951 to early 1953 were not as great as they were to become. It was not until early 1953 that the economy was operating at a boom level. Output then was near capacity, unemployment was down to 3 percent, and total spending was still expanding rapidly. Restrictive action thus seemed clearly in order and the Federal Reserve through open market operations cut down on the total reserves held by the banks and raised the discount rate to 2 percent, its highest level since 1934, to make it more expensive for the banks to get reserves by borrowing. In early 1953 the rate of growth of the money supply was cut in half. The pressures thus applied pushed market interest rates to their highest levels since the early thirties. Prices of long-term government securities fell as much as 10 percent below par.

In taking these actions during early 1953, the Federal Reserve moved in the right direction at the right time, but it moved too far. On this both monetarists and nonmonetarists tend to agree. There is less agreement as to whether Federal Reserve policy was appropriate during the recession that followed. Because the money supply showed little increase from the second quarter of 1953 through the second quarter of 1954, monetarists maintain that Federal Reserve policy aggravated the recession. Monetarists also note that, starting in mid-1954, the money supply began to grow at its 1951–52 rate, a strong increase in total spending followed, and recovery was under way. On the other side, nonmonetarists point to the various steps taken by the Federal Reserve starting in May 1953 to support their conclusion that the Federal Reserve acted in a way to shorten the recession and reduce its severity. In May the Federal Reserve began to purchase securities in the open market and by June had purchased $1 billion. In July it cut member bank reserve requirements to free $1.2 billion in reserves. And it reduced the discount rate in February of 1954 from 2 to 1 3/4 percent and in April to 1 1/2 percent. In the view of Federal Reserve officials and some others, the easing in credit conditions that followed from these actions was evidence that the actions taken were appropriate. Monetarists again disagree; they say credit conditions became easier because of the decline in the demand for credit, not because of the increase in the supply. For the Federal Reserve to have helped end the recession, it would have had to make credit conditions easier than they otherwise would have been. This, they maintain, it did not do. And apart from considerations like these, the fact that the money supply hardly grew during the recession is conclusive evidence to the monetarists that the Federal Reserve acted incorrectly. Recovery could not begin until the money supply grew more rapidly; as the monetarists point out, the money supply started to grow more rapidly in mid-1954, and the recession bottomed out a few months later.

The 1957–58 Recession

As recovery was well under way by late 1954, the Federal Reserve began to move away from the easy credit conditions it had helped to bring about during the recession. Then in response to a resumption of inflation and the appearance of balance of payments problems, it moved toward successively tighter credit conditions during 1955, 1956, and 1957. Starting in mid-1957 the economy suffered its next downturn, one that was more serious than the earlier postwar recessions. The unemployment rate rose from about 4 percent, where it had been for four years, to a peak of over 7 percent. Actual output, which had been 5 percent below potential, dropped to 10 percent below potential during the recession. And despite the sharp rise in unemployment and the underutilization of plant and equipment, prices continued to rise through the recession instead of falling as had happened in earlier postwar recessions. Consumer prices, which after four years of stability had risen by 1.5 percent in 1956 and almost 4 percent in 1957, rose another 3 percent in 1958, the recession notwithstanding.

During the years 1955–57, the rate of growth of the money supply was held down to about 1 percent per year, following the 5 percent rate at which it had grown in the last half of 1954. In addition, the Federal Reserve chose to make the restrictive policy it was following common knowledge through the statements that accompanied the successive increases in the discount rate. It raised the discount rate from 1 1/2 percent to 3 1/2 percent in seven steps from 1954 to 1957. In the face of rapidly growing credit demand and a slowly growing money supply, market interest rates also increased sharply over these same three years. Treasury bill rates went up from 0.65 percent in mid-1954 to 3.5 percent in mid-1957, and yields on long-term bonds went up from 2.3 percent to 3.7 percent over the same period.

The same questions raised in connection with the Korean expansion and the 1953–54 recession can now be raised here. Due to the return of inflation and balance of payments problems, economists in general would agree that a slowing of aggregate demand during the 1955–57 expansion was desirable. However, they differ as to whether or not this could have been done without precipitating another recession and one this time that was more serious in terms of the increase in unemployment and decrease in output that it involved. Again the monetarists point to the money supply and assert that the maintenance of the growth of the money supply at a more normal rate over the expansion years would have given us a less unfavorable outcome. The opposition replies that interest rates would then have risen less, aggregate demand would have risen more, prices would have risen more, and the end of such an inflationary expansion would have been followed by a more serious downward movement than the one that was actually suffered.

A similar difference between the two sides occurs in connection with Federal Reserve policy during the recession. As economic activity peaked in mid-1957, the money supply began to contract and continued to contract through early 1958, or right through the recession. To a monetarist there can be no question but that this aggravated the recession. The fact that the Federal Reserve sought to bring market interest rates down sharply during the recession carries little weight with them. The Federal Reserve reduced the discount rate four times between November 1957 and April 1958 and also reduced percentage reserve requirements and margin requirements on stock purchases. Treasury bill rates fell drastically from 3.6 percent in mid-1957 to less than 1 percent in mid-1958, and bond yields fell from 3.7 percent to 3.1 percent over the same period. But again there is the difficult question of whether such declines are little more than the result of the decline in business activity or whether they would have been much less than they were in the absence of the actions taken by the Federal Reserve. To the Federal Reserve the fact that interest rates fell sharply was evidence that its policy was appropriate, but to monetarists interest rates and credit conditions are a highly unreliable guide as to whether the Federal Reserve is following an appropriate or inappropriate policy. As has been repeatedly emphasized, Federal Reserve policy will be appropriate only if the Federal Reserve follows a money supply or other monetary aggregate target, according to the monetarists.

The 1960–61 Recession

The Federal Reserve had permitted the money supply to shrink through the 1957–58 recession and then took action that resulted in a rapid growth of the money supply at the same time that the economy began its recovery. But starting in 1959 the rate of growth of the money supply slowed, and for the three quarters starting with the third quarter of 1959 the money supply was actually reduced. During 1959 interest rates were allowed to reach their highest levels in thirty years. At the peak in December 1959, Treasury bill yields were around 4 1/2 percent, and long-term Treasury bond yields were about 4 1/4 percent.

The expansion from the 1957–58 recession was hardly so robust as to call for anything like the severely restrictive policy the Federal Reserve pursued. Unemployment, which had been 7 percent in the early part of 1958, declined to 4.9 percent by mid-1959 but then went up again and averaged 5.5 percent from mid-1959 to mid-1960. There was a record-long national steel strike of 116 days starting in July 1959. The increase in real GNP from the fourth quarter of 1958 to the fourth quarter of 1959 was only 4 percent, which is well below the rate the economy usually shows in the early stage of recovery from a recession. Prices, which had risen through the recession, continued to rise in 1959 but at the much slower rate of 1 percent during that year.

As has been pointed out, there is considerable agreement that a basis existed for the Federal Reserve to take some restrictive action during the expansions that culminated in the recessions of 1953–54 and 1957–58, although the actions taken may have been so restrictive in each case as to have contributed significantly to the recessions that occurred. However, in the case of the 1958–60 expansion, with unemployment as high as it was and the growth in output as slow as it was, it is not easy to see that any restrictive action was required. Actually it may be that no restrictive action was intended and that it was all an unfortunate error. According to a monetarist interpretation, the Federal Reserve was again led astray by its adherence to interest rates and credit conditions as a target. The unavailability of steel during the long strike had pervasive effects, one of which was on business inventories. Inventories, which had been growing at an annual rate of $9.1 billion during the second quarter of 1959, grew at only a $0.4 billion rate in the third quarter, one of the largest quarter-to-quarter changes on record. The liquidation of inventories in many areas that was forced by the steel shortage reduced the demand for credit and would of itself therefore have led to lower interest rates. However, it has been argued that the Federal Reserve did not adequately allow for the decrease in interest rates that would have occurred and chose an interest rate target that actually called for interest rates higher than they otherwise would have been. Then to hit this target the Federal Reserve decreased the money supply for three quarters in a row, and from the monetarist viewpoint this was enough to bring on the recession that began in the spring of 1960.

A quite different interpretation is that the Federal Reserve's restrictive policy was prompted by its fear of inflation. Although the rate of inflation had slowed in 1959, the fact that prices had risen appreciably right through the recession was something of a shock and had a significant impact on what the Federal Reserve officials judged to be appropriate policy once the recovery got under way. This 1957–58 experience combined with the fact that prices had been rising uninterruptedly for almost twenty years (apart from the recessions preceding 1957-58) may have suggested to these men the need to take a firm stand and let this process go no farther.

Whatever factors led to the actions that were taken, the actions are generally recognized to have been inappropriate for the circumstances that existed and a significant cause of the recession that began in May of 1960. Once the recession began, the Federal Reserve took steps toward easing credit conditions. It purchased securities in the open market and reduced member bank reserve requirements. The discount rate, which had been 4 percent, was cut to 3 1/2 percent in June and to 3 percent in August. These actions combined with the decrease in the demand for credit brought large declines in open market interest rates. For example, the Treasury bill yield of almost 4 percent in the first quarter of 1960 fell 1 percentage point in the second quarter and another 2/3 of a percentage point in the third quarter. However, in the area of the money supply, the Federal Reserve's action was not the expansionary kind that might have been expected. During the previous two recessions, it had brought about a rapid expansion of the money supply beginning with the onset of the recession; in late 1960 and early 1961 the money supply grew more slowly than its average rate. Judged on this monetarist criterion, Federal Reserve action did not contribute to bringing the recession to a quick end. The recession was, nonetheless, a mild one. It ran only nine months and produced a decline in real gross national product of less than 1 percent.

1961–70: THE LONG EXPANSION AND THE 1969–70 RECESSION

The 1960–61 recession turned out to be the last recession for almost a decade. A record-long period of unbroken expansion began in February 1961 and ended 105 months later in November 1969. This exceeded by two years the previous 80-month record expansion that included the years of World War II. Still, this expansion that began in February 1961 turned out to be a record-setter by the narrowest of margins. A downturn occurred in the first quarter of 1967 that was too mild and too short-lived (only one quarter) to qualify as a recession by the standards used by the National

Bureau of Economic Research, but it was still enough of a downturn to earn it the popular designation of a "mini-recession."

During most of the six-year period from the end of the recession in February 1961 to the minor downturn at the beginning of 1967, the economy moved ahead steadily. Unemployment, which had averaged almost 8 percent in the first quarter of 1961, declined gradually to average 4.6 percent in 1965. From the beginning of 1961 to the end of 1965, real GNP grew at a 6 percent annual rate, or faster than the growth in potential output, and thus closed most of the large gap between actual and potential output that existed in 1961. Prices moved up during these years at the relatively slow rate of less than 1 1/2 percent per year.

Then in 1966, with the marked enlargement of the U.S. role in the Vietnam war, a large jump in aggregate spending occurred. Federal spending for defense purposes jumped from $50 billion in 1965 to over $60 billion in 1966, or more than 20 percent in one year. Two years later defense spending had jumped further to $78 billion, or almost 30 percent above the 1966 level. As defense spending surged, there was no offsetting slowing in private spending: from 1965 to 1966, personal consumption expenditures rose 7.5 percent, and gross investment spending rose 10 percent. In the face of this rapidly expanding demand for goods and services, the unemployment percentage in 1966 fell below 4 percent, the first time that this had happened since 1953. The year also saw the rate of increase in consumer prices double, from 1 1/2 percent in 1965 to 3 percent in 1966.

With inflationary pressures already building in late 1965 and with much larger military expenditures widely anticipated at that time, many economists urged that tax rates be raised in 1966 to prevent the inflation that would result if the expected large increases in military spending were not offset by tax-induced declines in private spending. The slack that had existed in the economy from 1961 to 1965 was gone by the end of 1965; increases in aggregate spending would be absorbed in large part through a rise in prices. The Federal Reserve was so perturbed by the outlook in late 1965 that it took its first action to meet the danger in December of 1965; it raised the discount rate from 4 to 4 1/2 percent. The administration publicly criticized this move as premature and one that should have awaited the President's budget message in January. In retrospect, however, the Federal Reserve action does not seem to have been untimely, because that budget message did not allay the fears of greatly increased government spending and contained no recommendation to the Congress to raise tax rates to offset whatever increase in government spending might be called for as a result of our greater participation in the Vietnam war.

The Federal Reserve discount rate action was interpreted by the public as an expression of the Federal Reserve's fear of inflation and reinforced a similar fear already widespread among the public. The discount rate action may or may not have been the major causal factor, but this action was followed by an extraordinary increase in the demand for credit. Much of this increase in demand may have occurred in anticipation of still higher future interest rates and still higher future prices for the goods whose purchase the borrowing was to finance. In any event, interest rates responded sharply and quickly to the greater demand for credit and continued to rise through the summer of 1966. In September of that year, rates on Treasury bills reached 5.6 percent, on long-term Treasury bonds 4.8 percent, and on short term commercial paper 5.9 percent, the highest rates experienced in the United States since the twenties.

Perhaps because of the criticism that its December discount rate action had caused the sudden sharp rise in market interest rates, the Federal Reserve followed an easier open market policy during the first few months of 1966 than it might otherwise have done. It permitted bank reserves to grow sufficiently to support a 2 percent increase in the money supply from December to April. But then over the next six months, its open market policy was changed and led to an actual contraction in the total money supply. Over these months occurred the further upward surge in market interest rates to the peaks reached in September.

The pressure on interest rates came not only from the restrictive actions of the Federal Reserve but from the earlier noted extraordinary jump in the demand for credit over these months. The banks, especially the large ones, found themselves in a very difficult situation. In the normal course of business, banks commit themselves to providing firms with loans under "lines of credit" and during this period they were called upon to accommodate an unexpectedly large number of firms under these commitments, which the banks had permitted to grow to a larger total than they should have. To meet their commitments, they turned to every possible source. Borrowings by member banks from the Federal Reserve Banks increased from about $400 million in January to almost $800 million in September. The banks sold large quantities of their holdings of securities, especially state and local government obligations, in many cases at considerable losses. In the effort to attract more time deposits, they paid the maximum rates permitted on these deposits. Large banks even resorted to the Eurodollar market, time deposits denominated in dollars but on deposit in European banks, and paid a 7 percent rate to get dollars from this source. The imbalance between the demand for credit and the ability of the banks to meet that demand was so great during this period that it came to be described as a "credit crunch."

At the same time that "credit crunch" was on everyone's lips, another term came into popular usage: "disintermediation." Financial institutions such as savings and loan associations, mutual savings banks, life insurance companies, and the commercial banks in connection with their time deposit operations are commonly described as intermediaries in the sense that they receive a large part of the public's current saving out of income and lend these amounts to others, especially in the form of real estate loans. This process of intermediation is to be contrasted with the commercial banking system's operations in which their loans result in newly created demand deposits rather than the mere transfer of the public's saving. Focusing specifically on the process of intermediation, the ability of any particular group of financial institutions to lend depends on its ability to attract the public's saving, and this in turn depends in large part on the interest rates it stands ready to pay. In the case of the commercial banks, the rates that they may pay on time deposits are set by the Federal Reserve and the Federal Deposit Insurance Corporation, and at this time in 1966 these maxima ranged from 4 to 5 1/2 percent depending on the maturity of the deposit. Ordinary passbook saving accounts had the lowest maximum, 4 percent, and time deposits with maturities of a year or more had the highest maximum, 5 1/2 percent. As noted earlier, in the efforts to attract deposits the commercial banks had pushed the rates paid up to the maxima allowed. At the same time, savings and loan associations and mutual savings banks were unable to compete by raising the rates they paid to the same extent. They could afford to pay higher rates on *new* deposits because they could use these funds to make loans at correspondingly higher rates, but the same higher rates paid on new deposits must be paid on existing deposits. This, in effect, precluded a large increase in the rates they paid because the assets they already held were largely in the form of long-term mortgage loans made in earlier years at much lower rates. Commercial banks with only a small portion of their assets in long-term loans of this kind were not subject to the same constraint.

What ensued during the first three quarters of 1966 was a sharp reduction in the inflow of funds to the savings and loan associations and the mutual saving banks as savers turned elsewhere to get higher rates. During several months these institutions suffered a net outflow of funds. Life insurance companies faced the same pressures but in a different way. Because of the contractual nature of life insurance policies, premium payments, which in most policies include a large element of saving, continued to flow in, but now some policyholders produced a reverse flow by taking advantage of the provision in many outstanding policies that permitted policyholders to borrow amounts equal to the cash value of their policies at rates as low as 5 percent. It became profitable for policyholders to borrow on this basis and put the funds into other forms at a higher rate.

The principal victim of this disintermediation was the residential

328 The Influence of Money on National Income

construction industry, inasmuch as the principal sources of mortgage funds are the savings and loan associations, mutual savings banks, and life insurance companies. As the net inflow of saving into these institutions shrank and for a while even turned into a net outflow, the inevitable result was that these institutions had to turn away thousands of prospective borrowers seeking to obtain loans to finance the purchase of homes. The unavoidable result of this in turn was a depression in the housing industry as new private housing starts fell by October 1966 to a rate 40 percent below a year earlier.

By paying higher rates, the commercial banks had been able to attract funds from these other institutions to meet the demands of their business borrowers, but the commercial banks also faced disintermediation by late summer. With the rate on Treasury bills over 5 1/2 percent at the peak in September and with the ceiling rate the banks were permitted to pay set at 5 1/2 percent, the banks were unable to roll over all of their maturing certificates of deposit (CDs)—that is, not all holders chose to accept new certificates in exchange for matured certificates. The amount of these outstanding declined by about $3 billion in little more than a month during the fall. However, before the pressure on the commercial banks had led to even greater disintermediation, the Federal Reserve saw fit to move away from its policy of tight credit and high interest rates. During the last quarter, there were signs of a slowing in consumer and investment spending; in the case of the residential construction component of investment spending, it was an unmistakable fact. By the end of the year the Federal Reserve moved to increase bank reserves and bring interest rates well below their September peaks. The Treasury bill rate, for example, was down to 5 percent in December.

Mini-Recession, 1967

Despite this reversal in policy, the economy still suffered the short-lived downturn in the first quarter of 1967, one that is commonly attributed to the excessively restrictive policy pursued by the Federal Reserve during much of the preceding year. Monetarists in particular find Federal Reserve policy almost completely at fault. As we noted earlier, the money supply had spurted ahead in the first few months of 1966, despite the fact that the Federal Reserve in December of 1965 had recognized the need to slow the growth in total demand in view of the vast increase in military expenditures that loomed ahead. However, the restrictive actions taken by the Federal Reserve soon took hold, the growth of the money supply came to a halt, and for a six-month period starting in May 1966 the money supply actually declined. Simultaneous with this unusually restrictive monetary action there was strongly expansionary fiscal action as the budget of the federal government (at annual rates) swung from a surplus of $3.2 billion in the second quarter of 1966 to deficits of $0.7 billion in the third quarter, $3.3 billion in the fourth quarter, and $11.9 billion in the first quarter of 1967. With fiscal policy clearly expansionary and with no other major force working toward contraction, the contention that the restrictive monetary policy pursued in 1966 must be the cause of the contraction has considerable support. Monetarists seem to add to their case by noting that the mild contraction ended within a few months of the sharp reversal of monetary policy that produced an increase in the money supply of more than 3 percent during the first quarter of 1967. Real GNP, which had shown the tiny decline during the first quarter that made it a mini-recession, resumed its growth in the second quarter of the year. Of course, with both monetary and fiscal policy strongly expansionary during early 1967, one cannot as readily attribute the economic recovery to monetary policy rather than fiscal policy as he can attribute the contraction in early 1967 to monetary policy rather than fiscal policy.

The recovery from this mild contraction moved ahead vigorously. Unemployment, which had averaged just over 4 percent during the first quarter of 1967, was down to 3.3 percent during the first quarter of 1969. Aggregate demand increased almost 8 percent from the first quarter of 1967 to the first quarter of 1968 and almost 9 percent over the following year. The rise in consumer prices, which had been only 1 1/2 percent in 1965 and 3 percent in 1966 and 1967, accelerated to 4 percent in 1968 and 5 percent in 1969.

The cause of the rapid expansion of demand and of the worsening of inflation that followed this expansion of demand in a fully employed economy is not hard to find. At least for the period through mid-1968, the cause was the strongly destabilizing fiscal policy followed. For despite the huge increases in federal government spending for military requirements from 1965 to 1968 that culminated in a 1968 deficit of over $25 billion, the largest deficit since the deficits of World War II, no increase in tax rates was put through until June 1968. At that time a 10 percent income tax surcharge retroactive to January 1 was finally imposed on both personal and corporate incomes. With the level of income as it was in mid-1968, this increase in income tax rates would draw from the income stream a little over $10 billion at an annual rate.

A tax increase of this kind had been widely called for and talked about for several years, but action awaited mid-1968. Because of the feverish pace at which the economy was moving by early 1968 and the uncertainty at the time as to whether the Congress would at long last provide the needed restraint by passing a tax increase, the Federal

Reserve felt in the spring of 1968 that it had to provide that restraint by tightening credit. In two steps it brought the discount rate to a peak level of 5 1/2 percent by late April. Through open market operations it applied enough pressure on bank reserves to cut almost in half the rate of growth in bank credit from the 11.5 percent rate it had reached in 1967. Its actions caused interest rates to move up sharply by late May. Treasury bills reached almost 6 percent and high-grade corporate bonds over 7 percent, rates higher than those reached during the 1966 credit crunch.

Once the tax increase was passed by the Congress in June, the Federal Reserve believed a change in its policy was called for. In its judgment, the tax increase combined with the existing degree of monetary restraint was more overall restraint than the economy could take, "overkill" as it was popularly called, so it moved toward an easier policy during the summer of 1968. However, later in the year it began to appear that the surtax would not produce the considerable dampening effect on aggregate demand that had been expected from it. Consumers were apparently adjusting to their reduced take-home pay in very large part by cutting down on the portion of their incomes devoted to saving and were thus maintaining consumption close to the previous levels. With aggregate demand still excessive, the Federal Reserve by year's end began to move back toward restraint. The discount rate that had been cut to 5 1/4 percent in August was raised back to 5 1/2 percent in December. By year's end the Treasury bill rate was up to 6.3 percent, above its level in May, and likewise most other interest rates were then at their highs for the year.

The Federal Reserve policy of restraint was intensified in 1969, and this year turned out to be a mirror of 1966. In April the discount rate was lifted to 6 percent, and reserve requirements on demand deposits of all member banks were raised one-half percentage point. Market interest rates soared to exceed earlier peaks, but the earlier peaks were not now those of the last forty or fifty years but of a hundred years earlier. Financial writers commonly referred to interest rates as the "highest since the Civil War." The growth of the money supply, which had been allowed to reach a 7.2 percent rate in 1968, was slowed to a 4.4 percent rate during the first half of 1969 and then over the last half of the year was brought down to only a 0.7 percent rate.

As in 1966 the restriction on the supply of credit occurred at the same time that the demand for credit had become exceptionally strong. Apart from the high level of economic activity, the rapid rise in prices over the preceding few years and the widespread expectation of more of the same gave a further impetus to borrowing. Although demand for credit had grown sharply in 1966 as the economy reached capacity levels of output, inflation had not been a significant factor on the demand side at that time. It was, however, in large part because of this factor that interest rates rose to the extremes they reached in 1969, despite the fact that the rate of growth in the money supply was not as severely restricted in 1969 as it had been in 1966.

Because of the extraordinarily high open market interest rates reached in 1969, the disintermediation that appeared in 1966 reappeared in 1969 and this time struck hard at the commercial banks as well as the savings and loan associations, mutual savings banks, and life insurance companies. The maximum interest rates that the commercial banks were permitted to pay on various classes of time deposits had not been changed since April 1968, and market interest rates in 1969 had risen appreciably above these maxima. Thus, the highest rate the banks could pay was 6 1/4 percent, and this was limited to large CDs ($100,000 and over) with maturities of six months or more. The Treasury bill rate had risen above 7 percent by July and to almost 8 percent by December; the rate on prime commercial paper was not far from 9 percent by the end of the year. The banks, which counted among their deposits $22.8 billion in these large certificates at the end of 1968, saw this total shrink by more than half to $10.8 billion by the end of 1969 as holders of these deposits shifted into higher yielding assets such as Treasury bills and commercial paper.

As in 1966, in order to meet their customers demand for credit, the banks turned to every available source to replenish the funds lost by deposit withdrawals. Duplicating the 1966 experience, they sold large amounts of their holdings of U.S. Government and state and local government securities, and, despite the need to pay a 10 percent rate for such funds, the large banks borrowed heavily in the Eurodollar market. They also resorted to a new technique through which they obtained funds by the sale of commercial paper issued by subsidiaries and affiliates. Still they could not satisfy the demands of their customers, and the expansion of business loans slowed significantly in the last half of 1969.

Following the 1966 pattern, the savings and loan associations and mutual savings banks again experienced disintermediation—heavy withdrawals of funds occurred as market interest rates soared and depositors found they could get substantially higher rates than these intermediaries were able to pay. Until the Treasury closed this opportunity by increasing the minimum denomination issued to $10,000, even small savers were able to switch funds out of lower yielding deposits into higher yielding Treasury bills, a type of security ordinarily purchased by wealthy investors and financial institutions in large dollar amounts. The outflow of funds from the intermediaries had its expected effect. It was the housing industry that again felt the impact of the resultant shortage of mortgage credit and the extremely high interest rates on what was available, although the decline the industry suffered in 1969 was not nearly as severe as that of 1966. Private nonfarm housing (at its seasonally adjusted annual rate) fell from 1.7 million in the first quarter of 1969 to 1.5, 1.4, and 1.3 million in the next three quarters.

The 1969–70 Recession

Toward the end of 1969, the restrictive effect of monetary actions plus whatever restrictive effect had been produced by the tax surcharge were sufficient to produce a slowing in the economy. Real GNP showed a small decline from the third to the fourth quarter, the first time this had happened since the first quarter of 1967. However, the rate of price advance did not slow; the consumer price index had risen at a 5.6 annual rate from the second quarter to the third quarter and maintained this rate into the fourth quarter. In the face of such strong inflationary pressures, the decision of the Federal Reserve to shift from the policy of restraint it had followed through much of 1969 was not an easy one, but with output declining and unemployment rising sharply it did so shift early in 1970. However, the effects of the very tight policy of 1969 were still to be felt in 1970, and real GNP declined at an annual rate of almost 3 percent during the first quarter of 1970. By one rule of thumb, a decline in real gross national product for two consecutive quarters qualifies as a recession; in the spring of 1970, with a preliminary first quarter GNP figure available, it was recognized that the U.S. economy was in a recession. Real GNP showed small increases in the second and third quarters but in the fourth quarter declined at almost a 4 percent annual rate, a reversal attributed largely to the pervasive effects of a ten-week strike at General Motors, whose output accounts either directly or indirectly for about 1 1/2 percent of the nation's total output. Real GNP then resumed its rise in the first quarter of 1971, and the recession was later dated from November 1969 to November 1970.

During this year of recession the Federal Reserve acted to accelerate the rate of growth of the money supply. From the end of 1969 to the end of 1970, the money supply grew by 5.4 percent; during the last half of 1969, it had grown at an annual rate of only 0.7 percent. Except for a brief period in the second quarter of 1970, short-term interest rates declined sharply; by the first quarter of 1971, the Treasury bill rate was down to 3 1/2 percent, or less than half of the high of 8 percent it had reached during the earlier period of severe monetary restraint. As the effects of the restrictive 1969 policy wore off during 1970 and the effects of the stimulative 1970 policy began to be felt, aggregate demand for goods surged ahead. From the fourth quarter of 1970 to the fourth quarter of 1971, aggregate demand increased 8.6 percent. A good part of this was absorbed by higher prices, but the increase in real GNP over this year was a full 5 percent. Over the preceding four quarters there had been a decrease in real GNP of 2 percent.

1971–74: RECOVERY, BOOM, AND RECESSION

The economy in 1971 clearly had come out of the mild recession. The strong expansion that got under way in 1971 was followed by a year of boom-size expansion in 1972. From the fourth quarter of 1971 to the fourth quarter of 1972, aggregate demand increased 10.6 percent. The increase in real GNP for the year was 7 percent, one of the largest year-to-year real increases in recent experience. At the same time, the price record in 1972 was somewhat better than in 1971; the cost of living rose only 3.3 percent compared to 4.3 percent in 1971, an improvement perhaps attributable in part to the Phase II wage-price control program that had gone into effect in November of 1971.

The boom-size expansion of aggregate demand in 1972 was aided by monetary policy. The money supply grew by 8.2 percent from December 1971 to December 1972 compared with 6.2 percent in 1971 and only 5.4 percent in the recession year of 1970. Fiscal policy was also strongly expansionary in 1972, reflecting both rising government expenditures and tax reductions instituted in 1971 and 1972. Fiscal 1972 showed a deficit of $23.2 billion, a deficit even greater than the $23.0 billion of fiscal 1971. There had been a deficit of only $2.8 billion in fiscal 1970 and a surplus of $3.2 billion in fiscal 1969.

Unemployment at 3.5 percent in 1969 had been at its lowest since 1953. With the recession, the figure rose to 4.9 percent in 1970, and, despite a 5 percent rise in real output in 1971, it rose further to 5.9 percent in that year as strong cost-cutting efforts by firms in all sectors of the economy made possible more output per hour of labor input. With the further gain in the rate of output growth in 1972 and with little more room for increasing output per man hour, the unemployment percentage fell to 5.6, lower than in 1971 but still far above what most economists believed was the percentage consistent with full employment under the existing conditions.

The relatively favorable record on prices during 1972 did not carry over into 1973. Starting in late 1972, the cost of living started to rise at a more rapid rate than had been experienced since the Korean war.

Food prices were the primary problem, rising by 20 percent from December 1972 to December 1973. The cost of living index as a whole rose by 8.8 percent over these 12 months. Faced with a worsening of inflation, on the one hand, and an unacceptably high level of unemployment, on the other, a turn of policy toward restriction carried with it the danger of making a bad unemployment problem even worse. But given the existing pressures on prices and given little likelihood that restraint would come on the fiscal side either through an appropriate slowdown in the rate of government spending or an increase in tax rates, the Federal Reserve felt obligated to use its powers to slow the breakneck rate of expansion.

In the first half of 1973, however, its movement in the direction of restricting the growth of the money supply was in retrospect too gradual. The money supply grew at a 6 percent rate over these months, well below the 8.2 percent rate of 1972 but still too rapidly in view of the extraordinary strength of the demand for goods that already existed. Yet despite this considerable expansion in the money supply, interest rates still surged upward during this first half. So great was the demand for credit by business that the prime rate, which is the rate charged by commercial banks on short-term loans to large businesses with the highest credit standing, rose by one-third, from 6 percent at the beginning of the year to 8 percent at the beginning of July. The movement of this particular rate was widely reported in the press and on radio and television news and came to be the rate on which public attention was focused during this year of rapidly rising interest rates. Other short-term rates went up even faster; the Treasury bill rate jumped from 5 to 7 percent and the commercial paper rate from 5.4 to 8 percent over the same period. As these short-term rates rose, the Federal Reserve in six steps adjusted the discount rate upward from 4 1/2 percent in January to 7 percent in July. At 7 percent the discount rate was as high as it had ever been since the establishment of the Federal Reserve System almost sixty years earlier. Long-term interest rates also spurted ahead, in this case due in good part to the ability of lenders to get a larger inflation allowance as the rate of inflation accelerated during this period.

During July and August the Federal Reserve cut the growth of the money supply sharply to a 2 percent annual rate and in September held it virtually at zero. In the third quarter, interest rates rose even faster than they had earlier in the year. In eight one-quarter percentage point increases, the prime rate was raised from 8 percent in early July to an unprecedented 10 percent in mid-September. Other market interest rates went up in line. In mid-August the Federal Reserve discount rate was raised to 7 1/2 percent, a rate above the earlier peak that had been set during 1921 and matched in July 1973. From the perspective of fall

1973, the then record-high interest rates reached during the 1969 episode of severe monetary restraint no longer looked so awfully high.

During this 1973 period of restraint, the Federal Reserve followed a policy different from that followed in the two preceding periods of 1966 and 1969. In those two cases the Federal Reserve had made major use of its power to set the maximum interest rates the commercial banks were allowed to pay on their time deposits as a means of holding down the growth of the money supply. The highest of these rates, that on large denomination CDs, had been 5 1/2 percent in 1966 and 6 1/4 percent in 1969. Because holders of these CDs are very sensitive to interest rate differentials, they allow their CDs to run off and transfer the funds into Treasury bills, commercial paper, and other money market investments as soon as the differentials favor such action. As the commercial banks suffer a loss of CDs and other time deposits, they are forced to cut back their total assets in almost equal amount. Instead of acquiring more assets by providing their customers with the greater volume of loans they clamor for, the banks find it necessary to turn away loan customers. Interest rates are not necessarily so high as to discourage borrowers from seeking loans, but prospective borrowers discover that they are unable to get them in the amount desired because of the effect of disintermediation on the ability of the banks to provide more loans.

The Federal Reserve's policy in 1973 was to avoid reliance on an unavailability of funds at the commercial banks as in the two earlier periods and to depend instead on a rise in interest rates sufficiently large to discourage more and more businesses and consumers from seeking loans at the banks. In other words, one way the Federal Reserve can limit the growth in the loan volume of the commercial banks and in the money supply is to see to it that the banks do not have the ability to make loans in greater volume than the Federal Reserve deems appropriate, and another way to do the same thing is through a rise in interest rates so great that borrowers do not seek loans in greater volume than the Federal Reserve deems appropriate, although in the latter case the commercial banks retain the ability to make a greater volume of loans than they actually do make. To implement this new policy in 1973, the Federal Reserve had to eliminate the ceiling rate on certain time deposits. As of May 16, 1973, the commercial banks were no longer subject to any maximum on the rates they could pay on large denomination CDs, although ceilings ranging from 4 1/2 to 5 3/4 were in effect on other classes of time deposits. This change meant that the major cause of disintermediation pressure on the commercial banks, that arising from the loss of deposits through the runoff of large denomination CDs, would be avoided; the commercial banks could raise the rates paid on these deposits as needed to remain competitive with open market interest rates. In the fall of 1973, this required that the banks pay a full 10 percent rate on CDs to hold on to them as open market rates rose to this level.

Loans were available at the commercial banks but only at successively higher interest rates over the first three quarters of the year. In view of the hectic pace at which the economy was expanding, it is safe to say that the volume of these loans would have grown even more rapidly if interest rates had not risen so rapidly. Nonetheless, over the first nine months of the year, loan volume of the commercial banks still increased by a sizable 20 percent. This compares with an increase of only 7.8 percent in the first nine months of 1969 and 9.7 percent for the full year of 1969.

With the money supply and loan volume at commercial banks growing as fast as they did during the first half of 1973, it seems inappropriate to describe the first half as a period of monetary restraint. Still, interest rates rose sharply over these months and presumably squeezed out a lot of loan demand. It is when one looks at the impact of the rise in interest rates on particular sectors, however, that it becomes apparent that the period was one of considerable monetary restraint. As in 1966 and 1969, the area of real estate credit was hardest hit. Although commercial bank loan volume increased by 20 percent over the first three quarters of 1973, the amount of real estate loans outstanding at the commercial banks increased at less than half this rate. In addition, because real estate loans in recent years have made up only about one-fourth of all loans at commercial banks, in dollar amounts the commercial banks during 1973 were lending only about $1 in mortgages for every $8 they were lending for other purposes. There was a rising demand for real estate credit as for other kinds of credit during 1973, but the amount of real estate credit available at the commercial banks did not begin to satisfy the demand.

As in 1966 and 1969, intermediaries like savings and loan associations and mutual savings banks found it impossible to maintain their usual inflow of funds as savers found higher yields available in various open market securities. However, starting in July these intermediaries were permitted to raise the rates they paid to a scale ranging from 5 1/4 on ordinary passbook accounts to 7 1/2 percent on deposits with maturities of four years and in amount of $1,000 or more. These rates gave them a competitive edge over commercial banks in attracting smaller deposits and thereby reduced the pressure on them, although it must be recalled that the ability of most savings and loan associations to raise rates to the maxima permitted by government regulations was limited by the fact that the average rate of interest earned on the bulk of their existing assets is the lower rate at which long-term mortgage loans were made in earlier years.

With these intermediaries as the major source of home financing and with the demand for this kind of financing far exceeding their ability to meet it, mortgage loans became very difficult to secure except for borrowers able to make large down payments and with otherwise excellent credit records. The measures taken by the federal government through its housing agencies helped to soften the impact of the mortgage credit shortage, but it was still true, as in 1966 and 1969, that the impact of the policy of monetary restraint fell very disproportionally on the housing industry. From December 1972 to August 1973, private housing starts declined by 14 percent; over the corresponding months a year earlier they had risen by 18 percent.

The intense pressure on credit supplies and the resultant rise in interest rates reached a peak in September. After an unbroken march upward from 6 percent in January to 10 percent in September, the prime rate declined to 9 3/4 percent in November and to 8 3/4 percent in March 1974. The commercial paper rate peaked at 10 1/2 percent in September and fell to 7 3/4 percent in February 1974. Despite the easing in market interest rates, there was no evidence of a clearcut reversal in Federal Reserve policy. For the three months ending January 1974, the money supply grew at only a 3.3 percent annual rate. The Federal Reserve also maintained its discount rate at the 7.5 percent peak, despite the decline in open market interest rates.

The continuation of strong monetary restraint was apparently prompted by the Federal Reserve's fear of adding fuel to the inflationary fires then raging. The cost of living rose in the last half of 1973 at a 9.2 percent annual rate, even faster than during the first half. The dimensions of the energy crisis and the shortages of fuel and many other materials rather suddenly came to be recognized late in the year, although the problems were present earlier. One estimate was that the energy crisis alone would contribute 2 percentage points to the overall inflation rate in 1974. However, at the same time that inflation was worsening, there was evidence that the economy had begun to slow down in real terms. Certain areas had stopped growing as early as March. For example, sales of retail stores adjusted for price changes had been declining month by month since March. Spending on goods and services as measured by GNP continued to grow in real terms, but the annual rate of growth in the second half of the year was down to 2.0 percent from the 5.9 percent annual rate for the first half of the year.

With the new year, the slowing in the rate of growth of output was replaced by an actual decline in output. GNP in real terms declined from the fourth quarter of 1973 to the first quarter of 1974 at a 7.2 percent annual rate and in the next quarter at a 1.6 percent annual rate. The unemployment rate had declined from 5.9 percent in 1971 to 4.6 percent in October 1973 as a result of the rapid growth of output during 1972 and 1973. With the actual downturn in output over the first half of 1974, the unemployment rate rose to 5.3 percent in July.

By the widely used rule of thumb that two successive quarters of decline in real GNP constitute a period of recession, the U.S. economy had been in recession since at least January, 1974. However, as the decline in the first quarter of that year was so much a product of the special conditions created by the temporary Arab oil embargo and because the decline in the second quarter could also be attributed to some other special conditions, many observers felt that the rule of thumb was inappropriate in this case. However, with the release in October of the preliminary GNP figure for the third quarter, little disagreement remained as to whether or not a recession was underway. That figure showed a real decline in the third quarter at a 2.9 percent annual rate. In addition, the unemployment rate had risen from 5.3 percent in July to 5.8 percent in September. By October the only question being asked by most was how long and how severe a recession it would be.

Despite the slowdown in production and the sharp rise in unemployment over the first three quarters of the year, the consumer price index did not slow its rate of advance but rose at a 12.9 percent annual rate, much faster than the 8.8 percent rate during the boom year of 1973. During the early months of 1974 most economists had predicted that the rate of inflation would subside to about 7 to 8 percent later in the year. However, upward pressure on food prices as a result of bad weather conditions and the prospect of reduced oil output by the Arab states to prevent what otherwise would have meant a decline in the price of Mideast oil were two major factors that led economists to revise their price forecasts. With the staggering 3.7 percent and 3.9 percent increases in the wholesale price index for the months of July and August, the largest monthly increases in this index since the inflation just after World War II, a continuation of "double digit" inflation for the year ahead came to be the general expectation.

At the same time interest rates were surging to new peaks, and the likelihood of any appreciable decline was not much greater than the likelihood of an appreciably lower inflation rate. As noted above, interest rates had reached an earlier peak in September 1973 and had gradually fallen over the following six months. Then in March 1974 rates began a sharp climb to levels well above the 1973 peaks. In July 1974 the prime rate reached 12 percent; the 1973 peak had been 10 percent. The commercial paper rate approached 12 percent; its peak in 1973 had been 10.5 percent. In the next few months rates declined— the prime rate fell below 11 percent and the commercial paper rate fell below 10 percent—but these remained exceedingly high rates.

With the economy's output expected to continue to contract at least through the middle of 1975, with the unemployment rate expected to rise from the September 1974 figure of 5.8 percent to anywhere from 7 to 8 percent in 1975, with the rate of inflation expected to run far above an acceptable figure, and with interest rates close to their peak, the Federal Reserve authorities faced great difficulties. If they were to shift toward a more rapid expansion of the money supply, they might bring about some short-term decline in interest rates, some increases in the rate of growth of output, and some reduction in the unemployment rate. Various groups, especially the construction industry, urged such a policy. While there was a question during the summer of 1974 of whether or not the economy was in a recession, there was no question of whether this particular industry was in that predicament. Housing starts had declined by over one-third from a 2.1 million annual rate in the summer of 1973 to a 1.3 million annual rate in the summer of 1974. Unemployment in the construction trades was well over 10 percent and was expected to go higher, and bankruptcies among residential builders were commonplace. A major factor in the problem was the one noted several times above in examining other periods of high interest rates: disintermediation. With savers able to obtain from 8 to 9 percent on Treasury obligations during the summer and with savings and loan associations and mutual savings banks unable to pay such rates, there was an outflow of funds from these institutions. A decline in market rates would reverse this process, and the Federal Reserve had the power to bring about such a decline, at least in the short run, through a more rapid expansion of the money supply.

However, while such a decline would ease the housing industry's problem, likely bring about an improvement in the badly depressed stock market, and help the public utilities and other hard-pressed industries to find buyers for new stock and bond issues, these beneficial effects would probably be short-lived. Although there were opposing views, it appears that the consensus at this time was that to abandon a policy of strong monetary restraint would be to accept an even higher rate of inflation in the future as the increased money supply gradually exerted its effect on the price level. With this would come a return of the other problems in more virulent form than before. The policy of restricting the growth of the money supply is obviously painful in the short run, but the concensus was that only if such a policy were maintained could inflation finally be wrung out of the economy. With the problem having been built deeply into the economy over a period of years, the period required for its solution would also run into years. The quick solution—i.e., a massive depression—is, as all agree, a cure worse than the disease.

This consensus on what appropriate monetary policy was at the time was the view taken by the Federal Reserve authorities, a group whose view is clearly most important as it is the group that decides what policy will actually be. However, while there was broad agreement among most groups that a policy of monetary restraint was essential under the existing conditions, there was less agreement as to whether the degree of restraint being imposed by the Federal Reserve at the time was about right or too much or too little. Professor Friedman objected in September of 1974 that the restraint had been too little and too late; he noted that the rate of growth in the money supply had only slowed over the preceding three months and then only mildly. The rate of growth of M_1 from October 1973 to April 1974 had been 8.8 percent, and from April 1974 to July 1974 it had been 4.5 percent. In his judgment, there was as of September no strong evidence that the Federal Reserve had really shifted toward a fundamentally tighter policy. Nonmonetarists who tend to look not only at the monetary growth rate but also at interest rates in deciding on how easy or tight monetary policy is were led to conclude that interest rates such as the 11 percent prime then in effect did indeed suggest a fundamentally tighter policy than that of six months earlier. To some the fact that the Federal Reserve had raised the discount rate to a new peak of 8 percent in April 1974 was also an indicator of a turn to a basically tighter policy by the authorities.

The crucial issue is, of course, to achieve that particular degree of tightness which, in combination with the existing degree of ease or tightness in fiscal policy, will contribute most to the stabilization of the economy. As of the fall of 1974, the question of whether a more or less restrictive monetary policy would do more to check inflation, lower interest rates, reduce unemployment, and stimulate production was one not readily answerable. There were those who argued that the Federal Reserve should turn less restrictive than it had been over the preceding months, and there were others who argued that the Federal Reserve should not move in this direction.

With the danger that the recession then being recognized might become quite severe, there was pressure on the Federal Reserve to become less restrictive. With the danger that the rate of inflation, already intolerable, might become even worse, there was pressure on the Federal Reserve to maintain a tight policy. This is the same dilemma that the Federal Reserve has faced a number of times in the past but never before in such severe form. The economy in late 1974 was in a precarious balance. There was, on the one hand, a possibility that too restrictive a policy pursued too long could lead to a liquidity crisis, collapse of financial markets, massive business and bank failures, and a major depression and, on the other hand, a possibility that the opposite policy could lead to an even greater rate of inflation—15 or 20 percent per year or even more—which in turn might lead to the destruction of our system of society and government. The future of the economy would not be determined by the course of monetary policy alone, but if the course followed turned out to be seriously incorrect, the damage could be tremendous for an economy in the precarious position of the U.S. economy in 1974.

While monetary policy errors have not been uncommon, there is, in the fall of 1974, no reason to expect the grievous errors that would produce such disastrous results. The more likely results will be a gradual winding down of the inflation rate over a period of years obtained at the cost of little or no growth in production and higher unemployment. As unpleasant as even this is, the slow growth or zero growth in output and the higher unemployment appear to be unavoidable costs that must eventually be paid if the rapid inflation of recent years is finally to be brought under control.

A CONCLUDING NOTE

In this chapter we have reviewed monetary policy in the United States over the last few decades, starting with the period from 1941 to 1951, during which monetary policy exhibited zero flexibility as it was committed to maintaining fixed yields on U.S. Government securities, and continuing through the years since the 1951 accord, during which monetary policy regained the flexibility it had before 1941. For the period since the accord, the crucial question is whether the flexible monetary policy pursued by the Federal Reserve has made the recessions the economy has suffered over those years less severe and less prolonged or just the opposite. This question took on special meaning in 1974 as inflation raged and the recession that was then underway threatened to become something even worse. As the Federal Reserve adjusted its policy to attempt to meet these trying conditions, the danger was that it would err and make a bad situation even worse rather than better as it intended. There is also the possibility—or the "fact" as some monetarists see it—that some of the recessions the economy has endured would not have occurred at all in the absence of the flexible monetary policy pursued by the Federal Reserve.

If economists could definitively answer this question, we would be much closer to an end to the debate between Keynesianism and monetarism than we now appear to be. However, there are some who argue that, even if the flexible policy followed by the Federal Reserve has been procyclical rather than countercyclical, it does not automatically follow that a flexible policy is therefore inherently inferior to the kind of inflexible policy that monetarists favor. The argument here is that the errors were in the execution, not in the theory, of flexibility. But the monetarists insist that a repetition of past errors is unavoidable as long as the Federal Reserve takes as its target for policy anything other than the growth of the money supply or some other monetary aggregate.

Although this is not likely to happen in the near future and is something that antimonetarists insist should not be allowed to happen, a giant step toward answering the question posed here and toward resolving the Keynesian-monetarist debate would be taken by actually implementing the strict monetarist prescription over an unbroken period of years. There would, of course, be problems in getting a fair test. For one thing, if the economy somehow veered far off the path of stable growth despite strict adherence to a monetary rule that was supposed to keep the system on such a path, it is hard to visualize the responsible authorities not ordering a relaxation or abandonment of the rule and, depending on the situation, ordering an acceleration or a slowdown in the rate of growth of the money supply in the effort to push the economy back toward the path of stable growth. But if the monetarists are correct and if there were no shocks like wars, widespread strikes, Watergates, Arabian oil embargoes, or natural disasters to push the economy off a stable growth path, strict adherence to the monetary rule would mean that the instability of the past would become a thing of the past.

Unless there were an act of Congress ordering the Federal Reserve to pursue such a strict monetarist policy, this kind of ultimate test is not very likely to be made in the near future. In the years ahead economists will have to continue to evaluate as best they can the extent to which changes in Federal Reserve policy amount to movements toward or away from the kind of policy urged by the monetarists and compare this as best they can with the extent to which the responses of the economy to Federal Reserve policy changes appear to be in the direction or more or less instability. In a setting like this, with what will likely be only small shifts toward or away from the monetarist kind of monetary policy and with other factors always at work in the economy, the difficulties in trying to measure how much money matters will remain as great as they are today. Anything like a final resolution of the debate between Keynesianism and monetarism and between monetary policy by authorities and monetary policy by rules is not likely in the immediate future; the debate may never come to an end at all.

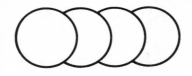

part four
MONEY IN THE INTERNATIONAL ECONOMY

seventeen
THE BALANCE
OF PAYMENTS

What we mean by "money" is the same whether we look at money in the United States, Britain, Italy, France, or any other country. The monetary unit, of course, varies from country to country—the dollar in the United States, the pound in Britain, the lire in Italy, the franc in France—but the underlying definition of what money is does not vary. For if it makes economic sense to define money as anything that is generally acceptable in payment for goods and services and in discharge of debts, it makes as much sense to do this in one country as in another.

Although the monetary and banking structure and practices of no two countries are the same, in each country one can identify those assets held by the public that meet this general acceptability criterion, and the total of these particular assets makes up the money supply narrowly defined, or M_1, for that country. As we saw in considering the U.S. case, one may also arrive at broader definitions of money by including certain assets that do not qualify as means of payment but can quickly and easily be converted into means of payment. These assets are not the same in all countries—for example, not all countries have the equivalent of our savings and loan shares, and not all central governments issue the equivalent of our U.S. Treasury bills—but in each case it is possible to identify those assets that are near-moneys and thus includable in a broader definition of money.

Control over the rate at which the money supply grows is clearly of great importance in every country, and each has a governmental apparatus of one kind or another whose function it is to exercise that control. There is a great diversity in the means employed, although the major industrial countries use techniques much like ours. The responsibility of managing the money supply typically rests with the central bank, and the major tools employed by the central bank to affect the lending power of the commercial banks are essentially the same ones employed by the Federal Reserve in this country. However, the relative importance of these tools varies considerably from country to country. For example, as a generalization, the use of the discount rate is more important in other major countries than it is in the United States.

If one's basic purpose is to see how money fits into and influences international economic transactions, it is not essential to enter into the technical differences of this kind that exist among the monetary and banking systems of different countries. When we look beyond our own system to those of other countries, the difference that is essential arises from the fact that each country has a different monetary unit—the U.S. dollar, the British pound, the French franc, the Italian lire, etc. And although more than one country may use the same name for its monetary unit—the U.S. dollar and the Canadian dollar, the British pound and the Israeli pound, the French franc and the Swiss franc—in terms of value each unit in these pairs of units may be as different from the other as they are from those with altogether different names.

With each country having its own unit, payments between persons, firms, and government units in any two countries involve converting units of one country's money into units of another country's money. These payments can be made in a bewildering variety of ways that only persons who actually work in this area are fully familiar with. However, a basic element in this payment mechanism is the use of deposit balances that commercial banks in each country carry with commercial banks in other countries for this purpose. The first section of this chapter examines briefly how international payments arising from certain kinds of transaction are made through the banking system.

MAKING INTERNATIONAL PAYMENTS

Every year trillions of dollars worth of payments are made in the United States to cover the purchase of goods and services, land, buildings, and securities and to meet tax obligations. These are payments made by persons and firms within the country, and these persons and firms seek to pay with U.S. dollars, which is the kind of money they in turn receive from others who make payments to them. As long as they are making payments to persons, firms, and government units within the country, we may expect that these payees or receivers want to be paid in U.S. dollars because, again, their payments will be made in this money. For the many trillions of dollars of payments of this kind made every year, nothing more is, therefore, involved than a movement of Federal Reserve Notes or other kinds of U.S. currency or of demand deposits in U.S. commercial banks from the accounts of various persons, firms, and government units to the accounts of others.

When we turn to the many billions of dollars of payments made every year by persons, firms, and government units in the United States to persons, firms and government units in other countries of the world, we find that such payments are not carried out in this same direct manner. To the extent that the transactions that give rise to the payments being made by U.S. parties to foreign parties call for payment in the monetary unit of the foreign parties, it becomes necessary for U.S. payers to obtain foreign moneys in exchange for the U.S. dollars they hold before they can make payment to these foreign parties.

The market in which persons, firms, and government units in each country convert units of their money into units of money of other countries is known as the *foreign exchange market*, and what is actually traded is known as *foreign exchange*. This will be either actual foreign currency or various kinds of claims on foreign currency. In by far the largest part of the transactions in this market what is bought and sold are claims on foreign currencies rather than the currency itself, but the simplest case is that in which actual currencies are exchanged.

As an illustration, take the case of a U.S. citizen who is leaving for a trip through Germany. Although for safety's sake he will probably carry the major part of his funds in traveler's checks, he may also want to have immediately available some German currency, Deutsche marks, or DMs, the money he will need to cover whatever payments he has to make in Germany. He obtains this DM currency from his bank in exchange for dollars. Where does the U.S. bank get the DM currency it sells? It may have some on hand as a result of purchases from other persons who have returned from Germany with some DM currency left over. Or, as need arises, it may buy some with dollars from firms in New York City that act as wholesalers in the foreign bank note market. Or it may have a German bank with which it does business ship DM currency to it in exchange for which it may ship the equivalent in U.S. currency to the German bank. Or if the German bank in question carries a demand deposit with this U.S. bank, the U.S. bank may make payment for the notes by crediting the German bank's account with it for the equivalent amount in dollars. Or if the U.S. bank has a demand deposit with the German bank, it may make payment by having the German bank charge its account for the amount involved.

If we were to look at the case of a German citizen leaving for a trip through the United States, we would have a similar case, except, of course, that the German citizen would want to purchase U.S. dollars with DMs back in Germany.

Apart from tourists, the demand by others who have to make payments in foreign currencies is primarily a demand for claims on foreign currencies and not the currency itself. The payments that persons and firms in each country must make to persons and firms in other countries as a result of the import of all kinds of goods and services and the purchase of securities—transactions that make up the largest part of the total of all international transactions—do not in most cases involve the use of currency at all but are settled by appropriate entries in the books of the banks in different countries. We may best see how this works out by tracing several transactions through T-accounts as we did in earlier chapters for purely domestic transactions. Our assumption initially is that amounts due to persons in other countries are to be paid in the monetary unit of the payee's country.

Let us take the case of a U.S. automobile dealer who has imported a number of Mercedes-Benz cars for an amount specified in DMs and who must thus purchase the number of DMs called for in order to make payment. U.S. banks maintain demand deposits in German banks that enable them to sell to their U.S. customers orders-to-pay drawn against German banks. If the U.S. firm must pay Mercedes-Benz 200,000 DMs, it will buy with dollars from its bank an order-to-pay, or a draft, in this amount and turn it over to the German firm in payment. That firm will collect the indicated number of DMs by depositing that draft, or check, in its bank just as it does checks it receives from its customers in Germany.

In the fall of 1974 the rate at which U.S. dollars could be

converted into DMs, or what is called the *foreign exchange rate*, between these two currencies was approximately 2.5 DMs to the U.S. dollar. This means that the U.S. automobile dealer who needs 200,000 DMs would pay $80,000 to his bank for a 200,000 DM draft drawn by his bank against its balance in a German bank. (In order to avoid the complications these create, we here skip over the bank charges and commissions that the automobile dealer would also pay.) The effects of this transaction on the assets and liabilities of U.S. banks and German banks are shown by the (a) entries in the T-accounts below. For U.S. banks, there is an $80,000 decline in the auto dealer's deposit balance and a 200,000 DM decline in the balance of a U.S. bank with a German bank, which at the going rate of exchange is equal to an $80,000 decrease in the deposit balances of U.S. banks with foreign banks. As all other assets and liabilities on the books of U.S. banks are expressed in U.S. dollars, the deposit balances of U.S. banks in foreign banks must also be converted to the equivalent in U.S. dollars for accounting purposes. For German banks there is a 200,000 DM increase in the deposit balance of Mercedes-Benz Company, the result of the receipt of this amount from the U.S. auto dealer, and a 200,000 DM decrease in the deposit balance of U.S. banks, the result of the 200,000 DMs sold by a U.S. bank to the U.S. auto dealer to pay the Mercedes-Benz Company.

Note that the net result of this one transaction is a decrease in the public's demand deposits in U.S. banks and a matching decrease in the deposits of U.S. banks in German banks. Other things being equal, this amounts to that much of a decrease in the U.S. money supply. This one transaction also results in an increase in the German public's demand

UNITED STATES BANKS

DM deposits in German banks:
  −200,000 DM = −$80,000 (a)
	Deposit of U.S. auto
	  dealer −$80,000 (a)
	Deposit of
	  RCA Corporation +$80,000 (b)
	Deposits of German bank −$80,000 (b)

GERMAN BANKS

U.S. dollar deposits in
  U.S. banks:
  −$80,000 = −200,000 DM (b)
	Deposit of Mercedes-
	  Benz Company +200,000 DM (a)
	Deposits of U.S. bank −200,000 DM (a)
	
	Deposit of German music
	  company −200,000 DM (b)

deposits in German banks and the aforementioned equal decrease in the deposits of U.S. banks in German banks. Because interbank demand deposits are not counted as part of a nation's money supply, these two changes are not offsetting; in Germany there is an increase in the money supply equal to the decrease in the money supply in the United States.

To take an opposite transaction, one involving a German import from the United States or a U.S. export to Germany, suppose a German music store purchases $80,000 worth of phonograph records from RCA Corporation in the United States and agrees to make payment in U.S. dollars. Given that the rate at which U.S. dollars can be converted into DMs is 2.5 DMs to the dollar, then the rate at which DMs can be converted into U.S. dollars must be $0.40 to the DM—one DM exchanges for 1/2.5 of a dollar, or $0.40. (As before, we overlook the commissions and bank charges, which would complicate our illustration considerably.) To obtain the $80,000 draft the music store needs to pay RCA thus requires that it turn over 200,000 DMs to its bank. German banks maintain demand deposits in U.S. banks, which enables them to sell such claims to dollars. RCA, on receiving the draft for $80,000 from the German importer, collects it in the same way as the checks received from its customers at home.

The effects of this transaction on the assets and liabilities of the German banks and U.S. banks are shown by the (b) entries in the T-accounts above. For the German banks, there is a 200,000 DM decrease in the deposit balance of the German music company and an $80,000 decrease in the balance of a German bank with a U.S. bank, which at the going rate of exchange is equal to a 200,000 DM decrease in the deposit balances of German banks with foreign banks. As U.S. banks must convert their foreign currency and deposit holdings into dollars for accounting purposes, German banks must convert into DMs for accounting purposes. For U.S. banks, there is an $80,000 increase in the deposit balance of RCA Corporation, the result of the receipt of this amount from the German music company, and an $80,000 decrease in the deposit balance of German banks in U.S. banks, the result of the $80,000 sold by a German bank to the German music company to pay RCA Corporation.

The net result of this one transaction is a decrease in the public's demand deposits in German banks and a matching decrease in the deposits of German banks in U.S. banks. That amounts to a decrease in the German money supply. This transaction also results in an increase in the U.S. public's demand deposits in U.S. banks and an equal decrease in the deposits of German banks in U.S. banks. This means an increase in the money supply in the United States equal to the decrease in Germany.

If we put the (a) and (b) transactions together, we have an export and an import of offsetting values for each of the two countries. We then find in each country that the increased deposit balance of the exporting firm is matched by the decreased deposit balance of the importing firm. For the two transactions combined, there is no effect on the money supply in either country—the import reduces it, but the equal-sized export increases it by the same amount. For the two transactions combined, the only net effect is that each country's banks show an equal decrease in the liability item "Deposit balances *of* foreign banks" and in the asset item "Deposit balances *in* foreign banks." If a country's banks were to show a change in deposit balances in foreign banks different from the change in deposit balances of foreign banks with domestic banks, that would be significant, but offsetting changes like those here are not particularly significant. It may be apparent that a bank in the U.S. and a bank in Germany may at any time increase (decrease) the balances each has with the other by simply adding (subtracting) offsetting amounts to (from) such deposit balances. In the illustration, deposits of U.S. banks in German banks and deposits of German banks in U.S. banks would be restored to the level they were at before these two transactions occurred if a U.S. bank were to credit the deposit balance of a German bank for $80,000 and that German bank were to credit the deposit balance of that U.S. bank for 200,000 DMs. These changes involve nothing but offsetting bookkeeping entries.

Behind the changes in the deposit balances of the four firms and of the U.S. and German banks in our illustration, it is worth noting that in real terms it is the U.S. export of $80,000 worth of RCA phonograph records that pays for the U.S. import of 200,000 DMs worth of Mercedes-Benz automobiles; or, what is the same thing, it is the German export of 200,000 DMs worth of Mercedes-Benz automobiles that pays for the German import of $80,000 worth of RCA phonograph records. These two equal-valued transactions could have been cleared by having the auto dealer turn over $80,000 to RCA and the music store turn over 200,000 DMs to Mercedes-Benz. In each country, the export pays for the import. As we can see in the T-accounts, the changes in the deposit balances of the four firms turn out to be just what they would be if the importer in each country had paid the exporter in that country. In the U.S., the auto dealer's (importer's) deposit balance is down by $80,000, and RCA's (exporter's) deposit balance is up by $80,000; in Germany, the music company's (importer's) deposit balance is down by $200,000 DMs, and Mercedes-Benz (exporter's) deposit balance is up by $200,000 DMs.

The settlement of a pair of transactions like these may also be effected in terms of only one currency. For example, the U.S. auto dealer may pay Mercedes-Benz in U.S. dollars if that is agreeable to

Mercedes-Benz, and the German music company may pay RCA in U.S. dollars. This will give the results shown in the following two T-accounts. As shown by the (a) entries, Mercedes-Benz sells the $80,000 check received from the U.S. automobile dealer to its bank in Germany for 200,000 DMs, which amount is credited to its deposit balance. The German bank in turn collects this dollar amount by having that amount credited to its deposit balance in a U.S. bank. As shown by the (b) entries, the effects of the German music company's paying RCA in dollars are the same here as in the preceding pair of T-accounts, where the same assumptions were made. Because in this case both transactions are settled in dollars, there is no activity in the deposit accounts carried by U.S. banks in German banks. There is activity in the deposit accounts of German banks in U.S. banks but no net change in the deposit balance. As before, there is also no *net* change in either country in the deposits of firms and persons as a result of these transactions. The full set of changes shown in each T-account will be seen to cancel out.

UNITED STATES BANKS

Deposit of U.S. auto dealer	−$80,000 (a)
Deposits of German banks in U.S. banks	+$80,000 (a)
Deposit of RCA Corporation	+$80,000 (b)
Deposits of German banks in U.S. banks	−$80,000 (b)

GERMAN BANKS

Deposits of German banks in U.S. banks: +$80,000 = +200,000 DM (a)	Deposits of Mercedes-Benz Company +200,000 DM (a)
Deposits of German banks in U.S. banks: −$80,000 = −200,000 DM (b)	Deposit of German music company −200,000 DM (b)

The opposite case, in which the pair of transactions is settled in terms of DMs only, gives us the entries shown in the following two T-accounts. As shown by the (b) entries, RCA Corporation sells the 200,000 DM check received from the music company in Germany to its U.S. bank for $80,000, which amount is credited to its deposit balance. The (a) entries, which show the effects of the U.S. automobile dealer's paying Mercedes-Benz in DMs, are the same as in the first set of T-accounts, where this same assumption was made.

As we found in the case where both transactions are settled in dollars, we find here also that the full set of changes in each T-account cancel out. There is no change in the deposits of U.S. banks in German banks or in the deposits of firms and persons in U.S. banks or in German banks.

UNITED STATES BANKS

Deposits of U.S. banks in German banks: −200,000 DM = −$80,000 (a)	Deposit of U.S. auto dealer −$80,000 (a)
Deposits of U.S. banks in German Banks +200,000 DM = +$80,000 (b)	Deposit of RCA Corp. +$80,000 (b)

GERMAN BANKS

	Deposit of Mercedes-Benz Company +200,000 DM (a)
	Deposits of U.S. Banks −200,000 DM (a)
	Deposit of music company −200,000 DM (b)
	Deposits of U.S. Banks +200,000 DM (b)

The several cases traced through here by no means exhaust all the possible ways in which the particular pair of transactions could be settled through the banking system, but they are sufficient to bring out the way that deposit balances of an importer and of an exporter in each country and of the banks in each country are affected by payments between parties in different countries. No matter which way its settlement occurs through the banking system, each individual transaction tends to cause changes in the deposit balances that banks in one country hold in another. If we look only at the U.S. automobile dealer's import of Mercedes-Benz cars, the result will be a decrease in the deposit balances of U.S. banks in German banks or an increase in the deposit balances of German banks in U.S. banks. If we look only at the RCA Corporation's export of records to the German music company, the result will be an increase in the deposit balances of U.S. banks in German banks or a decrease in the deposit balances of German banks in U.S. banks. When we later turn to the subject of explaining foreign exchange rates, for example, the U.S. dollar-DM rate, we will see that import transactions, like the U.S. automobile dealer's purchase of Mercedes-Benz automobiles, tend to reduce the number of DMs into which a U.S. dollar can be converted. Import transactions deplete U.S. banks' deposit balances in German banks and/or increase German banks' deposit balances in U.S. banks, both of which tend to add to the number of dollars available to the rest of the world and reduce the number of DMs available to parties in the U.S. and thus tend to raise the value of the DM relative to the U.S. dollar. Export transactions like RCA Corporation's sale of phonograph records to a German firm in a related way tend to have the opposite effect.

Before going into the explanation of foreign exchange rates, we must take into account the fact that a nation's international merchandise transactions are, of course, not limited to exports of goods to and imports of goods from one other country as in our illustration but in some cases involve a hundred or more of the other countries in the world. Furthermore, these transactions with these many other countries are by no means limited to exports and imports of goods or merchandise but include imports and exports of services (of which tourism is one kind), various remittances and transfers, and long- and short-term capital movements. The following explains briefly the nature of these less familiar international transactions and shows, for example, how all those transactions that result in payments from parties in the United States to parties in all other countries, or dollar *outpayments*, and all those transactions that result in payments from parties in all other countries to parties in the United States, or dollar *inpayments*, can be brought together in one statement to form what is called a nation's *balance of international payments*.

THE U.S. BALANCE OF INTERNATIONAL PAYMENTS

A balance of payments statement for the United States with data for 1973 is shown in Table 17–1. There are various ways in which the transactions that enter into the balance of payments can be organized, and economists are by no means in full agreement as to which is the best way. This question was much debated during the sixties, an outcome of which was the adoption by the Department of Commerce in 1971 of the kind of presentation given in Table 17–1. The official estimates prepared by the Department of

TABLE 17—1

U.S. BALANCE OF PAYMENTS,
1973 (in billions of dollars)

Merchandise trade balance		0.5
Exports	70.3	
Imports	−69.8	
Military transactions, net		−2.2
Travel and transportation, net		−2.7
Investment income, net		5.3
Other services, net		3.5
Balance on goods and services			4.4
Remittances, pensions, and other transfers		−1.9
Balance on goods, services, and remittances			2.4
U.S. Government grants (excluding military)		−1.9
Balance on current account			0.5
Long-term private capital flows, net		0.1
U.S. Government capital flows, net		−1.4
Balance on current account and long-term capital			−0.9
Nonliquid short-term private capital flows, net		−4.3
Allocations of Special Drawing Rights		0.0
Errors and omissions, net		−2.6
Net liquidity balance			−7.8
Liquid private capital flows, net		2.5
Official reserve transactions balance			−5.3
Financed by changes in:		
Liabilities to foreign official agencies		5.1
U.S. official reserve assets, net		0.2

Source: U.S. Department of Commerce, Bureau of Economic Analysis.

Commerce appear regularly in that agency's *Survey of Current Business* and also in the *Federal Reserve Bulletin*.

The statement in Table 17—1 is already somewhat condensed from the official statement, and it would be possible to condense it much further, even down to four lines, but an understanding of what the statement seeks to show requires that one look specifically at the quantitatively important items that enter it and the various subtotals or balances that are struck. We will go through these major items and subtotals one by one below, but at the outset several general features of the statement must be noted. From the viewpoint of the United States, transactions like exports of U.S. goods; provision of shipping, insurance, banking and other services to foreigners by U.S. companies; and sales of securities of U.S. companies or government units to foreigners or sales of real assets in the U.S. to foreigners are all transactions that give rise to inpayments, to what are known as *plus* entries, or *credits*. Transactions of the opposite kind, like imports by the United States of foreign goods; provision of shipping, insurance, banking and other services by foreigners to U.S. companies; and sales of securities of foreign companies or governments or of real assets in foreign countries to purchasers in the United States, give rise to outpayments, to what are known as *minus* (negative) entries, or *debits*, in the balance of payments. Any item like merchandise trade will give rise to both debits (for imports) and credits (for exports), but Table 17–1 is condensed to give only the net amount, plus or minus, for all items with the exception of merchandise trade. Thus, a plus sign on an item says that the inpayments, or credits, arising from this particular category of transactions exceeded the outpayments, or debits, arising from that category by the amount indicated; an item that carries a negative sign says the opposite.

For any particular item, the statement may show a credit or a debit balance. However, when all the transactions included under all of the items are combined, the credit and debit balances on individual items will cancel out to produce an overall balance of zero. The balance of payments must balance. This follows necessarily because of the double-entry system of accounting that is employed in preparing this statement. Every single transaction that enters into the total has an equal-sized credit and debit aspect. An export of goods from the United States is a credit, but it must in one way or another be matched or paid for, and, whatever the way is, it will involve a debit of equal size. There are many ways that this can occur, one of which is via changes in deposits in banks in the United States and in foreign countries. Suppose the U.S. exporter accepts payment by taking the amount involved in the form of a deposit in a foreign bank. As we will see below, this is in the nature of a loan; it is a short-term capital outflow, which is a debit in the U.S. balance of payments. Or suppose that the U.S. exporter secures payment as the foreign importer or his bank draws down the deposit balance held by the foreign importer or his bank in a U.S. bank. This amounts to a decrease in debt previously incurred to foreigners; it is a short-term capital inflow, which is a debit in the U.S. balance of payments. This U.S. export of goods, a credit in the U.S. balance of payments, is in the first of these two cases matched by an increase in U.S. bank balances abroad, a debit in the U.S. balance, and in the second by a decrease in foreign balances in U.S. banks, also a debit in the U.S. balance.

**From the Merchandise Balance
to the Net Liquidity Balance**

Turning to Table 17–1, we find that the first item shows the result of private transactions in merchandise. In terms of our earlier illustration, we would, of course, find the $80,000 of phonograph records sold by RCA to the German firm as part of the export total and the $80,000 worth of Mercedes-Benz automobiles purchased by the U.S. dealer as part of the import total. For 1973 the total of inpayments (credits) arising from exports of goods exceeded the total of outpayments (debits) arising from imports of goods by $0.5 billion to give us a positive balance on merchandise trade of that amount. In 1972 this figure had been a negative $7.0 billion.

While the first item in the list is limited to merchandise imports and exports of a private kind, the next four items, which bring us to the heading "Balance on goods and services," cover all other transactions in goods and services. In the second item, military transactions are seen to have been a minus $2.2 billion in 1973. In this year as in every year since World War II, the outpayments by the U.S. military in other countries have exceeded the inpayments to the United States that result from military sales by the United States to other countries.

Among the major services that enter into international trade are travel and transportation, the former covering tourism and business travel and the latter sea, air, and other forms of transportation. On both of these but especially on travel, the United States in recent years has shown greater outpayments than inpayments. Simply put, Americans spend more on travel abroad and on the purchase of transportation services provided by foreigners than foreigners spend on these same services in the United States. In 1973 this excess was $2.7 billion, which gives us the minus figure of that amount in the table.

The item "Investment income, net," is the difference between inpayments that result from earnings on U.S. investments made in other countries and the outpayments that result from earnings on the investments that foreigners have made in the United States. During 1973, inpayments in the form of interest and dividends received by U.S. nationals on their holdings of securities issued by foreign companies and foreign governments as well as profits remitted to the United States on businesses in other countries of the world owned by U.S. firms exceeded the outpayments resulting from foreign holdings of such assets in the United States. This figure, $5.3 billion in 1973, has been a positive figure for the United States for more than fifty years. The current size of this figure is related closely to the size of the nation's net long-term capital flows to other countries in earlier years, a balance of payments item we will come to below.

Combining the first five items in the statement gives us the first of a number of balances, or subtotals, that are struck in the overall balance of payments statement. This balance, known as the *balance on goods and services*, indicates whether transactions in goods and services taken by themselves would for the year in question result in net outpayments from the United States or net inpayments to the United States. For 1973 they indicate net inpayments of $4.4 billion—for 1973 the United States had a surplus of this amount on goods and services. We may also say that other countries of the world received $4.4 billion fewer U.S. dollars through U.S. outpayments made for their goods and services than the number of dollars they required to make payment for the goods and services obtained from the United States. Because of the huge $7.0 billion excess of merchandise imports over merchandise exports in 1972, U.S. outpayments for all goods and services had exceeded U.S. inpayments for all goods and services by $6.0 billion in that year. Given the $4.4 billion excess of inpayments in 1973, we see the very large $10.4 billion swing in the balance on goods and services that occurred from 1972 to 1973.

The next item, which is made up of things like gifts sent to relatives and friends in other countries and pensions paid to persons living in other countries, is regularly a minus item in the U.S. balance of payments—i.e., the amount of this flow from parties in the United States exceeds the amount of the flow in the opposite direction. As shown, the figure was minus $1.9 billion for 1973. Combining this item with the previous balance gives us the second subtotal, a balance that is called the *balance on goods, services, and remittances*.

Grants by the U.S. Government are picked up next and, like private remittances, are regularly a minus item, $1.9 billion in 1973. Combining all the items up to this point gives us one of the more important subtotals, the balance known as the *balance on current account*, $0.5 billion for the United States in 1973. All the items below the line for the balance on current account are, as might be guessed, items not classified as current; these are capital transactions, long term and short term, and official reserve transactions. These are of a quite different nature from such current transactions as imports and exports of goods and services, which dominate the transactions above the line on which the balance on current account is found.

Because the balance of payments must balance, it follows that if the sum of all the transactions that enter into the balance on current account is a plus figure, then the sum of all the capital transactions and official reserve transactions below this line will be an equal-sized minus figure. A minus balance for the balance on current account will, in the same way, mean an equal-sized plus balance for capital transactions and official reserve transactions.

Turning to capital transactions, we find included things like the purchase by U.S. persons and firms of stocks and bonds from foreign sellers or the expenditures by American companies for new plants or other facilities in foreign countries or increases in deposit balances in foreign banks by U.S. persons, banks, and other firms. Of course, there are similar capital movements in the other direction as citizens of other countries purchase securities from sellers in this country, as foreign firms acquire new plants and other real assets in this country, and as foreign persons, banks, and other firms increase their deposit balances in U.S. banks. Government transactions that involve loans to foreign countries or borrowings from them are also included under capital movements. (Government grants and government military transactions, it will be recalled, were included in the current account above; they are, in other words, not classified as capital movements.)

Capital movements are broken down into those of long term and those of short term. The purpose here is to distinguish between movements that are expected to persist over a period of a year or more and those that may be expected to be reversed in less than a year. If a U.S. firm spends $10 million to build a new plant in Germany, the capital movement that this involves is plainly meant to be a long-term one. At the other extreme, if a U.S. firm transfers $1 million from its checking deposit balance with a New York bank to its checking deposit balance with a German bank, this capital movement cannot be expected to be a long-term one. In preparing its balance of payments estimates, the government classifies bonds and bank deposits as short term or long term depending on whether they have more than one year before reaching maturity (repayment date). Stocks have no maturity date, and transactions in stock are all assumed to be long term. It is apparent that distinctions like these are somewhat arbitrary, but the available data permit nothing more exact.

In Table 17–1, under the line for "Balance on current account" appear the entries for private and government long-term capital flows, net. Net long-term private capital flows were $0.1 billion in 1973. Apart from 1968, this is the only other year since 1960 that this figure has been positive. The positive net figure for 1973 means that inpayments in that year were $0.1 billion more than outpayments, or that persons and firms in foreign countries spent that much more in purchasing U.S. securities or making direct investments in real assets in the United States than persons and firms in the United States spent for those purposes in foreign countries.

In most recent years the figure for the United States on long-term private capital flows has been minus. This has resulted from a minus figure for net direct investments sufficiently large to offset a plus figure for net transactions in securities. For example, in 1970, long-term private capital flows were −$1.4 billion. This resulted from direct investments by U.S. firms of $4.4 billion and direct investments of foreign firms in the United States of $1.0 billion, for a net figure of −$3.4 billion on direct investments. On securities, U.S. persons, banks, and other firms purchased $0.9 billion of foreign securities, but foreigners purchased $2.9 billion of securities in the United States to give the United States a figure of +$2.0 billion on long-term capital transactions in securities. The −$3.4 billion balance on direct investments and the +$2.0 billion balance on securities give the net balance of −$1.4 billion on all long-term private transactions.

The relatively large direct investments by U.S. firms abroad in recent years reflect the impact of various factors. A major one has been the circumvention of foreign tariffs, especially by producing within the European Common Market area and thereby enjoying the benefits of selling to all of the countries in this market on the same terms as firms domiciled within these countries. Lower production costs have also become important, so much so that for some goods it has become cheaper for U.S. firms to produce abroad and ship back to the United States for sale here. For sales in foreign markets, there is the added advantage of lower transportation costs and a better reception by foreign buyers to goods produced in their own area.

In regard to capital movements, confusion sometimes arises between movements that result in inpayments and movements that result in outpayments. If a U.S. firm makes a direct investment in the form of the construction of a new plant in Germany, this appears quite clearly as an outpayment or a minus item. Dollars are being supplied to pay for this project. However, for the case in which U.S. firms or persons purchase foreign bonds, a danger of error arises from the tendency to focus on this transaction as an export of capital. It does involve a loan, and a loan is an export of capital in the financial sense. Because exports of goods and services produce inpayments, or credits, to the exporting country, it is understandable that some persons will conclude that exports of capital will do the same. But exports of goods and services are things for which foreigners must pay the exporting country; exports of capital, which involve the purchases of bonds and making of loans to foreigners, call for payments by the capital-exporting country to foreigners. It is the *lenders* who must make outpayments for the foreign bonds or other promises to pay that they are buying from foreign borrowers.

Closely related to the outpayments that arise through capital exports are inpayments from the export of goods and services that may result directly from the capital outflow. In the case of the U.S. balance of payments, which in most years shows the U.S. to be a net lender on long term to the rest of the world, the amount in question may be used by foreign borrowers to finance the purchase of that much in goods and services from the U.S. Thus, the minus amount that appears for net private long-term capital flows as a result of a net export of capital may contribute an equal plus amount in the current account under the heading of exports of goods and services.

At the same time, it should also be seen that the sizable minus figures that the U.S. has run on long-term private capital flows over the years have gradually built up the figure for net investment income that is included in the balance on goods and services. Thus, although net long-term private capital flows abroad appear as a minus item in the balance of payments at the time they occur, the subsequent return in the form of interest, dividends, and repatriated profits that these flows produce appear as a plus item. In 1973 investment income on U.S. investments abroad was $14.0 billion; investment income earned by persons and firms in other countries on their investments in the United States was $8.7 billion. This yielded a *net* U.S. investment income on foreign investment of $5.3 billion. As long as the United States continues to show a minus figure for net long-term private capital flows year after year, it is to be expected that the figure for net investment income will continue to rise.

Long-term capital flows include flows between national governments as well as between private parties, and the next item in the table picks this up. Loans by the U.S. Government to other countries in recent years regularly have exceeded the amounts of repayments on earlier loans to produce a minus figure for this item. The amount in 1973 was −$1.4 billion, which, combined with the +$0.1 billion for long term private flows, gives a figure of −$1.3 billion for the total of net long-term capital flows.

By now combining this balance on long-term capital account with the earlier balance found on current account we have, as might be expected, what is called the *balance on current account and long-term capital*, or what is more popularly referred to as the *basic deficit*. This figure has been negative in every recent year; if in some future year it turns out to be positive, it will of course, be called the *basic surplus* in such a year.

As of this point, the balance, whether surplus or deficit in any time period, is the result of transactions in goods and services, remittances, pensions, and other transfers, U.S. government grants, and net long-term capital flows. The statement next moves on to bring in nonliquid short-term capital flows. These are short-term loans made by banks and nonbanking concerns to foreigners. In recent years the amount of such loans made by U.S. firms to foreigners regularly has exceeded the amount made by foreign firms to U.S. borrowers; accordingly, there is a net debit balance for this item.

The next item, "Allocations of Special Drawing Rights (SDRs)," popularly known as "paper gold," is the provision of a kind of international reserve asset to the various member nations by the International Monetary Fund (IMF) on a basis worked out among them. This is an asset like gold itself or like a nation's holdings of foreign currencies in that it is something the nation can use to make international payments. The allocation from the IMF is itself an inpayment and thus appears as a plus item during the period received. There were no allocations in 1973, so the entry for that year is zero. However, the total allocated to the United States over the preceding three years was $2.3 billion.

The item "Errors and omissions, net," covers unrecorded transactions and statistical errors. It is believed that most of the amount unaccounted for these reasons is the result of nonliquid short-term capital flows and is thus included in the overall statement at this point.

With these last three items now included, we have reached the *net liquidity balance*. This is perhaps the most important single balance in the series of balances derived in the statement since it provides a figure that, as will be seen, is an indicator of whether the nation has been drawing down or building up its international liquidity. If during the time period the amount of a nation's liquid claims against other countries increases more or decreases less than the amount of its liquid liabilities to other countries, there is a surplus in the net liquidity balance—and in the opposite case, a deficit. A deficit is a kind of warning signal to the country of a loss of liquidity that if continued will call for appropriate adjustment.

Autonomous and Accommodating Balance of Payments Items

The importance of the net liquidity balance is brought out by the distinction between autonomous items and balancing, or accommodating, items in the balance of payments. Apart from some question regarding the inclusion of nonliquid short-term capital flows, all the items that enter into the determination of the net liquidity balance— i.e., all the items above the line on which we find the net liquidity balance—are so-called *autonomous* items, and the items below the line in question are so-called *accommodating*, or *balancing*, items. Autonomous items cover all the transactions carried out by millions of persons, firms, and governmental units at their own initiative and independently of other transactions. They are transactions that occur in response to economic and political conditions in the different countries of the world. They are the kind of transaction most people think of when they think of what produces a nation's inpayments and outpayments: a U.S. automobile dealer importing Mercedes-Benz automobiles from Germany, RCA Corporation selling phonograph records to a German music store, a New York City schoolteacher taking a summer tour through Europe, a Canadian firm selling a new issue of bonds to investors in the United States, Ford Motor Company building a new plant in England. Every transaction of this kind is undertaken because it appears advantageous to the parties involved; each transaction is self-contained and independent of all others. There is for this reason no force at work to make the grand total of all of these transactions show a zero balance. Actually, until we add up all the transactions covered by the items above the line, we do not know whether the figure we will find on the line will be a minus or plus figure, a deficit or a surplus. As Table 17—1 shows, the figure on the line for 1973 was —$7.8 billion. It has been a minus figure for every year since 1960.

The amounts found for the items below the line differ from those above the line by being what they are simply because these are the amounts needed to accommodate (balance) the deficit or surplus that results from the amounts for the items above the line. The overall balance of payments, it will be recalled, must balance, and it is the items below the line that take on whatever value is needed for this purpose. In this sense, they are the very opposite of autonomous items, whose major distinguishing characteristic is their independence of other items. Since the net liquidity balance in 1973 was –$7.8 billion, there must be offsetting or accommodating items below this line that add up to +$7.8 billion to provide the required balance.

First among the below-the-line items that provide this balance are net liquid private capital flows. These cover changes in the amount of privately owned bank deposits and short-term securities (like Treasury bills and commercial paper) persons and firms in one country hold in other countries. The figure for a nation's *net* liquid private capital flows in any time period accordingly is derived from the changes in the amount of these short-term liquid assets that residents of one country hold in other countries and the change in the amounts of these assets that residents of all other countries hold in the first country. For example, if in a given year U.S. residents increase their holdings of this kind of asset abroad by $1 billion while foreign residents decrease their holdings of this kind of asset in the United States by $2 billion, the result shown for this item will be a *net* outflow of $3 billion, or a minus balance in this amount. For another example, if U.S. residents decrease their holdings of this kind of asset abroad by $3 billion while foreign residents increase their holdings in the U.S. by $1 billion, the result would be a *net* inflow of $4 billion, or a plus balance in this amount.

In what sense can we say that net liquid private capital flows act as a balancing item for a plus or minus figure in the net liquidity balance? If there is a minus figure in the net liquidity balance, why may we expect a plus figure for net liquid private capital flows? Or if there is a plus figure in the net liquidity balance, why may we expect a minus figure for net liquid private capital flows? The answer, in oversimplified terms, goes along these lines. A minus figure in the net liquidity balance means that outpayments were greater than inpayments for all the items above the net liquidity balance line. A situation like this automatically tends to produce an increase in foreign holdings of bank deposits in the United States and a decrease in U.S. holdings of bank deposits in other countries, or it automatically tends to produce a net liquid short-term private capital flow with a plus balance. This is readily apparent when one considers individual transactions. For example, go back to our U.S. automobile dealer's import of $80,000 (200,000 DMs) worth of Mercedes Benz automobiles from the producer in Germany. In considering earlier how payment might be made for this import, we saw that it could result in an $80,000 increase in the deposit balances in U.S. banks held by German banks or a 200,000 DM decrease in the deposit balances held in German banks by U.S. banks. Which will occur depends on the agreement between the two firms as to whether payment is to be in U.S. dollars or DMs, but in either case the transaction will contribute a +$80,000 amount to the U.S. total figure for liquid private capital flows. We also saw that our other transaction, the export by RCA Corporation of $80,000 (200,000 DMs) worth of phonograph records to a German music store, would result in an $80,000 decrease in the deposit balances in U.S. banks held by German banks or a 200,000 DM increase in the deposit balances in German banks held by U.S. banks, again depending on which currency was to be used for payment. In this case, regardless of the currency used, the transaction would contribute a −$80,000 amount to the U.S. total figure for liquid private capital flows.

These two transactions are clearly offsetting, but if we now take the millions of transactions in goods, services, military transactions, long-term capital flows, and the other items that enter into the determination of the net liquidity balance, we see in Table 17–1 that the United States had a −$7.8 billion balance in 1973. The U.S. balance of payments has shown a minus figure for this balance in every recent year, and it would, potentially at least, be possible for this minus balance to be accommodated by an equal plus balance in private liquid capital flows year after year. This plus balance, however, cannot be secured year after year by drawing down the balances held by U.S. persons and firms in foreign banks; the amounts in such deposits and in liquid assets held abroad that can be converted quickly into deposits are limited. However, they can be met year after year if foreigners are willing to allow their balances in U.S. banks to rise year after year. There is no limit in this direction other than the willingness of foreign private investors to hold more and more dollars in the form of deposits and other liquid assets in the United States. For many years following World War II, international monetary conditions were such that foreigners were willing to see their balances in these forms increase to an ever larger total. However, under more recent conditions, the decision to add to or reduce balances in these forms has come to depend more importantly on the rate of interest that can be earned on such assets in the United States in comparison with the rates in other countries and on expectations of changes in foreign exchange rates.

For example, net liquid private capital flows during 1971 were −$7.8 billion. They, therefore, did not help to offset or accommodate a net liquidity balance which in that year was a huge −$22 billion; rather they added to it. During 1971 interest rates that could be earned on dollar loans fell below the rates that could be earned on loans in foreign currencies, a development that caused banks to shift large amounts of funds from the United States to foreign loan markets to take advantage of the interest differential. To a lesser extent, the outflow that year was due to widely held expectations of a devaluation of the dollar, something that actually came to pass at the end of the year. Because devaluation of the dollar means that the dollar will purchase fewer units of other currencies than before, foreigners who hold dollars in bank deposits and other liquid assets and who expect devaluation can avoid the loss they would otherwise suffer on holdings of dollars by shifting into foreign currencies. U.S. banks and others can also profit by shifting their dollars from liquid assets in the United States to similar assets in foreign countries and then shifting back, if and when the dollar devaluation occurs.

In other years, for example 1969 and 1972, relative interest rates and the other conditions influencing liquid private capital flows were such as to produce a net plus figure for this item in the U.S. balance of payments. Therefore in these years this flow helped to offset or accommodate the minus figure in the net liquidity balance.

By now adding the amount for the year's net liquid capital flows, plus or minus as it may be, to the year's net liquidity balance, we derive what is called the *official reserve transactions balance*, the last of the series of balances in the balance of payments statement. Thus, in 1973 with a −$7.8 billion figure for the net liquidity balance and with a $2.5 billion figure for private liquid capital flows, the official reserves transactions balance was −$5.3 billion. To produce a final balance in 1973 thus called for official reserve transactions that totaled +$5.3 billion to offset the minus figure of that amount found in the official reserves transactions balance. Most of this amount appears as an increase in the number of dollars held by foreign central banks and other foreign official agencies in the form of deposits in U.S. banks and in other liquid assets like U.S. Treasury bills.

What lies behind this particular kind of official reserve transactions is an extension of a principle touched on earlier. If there is a deficit as a result of all the transactions that enter into the net liquidity balance—i.e., an excess of outpayments over inpayments for all the transactions viewed as autonomous—what follows in the ordinary course of handling the payments involved is a decrease in the balances of U.S. banks in foreign banks and an increase in the balances of foreign banks in U.S. banks. However, if the foreign banks see their deposit balances in U.S. banks rising above the amounts they regard as appropriate under the existing international monetary conditions, they will want to reduce these balances and will thus seek to exchange dollar balances for balances denominated in their own currency or in currencies of other countries. As will be explained more fully in the following chapter, the act of converting large amounts of dollar holdings into other currencies tends to produce an appreciation in the value of these other currency units relative to the U.S. dollar. For example, if the U.S. dollar—Deutsche mark exchange rate had been 2.5 DM per U.S. dollar, or $0.40 per DM, the attempt of private banks to switch out of dollars into DMs would, via the increased demand for DMs, lead to a rise in the price of the DM—the exchange rate would move above $0.40 per DM.

In an international monetary system in which nations seek to hold changes in exchange rates within a narrow range, pressures that would tend to push an exchange rate outside this range lead to official intervention. In the example above, if the upper limit of the range for the DM was established as $0.40, the Bundesbank, the German central bank, would buy up dollars with newly created DMs as required to prevent the price of the DM from going above $0.40. Central banks in other countries intervene in the same way to prevent a movement out of dollars into their currencies from pushing up the exchange rate on their currencies. During 1973 central banks of other countries and other official agencies absorbed 5.1 billion U.S. dollars in this way. The total amount that had to be offset in this year was $5.3 billion, and the remaining part of this total, $0.2 billion, was covered by the change in U.S. official reserve assets.

Foreign central banks can absorb U.S. dollars by exchanging their own money for these dollars as described above. The Federal Reserve and the U.S. Treasury can also absorb dollars of this kind by giving up official reserve assets. Through the sixties, the minus figure in the net liquidity balance not offset by a plus figure on liquid private capital flows was met to an appreciable extent by an outflow of gold from the

United States. To this extent, instead of foreign central banks getting U.S. dollar deposits in exchange for their newly issued money, they would get gold. However, as the U.S. gold stock was depleted through this process, an understanding was reached in the late sixties that other central banks would not continue to request gold from the U.S. Treasury in exchange for their holdings of dollars. Finally, in August 1971, convertibility into gold of U.S. dollars held by foreigners was ended by action of President Nixon.

Other official reserve assets are the government's holdings of SDRs (see p. 422), convertible currencies (or foreign exchange of those countries whose currencies are freely convertible into other currencies), and its gold tranche position in the IMF, which is the amount a member country of the IMF may borrow from the IMF in other currencies at any time at that country's discretion. If the U.S. Government faces the need to absorb dollars, each of these may be used. However, like a nation's holdings of gold, its holdings of these other reserve assets are limited in amount. There is no way for a nation to continuously replenish its holdings of reserve assets other than by running a surplus in its net liquidity balance (or by running a surplus in its net liquid private capital flows greater than the deficit in its net liquidity balance), and it is the fact of a deficit in the net liquidity balance and an unwillingness of foreign central banks to absorb more of that country's currency that causes official reserve assets to be depleted in the first place.

What this says, in sum, is that a nation that is not endowed with virtually unlimited official reserve assets—and no nation, including the United States, is in this position—must inevitably face the need to make some basic adjustment if that nation persistently runs a deficit in its net liquidity balance. Although the nation's overall balance of payments must always balance—there's a one dollar credit for every one dollar debit—in popular usage a nation's balance of payments is said to be out of balance if that balance is attained only through the cooperation of foreign central banks in absorbing more of that country's money than they would prefer to hold or through a depletion of that country's official reserve assets. Again, although the balance of payments must balance, it is common practice to say that the country has a deficit in its balance of payments under these conditions. The adjustment process by which a country eliminates a deficit in its balance of payments or achieves what is called balance of payments equilibrium is a central question in international monetary economics. The following chapter is devoted to an introduction to this very large subject.

eighteen

THE BALANCE OF PAYMENTS ADJUSTMENT

A nation whose goods, services, and capital transactions with all other nations are such as to lead to an increase in holdings of its currency by foreign banks and/or a depletion of its official reserve assets is a nation whose balance of payments is in deficit, according to the most common definition of this concept noted at the end of the last chapter. A nation in the opposite position is one whose balance of payments is in surplus.

Some ways that a nation might attack the problem of this kind of imbalance seem to be immediately suggested by an examination of the items that make up the balance of payments statement itself. One possibility is through the merchandise trade balance. Thus, a deficit country can reduce its imports by raising its tariffs and by imposing quotas on imports from lower cost countries; in addition, it can its exports by providing subsidies to domestic firms to enable them to undersell lower cost foreign producers in world markets. Another possibility is by imposing restrictions and taxes on capital outflows, including bank lending abroad, purchases of foreign securities, and direct investments abroad by domestic firms that are not financed abroad, the result of which is to restrict the flow of capital from countries where it is relatively abundant and its return is relatively low to countries where the opposite is true. All of these capital outflow restrictions, incidentally, were used by the United States from 1965 to 1974. Another possibility is for a country to reduce the amount of its foreign aid and also to require that the amount given must be spent in full in the granting country, regardless of the beneficiary countries' needs and of the possible availability of lower cost suppliers.

While it appears at first glance that they will do the job, restrictive measures such as these are not regarded by most economists as acceptable ways of meeting a balance of payments problem. For one thing, a nation that unilaterally introduces additional restrictions on imports and subsidies on exports—i.e., without the agreement of those countries whose export industries and import-competing industries will be affected—may gain no more than a short-term improvement in its balance of trade. Other countries may be expected to retaliate, in which event there may be no change in its merchandise trade balance and, other things being equal, no change in its balance of payments deficit.

But more fundamentally, economists generally criticize such actions even if a country may be able to get away with them for awhile. A nation's imports and exports of various goods ideally should conform to relative costs of production of such goods in different countries; the amount of this good imported or that good exported should not be determined by changes in tariffs, quotas, and subsidies whose purpose is to alter the merchandise trade balance so as to produce equilibrium in the balance of payments. Similarly in the case of capital: capital should flow to the nation in which it will have the greatest productivity and the highest rate of return, even though this means an outflow of capital from a country with a balance of payments deficit. Which countries give foreign aid and how much and which countries receive foreign aid and how much should depend on the overall affluence of each and not on which has a balance of payments deficit and which has a balance of payments surplus.

To the extent that international transactions in goods, services, and capital are guided by the market mechanism working in a competitive price structure, the result is an improvement in the economic well-being of all countries. Users of each good obtain it from the producer who can supply it at lowest cost, regardless of whether he happens to be a domestic or a foreign producer. Suppliers of capital send their capital to the market in which it has the highest rate of return, regardless of whether that market is at home or in another country. Interference with these processes that work toward the material betterment of all participants on the grounds that such interference will meet a nation's balance of payments problem is, in the judgment of most economists, bad economics.

What then is the "good" economics way in which nations adjust to balance of payments problems? Basically there are two. One is by means of an adjustment of the foreign exchange rates between deficit and surplus countries, and the other is by means of an adjustment of the level of costs, prices, and incomes in the different countries. Which of these will be used depends essentially on the kind of international monetary system under which the nations of the world have agreed to operate. If they have adopted a system that calls for fixed or stable exchange rates between currencies, balance of payments adjustments necessarily must come about by means of changes in costs, prices, and incomes in different countries. The extreme form of this system is the old-fashioned gold standard that prevailed in its pure form through much of the world up to 1914 and then again briefly during the late twenties. The other kind of system is one with freely fluctuating or flexible foreign exchange rates. Under this sytem, a nation's balance of payments deficit would tend to be eliminated automatically (or would be prevented from appearing in the first place) by an appropriate depreciation in the foreign exchange value of the deficit nation's currency. Between these two is the system of exchange rates with adjustable pegs that existed from the end of World War II until its demise in the early nineteen-seventies.

It is the purpose of this chapter to examine these alternative systems and to outline the adjustment process as it occurs under each. However, before getting into this, we must look briefly at the relationship between the balance of payments and foreign exchange rates to see why a deficit in the balance of payments tends to raise the price of foreign currencies in terms of the domestic currency or lower the price of domestic currency in terms of foreign currencies and why a surplus in the balance of payments tends to produce the opposite result. This tendency exists whether nations are operating under a system of fixed exchange rates, adjustable pegs, or flexible exchange rates, but, except in the last case, the tendency of the exchange rate to vary with a balance of payments deficit or surplus is held in check in ways we will note when we examine the balance of payments adjustment process under these systems.

THE BALANCE OF PAYMENTS
AND FOREIGN EXCHANGE RATES

In the absence of actions deliberately undertaken by central banks to influence foreign exchange rates, the rate at which one currency will be convertible into another will vary in response to changes in the free market supply of and demand for that currency. We can see what basically determines the amount of a nation's currency that is supplied and demanded in any time period by looking at that nation's balance of payments. Let us take the United States for illustration. All those transactions between parties in the United States and parties in other countries which require that the latter make payment to parties in the United States give rise to a demand for U.S. dollars, if payment is to be made in U.S. dollars, or to a supply of foreign currencies, if payment is to be made in the foreign currency. All those transactions between parties in the United States and parties in other countries which require that parties in the United States make payment to parties in other nations give rise to a supply of U.S. dollars to foreign parties, if payment is to be made in U.S. dollars, or to a demand for foreign currencies, if payment is to be made in foreign currencies.

As between currencies that are freely convertible into each other, it does not matter in terms of the supply of and demand for foreign exchange whether a payment owed to a party in the United States is made in dollars or in the currency of the payee's country or whether a payment owed by a party in the United States to, say, a party in Germany is made in DMs or in the currency of the payee's country. Therefore, so far as the supply of and demand for foreign exchange is concerned, we may look at all transactions of the parties in the United States as if they were settled in U.S. dollars. All transactions that involve inpayments, or payments from abroad, are transactions that give rise to a demand for dollars by foreigners, and all transactions that involve payments abroad give rise to a supply of dollars to foreigners. From this we may say that the number of dollars that are demanded in the foreign exchange market in any time period depends essentially on the dollar volume of U.S. exports of goods and services, remittances and pensions from abroad to persons in the United States, private and government long-term capital flows from other countries to the United States, and short-term loans from foreign lenders to borrowers in the United States. Correspondingly, the number of U.S. dollars that are supplied in the foreign exchange market in any time period depends on the dollar volume of U.S. imports of goods and services, U.S. military expenditures abroad, U.S. Government grants, private and government long-term capital flows from the United States to other countries, and short-term loans from U.S. lenders to foreign borrowers.

For each dollar supplied and for each dollar demanded, one can identify a dollar's worth of goods, securities, remittances, and the like moving between countries, but one does not actually also find a dollar's worth of payment moving between countries for each of these dollar's worth of goods, securities, and the like. The larger part of what otherwise would be movements of money between countries cancel out through a clearing mechanism; it is only the net balance that appears as an actual transfer between countries. The principle here is the same as that found in operation among banks in a community. Bank A may receive from its depositors during the day $1 million in checks drawn against Bank B, and Bank B may receive from its depositors during the day $900,000 in checks drawn against Bank A; $900,000 of the checks are offsetting, so all that is needed is that Bank B transfer $100,000 to Bank A to settle the difference. In the same way, it is only the difference between the number of dollars supplied and demanded that requires an actual transfer between parties in the United States and parties in other countries.

We may see this by returning again to the pair of transactions in the preceding chapter, the U.S. auto dealer's purchase of $80,000 worth of Mercedes-Benz automobiles from that company in Germany and the German music store's purchase of $80,000 worth of phonograph records from RCA in the United States. These transactions "clear" in the sense that the U.S. auto dealer in effect pays RCA and the German music store in effect pays Mercedes-Benz. The goods cross the Atlantic, but payment does not. On the assumption that both transactions have been stated in dollars, the German music store must make payment in dollars, but Mercedes-Benz has also received payment in dollars. Mercedes-Benz has no need for dollars as it makes its payments in DMs. The transfer of the appropriate number of DMs from the music store to Mercedes-Benz is then all that is required—the dollars cancel out. If one were to trace the transaction through the German banks, he would see that this in effect is what actually takes place. On the other side of the Atlantic, what in effect amounts to a payment of dollars by the U.S. auto dealer to RCA cancels out the amount paid for the U.S. import and the amount received for the U.S. export.

This, of course, is only one pair of transactions and one that we have conveniently set up to cancel out. All transactions giving rise to a supply of or demand for dollars do not cancel out, and the net difference is a measure of the excess of the supply of dollars over the demand for dollars, or vice versa, in the foreign exchange market. Thus, in a rough way, we may say that if the figure for the net liquidity balance is negative, the transactions that enter into that balance have produced during the year a supply of dollars greater than the demand for dollars in the foreign exchange market. If the net liquidity balance is positive, the transactions that enter into that balance have produced a demand for dollars greater than the supply of dollars flowing into the foreign exchange market during the year.

Suppose now that the United States has a deficit in its net liquidity balance. One effect of this is that persons and firms in other countries seek to sell to the banks in exchange for their own currencies a number of dollars greater than the number of dollars that other persons and firms in those countries seek to purchase from the banks in exchange for their own currencies. This excess supply of dollars leads to a bidding-up of the value of other currencies in terms of the dollar or a bidding-down of the value of the dollar in terms of other currencies. The dollar is depreciating, and other currencies are appreciating.

To be specific, let us look at one pair of currencies, those of the United States and Germany, and assume that the original exchange rate was \$1 = 2.5 DMs, or 1 DM = \$0.40. An excess supply of dollars means that German exporters and others who seek to convert claims they have for U.S. dollars into DMs will find the banks offering fewer DMs per dollar—e.g., 2.4 DMs per \$1. Also German importers and others who seek to exchange DMs for dollars will find that it takes fewer DMs to buy one U.S. dollar—e.g., 2.4 DMs per \$1 instead of 2.5 DMs. As the DM price of the dollar falls, there will be a rise in the number of dollars demanded and as the dollar price of the DM rises, there will be a fall in the number of DMs demanded. The rate of exchange will eventually be established at the level that clears the market—i.e., at which the quantity demanded and supplied are equal. The reason that the quantities of U.S. dollars and DMs supplied and demanded in the market change in the way described is because the falling DM price of the dollar leads to an increase in German purchases of goods and services in the United States, and the rising dollar price of the DM leads to a decrease in U.S. purchases of goods and services in Germany. Our focus at this point is on what determines the rate of exchange, but it may be apparent that in a system in which the rate of exchange is free to move with market forces, the equilibrium foreign exchange rate will be found at whatever level is consistent with balance of payments equilibrium.

The exchange rate between one nation's currency and other currencies will move in the way sketched here as long as there are no international arrangements among nations to produce a different outcome. However, if the nations of the world have agreed to operate under a system of fixed exchange rates or a system of adjustable pegs, the movement of exchange rates will be limited in one way or another to a narrow range over any short period of time. Thus, under both of those systems, exchange rates do not move over an unrestricted range as they potentially can with the system of flexible exchange rates. We will see what determines the degree of short-run fluctuation of exchange rates under the gold standard and under adjustable pegs in the sections below, where the adjustment process under these systems is covered. Still, under both of those systems, as under the system of flexible exchange rates, it is correct to say that the foreign exchange rates between one currency and others are determined by the supply of and demand for that currency in the market. The difference is that under those other systems there are forces that keep the supply of and demand for any currency in balance, at least over a limited period of time, without the need for potentially large variations in exchange rates.

BALANCE OF PAYMENTS ADJUSTMENT
UNDER THE GOLD STANDARD

The gold standard is a monetary arrangement in which the government legally defines the monetary unit as a specific quantity of gold and stands ready to sell the gold metal in exchange for money at that price and to buy the gold metal in exchange for money at that price, in both cases in unlimited amounts. Thus, over a long period ending in 1933, by act of the U.S. Congress the dollar was defined as 23.22 grains of fine (pure) gold, and the U.S. Treasury bought and sold gold unrestrictedly at this price. There are 480 grains to the ounce, so this amounted to buying and selling at a price of $20.67 per ounce—i.e., 480/23.22 = $20.67.

The government commitment to buy gold at the stipulated price meant that the market price of gold could not fall below the price at the mint. Nobody need sell 23.22 grains of gold for less than $1 because this much could always be gotten at the mint. On the other hand, the government commitment to sell gold at the same stipulated price meant that the market price of gold could not rise above $1 for 23.22 grains of gold. Nobody would pay more than $1 for 23.22 grains of gold in the market as long as he was able to purchase that amount of gold at the mint for $1. A final essential feature to be noted is the absence of any restriction on the import and export of gold. Foreigners who held dollars could freely convert those dollars into gold and ship the gold home; they could also ship gold into the country and freely convert that gold into dollars at the stipulated price.

What has been outlined here for the United States was also true for the other major countries of the world: each defined its monetary unit in terms of gold, permitted unrestricted convertibility, and free export and import of gold. With the world-wide depression in the early thirties and the financial panic that led people all over to try to convert their bank deposits and paper money into gold, country after country was forced to suspend convertibility and, in effect, go off the gold standard. In the years following, only the United States was able to maintain convertibility, and that was not the unlimited convertibility that had been available to all up to 1933.

Under power granted by Congress, President Roosevelt in 1933 ended the right of U.S. citizens to obtain gold in exchange for currency and furthermore required that they turn into the Treasury the gold coins they then held in exchange for currency or deposits. The President also devalued the dollar, redefining its gold content as 13.71 grains and thus raising the price at which the Treasury would buy and sell gold from $20.67 per ounce to $35.00 per ounce. Over the years that followed, the United States permitted foreign holders of dollars to convert their dollars into gold (and to sell gold for dollars) at this particular rate, but this right came to be more and more restricted until it was limited to foreign central banks only. Because of the massive balance of payments deficits incurred by the United States through the sixties and into the seventies, the U.S. gold stock was drawn down sharply. Finally, to prevent foreign central banks from withdrawing what remained, President Nixon on August 15, 1971 ended convertibility altogether. Although gold continues to play a role in international finance as one among the several assets that qualify as international reserve assets, the U.S. action of August 1971 in ending the limited convertibility that had existed up to then severed the last tie to the gold standard of the past.

The prospects that the nations of the world will ever choose to return to the old-fashioned gold standard are virtually nil, despite the fact that some French authorities insist that this is the only viable system. However, because this system prevailed over so long a period in the past and because an understanding of the balance of payments adjustment process under that system helps one understand the adjustment process under other systems, an outline of the way that system operates between countries is worth studying.

Mint Parity and Gold Points

Suppose that the nations of the world were today on the kind of gold standard that was in effect in earlier times. The United States defines the dollar as a specific amount of gold, for easy arithmetic let us say 10 grains, and other countries similarly define their currencies in terms of gold. To limit attention to two currencies, we take as before the DM, which we will assume is defined by the German government as 4 grains of gold. Defining the dollar as 10 grains of gold amounts to setting a gold price of $48 per ounce (480/10) and defining the DM as 4 grains of gold amounts to setting a gold price of 120 DMs per ounce (480/4). The mint parity, or par of exchange, between the U.S. dollar and the DM is then $1 = 2.5 DMs because the gold content of the dollar is 2.5 times that of the DM, or, in terms of the price of gold in each currency, the DM price of gold is 2.5 times the dollar price of gold.

Under gold standard conditions, these two countries (as well as others) freely convert their currencies into gold and gold into their currencies at this rate. What we must see first is that as long as this is true the exchange rate in the market between the U.S. dollar and the DM can move only a little above or below the mint parity. The upper and lower limits to this movement are set by what are called the gold export and gold import points, and the difference between the mint parity and either gold point is set by the cost of shipping gold between the two countries.

To illustrate, suppose that the cost of shipping 1,000 ounces of gold between the United States and Germany is $500. A U.S. Bank can then always secure additional DMs to sell to its customers at home at a cost to it no higher than $0.404 per DM. The arithmetic is as follows. The U.S. bank can obtain from the U.S. Treasury 1,000 ounces of gold in exchange for $48,000. It can then ship this gold to Germany and sell it there to the German government for 120 DMs per ounce or a total of 120,000 DMs. Allowing for the shipping cost of $500, it obtains 2.47 DMs per dollar (120,000 DMs/$48,500), or a cost of $0.404 per DM (1/2.47). Therefore, the maximum level to which the DM can rise in the U.S. market is $0.404; this is the U.S. gold export point.

In the other direction, U.S. banks holding DMs need not sell them for dollars in the market at a rate below $0.396 per DM. These banks can always get this price as a minimum by converting their DM holdings into gold in Germany and importing the gold. The arithmetic is as follows. A bank can purchase 1,000 ounces of gold from the German government with 120,000 DMs, ship the gold to the United States and obtain $48,000 by selling the gold to the U.S. Treasury. Deducting the $500 cost of shipping the gold, the proceeds to the U.S. bank are $47,500. This amounts to $0.396 net per DM ($47,500/120,000 DMs). Therefore, the minimum level to which the DM can fall in the U.S. market is $0.396; this is the gold import point.

The same illustration can be worked through from the viewpoint of banks in Germany with the same results. Assuming that the cost of shipping 1,000 ounces of gold between Germany and the United States is 1,250 DMs (equal to $500 dollars), working through the arithmetic will show that the gold import point in Germany is $0.404, necessarily the same as the gold export point in the United States. In selling dollars for DMs, banks in Germany will not give up more than $0.404 per DM as they can always get at least this much in DMs by converting their dollars into gold in the United States and shipping the gold to Germany to be sold there for DMs. Working through the arithmetic will also show that the gold export point in Germany is $0.396 per DM, necessarily the same as the gold import point in the United States. In buying dollars with DMs, German banks will not give up 1 DM for less than $0.396 as they can always get at least this much in dollars by converting DMs into gold in Germany and shipping gold to the United States to be sold there for dollars.

The range within which the exchange rate between the U.S. dollar and the DM can move is $0.396 and $0.404 per DM, or, expressed the other way, 2.53 DMs and 2.47 DMs per U.S. dollar.

The Price-Specie Flow Adjustment Mechanism

Let us now move on to the balance of payments adjustment process under the old standard. From an original equilibrium in which the supply of and demand for dollars is in balance—say, at an exchange rate of 1 DM = $0.40—we can upset the equilibrium by assuming, for example, a market change in U.S. tastes in favor of German goods, perhaps for VWs, Porsches, and other German automobiles. The resulting increase in U.S. imports, other things being equal, will increase the number of dollars flowing into the hands of German exporters while leaving unchanged the number of dollars demanded by German importers of U.S. goods and by others there who have dollar payments to make. This excess supply of dollars flowing into the German banks will cause the exchange value of the U.S. dollar to fall in terms of the DM—the exchange rate will move toward the German gold import point of 1 DM = $0.404. German exporters and others who have dollars to sell will get a little less in DMs per dollar as this occurs, but they are assured that they will not have to give up more than $0.404 to get 1 DM or that per U.S. dollar they will get at least 2.47 DMs. Skipping over the complication of bankers' commissions and profit margins, this result follows from the fact that once the exchange rate moves to the 1 DM = $0.404 level, dollars will be converted into gold in the United States and this gold, when sold to the German government, will yield after costs this much in DMs per U.S. dollar.

As long as the situation as described persists, there will be a continuing flow of gold from the United States to Germany to cover the deficit in the U.S. transactions with Germany. If the same is happening in the transactions of the United States with other countries, the overall deficit is that much greater, and the loss of gold could become sizable in short order. Of course, if this were to go on very long, the U.S. Treasury would be stripped of its gold reserve. Unable to meet the gold standard requirement of converting its currency into gold at the stipulated rate, the United States would be off the gold standard. However, the very outflow of gold presumably sets into motion a process that in reasonably short order checks that outflow and eliminates the deficit the gold-losing country is suffering.

The first basic relationship to be noted in this process is that between a nation's gold stock and its total money supply. Under gold standard conditions, the economy's money supply is linked closely to its monetary gold holdings. Because the government is committed to maintain convertibility of its paper money issue and other forms of money into gold, its total money supply may increase if the gold stock increases, but, having so increased, its total money supply must decrease if its gold stock decreases. Internationally, gold constitutes the reserves of the commercial banks, and gains or losses in reserves give rise to demand-deposit money increases or decreases equal to a multiple of the change in reserves in fractional-reserve banking systems. Gold, in brief, becomes the foundation of the money supply; the larger that foundation in any country, the larger that country's money supply.

The next basic relationship is the one that is the essence of today's monetarism: aggregate spending depends on the money supply. The rate of turnover of the money supply against goods and services is held to be reasonably stable, and therefore changes in the money supply result in proportional changes in the aggregate demand for goods and services. Depending on whether the economy is operating far below, close to, or at full employment, changes in aggregate demand may be matched by offsetting changes in the physical amount of goods produced, by offsetting changes in the prices of goods, or by some combination of the two. Thus, in an economy operating below full employment, it is to be expected that an increase in demand will be absorbed mostly by an increase in output with perhaps only some modest increase in prices. However, in the pre-Keynesian period, economic analysis was based on the assumption that the economy operates at the full employment level of output apart from infrequent and brief departures. Economists accordingly tended to translate increases in demand that resulted from increases in the money supply into proportional increases in the prices of goods and services. What is more, the process worked in both directions. Economists also then generally held that prices and wage rates were flexible downward as well as upward, so a decrease in aggregate demand would mean that prices of goods and services would fall about proportionally. To this extent, a decrease in demand would have little effect on the output of goods and services, and, with output little affected, employment would be little affected. In sum, the decrease in the gold stock leads to a shrinkage in the money supply, and this leads to a decline in aggregate demand, which, with flexible prices and wage rates, causes a decline in prices and wage rates.

This brings us to the next basic relationship: the decline in prices will lead to an increase in the demand by other countries for this country's goods. Under gold standard conditions, the price of its currency in the foreign exchange market is virtually unchanged, so the lower prices on the goods themselves make them that much more attractive to foreign buyers than before. Note also in this connection that the countries that have been gaining gold in payment for their expanded exports will, via the expansion in their money supplies, show rising prices for their goods and thus shrinking export markets for those goods. Each increase in the deficit country's exports and each decrease in its imports, of course, contributes that much of an improvement in its balance of payments.

The decline in the money supply in the deficit country also tends to raise interest rates in that country, and higher interest rates tend to bring about an inflow of capital. Foreign investors find the deficit country's securities more attractively priced than before, just as foreign importers find the deficit country's goods more attractively priced than before. At the same time, interest rates tend to fall in the countries gaining gold, and investors in the deficit country find securities in those countries less attractively priced, just as importers in the deficit country find goods in those other countries less attractively priced. The change toward a greater net capital inflow or a lesser net capital outflow contributes that much to an improvement in the deficit country's balance of payments.

It is in this simple and automatic way that the old-fashioned international gold standard presumably worked. A nation with a deficit in its balance of payments would see that deficit disappear as that deficit produced a gold outflow, a reduced money supply, a lower price level, and a rise in exports and decline in imports. That reduced money supply would also cause higher interest rates and a greater net capital inflow or a smaller net capital outflow. A nation with a surplus in its balance of payments would see that surplus disappear as the opposite set of changes came about.

Some Qualifications to the Adjustment Mechanism

It is generally conceded that the international gold standard functioned very effectively in the pre-1914 period, but economists have long questioned whether the balance of payments adjustment process under the gold standard occurred in fact in the way it was expected to occur in principle. For example, the record for the gold standard period from about 1870 to 1914 suggests that prices in major trading countries moved upward and downward together rather than divergently as would have been expected from the fact that some countries were gaining gold and others losing gold from time to time. An even more fundamental challenge arises from the evidence that central banks in major trading countries would frequently act to offset the influence that gold inflows and outflows would otherwise have had on the money supply. Thus, the effect of an inflow on commercial bank reserves could be neutralized by the central bank's sale of an appropriate amount of its security holdings in the open market. The central bank in a country incurring an outflow of gold could neutralize this by purchasing the appropriate amount of securities in the open market. To the extent that this happened, it was a flagrant violation of the "rules of the game," for the gold standard could not work as it was expected to unless the money supply responded to changes in a nation's gold stock. It may be apparent that this can help to explain why price levels in different countries did not move in accordance with gold inflows and outflows; to the extent that these flows were neutralized by the central banks, they simply were not permitted to work their way through to the money supply and so to the price level.

Starting in the forties, economists began to apply the new economics of Keynes to an explanation of how the adjustment process worked. Keynesian economics held that a decrease in demand in a country would result, not in falling prices and wage rates with unchanged output and employment levels, but in falling output and employment levels with virtually unchanged prices and wage rates. Thus, to take our earlier illustration, suppose there is a marked change in tastes within a country in favor of foreign goods. Starting from an original equilibrium, the result of the consequent expansion of imports is a deficit in the balance of payments, other things being equal. Under gold standard conditions, the exchange rate then moves to the gold export point, and gold starts to leave the country. As sketched above, what next happens according to the orthodox explanation is a declining money supply, falling price level, and rising exports. In contrast, what happens according to the Keynesian view—which in its extreme form holds that money doesn't matter—is that the shift in demand from domestic to foreign goods leads to a decline in output and employment in the domestic economy. At the same time, the increased demand for the goods of other countries leads to an increase in output and employment in those countries, if they were previously operating below full employment, or to upward pressure on their price levels if they were already operating at or near full employment. However, what must next be recognized is that as income declines in the domestic economy, total spending, both that for domestic goods and foreign goods, decreases. The decrease in spending thus tends to reduce the balance of payments deficit that the earlier increase in spending for foreign goods had created. At the same time this is occurring, the domestic economy may also show an increase in exports. To the extent that the earlier expansion in its imports had brought about a rise in output and employment in those countries that had met this demand, there will be an increase in income in those countries, which will result in an increase in demand, part of which will be for imported goods, and part of this may be for goods specifically from the country with the deficit. Or if the result had been a rise in prices and wage rates in those countries, again there will be an increase in demand for imported goods, in this case arising from the fact that those goods are now relatively cheaper than home-produced goods, and part of the increase in demand may be for goods specifically from the economy with the deficit. These feedbacks continue to interact on the output and income levels of the economy with the deficit and other economies, but over time they become smaller and smaller until output and income levels stabilize.

A conclusion of the greatest importance lies behind this: an adjustment to a balance of payments deficit that occurs via the Keynesian process of output and income changes is one that leaves the country that incurred the deficit operating at a lower level of output and with more unemployment than before. What makes this so important is that this way of adjusting is, for this reason, ordinarily unacceptable to the government and the public of a country if there is any other way at all. If the adjustment occurs in the way visualized by the traditional theory—i.e., through a deflation in prices and wage rates—it is still not without its problems, one of which is the fact that all prices and wage rates do not go down at the same rate, but adjustment that takes place in this way does not put the economy into a real decline and throw workers out of jobs. Adjustment that occurs in the way visualized by the Keynesian theory does do this.

To what extent the adjustment process during the gold standard period from 1870 to 1914 occurred through output and employment changes or along the lines indicated by Keynesian theory is hard to say. However, as we will see in the following section, the Keynesian theory came to be widely accepted in the years after World War II. A gold standard system, which establishes fixed exchange rates, or a system like that adopted at Bretton Woods at the end of World War II, which establishes exchange rates subject to change only under special circumstances, are systems that preclude or considerably restrict balance of payments adjustments occurring through changes in the external value of a nation's currency and require that all or part of the adjustment take place internally. Barring the imposition of controls as a means of keeping the balance of payments in equilibrium, the only way out for a nation in balance of payments deficit disequilibrium is then through braking the economy domestically so as to reduce its spending abroad. This objective unfortunately may at times be gained only through an unacceptably large contraction in output and employment.

In the following section we will look at the system that the nations of the world employed over the years from World War II to the early seventies in the effort to gain the benefits of stable foreign exchange rates without at the same time suffering the pains of adjusting to balance of payments deficits by forcing contraction in economic activity within their economies.

BALANCE OF PAYMENTS ADJUSTMENT
UNDER ADJUSTABLE PEGS

During World War I each of the belligerents—and this included most of the major countries of the world—financed its war effort in a way that involved great increases in its paper money supply. With gold reserves limited, maintenance of unrestricted convertibility of money into gold became impossible, and nations had to go off the gold standard. After national finances were brought into some degree of order in the twenties, the gold standard was restored, but in addition to other difficulties it was shortly faced with the depression that spread through the world in the early thirties. Nations again were unable to maintain convertibility and went off gold. What then followed through the thirties and the years of World War II was reliance on elaborate systems of controls as the means by which each nation sought to keep the amount of its international inpayments and outpayments in balance. In addition to the widespread use of tariffs and quotas on imports and subsidies on exports to influence a nation's trade balance, restrictions on the buying and selling of foreign exchange were adopted extensively. Persons and firms were not permitted to buy foreign exchange freely in the market but could do so only under government license. This meant that one could not buy goods abroad, however willing he might be to pay whatever import duties were imposed on these goods, unless he could also get permission to buy the required foreign exchange; one could not transfer funds into foreign bank deposits or foreign securities or foreign direct investments unless he were authorized to acquire the foreign exchange. At the same time, persons and firms who received foreign exchange via exports, remittances from abroad, and the like were not permitted to sell this freely in the foreign exchange market but had to surrender it to the government at rates fixed by the government. In contrast to the relatively free flow of goods and lending between countries that had occurred under the gold standard, the situation by the end of World War II had moved toward the other extreme. The real costs to the world in terms of reduced international trade and impeded capital flows that resulted from such comprehensive systems of controls were widely recognized. To enjoy once again the benefits that accrue to nations through a freer international flow of goods and capital, what was needed was a system that would enable countries to maintain equilibrium in their balance of payments without all kinds of controls.

As World War II drew to an end, there was general agreement among the world's monetary experts that the system to be established with the return of world peace could not be the old-fashioned gold standard system. For one thing, although the war had brought full employment, there was much fear that the return to a peace-time economy might be a return to depressed conditions like the thirties. There was also the belief, arrived at through the application of the then new Keynesian economics, that the adjustment process under the gold standard involved primarily output and employment changes rather than price and wage rate changes.

These two judgments taken together made the gold standard look like a national strait jacket. Under gold standard conditions, a country that might already be struggling with depressed output and high unemployment would be required to let a bad situation get even worse if it showed a deficit in its balance of payments. The adjustment process would call for further contraction in output and still greater unemployment to squeeze imports by the amount needed to restore equilibrium. This would not be very appealing to government leaders or anyone else under the best of circumstances, but it was clearly unacceptable with the suffering that had accompanied the mass unemployment and depressed output of the thirties still fresh in mind.

At the same time, a system whose adjustment process worked through freely fluctuating foreign exchange rates also was unacceptable to most countries. It was feared that the uncertainty of future exchange rates that would exist under this system would thoroughly disrupt international trade and capital flows. However, one cannot have it both ways: adjustment requires that nations with serious balance of payments deficits either undergo a contraction in their domestic output and price levels or a depreciation in the foreign exchange values of their currencies. To the degree that countries with persistent balance of payments surpluses permit expansion in their price levels and appreciation in the foreign exchange value of their currencies, they share in the adjustment process, but it remains that the process demands either the appropriate changes within economies or the appropriate changes in the rates at which the currencies of different economies exchange for one another.

The Adjustable Peg System Adopted at Bretton Woods

The system of adjustable pegs adopted by the major Western nations in meetings held at Bretton Woods, New Hampshire, in 1944 was a kind of compromise in which countries were not to be called on to sacrifice their domestic stability in order to secure stability of foreign exchange rates; nor were foreign exchange rates to be left to fluctuate freely. Exchange rates would change, but the changes were to occur in an orderly manner and under prescribed conditions. A nation whose balance of payments reflected what was called a "fundamental disequilibrium" was required to adjust its exchange rate in one step by the amount believed to be needed to correct the existing imbalance, but a nation was also expected to maintain the existing exchange rate as long as a balance of payments disequilibrium was not so serious as to qualify as a fundamental disequilibrium. The objective of the system was to secure the advantages of the gold standard fixity of exchange rates as far as possible but to permit nations to adjust exchange rates as required to meet structural changes in their economies that pushed them out of line with other economies.

As a key part of the adjustable peg system, there was set up in 1946 a new agency, the International Monetary Fund (IMF). Each member—at latest count 125 nations were members—is assigned a quota of gold and its currency that it must contribute on request to the IMF. This provision provides the agency with the means of making loans of foreign currencies to nations that seek to borrow. Thus, a country that incurs a deficit in its balance of payments has as one line of defense the gold and foreign currencies held by its Treasury and central bank and as another line of defense its drawing rights at the IMF or the amount of foreign exchange it can borrow from that agency, an amount that is limited by its quota.

The resources of the IMF are designed to meet the problems of nations suffering deficits of a transient nature, not deficits of a structural nature. If the deficit is transient, it is expected that the forces producing the deficit will disappear before long or that they will reverse themselves in time. Even if it were willing to resort to such a policy, a country in this situation would err if it adopted a contractionary domestic policy for the sole purpose of solving its balance of payments problem. To meet this kind of situation, it may appropriately rely on its reserve balances, including its drawing rights at the IMF. However, suppose that the deficits are structural in character. For example, they may be the result of the fact that the domestic economy has been suffering a higher rate of inflation than other countries, which damages its competitive position in world goods markets. Unless nations operate under the "rules of the game" of the gold standard system, the forces at work cannot be expected to reverse themselves automatically and correct the disequilibrium. If a deficit country does not deliberately take appropriate contractionary action at home, it will see its international reserves drawn down to zero. It cannot expect the IMF to bail it out with loans of more and more reserves; the limited resources of the fund are available to meet only transient as opposed to structural problems. If the problem is judged to be a structural one, the disequilibrium in the balance of payments is described as fundamental, and the adjustment to this is through an appropriate lowering of the exchange rate of the nation's currency unit. The foreign exchange value of the nation's currency is now pegged at this new lower level, hence the term "adjustable peg." Note that the availability of this adjustment mechanism is one of the features that distinguishes the adjustable peg system from the gold standard system, because in the latter system exchange rate variations were in effect ruled out, at least in the cases of the world's leading industrial countries.

A lowering of the foreign exchange value of a nation's currency is most commonly described as *devaluation*. Technically, devaluation (or its opposite, *revaluation*) is the governmental act of redefining the nation's monetary unit in terms of gold. For example, in 1949 the British pound was reduced from 54.8 grains of gold to 38.4 grains, and in 1967 it was further reduced to 32.9 grains. As the gold content of the dollar remained unchanged over these years at 13.71 grains, the British devaluation of 1949 meant that, in terms of the relative gold contents, the value of the British pound fell from $4.00 to $2.80 in 1949 and from $2.80 to $2.40 in 1967. At these new exchange rates, American imports from Britain became relatively cheaper and British imports from the United States relatively more expensive. The same occurred in Britain's position relative to other countries, with a resultant beneficial effect on Britain's trade balance over time.

Under the IMF, all member nations currently define their currencies in terms of gold—that is, gold is technically the numeraire, the common denominator in terms of which the values of all currencies are stated. It is important to see that this is not the same as saying that under the IMF arrangement all member countries stand ready to exchange gold for their currency or their currency for gold in unlimited amounts at the indicated rate. However, over the period from the establishment of the IMF until August 1971, the United States did stand ready to sell 13.71 grains of gold for each U.S. dollar presented and to pay a dollar of its currency for each 13.71 grains of gold presented. Thus, in defining their currencies in terms of gold, other nations also established a specific exchange rate between their currencies and the U.S. dollar. Then, as long as a nation could maintain that exchange rate, there was an indirect link between that nation's currency and gold because the U.S. dollar was linked directly to gold. In terms of the illustration above, over the period during which the British pound was held at $4.00, a British pound could be converted into four U.S. dollars, and these four U.S. dollars could be converted into 54.8 grains of gold, which made the pound convertible indirectly into gold at the rate of 54.8 grains per pound.

Exchange Rate Variations Under Adjustable Pegs

As we saw earlier, exchange rates were not perfectly rigid under the gold standard but fluctuated over the narrow range set by the gold points. Under the IMF arrangement, a range of fluctuation about the parity set by the relative gold contents of the currencies was established by agreement among the member nations. Each was obligated to maintain its exchange rate vis-à-vis the U.S. dollar within 1 percent on either side of parity. With the dollar convertible into gold, this indirectly maintained the value of each nation's currency in terms of gold within the same range. Countries whose currencies fell in value to the lower limit would have to use their gold and foreign currency reserves to buy up whatever amount of their currencies was necessary to prevent a decline below the lower limit. Countries whose currencies rose in value to the upper limit would sell more of their own currencies for other currencies to prevent the value of their currencies from rising above the upper limit.

From the time the IMF adjustable peg system was set up at the end of World War II until the end of 1971, this obligation of member IMF member countries to keep their exchange rates within 1 percent of parity remained unchanged. To introduce greater flexibility into the system, the figure was raised by mutual agreement to 2.25 percent in December 1971. Over the preceding quarter of a century, holding to that 1 percent requirement appeared to provide the world with a stable exchange rate system—the rates could move only over this 2 percent range, a range comparable to that set by the gold points under the gold standard. But what may also be apparent is that this is a somewhat artificial kind of stability. If a nation finds itself running balance of payments deficits of more than a transient nature, it is not allowed to respond to the deficits by simply letting the foreign exchange value of its currency decline gradually in response to the market forces at work. Instead, once these forces have pushed its currency value 1 percent below parity, the country in question is expected to support it against further decline. As we will see below, over the period of experience under the adjustable peg system, nations often made valiant attempts to do this, but, if the underlying forces involved structural changes, they sooner or later had to yield. To yield in this sense is to devalue, and to devalue is to adjust the peg downward in one step to the new lower level at which it is believed the existing underlying forces will once again be in equilibrium. The adjustable peg system, in other words, did not eliminate changes in exchange rates but substituted less frequent and relatively large "one-time" changes for what alternatively would have been more frequent, even continuous, relatively small changes.

Even so, when one looks back at the record, the number of times that nations changed their exchange rates was not as small as is often believed. An IMF study shows that 97 of the then 109 member nations had changed their exchange rates relative to the dollar at least once between 1948 and 1967. The United States, Switzerland, Japan, and nine less developed countries were the only ones that held their rates unchanged over these years. Twenty-one countries devalued four or more times, and the cumulative devaluation over these years of more than half of all member countries exceeded 40 percent. Only a few countries revalued their currencies at all during this period—e.g., Germany and the Netherlands in 1961.

Supporters of the adjustable peg system use this same evidence to show that there were periods running years in length during which the exchange rate of many currencies did not move outside the range of 1 percent above or below parity and assert that this degree of stability, however far short of complete stability, is still that much better than an alternative that would give much less. While this contention is superficially correct, the degree of exchange rate stability obtained through the adjustable peg system is gained only at the price of sacrifices made in other directions. The adjustable peg system has shortcomings that other systems do not have.

Some Shortcomings of the Adjustable Peg System

The fact that a country was required under the IMF rules to put off a change in its exchange rate until a balance of payments difficulty had developed into a "fundamental disequilibrium" gave rise to problems, one of which was the perverse foreign exchange speculation that made a government's already difficult balance of payments problem even more difficult. By deferring an adjustment in a nation's exchange rate so long that it was clear to almost everyone that an adjustment was unavoidable, the system presented speculators with an almost risk-free opportunity. The possible losses were minor and the possible gains huge. Take speculators whose study of a country's international position convinces them that a devaluation of the currency is bound to occur. They move out of this currency into a "strong" currency. If they then turn out to be correct and devaluation does occur, the earlier capital outflow is reversed by a capital inflow, but the speculators now buy back the devalued currency at a lower price per unit than that at which they earlier sold it. The greater the devaluation, the greater their profit per unit. If they turn out to be wrong and devaluation does not occur, they can buy back their country's currency at a price near the price at which they sold it. Even if they are wrong, they cannot suffer a large loss because they are protected in the other direction by the narrow range over which the exchange rate is permitted to move.

Short of imposing controls on short-term capital movements or otherwise interfering with the operation of free markets, governments are unable to do much to prevent this perverse speculation that occurs under the system of adjustable pegs. It is true that a nation with balance of payments difficulties will not find the origin of its difficulties in an outflow of capital initiated by the expectation of a devaluation of that nation's currency; a speculative capital movement of this kind does not become appreciable until the nation's balance of payments problem has become difficult. However, up to the time of the speculative attack on the currency, it may still have been possible for the government in time to have corrected the difficulties before they made devaluation unavoidable. A speculative onslaught of sufficient strength will deny the government this chance. Its depleted international reserves are simply unable to cope with a massive capital outflow. The situation reaches the crisis stage, and the government devalues. Of course, government officials maintain right up to the moment of devaluation that the crisis will be met and devaluation will not occur, but the speculators over the years have learned how to evaluate these official pronouncements.

Another shortcoming under the adjustable peg system is that a government's monetary officials cannot gauge very accurately how much of an adjustment in exchange rates is needed if the nation's balance of payments has been permitted to remain out of equilibrium for some period of time and the required adjustment is sizable. If the disequilibrium is on the side of deficits, the country will have depleted its reserve assets, and the exchange rate it moves to would ideally be one that would not only remove the deficit but yield a surplus. This would enable it to build up its depleted reserves, but then this rate would before long have to be changed again to that consistent with neither a deficit nor a surplus in the balance of payments. However, to accomplish something like this requires more than the relatively infrequent changes in exchange rates that the system of adjustable pegs permits.

Another weakness is the asymmetry of pressures that the adjustable peg system imposes on deficit and surplus countries. To meet the pressures working toward a decline in the value of its currency, a deficit country must use its own reserves or borrow from the IMF or from other countries that might be willing to lend to it, but it will inevitably reach a limit in this direction. If the deficits persist, devaluation must ultimately follow. In contrast, there is no such limit to the amount of reserves that a surplus country can accumulate. To prevent the value of its currency from rising more than the allowable percent above parity, the central bank of the surplus country must issue more and more of its currency to buy up foreign currencies in the foreign exchange market. There is, of course, no limit to the amount of its currency that it can create. However, if carried too far, an overexpansion of its money supply originating in this way, like an overexpansion originating in any other way, may be inflationary. The central bank can offset this to some degree with appropriate monetary policy, but it may still have to accept some greater domestic inflation. Nonetheless, a surplus nation can avoid a revaluation of its currency almost indefinitely. The upshot of this asymmetry in the pressures on deficit and surplus nations under the adjustable peg system is that the system has a bias toward devaluation. Surplus countries ordinarily prefer not to revalue their currencies, and they are able to avoid revaluation because they have the means to resist the pressures working in this direction. The required adjustments in exchange rates, therefore, come about almost entirely through devaluations, which deficit countries can only resist up to a point.

While the adjustment process under the adjustable peg system is thus one that works primarily through devaluation, it is oddly also a system in which countries typically resist devaluation to the last ditch. If exchange rates were allowed to move freely in response to supply and demand in the foreign exchange markets and if a structural change required it, a nation's currency might gradually depreciate 10 percent over the course of a couple of years without a great deal of attention being paid to this by others than those who regularly buy and sell foreign exchange. However, under the adjustable peg system a devaluation involves a significant decrease in the foreign exchange value of the nation's currency on a particular day, and this momentous act makes that day a day that goes down in the nation's history.

If there were fairly clear-cut evidence that the currency is overvalued, one would think that the national authorities would be anxious to devalue in order to get the balance of payments back in equilibrium, but this is frequently not the case. There is often an irrational response by the authorities to the relatively large, one-step adjustment in the external value of the currency that is needed to allow for pressures built up over a period of years. As indicated by experience under the adjustable peg system, devaluation came to be viewed as a disturbing reflection on a nation's honor and its international position; it came to be viewed as an embarrassing admission of failure in maintaining the integrity of the currency and as a symbol of political defeat for the nation's leaders.

If they are to avoid devaluation, governments must obviously seek other ways out. Forcing a contraction of income, output, and employment at home through restrictive monetary and fiscal policy is another way out, but resort to this would be interpreted as admission of an even greater failure on the part of the nation's leaders. Maintaining output and employment is ordinarily a national goal that stands second to none. This means that the avoidance of devaluation leaves a government no alternative but to adopt trade and other restrictions, at least as far as they can do so without producing retaliatory actions by other countries that feel the effect of these restrictions.

This reluctance of nations to resort to devaluation, even when a balance of payments problem has advanced from a difficulty to a "fundamental disequilibrium," means that international payments could be out of equilibrium much of the time. Inappropriate exchange rates permitted to persist influence imports and exports among nations in ways that involve misallocation of resources and a sacrifice of economic welfare among nations. Furthermore, the resort to restrictive devices in the effort to maintain the existing exchange rate makes the misallocation of resources and sacrifice of welfare that much greater.

Some economists assert that, in the final analysis, it is this re-source misallocation and the welfare-reducing distortions that result from the way that the adjustable peg system works in practice that are its most serious shortcomings. These economists argue that under competitive conditions each nation would be free to direct its domestic policy at maintaining a stable economy with full employment and at the same time avoid the encouragement to foreign exchange speculation and the real loss of production through resource misallocation that occurs under the adjustable peg system. What is needed, according to these critics, is to replace the system of adjustable pegs with a system of freely fluctuating exchange rates.

BALANCE OF PAYMENTS ADJUSTMENT
UNDER FLEXIBLE EXCHANGE RATES

While admitting its drawbacks, sup-porters of the system of adjustable pegs point to the fact that the system served the world quite well for more than two decades following World War II. Economic growth through most of the world over these years was truly remarkable, and proponents of the adjustable peg system maintain that a good part of this growth can be traced directly to the expansion of international trade that was made possible by that exchange rate system. As they see it, those interruptions in international trade and world economic growth that did occur over these years may be explained more from conditions arising within countries than specifically from the system of pegged exchange rates that was in use. On the other side are those critics who assert that, whatever the success of that system over more than twenty years, the world would have been still better served by a system that allowed for greater flexibility in exchange rates.

However high or low a rating one gives to the system of adjustable pegs in the earlier years, that system began to come apart at the start of the seventies. As we have seen, the rules of the IMF under which the adjustable peg system operates require that each country support its exchange rate within the specified band around parity or, in the face of a persistent balance of payments problem that builds up to a fundamental disequilibrium, that the country devalue or revalue. However, from the experience in the fall of 1969, when the German government left its currency free to "float" for a period of time before it revalued it by 9.3 percent, to the experience in the spring of 1973, when governments of most major countries abandoned attempts to maintain exchange rates at previously negotiated levels and resorted to "floats," the system of adjustable pegs underwent a gradual demise.

The following chapter will examine in detail the developments of these last few years that brought the Bretton Woods system of adjustable pegs to an end. But before looking at the specifics of the recent record, we must look at the way the adjustment process works in general under a system of flexible exchange rates. That is the purpose of the final section of this chapter. We will also note the major shortcomings of the flexible exchange rate system as we did the shortcomings of other systems.

Flexible Exchange Rates and the Trade Balance

Under a system of flexible exchange rates, there is nothing like the gold standard system's requirement of price level and income level variations or the adjustable peg system's requirement of devaluation or revaluation of a nation's currency. Under a system of freely fluctuating exchange rates, the adjustment process occurs simply by permitting foreign exchange rates to change by the amount needed to bring about the changes in a nation's imports and exports that will restore the balance of payments to equilibrium. As long as nations do nothing to prevent this from occurring, the required changes in the external value of their currencies will occur automatically. As we saw earlier in this chapter in examining the relationship between the balance of payments and the supply of and demand for foreign currencies, a deficit in a nation's balance of payments increases the supply of its currency relative to the demand for that currency in the foreign exchange markets, which tends to produce a decline in the value of that currency in terms of other currencies. As this occurs, that nation's exports tend to increase and its imports to decrease, changes that bring the balance of payments back into equilibrium. A surplus in a nation's balance of payments, of course, has the opposite effects.

That changes in foreign exchange rates will affect exports and imports in the ways indicated may be apparent—simply because a decrease in the foreign exchange value of a currency makes the goods in that country proportionally cheaper to foreigners, while an increase makes them proportionally more expensive to foreigners. In terms of our familiar illustration, if the dollar price of RCA phonograph records in the United States remains the same, a 10 percent decrease in the foreign exchange value of the dollar is equal to a 10 percent cut in the price of that product to foreign purchasers. Some increase in U.S. exports of RCA phonograph records may be expected, other things being equal, and the same in general may be said for other U.S. goods. Given the DM price of Mercedes-Benz automobiles in Germany, a 10 percent decrease in the foreign exchange value of the dollar is also equal to about an 11 percent rise in the price of that product to U.S. purchasers. Some decrease in U.S. imports of Mercedes-Benz automobiles may be expected, other things being equal, and the same in general may be said for other goods imported from Germany. If we extend this illustration and assume a decrease in the value of the dollar relative to all other leading currencies, we may expect a correspondingly large increase in exports and decrease in imports. And the greater the decline in the value of one currency relative to other currencies, the greater will be the increase in that country's exports and the greater the decrease in its imports.

Flexible Exchange Rates and the Forward Exchange Market

The major criticism directed against the system of flexible exchange rates is that when rates are free to move without limit they may move widely and even wildly. The danger in this is the restrictive effect that sizable and rapid fluctuations in exchange rates can have on the volume of international trade. Any degree of fluctuation in exchange rates adds to the risk of doing business internationally, and substantial fluctuations impose a degree of risk that may seriously disrupt international business. The fact that importers and exporters can protect themselves against this kind of loss by dealing in what is called the forward exchange market is only a partial answer to this objection.

To see how this market works and its relevance here, suppose in our illustration that Mercedes-Benz has agreed to take payment from the U.S. automobile dealer in dollars and to receive payment 90 days following delivery of the cars in the United States. At the time it works out the terms of the sale, Mercedes-Benz can check the U.S. dollar-DM rate in the forward exchange market—i.e., the number of DMs per dollar that foreign exchange dealers will *today* commit themselves to pay for dollars to be delivered to them at a specific future date. The company thus knows how many DMs it will be able to get in 90 days in exchange for the dollars it will then receive in payment for its shipment to the U.S. dealer. By making use of the forward market it protects itself against a loss in the event that the dollar falls in terms of the DM, but it also rules out the gain that would follow in the opposite case.

To consider the case of an importer, suppose that the German music store has agreed to pay RCA in dollars in 90 days. The music store can determine at the time it arranges the purchase from RCA how much it will cost in DMs to get the number of dollars to be paid to RCA when those dollars are needed 90 days later. This is given by the U.S. dollar-DM rate in the forward exchange market—i.e., the number of dollars per DM (actually the fraction of a dollar per DM) that foreign exchange dealers will *today* commit themselves to give in exchange for DMs to be delivered to them at a specific future date. By making use of the forward market, the music store protects itself against a loss in the event that the dollar rises in terms of the DM, but it also rules out the gain that would follow in the opposite case.

Mercedes Benz is in the business of manufacturing automobiles, and the music store is in the business of selling phonograph records and related goods; neither is in the business of gambling on future foreign exchange rates. They and most other exporters and importers will thus ordinarily use the forward market in which other firms whose business it is to buy and sell future exchange relieve them of the risks involved. In our illustration, a foreign exchange dealer who handled both of these transactions could exactly match one against the other. Whatever the U.S. dollar-DM exchange rate might be 90 days later, his loss on one transaction would be just matched by his gain on the other. However, the total of all transactions does not balance out like this, and dealers must operate in a way to permit an appreciable margin. This works out through the competitive forces of the market in the form of a spread between the price at which dealers will buy future exchange and the price at which they will sell future exchange.

If foreign exchange rates are expected to show wide fluctuations, dealers will offer lower prices in buying future exchange and ask higher prices in selling future exchange. Changes in this direction in effect involve increases in the cost of doing business internationally. Just as increased transportation costs between countries will reduce the volume of trade, increased costs to importers and exporters of protecting themselves against changes in exchange rates under a system of freely fluctuating exchange rates will reduce the volume of trade between countries. Whether or not so-called forward cover will be available at reasonable costs thus becomes a major question in determining how well a system of freely fluctuating exchange rates works. If these costs become so high as to seriously shrink the volume of trade, freely fluctuating exchange rates do not qualify as an acceptable alternative.

Fluctuating exchange rates can be even more restrictive to other transactions in which forward cover may not be available at all. Foreign exchange dealers regularly buy and sell forward exchange over a long enough period to cover the needs of most importers and exporters, but they do not do this over the long period of time that is involved in long-term capital movements. Even if such protection were to be made available, it would likely be very expensive. Therefore, given the extreme uncertainty that accompanies very long time periods and the lender's inability to purchase exchange rate protection over it at reasonable cost, a U.S. lender, for example, would understandably hesitate to use his dollars to buy a German corporation bond that promises to pay a certain number of DMs in interest each year plus the principal in DMs at the end of, say, 20 years. A depreciation in the DM relative to the dollar of only 2 percent a year will wipe out about half of the lender's investment over the 20 years. The corporate borrower in Germany will also be reluctant to agree to repay the amount in dollars, because the same development will mean that, apart from interest, the company will have to pay about half again as many DMs to purchase the dollars needed to repay the debt at maturity that it obtained when the debt was incurred. However, while the risk in long-term international lending may thus appear to be greater under a flexible exchange rate system, it is to be noted that such risks were by no means absent during the post-World War II period under the adjustable peg system. As was pointed out earlier, the cumulative devaluations of the currencies of more than half of all IMF member countries over 1948–67 exceeded 40 percent. A U.S. lender who in 1948 had bought a 20-year bond issued in any of these countries and payable in the currency of that country would have lost almost half of his investment through devaluations over those 20 years.

The Degree of Exchange Rate Variation Under Flexible Rates

Whether the flexible exchange rate system will have seriously adverse effects on the flow of long-term capital and on the volume of international trade depends fundamentally on how widely exchange rates will fluctuate under such a system. Long-term capital movements may be reduced markedly at first under a fully flexible rate system, but a few years of successful operation without wide swings in exchange rates, if things work out that way, may overcome fears and restore the flow of long-term credit to normal levels. In the area of international trade, if the movements in exchange rates are not wide, the costs to business of purchasing protection against such movements will not be so great as to seriously restrict world trade. Some sacrifice of international specialization and some reduction in international welfare may be unavoidable, but proponents of flexible rates argue that it is worth paying some price to have an exchange rate system that escapes many of the problems faced under the system of adjustable pegs.

The all-important question clearly is: Will exchange rates fluctuate widely if they are left to fluctuate without limit? The answer has been much debated over the years, and there has not been enough actual experience with the flexible rate system under anything approximating normal conditions to resolve the question conclusively. However, the experience provided by the resort to "floating" of their currencies by many of the leading trading nations of the world in the spring of 1973 did not lead to the very large exchange rate fluctuation or to other difficulties that were forecast by many. On the contrary, the earlier international monetary "crises" that drove countries to floating or flexible exchange rates in 1973 seem to have become a thing of the past. No system is without its shortcomings, but recent experience with a system of floating rates suggests that its shortcomings may have been greatly exaggerated.

Supporters of the flexible rate system assert that there is no inherent reason for exchange rates to fluctuate widely merely because they are flexible. Barring conditions such as serious inflation or depression, conditions under which no adjustment system will work smoothly, neither widely nor rapidly fluctuating exchange rates are required to maintain equilibrium in the balance of payments. After all, under such a system market forces act to force a depreciation in the currency of a country with a balance of payments deficit shortly after the appearance of the deficit. As we saw earlier, under the system of adjustable pegs, countries often maintain the foreign exchange value of their currencies at the existing peg despite a build-up of pressures that call for a lower exchange rate. Usually only when the central bank's official reserve assets are badly drawn down and the nation faces a balance of payments "crisis" is there an adjustment, and this is then, in one fell swoop, the relatively large adjustment needed to correct for the cumulated imbalance that has occurred. By adjusting continuously to changes in supply and demand conditions, the flexible exchange rate system may avoid the relatively large, wrenching changes that occur as the peg is periodically adjusted under that alternative system.

While conceding that the flexible exchange rate system may be able to maintain balance of payments equilibrium without the necessity of large and rapid swings in exchange rates, some critics of this system assert that such large swings may, nonetheless, occur as a result of speculation. Under the adjustable peg system of exchange rates, there is a relatively narrow range over which the exchange rate can move (as long as the peg is maintained), but under the flexible exchange rate system there is no such limit. In this open-ended case, speculation, if it is of a destabilizing rather than stabilizing nature, can cause large movements in exchange rates away from the rates consistent with balance of payments equilibrium. By one definition, speculation is said to be stabilizing if speculators buy a currency when it is relatively weak in the expectation that it will become less weak or sell a currency when it is relatively strong in the expectation that it will become less strong. Speculation is said to be destabilizing if speculators sell a currency when it is relatively weak in the expectation that it will become even weaker or buy a currency when it is relatively strong in the expectation that it will become even stronger. The destabilizing action here is similar to that which occurs in the stock market. It is not uncommon for speculators to purchase a stock whose price is already well above what they believe its longer-run equilibrium price will be because they also believe that the concensus of opinion in the market is that the stock is going to rise. Such purchases are destabilizing in the sense that they will tend to push the price still farther from its longer-run equilibrium price, but such purchases are also profitable to the speculators who have called the movement correctly and who manage to sell before the price starts down. In a similar way in the foreign exchange market, speculators may, for example, use holdings of dollars to buy DMs, despite the fact that the DM is already strong. They believe the longer run equilibrium value of the DM in terms of the dollar will be lower than it is at the moment, but they also believe that this is not the concensus among participants in the foreign exchange market. They thus buy DMs, causing a further rise in the DM and a further fall in the dollar, movements away from and not toward the equilibrium rate of exchange.

Because it imposes no limits on the movement of exchange rates, the flexible rate system does expose itself to the dangers of large movements in exchange rates, but it must be seen that this absence of limits at the same time decreases the possibility of destabilizing speculative action. We saw under the adjustable peg system that speculators had almost a "sure thing." They would "attack" a currency that had weakened and appeared likely to be devalued. If devaluation occurred, a good gain was made; if it did not, at the most a minor loss was suffered. However, under the flexible rate system, they have no such protection—they now face the possibility of equal-sized gains and losses. Speculators who sell a weak currency cannot look forward to, say, the approximately 10 percent lump-sum gain that would be provided by a 10 percent devaluation, because devaluation (and revaluation) no longer occurs. The sellers will gain only if the currency grows weaker; they will lose if it grows stronger. This change in the odds is bound to limit the intensity of speculation, but it by no means will rule it out. Without the limits imposed by an adjustable peg system, some danger remains that a flexible rate system will be a system of unstable rates because of the recurrent destabilizing speculation that may occur. The belief that this is always a very real danger has long prevailed among many central bankers and many government officials and as much as anything else has kept the flexible exchange rate system in disrepute in these quarters.

Destabilizing Short-Term Capital Movements
Under Flexible Exchange Rates

Another major objection to the flexible rate system is that changes in rates, even though fairly moderate in size, may still have quite damaging effects on nations' trade balances under certain conditions. Take a country with a high ratio of imports and exports to domestic production and with its balance of payments in equilibrium. Suppose that, due to a political disturbance in another country, there is a large inflow of short-term capital that produces an appreciation in the value of its currency. This will raise the prices of its goods in terms of foreign currencies and discourage exports; this will also lower the prices of foreign goods in terms of its currency and encourage imports. The existing equilibrium in its merchandise trade will be upset. With imports and exports playing a relatively large role in its total economic activity, the overall effect can be a serious decrease in domestic output and employment. However, if there is then another change in conditions that produces a large outflow of short-term capital, the country's exchange rate would move in the opposite direction. Exports would be stimulated and imports discouraged, with the result that output and employment would expand. For countries in which exports and imports play a large role, the expansion and contraction of output and employment that can come about in this way is not something that can be readily absorbed as would be the case in countries in which imports and exports play only a small role.

In addition to their effects on output and employment, these short-term capital movements may also have destabilizing effects on prices. Take a country in which a large short-term capital outflow occurs and in which the foreign exchange value of the country's currency is allowed to fall freely in response to the resultant pressures. The rise in the values of foreign currencies means a rise in the cost of imports and, for a country in which imports are large relative to domestic output, this means an appreciably higher domestic price level. This leads to a demand for higher wages as labor seeks to catch up with the now higher cost of living. The higher wages, which are not accompanied by any greater labor productivity, in turn lead to a further rise in domestic prices as firms pass on the higher wage costs of domestically produced goods. At this point a further depreciation in the foreign exchange value of the currency can occur to offset the rise in domestic prices. This then means still higher costs for imported goods, a still higher domestic price level, a demand for still higher wage rates, etc. A standard price-wage spiral is in operation.

These problems do not appear under the system of adjustable pegs, at least not as long as nations are able to maintain the existing pegs. Under this sytem, central banks enter the foreign exchange market and buy or sell currencies as needed to offset the pressures on exchange rates that originate with short-term capital movements. Rates are allowed to move only within the limits set by the band. In contrast, under the flexible rate system, rates are allowed to move as far as market forces may carry them, and it would apparently not take massive short-term capital movements to move rates well outside the narrow band that nations adhered to under the Bretton Woods agreement. Movements of this degree would then presumably be all that is needed to produce the output, employment, and perhaps the inflationary consequences outlined here.

Government Intervention

Because a system in which exchange rates are left to respond freely to changes in the supply of and demand for foreign exchange may under certain conditions and at least for some countries produce results that are socially and economically unacceptable, even supporters of flexible rates grant that there are circumstances under which government intervention is appropriate. What is here intended is not the kind of intervention practiced under the adjustable peg system in which the objective is to keep the rate within the prescribed band, but intervention designed only to counter exchange rate changes that appear to be inconsistent with longer run equilibrium in the balance of payments. While this seems to be quite appropriate policy, the difficulty it presents may be obvious: government officials are not omniscient and cannot be sure whether any given change in exchange rates is consistent with or inconsistent with longer run equilibrium. Given their limited knowledge and fallibility in judgment, it may be argued that their intervention under a flexible rate system should not go beyond that needed to prevent "disorderly movements" in foreign exchange rates. That is, the amount by which rates are allowed to move should not be limited, but the speed with which they move may be influenced by official intervention. If intervention goes so far beyond this as to prevent even "orderly movements" in excess of some prescribed amount, the intervention becomes virtually the same as that found under the system of adjustable pegs, and the system can no longer be properly described as a flexible rate system.

Furthermore, intervention that goes beyond the maintenance of orderly markets may be intervention whose intent is not to offset changes judged inconsistent with the longer run equilibrium in a nation's balance of payments, but is to increase a nation's net export balance or reduce its net import balance. Granting the difficulties in determining whether any given movement in the foreign exchange value of a nation's currency is consistent with longer run equilibrium in its balance of payments, there is an understandable tendency for government to intervene as it sees the foreign exchange value of its currency rise appreciably at the same time that its price level is rising as rapidly as the price levels in the countries with which it trades. For under these conditions, there will be more than the normal pressure for intervention exerted by export firms, which see their foreign markets shrinking, and also by firms producing for the home market, which see foreign firms now able to compete with them in these markets. To the extent that there is unemployment at home, the pressure from business becomes that much greater, and the government's interest may coincide with that of business as government seeks ways of meeting the unemployment problem.

Intervention may occur not only to prevent unwanted exchange rate changes but to initiate desired changes. In the face of unemployment, a nation may seek to drive down the foreign exchange value of its currency in order to increase the sales of its export firms and to decrease the competition faced from abroad by its firms producing for the home market. If there is unemployment, there is pressure on a country to pursue this beggar-my-neighbor policy even though it has a surplus in its balance of payments. But the attempt of a nation to protect its existing net export balance by intervening to prevent a rise in the foreign exchange value of its currency or the attempt to improve its net export balance by intervening to force a decrease in the foreign exchange value of its currency is likely to produce retaliation by other countries. The outcome can be exchange rate warfare among nations as occurred during the depression of the thirties. The result of this in turn is a drastic shrinkage in the volume of international trade and foreign lending to the detriment of all parties concerned.

Under the system of adjustable pegs, there is little opportunity for nations to practice that kind of disruptive intervention. The rules of the game require that government intervene to maintain rates within the prescribed band, but this band is too narrow to provide any appreciable competitive advantage to a nation moving within it. For a country to move outside it on the lower side requires a devaluation, and the rules require a fundamental disequilibrium in the balance of payments before a nation takes this action. In contrast, because the system of freely fluctuating exchange rates may at times call for sizable movements in exchange rates as a part of the process of adjusting a nation's balance of payments, it does lend itself to this kind of self-serving intervention. It is not always apparent whether a decline in the value of a nation's currency is occurring as a result of the free operation of market forces working to correct a disequilibrium or as the result of government intervention designed to cheapen its currency in order to boost its exports and choke off imports.

Governments will be tempted to try to get away with this kind of unfair intervention when subject to the pressures of unemployment at home. For this reason a system of flexible exchange rates is likely to work best when countries pursue domestic policies that are successful in promoting full employment and providing reasonable price stability. If there is then minimum government interference with international trade and capital movements, the changes that do occur in foreign exchange rates under a system of freely fluctuating rates may be expected to be changes that work toward correcting disequilibrium situations, apart from the perhaps uncommon cases in which changes result from destabilizing speculation.

A CONCLUDING NOTE

It is common practice among economists today to distinguish among the three basic kinds of international monetary systems that we have considered in this chapter. However, some choose to reduce the basic number to two by speaking initially of systems with pegged exchange rates and systems with flexible exchange rates. From this viewpoint, both the gold standard system and the adjustable peg system are included under the heading of pegged exchange rate systems. But while both of these are readily distinguishable in principle from the flexible rate system, they are also readily distinguishable from each other in terms of the degree of exchange rate flexibility that each provides. So far as the world's major currencies are concerned, the old gold standard system was one in which exchange rates remained unchanged at the established pegs over long periods of years, but under the adjustable peg system, as the name itself implies, exchange rates changed at more frequent intervals as the pegs were adjusted from time to time. On this basis alone, it seems more informative to view the gold standard system and the adjustable peg system as basically different systems, despite the fact that they both operate with pegged exchange rates. And beyond this, as we have seen in examining the balance of payments adjustment process under each, these two systems are basically different in that regard.

While this three-way classification seems to be the most appropriate if our purpose is to list the basic kinds of international monetary system from which a choice must be made, experience during recent years has been limited to the adjustable peg system and the flexible exchange rate system. The final chapter looks at the experience over the years from 1970 to 1974, which saw the adjustable peg system established at Bretton Woods expire and a system of flexible, or floating, exchange rates at least temporarily take its place.

nineteen

THE INTERNATIONAL MONETARY SYSTEM: 1970-74 AND BEYOND

The Bretton Woods system prescribed certain kinds of action that nations were to take under certain kinds of condition. During the quinquennium 1970–74 leading nations took a series of actions that departed so radically from the kinds to which they were supposed to restrict themselves under that system as to bring the system effectively to an end. The developments that began in 1970 reached a climax in 1973–74, when the values of many of the world's major currencies were left to float more or less freely, month after month, in response to short-run changes in the supply of and demand for each currency. In place of the short-run exchange rate stability obtained under the Bretton Woods system by nations' supporting exchange rates within a prescribed range, there was a degree of short-run instability that resulted from floating—that is, from the withdrawal of the kind of close support that previously had been provided. Although this arrangement was viewed by many academic economists as a viable one that could continue on a permanent basis, to many central bankers what was needed was a successor to the Bretton Woods system that would provide, as that system had, short-run exchange rate stability with some device to bring about periodic adjustments in the parity rates about which this short-run stability was maintained. However, at the time of writing in the fall of 1974, there appeared to be practically no chance of the kind of full-scale reform that would make possible a return to a system of fixed exchange rates.

In this final chapter we will look back at the major international monetary developments of 1970–74 that brought the Bretton Woods system to an end. Our restriction to the last few years is not meant to suggest that all was well before 1970. The system had been subject to pressures in earlier years, but there was room within its basic structure for reforms that managed, at least temporarily, to absorb these pressures and thus avoid a breakdown. However, these pressures, especially those resulting from the long series of U.S. balance of payments deficits, were not removed in this way, and they grew stronger over time. In the last few years we witnessed the specific actions that finally brought the system to an end, and it is to these few years and the actions during them that we will limit attention.

1970

In one way, the first year of the seventies was like each year of the sixties: the United States again ran a deficit in its balance of payments. Measured by the net liquidity balance, there had been a deficit every year since 1952 with the single exception of 1957. But in another sense, 1970 was different from those earlier years in that certain countries had by then virtually reached the absolute limit of their willingness to absorb more U.S. dollars. Measured by the net liquidity balance, the U.S. deficit over the 10 years 1960–69 totaled $31.2 billions. Recall that this measures the net outflow of U.S. dollars resulting from transactions on current account, long-term capital flows, and nonliquid private capital flows. It is an amount that is matched by that much of an increase in liquid dollar assets like U.S.

currency, bank deposits, and short-term securities held by parties in the rest of the world. Initially this $31.2 billion flowed into the hands of private parties, but private parties did not have to hold more of these dollars than they wished to hold. It became necessary for foreign central banks to absorb whatever amount private parties chose not to hold, or the sale of these unwanted dollars in the foreign exchange markets by unwilling holders would have raised the prices of the currencies into which dollars were being converted beyond the 1 percent limit over the parity rate. To avoid appreciation of their currencies, foreign central banks were forced during the decade to buy $11.0 billion of the $31.2 billion total. This is another way of saying that the U.S. deficit for those years as measured by the official reserve transactions balance was $11.0 billion. Foreign central banks exchanged $4.6 billion of this for U.S.-owned gold and other official reserve assets; the other $6.4 billion they added to their holdings of liquid dollar assets.

The rate at which foreign central banks found it necessary to add to their dollar holdings increased rapidly during 1970. Although the U.S. net liquidity balance showed a smaller deficit in 1970 than in 1969 and thus produced a smaller addition to the rest of the world's liquid dollar asset holdings than in the preceding year, there was during the year a massive move by holders of existing dollars out of dollars into foreign currencies. During the year foreign central banks and official agencies had to absorb $9.8 billion dollars (or the deficit as measured by the official reserve transactions balance was $9.8 billion). Of this $2.5 billion was converted into official reserve assets, including $0.9 billion of the U.S. gold stock, with the balance of $7.3 billion made up of that many more dollars held in liquid assets by foreign central banks and official agencies. That $7.3 billion figure for the single year of 1970 was thus greater than the number of U.S. dollars absorbed by these banks and official agencies over the preceding 10 years.

The movement by holders of short-term dollar funds into foreign currencies continued in 1971. During 1970 and the first couple of months of 1971 much of the movement was in response to higher interest rates abroad; the United States had been in a recession during 1970, and interest rates had fallen to relatively low levels here. Part was also due to a fear for the future of the dollar arising from the deterioration of the U.S. balance on goods and services. By March the situation had reached the point at which many speculators were convinced that the dollar would have to be devalued, and a speculative movement out of the dollar was added to the movement arising for other reasons. In the course of the next few months this movement grew by leaps and bounds, especially into Germany. In addition to the billions of U.S. dollars purchased over the preceding few years, the German central bank found it necessary to buy several billions more in the course of just three days, May 3–5.

THE MAY 1971 FLOAT

In the face of this onslaught, the German central bank on May 5 announced that it would buy no more dollars. The central banks in Austria, Belgium, Netherlands, and Switzerland promptly followed the action of the German central bank. The DM and the Dutch guilder were allowed to float upward against the dollar. Austria and Switzerland took more orthodox action; the Austrian schilling was revalued by 5.05 percent and the Swiss franc by 7.07 percent. But despite these actions there was widespread belief that these and other currencies would rise even higher, and the flight out of dollars into these and some other currencies persisted.

During the first six months of 1971, the deficit in the U.S. net liquidity balance was $8.4 billion. During this period not only did private parties abroad choose not to add any of these extra dollars to their holdings, but they decided to reduce their existing holdings by $3.6 billion. This meant a deficit in the U.S. official reserve transactions balance of $12.0 billion or that $12.0 billion additional dollars were absorbed by foreign central banks and official agencies, more than the $9.8 billion for the full year of 1970, which itself had set a record for any one year. Then in the third quarter, the deficit in the net liquidity balance soared to $9.5 billion. With short-term liquid capital flows into foreign currencies of $2.4 billion for the quarter, foreign central banks absorbed another $11.9 billion dollars. Therefore, for the nine months, they bought the staggering total of $23.9 billion U.S. dollars.

From the first of the year to mid-August, approximately $3 billion of this vast increase in official foreign dollar holdings was converted by foreign central banks into gold and other official reserve assets, about 40 percent of which was taken in the early days of August. This $3 billion amounted to roughly 20 percent of U.S. total reserve assets of approximately $15 billion at the beginning of the year. If foreign central banks had sought to convert any appreciable part of their massive holdings of dollars, something they knew they could not do if all were to try to do it at the same time, the remaining U.S. official reserve assets would have been paid out to these banks in very short order.

THE SUSPENSION OF DOLLAR CONVERTIBILITY

One way to avert this eventuality and also reduce the seemingly insatiable demand of holders of dollars for other currencies was to suspend the convertibility of the dollar and to allow the dollar to float downward against other major currencies. On August 15 the President took this action: effective that date, foreign central banks could no longer obtain gold or other official reserve assets from the United States. Actually, the dollar had been inconvertible *de facto* for some time insofar as large conversions were concerned, although there had been, as one writer put it, nibbling at the U.S. gold stock by small conversion. On August 15 the inconvertibility became *de jure*.

The suspension of convertibility amounted to a withdrawal of U.S. support for the old exchange rates between the dollar and foreign currencies; the value of the dollar in terms of other major currencies was to be determined by permitting the dollar to float against these currencies. But, like the suspension of convertibility, this withdrawal of support was more *de jure* than *de facto*. For in fact the United States had been contributing little to the support of the old exchange parities. The rates of other major currencies against the dollar were kept from breaking through the 1 percent upper limit of their parities primarily by other countries' purchases of dollars with their currencies in the amount needed to stop their currencies from rising beyond this limit.

In the weeks following the August 15 announcement, few countries stepped aside to permit the values of their currencies vis-à-vis the dollar to respond freely to market forces. They permitted the float to raise the value of their currencies well above the 1 percent upper limit of the parity rates, but they adopted various measures such as regulation of capital inflows, exchange controls, and central bank intervention in the market to keep the appreciation of their currencies under control. Japan at first even tried to maintain its rate completely unchanged, but it found the number of dollars it had to buy overwhelming. During August alone the Japanese central bank bought $4.4 billion, which amounted to much more than a doubling of its $2.9 billion total dollar holdings as of the end of 1970. The yen was then allowed to float upward, but the central bank continued to intervene to dampen the rate at which this occurred. France tried and succeeded in maintaining the parity in a qualified way by resorting to a segregated foreign exchange market, with one exchange rate for transactions related to international trade and another rate for other transactions.

By intervening in the former market, the central bank prevented the franc from rising above its parity with the U.S. dollar for at least these transactions.

TOWARD REALIGNMENT: BY FLOATING
OR BY NEGOTIATION?

The floating of currencies was accepted at the time by the world's central bankers as appropriate for a transition period, but a return to a system of fixed exchange rates was generally viewed as the only viable arrangement in the longer run. The central question became that of determining the realignment of exchange rates that would be consistent with balance of payments equilibrium among nations. An answer to this question, of course, could not be arrived at independently of related questions such as changes in tariff, quota, and other trade restrictions between countries and, for the United States and her European allies, changes in the way that mutual security costs were shared. But with these qualifications in mind, the U.S. position in the fall of 1971 was that an equilibrium pattern of exchange rates could best be arrived at by permitting exchange rates to float freely during a transition period. The critical requirement here was that the float be free, or what came to be called "clean." To the extent that nations intervened to produce exchange rates different from those that would be determined by free market forces, the float came to be called "dirty," and the pattern of exchange rates that resulted under these conditions could not be considered an equilibrium pattern. As already noted, in the months following the August 15 announcement most countries did not allow their currencies to appreciate relative to the dollar by the amount that would have occurred under a completely free float. They did not deny the need for a major realignment of currency values, but their position was that the new pattern of equilibrium rates had to be arrived at by negotiations.

A number of reasons may be noted for their objection to a float of currencies as the way to answer this question. First, there was the resistance to a rise in the values of their currencies relative to the dollar because of its effect on their trade balances. This resistance would exist whether the appropriate increase in the value of their currencies was determined by a float or by negotiations, but in the present context it became a reason for resisting a free float. The argument here is the familiar one that a rise in the exchange value of a nation's currency reduces the price competitiveness of its export industries and increases the price competitiveness of the export industries of other countries in its home markets. In an economy that manages to maintain full employment, government leaders may be able to base policy on the fact that the benefits to the general public that result from being able to get goods from abroad at lower real cost outweigh the costs imposed on certain export and import-competing industries at home, but in an economy suffering unemployment, the cries of anguish from the injured export industries and import-competing industries cannot be disregarded in policymaking by government leaders who want to stay in power. They will seek to keep the nation's currency as cheap relative to others as is feasible.

A second issue is closely related to the preceding. Although various nations may have accepted the fact that international payments equilibrium required that they revalue their currencies in terms of the U.S. dollar, each would be reluctant to determine the amount of that revaluation on the basis of the rates established in the market through floating as long as any important nation was intervening to influence the value of its currency in the market. Despite the suspension of the convertibility of the U. S. dollar on August 15, the U.S. dollar for the time being remained the common denominator in terms of which other currencies were valued. In other words, a nation that revalued at this time in terms of the dollar also revalued to the same extent in terms of all other currencies that remained unchanged in terms of the dollar, and, while a revaluation in terms of the dollar may have been warranted, a revaluation in terms of other currencies may not have been. Therefore, if some countries permitted their currencies to float freely and one or more important countries intervened, nations could not float toward a new equilibrium pattern of exchange rates.

To illustrate, suppose that the currencies of both Countries A and B would rise by 10 percent in terms of the dollar if both were left to float freely, but country B intervenes to prevent its currency from appreciating relative to the dollar and Country A allows its currency to float upward by the full 10 percent. If then there is a realignment of exchange rates in accordance with what emerges from the float, Country A will find its currency revalued relative to Country B by 10 percent, even though no adjustment was called for between these currencies. Under these conditions Country A will clearly be unwilling to accept the 10 percent revaluation relative to the dollar, despite the fact that 10 percent may be the appropriate adjustment between these two currencies.

It was this sort of situation that developed between the DM and the French franc in the fall of 1971. The DM was left free to rise against the dollar and moved up about 10 percent over the existing parity. However, the French franc was held at its parity with the dollar so that the DM also increased 10 percent against the French franc. As

France is Germany's largest customer, the effect of a 10 percent more expensive DM on German exports to France would be sizable. The unwillingness of Germany to revalue by an amount indicated by the float is understandable under these conditions.

There were still other objections to relying on a float as the basis for determining the appropriate realignment of currency values. These centered about the relationship between gold and the realigned values. Although the role of gold in the international monetary system was substantially altered by the U.S. suspension of convertibility on August 15, it was agreed by the leading countries that gold would continue for the time being to be the common unit in terms of which each country would define its currency. During the discussions in the fall of 1971, some consideration was given to dropping gold from this role, but no agreement could be reached on an alternative. The special drawing right issued by the IMF was also defined in gold, so it was no real alternative to gold itself. The only practical alternative at the time appeared to be the U.S. dollar, and few countries were in favor of this. (Continuing to define each currency unit in terms of a thing into which none of these currency units is any longer freely convertible at the stated rate may sound meaningless, but the absence of convertibility of currency into that thing in no way precludes the use of that thing as a common denominator for measurement purposes.)

Given then that each currency is defined in terms of gold, it will be seen that reliance on a float as the basis for determining the appropriate realignment of currency values would leave the U.S. dollar unchanged in terms of gold while other currencies would rise in terms of the dollar and therefore in terms of gold. This is something a number of foreign countries, especially France, were unwilling to accept. To grasp what is involved here, we must note all of the ways in which the objective of a higher value for other currencies relative to the dollar could be achieved.

Suppose the dollar was defined as 10 grains of gold. Given that 1 ounce equals 480 grains, the official price of gold in terms of the dollar would therefore be set at $48.00 per ounce. A 10 percent devaluation of the dollar would reduce the dollar in terms of gold from 10 grains to 9 grains and raise the official price of gold in terms of dollars from $48.00 to $53.33 per ounce (480/9 = $53.33). This would mean a 10 percent decrease in the value of the dollar in terms of any other currency whose definition in terms of gold remained unchanged. Note next that this same 10 percent decrease in the value of the dollar in terms of any other currency could be achieved just as easily by an appropriate increase in the amount of gold that other currency is defined as. If the DM had been defined as 4 grains of gold and the price of gold had therefore been set at 120 DMs per ounce, a 10 percent revaluation of the DM in terms of gold would increase the DM from 4 to 4.4 grains and decrease the official price of gold in terms of the DM from 120 DMs to 109.09 DMs per ounce. With the dollar still defined as 10 grains of gold, this revaluation of the DM alters the parity between the dollar and the DM from 2.5 to 2.272 DMs per dollar, in which it will be seen that the original rate of 2.5 DMs per dollar is a rate 10 percent higher than the new rate of 2.272 DMs per dollar. Finally, note that this same 10 percent decrease in the value of the dollar in terms of the DM could also be achieved through any number of different combinations of changes in the two currencies. If one-fourth of the 10 percent were to occur via a devaluation of the dollar and three-fourths via a revaluation of the DM, the dollar would be devalued from 10 to about 9.75 (or more exactly 9.7534) grains of gold, and the DM would be revalued from 4 to about 4.3 (or more exactly 4.2915) grains of gold. The official price of gold in terms of the dollar would rise to $49.21 per ounce and would fall in terms of the DM to 111.85 DMs per ounce.

Foreign countries were anything but indifferent to which of these various ways was to be used to accomplish any given change in relative currency values. France and other countries that held a major part of their official reserves in gold wanted to see a rise in the official price of gold and thereby a corresponding rise in the balance-sheet value of their existing gold holdings. The only way that they could realize this would be through a devaluation of the dollar. To the extent that currency realignment occurred through revaluation of other currencies with the dollar unchanged, there would be no increase but a decrease in the value of the existing gold holdings of those countries whose currencies were revalued. Thus, assuming the DM had been defined as 4 grains of gold and that the country's existing stock of monetary gold valued on this basis had been 10 billion DMs, a 10 percent revaluation to 4.4 grains per DM would reduce the value of the existing stock of gold to 9.09 billion DMs, the decrease in value of approximately 0.91 billion DMs being 10 percent of the new valuation, 9.09 billion DMs. The same sort of balance sheet loss follows from revaluation for a nation's holdings of other reserve assets, notably U.S. dollars. However, to the extent that currency realignments were to be brought about by a devaluation of the dollar or an increase in the dollar price of gold, other nations could avoid this loss on their gold holdings. If the realignment between the dollar and another currency were split evenly between dollar devaluation and revaluation of the other currency, the other country would come out approximately even with respect to the value of the gold component of its official reserve assets.

Another reason that other countries wanted part of the realignment to come about via a devaluation of the dollar is that, whatever the overall realignment called for, revaluation of their currencies could thereby be that much smaller. Revaluation carries a political onus and generates economic repercussions. Export industries and import-competing industries never welcome revaluations. But while the economic impact on those industries of a given-sized parity change will be the same whether it comes about by devaluation of the dollar or revaluation of a nation's own currency, that country's leaders will face a smaller outcry from the injured parties at home if the consequences follow more from actions taken by the United States than from actions taken by themselves.

Devaluations also carry a political onus. Over the years of experience under the Bretton Woods system, devaluation had come to be interpreted as an admission of national economic weakness or failure on the part of the government and was accepted only when conditions had built up to a crisis. There were more than a few foreign leaders who relished the idea of administering a strong dose of the bitter devaluation medicine to the United States despite its protestations that it was far too healthy to require such treatment. Into the fall of 1971 the U.S. authorities insisted that devaluation of the dollar would not be considered. Their position was that other countries were the source of the difficulties and that it was up to those countries to take the necessary corrective actions. Some other countries led by France maintained just as strongly that the United States was to blame for the disruption in the system and that it was appropriate that the blameworthy party admit as much by devaluing its currency.

If the realignment was to include a devaluation of the dollar and a rise in the official value of gold as France insisted, the realignment could not be achieved through a float, only through bilateral and multilateral negotiations. Several other objections to floating to new currency values have been noted here, and each of these added to the case for negotiating the problems. The idea of setting new parities entirely by a float never won much support outside of the United States, and negotiations to work out a realignment of parities were under way among the United States and other major countries not many weeks after the August 15 announcement. Over time compromises were reached in which the United States granted that a small devaluation of the dollar would be appropriate and other countries recognized that revaluations of their currencies would have to be accepted.

THE SMITHSONIAN AGREEMENT

The negotiations culminated in an agreement signed by representatives of the 10 major industrial countries known as the Group of Ten at the Smithsonian Institution in Washington in December 1971. Foremost among the major changes was a realignment of exchange rates that combined the results of negotiations and the market changes in rates that had occurred over the months during which some rates had been allowed to float.

Specifically, the U.S. representatives agreed to ask Congress to devalue the dollar by 8.57 percent. This would call for a rise in the dollar price of gold from $35 to $38 per ounce, and, for the definition of the dollar in terms of gold, this would mean a reduction from 13.71 to 12.63 grains per dollar. The indicated devaluation would raise by 8.57 percent the price in dollars of the currencies of those countries that did not change the definition of their currencies in terms of gold. Under the terms of the agreement, France and the United Kingdom would follow this policy so that these two currencies would become 8.57 more expensive in terms of dollars than they had been under the old parities. Five other major countries agreed to revalue their currencies in terms of gold so that these currencies would increase more than 8.57 percent in terms of the dollar. Relative to the parity rates in effect on January 1, 1971, the agreed percentage revaluations of these currencies combined with the 8.57 percentage devaluation of the dollar would increase their exchange value in terms of the dollar by the following percentages: Japanese yen, 16.88; Swiss franc, 13.88; West German mark, 13.58; Netherlands guilder, 11.57; and Belgian franc, 11.57. The Swedish krona and the Italian lira were devalued by about 1 percent so that these two currencies would rise relative to the dollar by that much less than the devaluation of the dollar. Compared to the January 1, 1971 parities, the figures were 7.49 and 7.48 percent respectively. The remaining country in the Group of Ten, Canada, continued to allow its dollar to float. The Canadian dollar at the end of December 1971 was 99.79 U.S. cents, or 7.9 percent greater than its pre-May 1970 par value of 92.5 U.S. cents.

A second important change embodied in the Smithsonian agreement was a widening of the band within which each country would be expected to maintain the exchange value of its currency. Recall that under the Bretton Woods arrangement a country was required to hold its rate within 1 percent on either side of its parity, barring a fundamental disequilibrium that was the basis for a change in the parity itself. Under the December 1971 agreement, those countries which chose to could expand the range from 1 percent to 2.25 percent on each side of parity.

Another important change was the removal of a 10 percent surcharge on dutiable imports that had been imposed by the United States on August 15 as another in a package of changes that included the previously discussed suspension of the convertibility of the dollar into gold. In the course of the negotiations with other countries in the fall of 1971, the U.S. objective had been to secure changes that would improve its "basic balance" (the balance on current account and long-term capital) by approximately $13 billion per year. In dropping the 10 percent surcharge as part of the Smithsonian agreement, the United States made clear that it would seek better treatment for its exports and some limitations on specific goods among its imports. The currency realignments would help to move the U.S. basic balance closer to a position of stable equilibrium, but the U.S. evaluation of the situation indicated that trade concessions by other countries would be needed as well.

The increase in the U.S. official price of gold, which was a key provision of the Smithsonian realignment of currency values, could not become effective without the approval of Congress, and this was put off for several months, according to some as a means of extracting additional trade concessions from some other countries. The devaluation of the dollar was signed into law on March 31, 1972.

Even before the Smithsonian realignment was fully established weaknesses in the new rate structure began to appear. The dollar was subject to downward pressure in relation to most other currencies, but it strengthened during the spring and later in the year. However, the pound found itself in serious difficulty. The United Kingdom, which had enjoyed a large surplus in its balance for 1971, saw its balance slide into a substantial deficit during the first half of 1972. Considerable doubt arose regarding the viability of the parity for the pound set under the Smithsonian agreement, and a strong speculative movement against the pound was under way. The British authorities gave up a large amount of their reserves in trying to prevent the pound from falling below the Smithsonian floor—during six days in June the Bank of England bought 2.6 billion pounds in defending the parity. But the pressure was too much, and the British authorities were forced to allow the pound to float. Six months later the pound had floated downward to a point 10 percent below the parity established for it by the Smithsonian agreement.

Another problem but of the opposite kind was the Japanese yen. Japan showed a sizable surplus in its balance of payments and found its currency under strong upward pressure during the second half of the year. The Japanese authorities were forced to purchase large amounts of dollars in the foreign exchange markets to hold the yen within the Smithsonian ceiling. This was done; the yen was not set free to float upward.

Apart from the several cases of strong pressures noted, the Smithsonian rates held up reasonably well during their first year. There was some confidence late in the year that the rate realignment adopted in December 1971 would hold for some time to come. However, it turned out that this confidence was misplaced; in early 1973 most of the world's major currencies were once again floating.

THE MARCH 1973 FLOAT

The beginning of the end of the Smithsonian rates came with a massive outflow of funds from Italy into Switzerland in January. The Italian authorities permitted the lira to float downward below its Smithsonian floor. Switzerland, which was also getting heavy inflows of currencies other than lira, decided to permit its franc to float. The alternative would have been a large increase in the Swiss money supply, which would have aggravated an already difficult inflation problem in that country. The floating of the Swiss franc reinforced expectations among speculators that other strong currencies might also soon be set free to float upward. Japan and Germany with their large balance of payments surpluses were the most likely candidates, and large speculative purchases of these two currencies for dollars commenced. However, as these purchases grew larger and larger, the German and Japanese authorities did not simply yield by permitting their currencies to float upward; instead, in agreement with other countries, they temporarily closed the foreign exchange markets and began high-speed consultations with the United States and other countries to work out some cooperative plan of action to meet the problem without completely abandoning the existing alignment of parities.

The most striking and surprising of the actions agreed upon was a 10 percent devaluation of the dollar that the administration would ask the Congress to approve. In addition, a number of coordinated adjustments in the Smithsonian exchange rates among the currencies were worked out. However, despite the devaluation of the dollar and these other changes, confidence was not restored in the full pattern of rates. When the exchange markets reopened, the speculative movement out of dollars into DMs and some other currencies resumed. On one day, March 1, European central banks bought 3.6 billion U.S. dollars. Foreign exchange markets were closed again on March 2.

The foreign exchange markets remained closed until March 19, although private trading of currencies continued in the meantime. Instead of trying to work out another set of temporary adjustments in the rate structure during this period, the authorities of the major countries reached the decision to let their currencies float. When markets reopened on March 19, five member countries of the European Community—Belgium, Denmark, France, Germany, and the Netherlands—permitted their currencies to float as a bloc against other currencies including the U.S. dollar but maintained the exchange rates between every pair of their own currencies within a band of 2 1/4 percent or 1 1/8 percent on each side of the agreed central rates. Subsequently these countries were joined by Norway and Sweden. The Japanese yen, Swiss franc, Italian lira, and Canadian dollar were all allowed to float independently.

After holding fairly steady for the first couple of months after the float began, the U.S. dollar dropped rapidly in terms of the major European currencies from May to July. In this short period, the dollar declined by approximately 20 percent against the DM, 17 percent against the Swiss franc, and 15 percent against the French franc. Contributing to this was a continuation of a deficit in the U.S. basic balance of payments vis-à-vis Europe. Dollars were also flowing into Europe from other countries that had deficits at the time vis-à-vis Europe. These countries tend to finance their deficits with the dollars they hold as part of their international reserves, and an inflow of these dollars, like that of dollars from any other source, tends to cause a fall in the value of the dollar in the foreign exchange markets. Finally, there was a movement out of dollars by private holders of dollars. They had seen the dollar decline almost uninterruptedly for nearly two years, and the fact that various actions taken had failed to arrest the decline led them to believe that still more decline lay ahead.

But the dollar then staged a recovery beginning in July, and by the end of the year its value was back to the level in effect when the float began in March. One reason for the recovery is the fact that the sharpness of the decline from May to July gave rise to a widening body of opinion that the dollar had already declined too far and had become undervalued. This view was strengthened by a rapidly shrinking deficit in the U.S. merchandise balance and the emergence of a surplus on goods and services. Another assist came from the decision of the Federal Reserve authorities to replace their policy of hands-off the foreign exchange markets with a policy of intervention as needed to maintain orderly market conditions. Finally, and of considerable importance, was the impact starting in the last quarter of the year of the skyrocketing import costs of oil to the Western nations. Because European countries and Japan are so heavily dependent on imported oil and the United States much less dependent, the rising costs of imported oil will involve relatively large debit items in these other countries' balances of payments. To the extent that this can not be offset, it results in shrinking surpluses or expanding deficits. The value of the currency of countries in this situation naturally tends to decline in terms of the currency of the United States, which is not in an equally trying situation.

After going through a large decline and recovery in value over the months from May 1973 to early 1974, the dollar fluctuated within a narrower range from early 1974 to the time of writing in the fall of 1974. Except for the short episode of disorderly conditions in June and July of 1973, the foreign exchange markets continued to function efficiently under the regime of floating exchange rates. Forward exchange could be purchased at reasonable cost, and the volume of world trade did not appear to have been affected adversely by the float. The extent to which longer term transactions including long-term capital movements have been affected adversely by a continuing float is hard to say. These are transactions for which protection against exchange rate changes cannot be readily obtained in the forward exchange market, but it may be that the risk in these transactions under the floating system is no greater than under a pegged system in which rates are adjusted intermittently, as was the case under the Bretton Woods arrangement.

The float that began with the German mark in May 1971 and spread with the suspension of the convertibility of the U.S. dollar in August 1971 was relatively short-lived. In December, just four months after the latter action, the Smithsonian agreement returned the United States and other major countries to a regime of pegged exchange rates, albeit with a wider band around the central rates than before. In contrast, as the Smithsonian agreement disintegrated and another general float began in March 1973, there was not the same sense of urgency on the part of the authorities around the world to end the float. As the float worked far better than most critics had predicted, it appeared to be a system that the major countries could live with for some time. In any event, the balance of payments uncertainties for Japan and the nations of Europe that were created by the tripling in the price of imported oil late in 1973 were in themselves enough to rule out any early return to a system of fixed exchange rates with adjustable pegs. However, as of a date not much more than a year before this, that was the kind of international monetary system that the authorities of most of the leading nations believed could be attained in the not too distant future.

As the Bretton Woods system was coming apart, the IMF in July of 1972 had established an international group known as the Committee of Twenty (C-20) to prepare a plan for monetary reform that would meet the current and future needs of the world economy. At the annual meeting of the IMF in Nairobi, Kenya, in September 1973, the committee submitted a report called *First Outline of Reform*, which noted those issues on which some agreement had been reached and those on which the opposite was true and set forth suggestions by committee members on ways of resolving the outstanding issues. That outline suggested strongly that the international monetary system should entail a return to fixed exchange rates. Specifically, it said: "The main features of the international monetary reform should include: an effective symmetrical adjustment process, including better functioning of the exchange rate mechanism, with the exchange rate regime based on stable but adjustable par values and floating rates recognized as providing a useful technique in particular situations."

It is interesting that the committee's report was released just before the turbulence in world oil supplies and prices began. As was noted above, if a system of exchange rate parities had been established by October to succeed the float that began in March, those fixed parities would surely not have survived the developments of the next few months. Although more such violent disturbances may not occur for years to come, the near future may still not be so tranquil internationally as to make a return to fixed parities feasible. Apart from disturbances from new sources is the potential for major disturbance that arises from the fact that the oil exporting countries will be accumulating massive amounts of foreign currencies in the years ahead. For 1974 alone it has been estimated that these countries will take in $60 billion more from the rest of the world than they pay out to the rest of the world for imports, and much of this will be held in the United States and European countries in liquid balances. While it is to be hoped that these large balances will be managed with allowance for their international monetary repercussions, management of a different kind can in itself be extremely disruptive to the system. Practically all observors looking at the instability and turbulence in the world in 1974 and the potential for more ahead find it hard to believe that anything but a regime of flexible or floating exchange rates will work in the next several years. By the time of its final meeting in Washington in June of 1974, the Committee of Twenty (which is to be succeeded by a differently constituted group) had come around to the position that there was no alternative to flexible or floating rates for at least the near future. With floating to be a continuing reality, the committee recognized that the immediate need was to reach agreement on rules for floating to avoid the dangers otherwise inherent in such a system. Due in part to the pressures exerted by world-wide inflation and the deteriorating position of various economies, the members of the committee managed to compromise their differing views and reach an agreement on such rules.

Many of the technical aspects of the rules remained to be worked out, but the broad outline was set at the meeting. The monetary authorities of each country in consultation with the IMF staff will establish confidential "target zones," or ranges of fluctuation, for each country's currency. Thereafter, a country would be expected to keep its currency value within this zone and to intervene as necessary to do so. At the same time, to avoid the competitive devaluations that a country might at times resort to as a means of improving its export position, a country would not lower its "target zone" unilaterally. Such reduction may be appropriate at times to correct past mistakes or to accomodate future economic policy, but this is something to be worked out in consultation with the IMF staff. The IMF staff may also, on the basis of its own studies, recommend that a nation should at times raise or lower its zone. Initially the zones that are in effect will be confidential, but it is hoped that within a year or two they will be publicly stated. Initially they will also presumably be relatively wide, but the hope here is that they eventually will be reduced to something like the "wider bands" that were temporarily in effect under the Smithsonian agreement.

Substantive agreements were also reached in a number of other areas at the June 1974 meeting, and some of these will be referred to in the concluding note to this chapter.

A CONCLUDING NOTE

Among the many questions that must be answered in constructing an international monetary system, the most basic is the question of the method by which each country sees to it that over time its payments of foreign currencies equal its receipts of foreign currencies. Should nations maintain this balance through a free market in which currencies are exchanged at whatever rate will clear the market, subject only to a set of rules to see to it that nations do not intervene to manipulate exchange rates to their selfish advantage? Or, in the Bretton Woods tradition, should a system of stable but adjustable exchange rates be created in which a set of rules is agreed upon to specify when countries may or should intervene in the market to support existing exchange rates and when they may or should allow exchange rates to adjust to a new level? Or should the system be something in between that leans closer to one or the other of these two arrangements? As was noted just above, at least for the time being, the world's monetary authorities have agreed on one that leans closer to the former, and the immediate problem faced by the experts is to work out the technical aspects of the "rules of the road" for a system of rates that float within "target zones."

In this and the preceding chapter our focus has been on this question of the balance of payments adjustment process under different international monetary arrangements. Although the question of the kind of exchange rate regime that will be used for adjustment purposes is the central question faced in reforming the international monetary system, there are many closely related questions that also must be answered. As with the question of the balance of payments adjustment process, one needs a chapter or more to come to grips with the basic elements involved in some of these. In this final note, we do little more than identify a few of these other questions.

The Role of Gold

The one that is the most interesting to the general public is the future role of gold in the international monetary system. With the suspension of convertibility of the U.S. dollar into gold on August 15, 1971, there was not a single national treasury in the world at which a nation's currency could be converted into gold. But despite this inconvertibility, each country for the time being continued to define its currency in terms of gold. That is, gold formally remained the numeraire, or the common denominator in terms of which the par values of currencies were expressed. But gold's long established role as numeraire is now to end. The Committee of Twenty at the June 1974 meeting agreed that the SDR will become the numeraire. This will be considered in the following section. The SDR will also become the principal reserve asset of nations, and the role of gold as a reserve asset will be reduced.

As of 1974, however, gold very much remained an international reserve asset, and gold transactions between countries remained subject to IMF rules. One rule was that such transactions between countries were to take place at the official price of gold. This was $42.22 per ounce following the February 1973 devaluation of the dollar. At the same time, the price of gold in the free market was well above this, and under the pressure of world-wide inflation the price rose still higher or from $90 per ounce in late 1973 to as much as $180 per ounce in late 1974.

Various countries with sizable gold reserves had been arguing over the preceding several years that the official price was completely unrealistic and that gold should be officially revalued to a price in line with market quotations. Starting in late 1973 they sought to bolster their case with the argument that such a large official revaluation of their gold reserves and those of other countries was needed to help them pay for their much more costly oil imports. Under existing international monetary agreements, countries are not prohibited completely from selling gold in the open market at whatever price they can get, so it does not appear that an official revaluation of the price of gold was needed to enable them to get the market value. However, the countries recognized that any large movement of gold out of monetary reserves into the free gold markets might cause a collapse of the free market price. Valued at $42.22 per ounce, monetary gold reserves of central banks and governments totaled about $50 billion in mid-1974. At the then market price of, say, $155 per ounce, the same pile of some 37,000 metric tons would be worth about $184 billion. At normal rates of consumption of gold in industry, jewelry, dentistry, and the like, the physical amount in monetary reserves equals about twenty years' supply. What would happen to the price of wheat if an amount equal to twenty years' consumption were to come on the market during a year? With the private gold market dwarfed by official gold holding, not very much of these holdings could be unloaded at existing prices. However, if officially revalued to a level in line with market prices, countries could then use their gold to settle balances with other countries on more favorable terms than otherwise.

A side effect of an official revaluation of this extent would be to secure a place for gold in the world monetary system for years to come. The United States and other countries that believe a rational international monetary system requires a lesser role for gold or the outright demonetization of gold have firmly opposed the proposal to permit movements between countries of gold held in their international monetary reserves at a price in line with the recent free market price. Still, a way was needed to permit nations to use their gold reserves short of selling such reserves at $42.22 per ounce, something no nation could understandably bring itself to do. At the June meeting of the Committee of Twenty a compromise was worked out. Nations would be enabled to use their gold reserves at a value close to the existing market value by putting up their gold as collateral for loans from other nations. Germany, which was running a large surplus in its balance of payments, suggested that it might make loans to Italy, France, and other countries suffering deficits if it could take gold as collateral at something near the market price. The first of such loans was then negotiated in August. The German central bank agreed to lend $2 billion in U.S. dollars to Italy, with the Italian central bank putting up about 500 tons of gold as collateral for the loan.

The collateralizing of gold at whatever terms are agreed upon between lending and borrowing countries does not elevate the position of gold in the international monetary system as would a correspondingly higher official valuation for gold. Many of those who believe that the most rational exchange rate system is one with floating currency values also believe that gold should be given parallel treatment: simply demonetize gold by abolishing the official price of gold altogether and permit the price of that metal to find its level in response to world market forces as is the case with the prices of currencies in a floating exchange rate system.

Demonetization of gold would mean that the large part of the total demand for gold that originates with its use in official monetary reserves would disappear, at least in a formal sense. As they have done for centuries, people would continue to hoard gold as a store of value. Its value would be determined in the free market by supply and demand, but now the demand would no longer include an official monetary demand. Furthermore, if gold were officially demonetized a likely consequence is that it would also lose some of its appeal as a store of value for individuals. In any event, from the demand side its value would be determined predominantly by its use in industry, jewelry, and the like. In a world in which inflation runs on unchecked, its price would, of course, rise together with the rises in prices of other commodities. However, if inflation were brought under control internationally, it might turn out that gold, if demonetized, would be worth a lot less than the prices at which it was selling in late 1974.

In the summer of 1974 President Ford signed legislation that makes legal the ownership of gold bullion by U.S. citizens as of January 1, 1975. Over the preceding forty years they had been limited to the holding of gold contained in jewelry, coins, or their teeth. What impact this change will have on the market price of gold is extremely uncertain, although at first glance one might expect that the addition of the potentially huge demand of the wealthy American public would send the price of gold bullion zooming. Perhaps an equally likely possibility is that a movement of the price much above the $180 level will be checked as central banks deem it opportune to sell off part of their massive holdings at such a level. This could hold the price in the $180 neighborhood for the indefinite future and deny any profit to those who have bought in around this price. Of course, a continuation of inflation at the 1973–74 rate or an even higher rate might lead the central banks to hold back for still higher prices. The price might then rise above the $200 level and even to the $300 or $400 level that some investment advisers and gold promotors foresee. Another possibility is that noted earlier: that international inflation will subside and that gold will be demonetized or become just another metal, albeit still a precious one. Its price might drop far below the $180 per ounce level—even a return to the neighborhood of the present official price of $42.22 per ounce would not then be beyond possibility. Needless to say, we will not know even approximately what that price will be a couple of years from now until a couple of years have passed.

The Question of the Numeraire

As it had been over the long period of experience under the gold standard, gold was the numeraire under the Bretton Woods system. The currency of each country was defined as a specific amount of gold—as each country did this, the exchange rate parity between every pair of currencies was established. But under the Bretton Woods system it was only in a formal sense that gold served as the numeraire; in practice the U.S. dollar took over this role. The par value of each currency was expressed as some fraction or multiple of the U.S. dollar. This followed from the fact that over the years following World War II the dollar came to be the most important asset in other countries' official reserve assets as well as in the reserve assets of private parties. Over most of this period the dollar retained its fixed tie to gold, and it was as good as gold to foreign holders of dollars. However, with the formal suspension of convertibility on August 15, 1971, the fixed tie to gold, which had even earlier been severely weakened, was legally severed.

If they were of such mind, other countries could continue to use the dollar as numeraire, but, despite the fact that the dollar remains the most widely used currency through the world, with inconvertibility it has lost its unique position as the linchpin in the international monetary system. Furthermore, with devaluations in 1971 and 1973, the dollar came to resemble other currencies whose values in terms of other currencies are subject to change by actions of the nation's monetary authorities. To use a currency whose value changes in this way as numeraire would be like measuring distances with a foot that varies over time from less than 12 inches to more than 12 inches.

The most feasible alternative to the dollar as numeraire was the SDR, and at the June 1974 meeting the Committee of Twenty agreed that this internationally created reserve unit would be the numeraire. Following agreement among its membership in 1967, the IMF had begun in 1970 to issue SDRs. At this time the SDR was defined in terms of gold. However, with the dollar formally not convertible into gold after August 1971, the SDR lost its fixed tie to gold. Just as other currencies were no longer able to maintain a fixed tie to gold by maintaining a fixed value in terms of the dollar, the same was true for the SDR. An alternative method of placing a valuation on the SDR was needed. At the June meeting the Committee of Twenty agreed on the "basket of currencies" technique for valuing the SDR. Its value will be based on an average of the values of 16 world currencies of which the U.S. dollar will be the most important. The fraction of the total basket accounted for by the U.S. dollar is 33 percent with other major currencies like the

DM, the French franc, and the British pound accounting for sizable fractions. The value of SDR 1.00—i.e., one SDR—in terms of any one currency will be the value of the amounts of each of the currencies in the basket expressed in terms of this one currency at the prevailing exchange rates. Any one currency may show a sizable change in value in terms of others, but a decline in one currency is, in a relative sense, a rise in another. The average value of a collection of the world's major currencies, which is what the basket of 16 is, should not show appreciable short-run change and accordingly should serve well as the thing in terms of which the SDR as numeraire is valued.

International Liquidity

One of the major questions faced under the Bretton Woods system was the provision of the appropriate level of international liquidity. Within a nation, an expanding volume of business activity requires an expanding money supply, and the central bank expands the banking system's reserves at a rate deemed appropriate to these requirements. In the same way, a growing volume of international reserves is needed in the world to handle an expanding volume of international trade and financial transactions. It was to supplement the sum of monetary gold holdings, regular drawing rights at the IMF, and reserve currency holdings of its members that the IMF in 1970 began to issue special drawing rights. For years international liquidity had grown primarily through U.S. deficits that added to the world's holdings of reserve currencies, but this process could not go on indefinitely. The SDR was designed to be the answer to the problem.

There would be virtually no problem of international liquidity if the world operated with freely floating exchange rates. Reserves are needed to bridge temporary balance of payments deficits, but with freely floating exchange rates the market sees to it that the balance of payments is always in equilibrium. In such a world there would be no need for SDRs or even for the normal resources the IMF makes available to its members to temporarily supplement their reserves. However, completely free floating is an extreme case and not one found in practice. Some degree of intervention will always occur, if only to prevent any too erratic variation in exchange rates. But as long as intervention does not go much beyond this, the need for reserves under floating rates is relatively small in comparison with the need under an adjustable peg system. The system of "target zones" for exchange rates agreed upon by the Committee of Twenty at the June 1974 meeting does not mean an end to the floating rates that have been in effect since the spring of 1973. One purpose of the system is to work toward a lesser degree of fluctuation in rates than otherwise would occur, but this is a far cry from the stable but adjustable rates to which many monetary authorities want eventually to return. If the world should some day move back to such a system, the rate of expansion in international liquidity will have to be more rapid than otherwise.

As a result of the decisions reached at the June meeting, it appears that whatever the international liquidity requirements of the future, the SDR will play a major role in meeting them. A total of 9.3 billion SDRs was issued during 1970—72 and none since then; these made up about 5 percent of total international reserves as of the end of 1973. As the agreed-upon plan to make the SDR the principal reserve asset and reduce the role of gold and the U.S. dollar as reserve assets is carried out in the years ahead, the volume of SDRs may be expected to expand significantly. How much will depend, among other things, on the growing liquidity requirements of the world's nations.

The Issue of Convertibility

This refers to the convertibility of national currencies into gold or SDRs, the so-called primary reserve assets. An objective is to achieve a system in which all imbalances in international payments, including U.S. imbalances, will be settled, at least partially, in such assets. The problem that was confronted in recent years was that surplus countries found it necessary to absorb deficit countries' currencies, especially the U.S. dollar, to prevent an appreciation in the value of their own currencies. The issue this raises is whether or not a deficit country should be obligated to buy back its currency with primary reserve assets. If there is no such obligation, a surplus country by exchanging its currency for that of the deficit country finds that it must finance the other country's deficit. There is then little pressure on the deficit country to take action to eliminate the deficit. On the other hand, if a deficit country has such an obligation, this does put pressure on it to take corrective steps, especially if the cause of the deficit is overly expansionary policies pursued in the home economy.

While the call for convertibility is a general one, it is aimed primarily at the U.S. dollar. Europeans see the need to impose financial discipline on the United States; to compel at least partial convertibility of the dollar would be a way of doing this. However, the United States maintains that there can be no convertibility of the dollar until the U.S. balance of payments is brought back to normal. From the U.S. viewpoint, this comes first, and convertibility may then follow. For the United States to accept the other would be to subordinate its domestic policies to the needs of the balance of payments, and there is great resistance to such a policy in the United States as there is in other major countries.

The question of convertibility would lose its urgency in a world that continued to operate with floating exchange rates. The situation in which one country finds it necessary to absorb large amounts of another country's currency does not occur with floating rates; exchange rates adjust as needed to keep the private market supply of and the private market demand for each currency in balance. The major nations have now been operating with floating exchange rates for a year and a half. As long as they continue to so operate, the convertibility question is one that may be discussed and debated but will not be directly faced. However, even with a regime of floating rates, a closely related question is confronted that we turn to next.

The "Dollar Overhang"

Floating rates will prevent the accumulation of large amounts of deficit country currencies by surplus countries, but floating rates will not remove the stock of such currencies already accumulated by surplus countries. As a result of the purchases made over earlier years to prevent their currencies from appreciating in terms of dollars, foreign central banks and official agencies have on hand a stock of about $70 billion. As we saw earlier, a good part of this accumulation occurred during 1970 and 1971, when dollars flowed into Europe and Japan in massive quantities. What are the prospects that the official holders of these billions will be able to convert them into primary reserve assets?

If the IMF rules were changed to permit countries to sell gold to each other at prices near the market price, convertibility of these dollars would become at least a possibility. At the mid-1974 market price of about $150 per ounce, the U.S. monetary gold stock would be worth about $43 billion. With the likelihood that the dollar will remain fairly strong relative to European currencies in the foreseeable future, foreign official holders would not wish to convert all of their dollar holdings, and a $43 billion U.S. gold stock might be adequate to make a return to convertibility possible. However, as noted above in discussing the future role of gold in the world system, the United States will not agree to an official revaluation of a magnitude like that indicated, one that would lock the place of gold into the world monetary system for years to come.

As such a revaluation is not likely to occur with the U.S. position being what it is, is there any other way for the foreign central banks to reduce their huge holdings of unwanted dollars? If the dollar remains fairly strong and world confidence in it gradually improves, there is the prospect that private holders may move large amounts from other currencies back into dollars in the years ahead. As private holders increase their dollar holdings, official holders will be able to decrease theirs. Furthermore, if there is renewed confidence in the dollar, the number of dollars that foreign central banks and official agencies want to hold will also grow larger. This does not reduce the total number of dollars they actually hold, but it helps to meet the overhang problem by reducing the number unwillingly held.

There are numerous other possibilities, practical or impractical depending on the point of view. Foreign central banks could use dollars to buy back from U.S. investors corporate stocks and bonds issued by companies in the countries of these central banks. It was through the purchase of these securities by Americans, so-called long-term capital exports, that many billions of these dollars came into foreign hands. The foreign central banks would then have rid themselves of the unwanted dollars and replaced them in their portfolios with stocks and bonds of domestic firms. Another possibility, although quantitatively too small to make a large dent in their massive dollar holdings, would be for some foreign governments to use dollars to finance attendance at U.S. universities by students who are unable to enter overcrowded universities at home at a time when U.S. universities have thousands of available places. This is now occurring on a small scale. Along this same line, subsidies in dollars could be provided to promote travel in the United States by citizens in those countries whose central banks are so anxious to unload dollars, though this would raise howls of protest by companies at home that would lose business as a result. Farther out than these and totally unacceptable to the foreigners involved is the suggestion of an outright cancellation of a portion of the dollars held by central banks in certain countries. They could be replaced in the portfolios of the central banks with noninterest-bearing obligations of the country's treasury. In the judgment of some, such cancellations might be no more than fair in view of the large amounts of aid extended during and after World War II to various countries in Europe whose central banks are now bulging with unwanted dollars.

The several questions introduced in the last pages will be prominent in the discussions of the monetary authorities of the world's major countries in the years ahead. However important, they will remain subsidiary to the question of the exchange rate regime, which is the question on which we have focused in these chapters. As suggested several times in these chapters, the probability for the next few years is the continuation of the float but in the qualified form of "target zones" for fluctuation of exchange rates agreed upon by the finance ministers at their meeting in June 1974. This is the best that can be expected under existing circumstances, and it may turn out that even the degree of cooperation needed for this will be unobtainable.

INDEX

Accommodating items, in balance of payments statement, 362–67

Adjustable pegs: balance of payments adjustment under, 382–90, 394; compared with flexible exchange rates, 395, 398; exchange rate variations under, 386–87, 390–91; and government intervention, 398–400; shortcomings of, 387–90

Aggregate demand: excessive, 330; slowing of, 321–22

Aggregate spending, 325; and change in interest rates, 298; and gold standard, 378–79

Anderson, L. C., 286n, 287

Assets: and cash withdrawn from banks, 26; of commercial banks, 37–38, 39, 40–43, 45, 46, 47–51, 72–75, 125; effect of reserve requirements on, 75–81; and excess reserves, 103; of Federal Reserve Banks, 39, 40–43, 44, 45, 46; qualifying as legal reserves, 63–64; and savings, 30; and T-account for public, 26; and variations in public currency holdings, 94–100

Autonomous items, in balance of payments statement, 362–67

Balance on current account, in U.S. balance of payments statement, 358–59; see also Basic deficit; Basic surplus

Balance on goods and services, in U.S. balance of payments statement, 357, 358

Balance of payments, and convertibility, 424–25; see also Balance of payments adjustment; U.S. balance of payments

Balance of payments adjustment: under adjustable pegs, 382–90; and devaluation, 410–11; under flexible exchange rates, 390–400; and foreign exchange rates, 371–74; under gold standard, 374–82; and government intervention, 398–400; and Keynesian economics, 380–82; methods used for, 368–70

Balance sheet, 21–22; for commercial banks, 39–43, 45, 46, 47–53, 80–81; for Federal Reserve Banks, 39–43, 44, 45, 46; identity, 218; and transactions, 23

Balanced budget, 174

Bank reserves, see Legal reserves

Barter, 6–10

Basic deficit or surplus, 361

Borrowers: funds available to, 32; and loan proceeds, 49–50; see also Borrowing

Borrowing: and business activity, 207; by commercial banks, 72, 122–24; and floating discount rates, 129–32; by public, and money supply, 270; by Treasury, 158–72, 185–88; and Vietnam War, 326–28; see also Demand for money; Interest rates

Bretton Woods system, 381, 402–403, 411, 416; see also Adjustable peg system

Business activity: and interest rates, 297–98; and spending, 206–207; see also Business cycle; Business cycle turning-points

Business cycle: and employment, 225; and monetary policy targets, 312; see also Depression; Expansion; Recession

A 5
B 6
C 7
D 8
E 9
F 0
G 1
H 2
I 3
J 4

understanding
MONEY